COLLEGE LAW

A Guide for Administrators

COMMITTEE ON A HANDBOOK OF COLLEGE LAW FOR ADMINISTRATORS

Appointed by the American Council on Education

NORMAN P. AUBURN, *Chairman*
President, University of Akron

RALPH F. FUCHS
Professor of Law, Indiana University

HOWARD F. LOWRY
President, College of Wooster

JOHN W. MACDONALD
Professor of Law, Cornell University

A. W. PETERSON
Vice-President, Business and Finance, University of Wisconsin

MARCUS ROBBINS
Comptroller, Yale University

JOHN DALE RUSSELL
Director of Office of Institutional Research, New York University

ARTHUR S. ADAMS, *ex officio*
President, American Council on Education

ROBERT QUICK, *Secretary*
Manager of Publications, American Council on Education

THOMAS EDWARD BLACKWELL

COLLEGE LAW

A Guide for Administrators

AMERICAN COUNCIL ON EDUCATION

Washington · D.C.

PRINTED IN THE UNITED STATES OF AMERICA BY
GEORGE BANTA COMPANY, INC., MENASHA, WISCONSIN

Foreword

Eᴠᴇʀʏ experienced college administrator today knows, or soon comes to learn, that he frequently has to deal with situations which require knowledge and understanding of related legal problems. Relationships to governmental agencies in research and taxation, to college employees in employment and tenure, to donors of gifts in relation to terms and conditions are only a few of the situations which require the college administrator to have an acquaintance with legal principles.

This book does not represent an attempt to make every college administrator his own lawyer. Its primary purpose is to give the college administrator an awareness and understanding of basic law and legal concepts as they relate to the colleges. It is intended to assist him in planning procedures in order to avoid the possibility of litigation. By calling attention to the importance of reviewing day-by-day procedures to make sure they include sound legal safeguards, it is intended to encourage the recognition of incipient legal difficulties that require the services of an attorney. Although not especially addressed to lawyers themselves, I am sure this book will be a useful guide to those attorneys with colleges as their clients.

The Council was indeed fortunate in obtaining T. E. Blackwell as the author of this book. During his long service as vice-chancellor of Washington University and as editor of *College and University Business Administration*, Dr. Blackwell became aware of the importance of legal problems in the administration of higher educational institutions. For a number of years he has been the author of a series of articles on "Legal Problems of Colleges and Universities" in *College and University Business*. By drawing upon his wide background and varied experience, Dr. Blackwell's work represents a significant contribution in this area.

The Council acknowledges with grateful appreciation both the financial support of the project from funds granted to the Council by the United States Steel Foundation and the services by the members of the Council's advisory committee for the book, who gave the manuscript careful scrutiny and made numerous useful suggestions.

Aʀᴛʜᴜʀ S. Aᴅᴀᴍs, *President*
American Council on Education

v

Contents

CHAPTER I

Basic Legal Concepts

THIS handbook on college law is addressed to administrators, not to lawyers, although it is hoped that lawyers may find it a convenient reference volume. It is not intended to make the administrator his own lawyer, but to help him to recognize incipient legal issues so that he may seek appropriate advice in time to avoid controversy and expense. In order that lawyer and client may understand one another more clearly, that is, in order that they may have a common vocabulary with which to converse, it would seem desirable to define a few basic concepts of the law.

The word "law" itself has many meanings.[1] As used in this and in other legal texts, a law is a rule of human conduct that we, the people, have agreed should be enforced by the state through its courts. We are under the pressure of public opinion to conform to generally accepted concepts of morality and ethics, but these concepts do not have the force of law unless they are implemented by the power of the state.

THE COMMON LAW. The term "common law" has several related meanings. It first came into use to designate the system of justice administered in the king's courts as contrasted with that to be obtained in the courts of the feudal barons. Prior to the reign of Henry II (1154–1189), each baron claimed the right, either by royal grant or

---

[1] Those interested in the history of the development of our concepts of justice and our Anglo-American system of jurisprudence should begin their reading with a modern text; for example: William Seal Carpenter, *Foundations of Modern Jurisprudence* (New York: Appleton-Century-Crofts, 1958). The most comprehensive history of English law is William S. Holdsworth, *History of English Law* (13 vols.; London: Methuen, 1922–52). For a less detailed analysis, see John Chipman Gray, *The Nature and Sources of the Law* (2d ed.; New York: Macmillan Co., 1921); Oliver Wendell Holmes, Jr., *The Common Law* (Rev. ed., 1923; Boston: Little, Brown & Co., 1881); Theodore Frank Thomas Plucknett, *Concise History of the Common Law* (5th ed.; Boston: Little, Brown & Co., 1956).

1

by usurpation, to adjudicate the disputes of his vassals and serfs. The Plantagenet kings of England, realizing the importance of gaining control of the legal system of the country, initiated a plan calling for the use of itinerant judges. These circuit courts of the king, holding session in every large community, brought to the people a much-needed system of uniform justice, common to the entire realm. Thus came into use the term "the common law of England."

EQUITY AND THE COURT OF CHANCERY. "Equity" has a special connotation to the lawyer. The law courts of early England, bound by rigid adherence to precedent and primitive procedures, did not always meet the need for justice in the settlement of disputes. When unable to obtain justice from the feudal or from the common law courts, the dissatisfied litigant might appeal to the king, long considered to be the fountainhead of justice. The king would usually turn to his chancellor, the scribe or secretary of his council. Since few outside the hierarchy of the Church possessed the skill of writing in those early days, the chancellor was a cleric trained in the law of the Church, which was based upon Roman or civil law. Under this system of jurisprudence, prior decisions were not binding, procedure was not a hindrance. Thus, the king, through his chancellor, was able to offer a more flexible system of justice.

When the demand for his services increased, the chancellor organized his own court, which came to be known as the court of chancery, or what we now know as equity, with its own rules and precedents. For centuries, law and equity functioned as separate and sometimes as competitive legal systems. Gradually, the obvious logic of coordination compelled their merger, and today, in the majority of jurisdictions, the same court will administer both law and equity, as the needs of the case before it require.

THE LAW MERCHANT. The common law of early England had another alien competitor in the law merchant. The trade of the Western world during the Middle Ages was in the hands of a comparatively small number of merchant associations or guilds. They developed their own customs and procedures for the quick settlement of disputes arising in the course of trade. With family or guild connections in the principal trading centers of Europe, these merchants and moneylenders devised a system for the transfer of funds by the use of drafts, letters of credit, and promissory notes, thereby obviating the costly and hazardous procedure of shipping gold and silver coin or bullion. These fiscal obligations were enforced, and the disputes arising from the purchase and sale of goods by these early international traders were adjudicated by special courts, according to the law merchant. The law merchant included what is now known as the law of negotiable instruments, sales, bankruptcy, and insurance. By 1756 William Murray, the Lord Chief Justice, succeeded in incorporating the principles of the law merchant into the body of English common law. Both equity and the law merchant, although now part of the general system of Anglo-American jurisprudence, have left a distinctive impression upon the structure of our law.

THE CIVIL LAW. In its broadest connotation, the term "the common law" is used to contrast our system of jurisprudence with the civil law. As we have noted, civil law is based upon Roman law as codified (528–534) under the direction of the emperor Justinian I. This famous legal code, known as Corpus Juris Civilis, is the foundation of law in most of continental Europe today, and in the areas of the world colonized by Spain, France, and the other continental powers. It has strongly influenced the law of those states of our American union with a Spanish or French colonial background, including Florida, Louisiana, Texas, New Mexico, Arizona, and California. The territorial legislature of Louisiana before its admission as a state adopted a civil law code based upon the Code Napoléon of France. The present constitution of Louisiana forbids the state legislature to adopt, by reference, the common law or any other legal system.[2]

THE RECEPTION OF THE COMMON LAW IN THE UNITED STATES. The common law of England was carried by her colonists to what are now the United States of America, Canada, Australia, New Zealand, and South Africa. Shortly after the Declaration of Independence, a general convention held in the colony of Virginia adopted an ordinance—one of extreme importance to our present legal system, since it has been enacted, almost verbatim, by many state legislatures and constitutional conventions—which reads as follows:

And be it further ordained that the common law of England, all statutes or acts of Parliament made in aid of the common law prior to the fourth year of the reign of King James the First, and which are of a general nature, not local to that kingdom . . . shall be considered in full force until the same shall be altered by the legislative power of the colony.[3]

---

[2] *La. Const.* art. 3, par. 18.

[3] 9 *Laws of Virginia* 126 (Hening 1821). See also Ford W. Hall, "The Common Law: An Account of Its Reception in the United States," 4 *Vand. L. Rev.* 791 (1951).

Thus, the decisions of English courts and the general acts of the English parliament prior to the reign of the Stuart kings are considered an integral part of our American legal system. It is not uncommon for a lawyer to cite an English or Canadian court decision in his brief, and a legal scholar is expected to be familiar with significant trends in the common law in his field throughout the English-speaking world.

STATUTORY LAW. In a more restricted sense, the term "common law" is used to differentiate the law as enunciated by the judge from the bench from law enacted by legislative bodies, that is, "case law" in contradistinction to "statutory law." One not trained in the intricacies of the law may have gained the impression that law is primarily the creature of the legislature. Quite the contrary is true. The vast bulk of legal reference material is not to be found in the statute books but in the case books and in the regulations and rulings of administrative agencies of government. Law libraries are crowded with volumes containing the recorded decisions of state and federal courts.[4] Two rows of shelves are sufficient to contain the legislative product now in force.

---

[4] There are several sources for the published opinions of the state and federal courts. Every important court of record authorizes and supervises the publication of its own decisions. In addition, the West Publishing Co., St. Paul, Minn., publishes what is known as the National Reporter System. This system is made up of the *Atlantic Reporter:* the cases argued and determined in the state courts of Connecticut, Delaware, the municipal appellate court of the District of Columbia, the state courts of Maine, Maryland, New Hampshire, New Jersey, Pennsylvania, Rhode Island, and Vermont; *North Eastern Reporter:* Illinois, Indiana, Massachusetts, New York, and Ohio; *North Western Reporter:* Iowa, Michigan, Minnesota, Nebraska, North Dakota, South Dakota, and Wisconsin; *Pacific Reporter:* Arizona, California, Colorado, Idaho, Kansas, Montana, Nevada, New Mexico, Oklahoma, Oregon, Utah, Washington, and Wyoming; *South Eastern Reporter:* Georgia, North Carolina, South Carolina, Virginia, and West Virginia; *Southern Reporter:* Alabama, Florida, Louisiana, and Mississippi; *South Western Reporter:* Arkansas, Kansas, Missouri, Tennessee, and Texas. Because of the large volume of litigation in New York, the National Reporter System includes a supplementary series for the state entitled *New York Supplement:* New York Court of Appeals; New York Supreme Court, Appellate Division; New York Supreme Court; and other courts of record within the state. The West Publishing Co. has recently announced plans for the *California Reporter,* similar in character to the *New York Supplement.*

The decisions of the Supreme Court of the United States are now published by the Government Printing Office in the official series known as the *United States Reports.* Until 1875, cases were reported by individuals, and citations to such cases show the name of the reporter, e.g., Dallas (Dall.), Cranch (Cr.), Wheaton (Wheat.). The National Reporter edition is termed the *Supreme Court Reporter.* Another edition, published by the Lawyers' Co-operative Publishing

ADMINISTRATIVE LAW. In addition to statutory law, enacted by Congress and the legislatures of the states, and case law, enunciated from the bench by judges, a multitude of administrative agencies of government issue regulations and rulings that have the compulsion of law until modified by statute or by the decision of a court of competent jurisdiction.⁵ Some students of government have deplored what they consider to be a usurpation of power by these administrative agencies exercising executive, legislative, and even judicial functions. Gordon Hewart, Lord Chief Justice of England from 1922 to 1940, branded it as the "new despotism."⁶

It will be recalled that those responsible for the drafting of our federal Constitution considered the separation of these three functions the very essence of good government. However, the growing complexity and magnitude of our business and fiscal transactions seemed to demand more effective regulation than could be effected by Congress and its committees.

In order to control what was considered at that time an abuse of monopolistic powers by the railroads, Congress created the Interstate Commerce Commission in 1904. This was followed by the establishment of the Federal Trade Commission in 1914, the Securities Commission (now the Securities and Exchange Commission) in 1933, and

Co., Rochester, N.Y., is entitled *United States Supreme Court Reports*, Lawyers Ed., Annotated.

The decisions of the lower federal courts are published as part of the National Reporter System in *Federal Reporter*: Courts of Appeals, Court of Customs and Patent Appeals, and the Emergency Court of Appeals; *Federal Supplement*: District Courts, Court of Claims, and the Customs Court.

The West Publishing Co. issues the *General Digest*, giving a summary of the decisions of all state and federal courts published in detail in the National Reporter System. The *General Digest* is issued monthly throughout the year in temporary pamphlets and subsequently in annual and decennial volumes. For some time, the Commissioners on Uniform State Laws have been concerned about the lack of a digest of the statutory laws of the states, comparable to the case law digests, such as the *General Digest*, which permit a lawyer to get leads quickly to all of the cases in all of the states on the particular legal point on which he may be working. Consequently, the National Conference of Commissioners has proposed that the American Bar Foundation undertake a survey of American statutory law as one of its major projects. The address of the American Bar Foundation and of the National Conference of Commissioners on Uniform State Laws is: American Bar Center, 1155 East 60th St., Chicago 37, Ill.

⁵ The following are two modern texts on administrative law: Kenneth Culp Davis, *Administrative Law Treatise* (St. Paul, Minn.: West Publishing Co., 1958); and Morris D. Forkosch, *Administrative Law* (Indianapolis, Ind.: Bobbs-Merrill Co., 1956).

⁶ Gordon Hewart, *The New Despotism* (London: E. Benn, 1945).

the National Labor Relations Board in 1935. In addition, other agencies of government are empowered by Congress to issue mandates enforceable by judicial proceedings, including the Federal Reserve Board, the Federal Communications Commission, the Federal Power Commission, the Federal Trade Commission, the Civil Aeronautics Board, the Atomic Energy Commission, the Postmaster General, the Immigration Service, the Department of Agriculture, and the armed services. State agencies, such as labor mediation boards and workmen's compensation boards, are also authorized to create administrative law.

The regulations and rulings of these administrative agencies form a substantial portion of the physical bulk of the published material demanding attention and study by the lawyer. One major objection to the proliferation of administrative rulings is the difficulty of finding out—even by the most expert—what the law is at any given time. This difficulty has been reduced by the establishment of the *Federal Register*,[7] a governmental publication, and by the availability, on a subscription basis, of these regulations and rulings, indexed and classified in great detail. The modern reporting services,[8] with both code and current material in loose-leaf volumes, may be found in any good law library. The college administrator is advised to become familiar with the resources of the law library on his campus or in his community and to accumulate his own reference file of statutes,

---

[7] Congress established the *Federal Register* in 1935 and requires that all Presidential proclamations and administrative regulations prescribing a penalty for their violation be published therein. The scope of the *Federal Register* was expanded by Congress in 1949. (Federal Administrative Procedures Act of 1949; 5 *U.S.C.* § 1001.) Regulations published in the *Federal Register*, except those of short duration, are subsequently published in the *Code of Federal Regulations*. These governmental publications may be obtained from the Superintendent of Documents, U.S. Government Printing Office, Washington 25, D.C.

A commercial service, known as the *United States Code Congressional and Administrative News*, is published by the West Publishing Co., St. Paul, Minn., and Edward Thompson Co., Brooklyn, N.Y. It is issued as semimonthly pamphlets while Congress is in session and monthly thereafter. Cumulative bound volumes are published each year. This service provides the full text of current federal public laws, the legislative histories of the more significant, and selected regulations of government agencies, including current federal tax regulations.

In New York, Indiana, California, Iowa, Wisconsin, Kentucky, and Michigan, the state administrative regulations and rulings are officially codified and kept up to date. Some are now available in loose-leaf reporter services.

[8] The leading publishers of federal and state administrative regulations and decisions are: Bureau of National Affairs, Washington, D.C.; Callaghan & Co., Chicago, Ill.; Prentice-Hall, Inc., Englewood Cliffs, N.J.

opinions of the attorney general of his state, and administrative regulations and rulings, especially in the field of taxation.

CODIFICATION OF STATUTORY LAW. The first official classification of the general and permanent laws of the Federal Government was made in 1874. The second attempt to classify and compile the mass of statutes was begun in 1919 by the appointment of a Committee on the Revision of the Laws of the House of Representatives. This project was brought to a conclusion in 1926 by the enactment of a new federal code. The code[9] itself is published by the Government Printing Office, but the task of publishing an annotated edition was delegated by Congress to two legal publishing companies. The annotated edition[10] is in seventy volumes, with a current supplement in a pocket at the back of each volume. The annotations include a brief legislative history of each section of the code and a summary of the judicial decisions in interpretation thereof.

In like manner, each of the state legislatures has authorized the publication of a codification of its general statutes, usually in an annotated edition.

RESTATEMENT OF THE LAW. For many years legal scholars expressed grave concern because of the ever increasing volume of case law and the apparent conflict of opinions of our state and federal courts. To bring order out of this chaos, the American Law Institute was established in 1923. It was the belief of those responsible for its formation that it would be possible to reconcile this conflict and to restate the principles and rules of the common law in simple language—as simple as the character of our complex civilization would permit. The project was financed by a grant of almost $2.5 million from the Carnegie Corporation. As the project progressed, it was found that the conflict and confusion of the common law was more apparent than actual. The impression that it was a mass of contradictions was due, to a large

---

[9] The fifth or 1952 edition of the *United States Code*, with supplementary volumes, may be purchased from the Government Printing Office. The work of preparing and editing the material for this official edition of the code has been delegated by Congress to the West Publishing Co. and the Edward Thompson Co. under the supervision of the Committee on the Judiciary of the House of Representatives.

[10] An unofficial annotated edition of the *United States Code* is published jointly by the West Publishing Co. and the Edward Thompson Co. under the title *United States Code Annotated*. Another unofficial annotated edition is published by the Bobbs-Merrill Co., Indianapolis, Ind., under the title *Federal Code Annotated*.

degree, to variations in judicial language. When the restatement was completed in 1945,[11] it was found that less than 2 percent of the judicial opinions in the case books were contrary to the legal principles and rules therein enunciated.

Although the rules are expressed in the form of a code, the restatement is not and was not intended to be a legal code, similar to the civil codes of continental Europe. A civil code is the actual law of the land, and it is the function of the courts of each country making use of such a code to enforce it, not to interpret it.

The restatement has no official status. It is intended merely for the information and guidance of bench and bar. Although frequently cited by lawyers in their briefs and by judges as support for their opinions, it cannot be used as precedent for the actual decision of the court. It is, however, having a powerful influence upon the development of the common law because of the reputation and prestige of its sponsors.

SUPREMACY OF THE JUDICIARY. Although Congress and the state legislatures enact the statutes, it is the courts that, under our system of jurisprudence, interpret them. Consequently, one must look to their decisions for the last word. Until the judge on the bench has spoken, no one can be certain what the law really is. This judicial power to interpret the federal and state constitutions and to declare a statute, enacted with all appropriate formality by Congress or by a state legislature, unconstitutional and therefore void, was for many years a unique feature of our American system of government. Today, however, the courts of Argentina, Australia, Austria, Bolivia, Brazil, Colombia, Cuba, Czechoslovakia, Eire, Haiti, Honduras, Mexico, and West Germany have acquired this power.[12]

---

[11] The First Restatement of the Law includes the following subjects: agency (2 vols.), conflict of laws (1 vol.), contracts (2 vols.), judgments (1 vol.), property (5 vols.), restitution (1 vol.), security (1 vol.), torts (4 vols.), trusts (2 vols.).

For a more detailed history of this important project and for an appraisal of its effects upon the common law, see Restatement in the Courts (St. Paul, Minn.: American Law Institute, 1945); Herbert F. Goodrich, "The Story of the American Law Institute," 1951 Wash. U.L.Q. 283; and William Draper Lewis, History of the American Law Institute and the First Restatement of the Law (Philadelphia: American Law Institute, 1954).

The Second Restatement of the Law by the American Law Institute is now in preparation. The first of the new series, the Second Restatement of the Law of Agency, was published in 1958. The project is being financed by a grant from the A. W. Mellon Educational and Charitable Trust.

[12] Charles Graves Haines, The American Doctrine of Judicial Supremacy (New York: Russell & Russell, 1959), pp. 6–19; see also George M. Vetter, Jr., "Who Is Supreme: People, Court or Legislature?" 45 A.B.A.J. 1051 (1959).

The supremacy of the judiciary explains the significance of the multitude of quotations from court decisions in all legal articles and textbooks. Authors and lawyers are aware of the fact that no statement of a legal principle will be accorded respect by bench or bar unless supported and confirmed by a decision.

This supremacy of the bench is also the reason why a lawyer usually finds it so difficult to give his client an unqualified opinion as to the status of the law governing a specific situation or proposed action. Even if the language of the statute or administrative regulation seems clear and unambiguous, and even though the attorney has been able to find a case exactly in point, he must always express his opinion of the law in terms of probability, not of certainty. Until the judge has delivered his opinion, the issues of the case are in doubt. What was considered the law yesterday may not be the law of today and tomorrow. The common law is fluid, dynamic, constantly evolving. This is its strength as well as its weakness.

Torts. Another term used by lawyers that requires explanation is the word "tort." It is derived from the same Latin verb that gave us the English words "tortion" and "torture." Until the middle of the eighteenth century, it was in common use in England and America as a synonym for "wrong." Gradually its usage was restricted to the technical vocabulary of the lawyer. It is now defined as any wrongful act, other than a breach of contract, which may serve as the basis for a suit for damages.[13]

The same act may be both a tort against an individual or group of individuals and a crime against the state. For example, if one kills a pedestrian by the negligent operation of a motor car, those legally dependent upon the deceased may bring a civil action for the tort and recover monetary compensation. The state may indict for manslaughter for the same act. A crime is an offense against the public for which the state, as the representative of the public, will bring proceedings in the form of a criminal prosecution. On the other hand, the civil action for a tort is initiated and maintained by those injured physically, mentally, or financially by the wrongful act.

---

[13] The following are a few modern texts on torts: Fowler V. Harper and Fleming James, Jr., *The Law of Torts* (3 vols.; Boston: Little, Brown & Co., 1956); Sir Frederick Pollock, *Law of Torts* (15th ed.; London: Stevens, 1951); and William L. Prosser, *Handbook of the Law of Torts* (2d ed.; St. Paul, Minn.: West Publishing Co., 1955).

EQUITABLE RELIEF. Although both common law and equity may be administered from the same bench in some jurisdictions, it is well to remember that a judge or chancellor administering equity is able to take affirmative action by issuing commands or injunctions directed to specific individuals or groups of individuals. Noncompliance with a writ of court can bring summary imprisonment and fine for the contumacious. With this power of positive action, this ability to act in personam (that is, against the person), a judge can prevent a threatened wrong instead of waiting, as the common law judge must, until after the wrong has been committed and then granting merely monetary recompense or damages to the injured party.

EQUITY AND THE TRUSTEE. Since the Church courts, from earliest times, claimed jurisdiction over the administration of property left for the support of widows, orphans, and other charitable purposes, the chancellor, as a churchman, developed those legal principles and procedures that must guide us in our consideration of the problems of trusteeship.[14] It is to the judge, sitting as a court of equity, that a trustee must look for instructions if in doubt as to his powers and duties and for any modification of the provisions of his instrument of trust should he find it impossible of administration. If he acts in strict conformity with the instructions and commands of the court, he is relieved of personal liability should he be charged with maladministration of the trust.

THE CHARITABLE TRUST AND THE CHARITABLE CORPORATION. The terms "trust," "charitable trust," and "charitable corporation" will be used frequently in this volume. This must be so since every gift, grant, and bequest to a college or university made subject to restrictions as to use creates in effect, if not in fact, a separate charitable trust when accepted for administration. Furthermore, almost all colleges and universities in America, except those organized and administered as in-

---

[14] See the sections on charitable trusts in George G. Bogert, *The Law of Trusts and Trustees* (4 vols.; Kansas City: Vernon Law Book Co., 1946–55): II, §§ 321–40: "The Creation of Charitable Trusts"; §§ 341–60: "Charities"; IIA, §§ 361–90: "The Charitable Trust"; §§ 391–410: "The Administration of Charitable Trusts." See also Austin W. Scott, *The Law of Trusts* (2d ed.; 5 vols.; Boston: Little, Brown & Co., 1956): IV, chap. 11, "Charitable Trusts"; Topics 1, General Principles; 2, Creation of Charitable Trusts; 3, Nature of Charitable Purposes; 4, Administration of Charitable Trusts; 5, Failure of Charitable Trusts; 6, Liability to Third Persons. Both Bogert and Scott are maintained on a current basis by means of cumulative revision pamphlets inserted in pockets in the inside back cover of each volume.

strumentalities of the federal, state, or local governments, are charitable corporations.

THE TRUST. The "trust" or "use" has been recognized, under various designations, since the early Roman period. During the Middle Ages, it was found to be a most useful device to circumvent the feudal burdens incident to the direct ownership of land. By means of a trust agreement, the title or fee of a tract of land could be retained by an individual able and willing to fulfill the obligation to bear arms in defense of his feudal lord, with the income, benefit, or profit derived therefrom payable to another. Since the payment of the use or benefit from the trust was enforceable by the chancellor in his court of equity, the right to receive such income became known as the equitable title to the property, in contradistinction to the legal title or fee.

THE PRIVATE TRUST. If one or more designated individuals are named as beneficiaries of the trust, it is known as a private trust. Since land was the primary source of income until comparatively recent times, land usually formed the "corpus," body, or principal of the trust. As other forms of capital, such as stocks and bonds, became available, the trust agreement developed into a convenient instrumentality whereby the legal title and physical custody of securities could be separated from the equitable right to receive the income therefrom.

THE CHARITABLE TRUST. If the beneficiaries of a trust are not specifically designated, that is, if the trust is established for the benefit of the general public or for a large segment thereof, it is deemed to be a charitable or public trust or use. "Charity," in its popular sense, means whatever is bestowed upon the needy or suffering for their relief. In the eyes of the law, charity is not confined to mere almsgiving but has a much wider significance, embracing the improvement of social conditions and the promotion of the happiness and well-being of mankind. At the same time, courts have made it clear that, while all charity may be motivated by benevolence, all benevolence is not necessarily charity, in the legal sense. A charity, in legal terminology, must be public in character. A quarter to a beggar, a gift to an individual, the tuition paid for a designated scholar may be motivated by generosity, but it is not charity as defined by the courts. If the beneficiaries of a trust are identified in the trust instrument, or if they are, as a class, too few in number, the trust must be considered private rather than charitable or public. Where charity, in the legal sense, is involved, the peculiar provisions of the law of charitable trusts are applicable. The word "peculiar" is used to sharpen the distinction that must be maintained when one is called upon to interpret and to administer the provisions of a charitable trust as contrasted with those of an ordinary agreement or contract. In the eyes of the law, the parties to a contract negotiate "at arm's length." The bargain is struck, and its terms and conditions are to be interpreted within the framework of the normal conflict of interests encountered in our competitive business environment.

On the other hand, the law demands that there be a complete disclosure of all pertinent facts and factors in the drafting of a trust instrument. In its administration, the trustee must avoid being placed in a position in which his interests as an individual are, or can be, in conflict with his duties and responsibilities as trustee. If he finds himself in such a position, he is under a duty to confer with the court, act under its instructions, or withdraw from the position of trustee.

A charitable trust may have perpetual existence, whereas a private trust must terminate, according to ancient custom subject to local variations, within twenty-one years after the death of a designated individual in being at the date of the creation of the trust.

THE CHARITABLE CORPORATION. In the contemplation of the law, all gifts and bequests for the benefit of the general public, such as those designated for the establishment and maintenance of hospitals, libraries, art museums, colleges and universities, are charitable in character. Consequently, it is proper, in the legal sense, to refer to a college, thus established and maintained without profit to an individual or group of individuals, as a charitable corporation, even though it may charge substantial fees for the use of its facilities.

JURISDICTION AND POWER. Every sovereign state has inherent jurisdiction over its own physical resources and over the person and property of its citizens. The states of the American union surrendered a portion of their inherent sovereignty by the acceptance and adoption, by their citizens, of the federal Constitution and by their admission to the union.

The Federal Government thus formed is one of limited powers. By virtue of the provisions of the Tenth Amendment, the states and their people retained all powers not granted to the Federal Government, explicitly or implicitly. Moreover, in most areas of the law of interest to the colleges, the state legislature and the state courts are supreme.

Despite the tendency of the public press to focus attention upon the actions of Congress and the Supreme Court of the United States, college administrators should remember that state legislation, state court decisions, municipal ordinances, and rulings and regulations of local agencies of government may be of more immediate concern to their institutions.

Since the powers of the Federal Government are limited and not plenary, the jurisdiction of the federal courts, the power of Congress to legislate, and the authority of the executive and administrative agencies of the Federal Government to administer and regulate, must be found in the federal Constitution, as interpreted by its courts.

The Supreme Court of the United States, by its interpretation of the provisions of the Constitution,[15] especially that portion of Section 8 of Article I giving Congress power "to regulate commerce . . . among the several states," has greatly enlarged the extent and scope of the power of the national government at the expense of state power.

The people of the several states, by their adoption of state constitutions, have established definite limits to the exercise of the power and authority of their state and local governments. This concept of the plenary power of the people to limit the power of government by the adoption of written constitutions is probably our most significant contribution to the art of living together on this planet.

CONSTITUTIONAL LIMITATIONS OF POWER. The power of a state to tax its citizens is an inherent attribute of sovereignty, but the public, in many of our American states, has seen fit to impose constitutional

---

[15] The decision of the Supreme Court of the United States in the case of Massachusetts v. Mellon, 262 U.S. 447 (1923) illustrates the extent to which the court has permitted the Congress to expand federal power by the use of federal funds and the extent to which the court itself feels free to assert the supremacy of the Constitution over all statutory law, state and federal.

The Maternity Act of 1921 provides for an annual expenditure of federal funds for a period of five years, "to be apportioned among such of the several states as shall accept and comply with its provisions" for the purpose of reducing maternal and infant mortality and of protecting the health of mothers and infants. The Commonwealth of Massachusetts brought an action to enjoin the federal officials from attempting to enforce the provisions of the act. In its brief, the state asserted that the act imposed upon it an option either to yield a part of its powers of government reserved by the Tenth Amendment, or to give up its share of appropriations under the act. It declared, in effect, that the protection of the health of mother and child was a function of state, not national, government; that the appropriations of federal funds for such purposes constituted an effective, but unconstitutional, method of inducing the states to yield a portion of their sovereignty. The Court rejected these contentions and declined to grant the injunction.

limitations upon its power to borrow. These constitutional debt limitations and their interpretation by the courts have had an important influence upon the methods adopted by tax-supported colleges and universities to finance the construction of needed dormitories and other income-producing campus buildings.[16]

The Federal Government, being one of limited powers, must look to its Constitution for its power to tax. The power to levy a tax on imports and an excise tax on commodities is to be found in the Constitution as originally adopted,[17] but the power to tax the income of its citizens and corporations was conferred by the adoption of the Sixteenth Amendment in 1913. Congress was thereby given power "to levy and collect taxes on income, from whatever source derived."

In 1861 Congress levied the first tax upon income in order to finance the cost of the Civil War. Its power to tax income was not contested until 1880. At that time, the Supreme Court[18] was of the opinion that this was a valid exercise of power, despite the constitutional limitations upon the imposition of direct taxes. The Civil War income tax laws expired in 1872, and it was not until 1884 that Congress decided to again exercise this asserted power. This time, the Supreme Court declared that the tax was unconstitutional.[19]

After much debate, the American people decided to give Congress the power to tax their income by the adoption of the Sixteenth Amendment, but this congressional power to tax is still limited by the power of the judiciary to define the word "income." For example, since the Supreme Court has declared that a true stock dividend is not income,[20] Congress is powerless to declare that it is, and thus subject it to taxation.

TAX LEGISLATION. Beginning in 1913, Congress has enacted a series of income tax statutes. Prior to 1939, in order to ascertain the law of taxa-

---

[16] See "Constitutional Debt Limitations," pp. 259–65.

[17] Art. I, § 8 (1): "The Congress shall have power to lay and collect taxes, duties, imposts and excises . . ."

The following are modern texts on the Constitution of the United States: Edward S. Corwin, *The Constitution and What It Means Today* (12th ed.; Princeton, N.J.: Princeton University Press, 1958). A. T. Mason and W. M. Beaney, *American Constitutional Law* (Englewood Cliffs, N.J.: Prentice-Hall, 1954). This text has been used for teaching courses in constitutional interpretation in liberal arts programs at Princeton University.

[18] Springer v. United States, 102 U.S. 586 (1880).

[19] Pollock v. Farmers Loan & Trust Co., 157 U.S. 429 (1895).

[20] Eisner v. Macomber, 252 U.S. 189 (1920).

tion on any given question, it was necessary to consult many of the older statutes. In that year, all tax legislation of the Federal Government, except that relating to customs, was consolidated and re-enacted as the Internal Revenue Code of 1939.[21] Between 1939 and 1954, all new revenue laws, their repeal or modification, were enacted as amendments to the code of 1939. In 1954, an entirely new code was adopted. However, in the opinion of many authorities, there is a great need for a complete restudy and revision of our national tax structure, federal and state.

TAX REGULATIONS AND RULINGS. Congress, by the enactment of tax codes and amendments thereto, determines the general structure of our system of federal taxation. It delegates certain powers of interpretation to the Secretary of the Treasury. He, in turn, delegates many of his powers to the Commissioner of Internal Revenue. Under this delegation of power, the Commissioner formulates regulations as his interpretation of the intent of the Congress. The more important of these regulations must be approved by the Secretary of the Treasury and are known as Treasury Decisions. They are the only regulations considered by the Treasury Department to be binding upon its own actions. Regulations and rulings of lower rank, published in the *Internal Revenue Bulletin,* are termed I.R.B. rulings, and its Commissioner does not consider that he is bound to follow such rulings in the disposition of subsequent tax cases.

Both the taxpayer and the Internal Revenue Service may request a ruling from the Commissioner as to the application of the tax laws to a specific transaction. These are known as letter rulings and are also not binding precedents, even with reference to the specific transaction in question. In general, however, if the taxpayer has made a full disclosure, in good faith, a letter ruling will not be revoked, so far as it applies to his case. They cannot be relied upon by other taxpayers, except as an indication of the trend of thinking of the Commissioner and his staff on the subject. In point of law, no statement of any official of the Internal Revenue Service, oral or written, is conclusive and

---

[21] Jacob K. Lasser (ed.), *Encyclopedia of Tax Procedures* (Englewood Cliffs, N.J.: Prentice-Hall, 1956). Randolph E. Paul, *Taxation in the United States* (Boston: Little, Brown & Co., 1954); this is a history of taxation in the country and an appraisal of the present system. *Federal Taxes* (16 vols.; Englewood Cliffs, N.J.: Prentice-Hall, 1956–). See Vol. 2A of this loose-leaf service, the following paragraphs: "General Principles," ¶¶ 28, 001–429; "Internal Revenue Service: Organization and Procedure," ¶¶ 21, 001–396; "Tax Court of the United States," ¶¶ 21, 401–851.

binding upon the service except those contained in what is known as a "closing agreement."[22]

TAX DECISIONS. If a taxpayer does not concur with the determination of his tax liability by members of the staff of the Internal Revenue Service, he is entitled to an informal conference in the District Director's office in his community. If an agreement is not reached at the conference, the taxpayer will receive what is known as a "thirty-day letter," with a copy of the final conference report. If he files a written protest within the statutory period, his case is referred to the Appellate Division of his region. After hearing, the decision of the Appellate Division is final, so far as the Internal Revenue Service is concerned, unless the District Director refers the case to Washington, in accordance with the provisions of the statute. If, after final hearing and determination by the IRS, the taxpayer is still unwilling to accept the decision, either he may pay the tax under protest and file claim for refund in the Court of Claims or, in some cases, in the U.S. District Court, or he may contest the collection of the tax thus assessed in the Tax Court of the United States.

Prior to 1924, a taxpayer, unable to reach an agreement with the Commissioner, had no choice in the matter. He was compelled to pay the tax as assessed and then seek to recover it by long and costly litigation. To remedy this unfair burden upon the citizen, Congress created a Board of Tax Appeals. In 1942 the name was changed to that of the Tax Court of the United States. Either the taxpayer or the Commissioner may file a petition for a review of the decisions of the Tax Court with the appropriate United States Court of Appeals. Both the government and the citizen may request the United States Supreme Court to review the decision of the lower court. If the high court declines to review, as it so frequently does in tax cases, the decision of the United States Court of Appeals is final, so far as the specific case is concerned. However, the Commissioner does not consider himself bound to follow the precedents established by decisions of lower federal courts. The only decisions he is required to follow in the settlement of subsequent tax disputes are those of the United States Supreme Court. In other words, this administrative officer can compel the citizens of this country to litigate the same basic tax questions time after time, until the issue has been settled by the highest federal court or by congressional action.

---

[22] *Int. Rev. Code of 1954*, § 7121.

THE NATURE OF THE JUDICIAL PROCESS. The very foundation of our Anglo-American system of common law, the rock of stability on which our concept of justice through law is erected, is expressed by the ancient maxim "stare decisis." This is the doctrine that declares that a court, when it has once laid down a principle of law as applicable to a certain state of facts, will adhere to that principle and apply it in all future cases when the facts are substantially the same. Dean Pound has said:

> The chief cause of success of our common law doctrine of precedents as a form of law is that it combines certainty and power of growth as no other doctrine has been able to do. Certainty is insured within reasonable limits in that the court proceeds by analogy of rules and doctrines in the traditional system and develops a principle for the cause before it according to a known technique. Growth is insured in that the limits of the principle are not fixed authoritatively once for all but are discovered gradually by a process of inclusion and exclusion as cases arise which bring out its practical workings and prove how far it may be made to do justice in its actual operation.[23]

DUE PROCESS OF LAW. The people of this country, before they would accept the proposed federal Constitution, demanded the adoption of a series of amendments, known as the Bill of Rights, to protect them against the exercise of arbitrary power by the new national government. The Fifth Amendment declares that no person shall be deprived of "life, liberty, or property, without due process of law." Due process has been interpreted to be synonymous with "the law of the land." What does this mean? It cannot refer to the general body of law, common and statutory, as it was at the time the federal Constitution took effect, for this would make it impossible for Congress and the courts to alter and modify the law of the land. The courts have declared that it refers to certain fundamental rights which men have always recognized as essential to their freedom. This concept is to be found in an edict of an emperor of the Holy Roman Empire. Conrad II, in 1037, declared that no man shall be deprived of his land but by the laws of the empire and the judgment of his peers.

At Runnymede in 1215, the barons of King John compelled him to grant these rights in the thirty-ninth section of Magna Carta,

---

[23] Roscoe Pound, *The Spirit of the Common Law* (Boston: Marshall Jones Co., 1921), p. 182. See also Benjamin N. Cardozo, *The Nature of the Judicial Process* (New Haven, Conn.: Yale University Press, 1921); William O. Douglas, *Stare Decisis* (New York: Association of the Bar of the City of New York, 1949); A. L. Goodhart, "Precedent in English and Continental Law," 50 *Law Q. Rev.* 40 (1934).

no freeman shall be taken, or imprisoned, or disseised, or outlawed, or exiled, or in any way destroyed, nor will we go upon him, nor will we send upon him, except by the legal judgment of his peers or by the law of the land.

The exact phrase "due process of law" was used in 1354 in one of the many confirmations of the Great Charter, sometimes called the Statute of Westminster of the Liberties of London.[24]

It was not until almost fifty years after the adoption of the Fifth Amendment that the United States Supreme Court gave this country an authoritative interpretation of the phrase, "due process of law." In a case[25] involving an act of Congress providing for summary procedures in the collection of debts owed to the government, Mr. Justice Curtis stated:

The article is a restraint upon the legislative as well as on the judicial powers of the government, and cannot be so construed as to leave Congress free to make any process "due process of law" by its mere will.

Shortly after the Civil War the voters, by their adoption of the Fourteenth Amendment, imposed similar restraints upon the power of the states. Thus, the courts, by this interpretation of due process, may declare any legislative, executive, or administrative action invalid, as contrary to the Constitution, if it is in the opinion of the judges contrary to common right and reason.[26]

The House of Lords, sitting as the supreme court of Great Britain, considers itself bound by its own decisions, but our federal and state courts do not hesitate to depart from precedent when they are persuaded that the justification to do so is sufficiently strong and compelling.[27] Frequent departures of the Supreme Court of the United States from the doctrine of stare decisis during recent years have evoked much criticism, both by legal scholars and by individual members[28] of the high court itself.

---

[24] 28 Edw. 3, c. 7.

[25] Murray v. Hoboken Land & Improvement Co., 59 U.S. (18 How.) 272 (1856).

[26] The provisions of the ten amendments, our Bill of Rights, are limitations upon the power of the national government, not upon the power of the states. However, the Supreme Court of the United States by its interpretation of the phrase "due process of law" in the Fourteenth Amendment has, to some extent, imposed upon the states these same limitations of power. For an illustration of this, see "Constitutional Restrictions on the Use of Public Funds for the Support of Church-Related Colleges," p. 32. See also Calder v. Bull, 3 U.S. (3 Dall.) 386 (1798).

[27] Roscoe Pound, "The Theory of Judicial Decision," 36 *Harv. L. Rev.* 641 (1923).

[28] The following is an excerpt from the dissenting opinion of Mr. Justice Roberts in the case of Mahnich v. Southern Steamship Co., 321 U.S. 96 (1944) in

THE INTERPRETATION OF STATUTES. It is the function of the courts to interpret the statutes enacted by Congress and by the state legislatures. The supreme court of each state is the final authority as to the meaning of a statute enacted by its legislature just as the United States Supreme Court has the final word as to the meaning of an act of Congress. In this process of interpretation, a court attempts to ascertain the intention of the legislative body. When the intent is not clear to the court from the language of the statute, it may refer to the record of legislative hearings, debate, and committee reports while the act in question was under discussion. Consequently, an attorney, when he is called upon to prepare an opinion as to the probable action of a court with reference to a legal issue not fully adjudicated, finds it useful to refer to the legislative history[29] of the statute involved.

THE AMERICAN JUDICIAL SYSTEM. Our Federal Government being one of limited powers, its courts have only that jurisdiction conferred upon them by the federal Constitution and legislation enacted in consonance therewith. The scope of their jurisdiction is to be found in Article III, subject to the limitation subsequently imposed by the adoption of the Eleventh Amendment.

Section 1 of Article III states, in part, that:

The judicial power of the United States shall be vested in one Supreme Court, and in such inferior courts as Congress may, from time to time, obtain and establish . . .

The jurisdiction of these courts is defined and limited in Section 2 (1), which reads as follows:

The judicial power shall extend to all cases, in law and equity, arising under this Constitution, the laws of the United States and treaties made or which shall be made, under their authority; to all cases affecting ambassadors, other public ministers, and consuls; to all cases of admiralty and maritime jurisdiction; to controversies to which the United States shall be a party; to controversies between two or more states; between a State and a citizen of

---

which he was joined by Mr. Justice Frankfurter: "The evil resulting from overriding earlier considered decisions must be evident. . . . The tendency to disregard precedents . . . has become so strong in this Court of late as, in my view, to shake confidence in the consistency of decision and leave the courts below on an uncharted sea of doubt and difficulty without any confidence that what was said yesterday will hold good tomorrow."

See also Frank W. Grinnell, "Stare Decisis and the Supreme Court of the United States," 27 *J. Am. Jud. Soc'y* 183 (1944).

[29] The history of the more recent federal statutes may be found in the *United States Code Congressional and Administrative News.* (See note 7 for a description of this publication.)

another State, between citizens of different States; between the citizens of
the same State claiming lands under grants of different States, and between
a State, or a citizen thereof, and foreign States, citizens, or subjects.

The Eleventh Amendment was adopted in 1798 after the United
States Supreme Court had ruled[30] that the "sovereign State of Georgia"
could be compelled to appear before a federal court to answer the suit
of a citizen of another state. To avoid a second affront to the dignity of
a state, the following limitation upon the jurisdiction of federal courts
was imposed:

The judicial power of the United States shall not be construed to extend
to any suit in law or equity commenced or prosecuted against one of the
United States by citizens of another State, or by citizens or subjects of any
foreign State.

Section 2 (2) of Article III of the federal Constitution further defines
the jurisdiction of the Supreme Court as follows:

In all cases affecting ambassadors, other public ministers and consuls, and
those in which a State shall be a party, the Supreme Court shall have original
jurisdiction, both as to law and fact, with such exceptions, and under such
regulations, as Congress shall make.

Under the delegation of power in Section 1 of Article III, Congress
created a number of "inferior" courts, including the Circuit Courts of
Appeals, the federal district courts, and the Court of Claims. Congress
had also established courts for the territories, the District of Columbia,
and the special courts to hear appeals from the rulings and decisions
of administrative officers of the Federal Government.[31] These include
the Customs Court, the Court of Customs and Patent Appeals, the Tax
Court, and the Court of Military Appeals.

Every state has its own judiciary similar in structure to the federal
system, including a supreme court, although not always so designated,
appellate courts, district and county courts, and minor and special
courts. In rural areas and small communities, the justice of the peace
disposes of minor disputes with little formality. Some states have replaced him with a legally trained magistrate. In metropolitan areas one
will usually find courts with specialized functions and limited jurisdiction, such as probate courts, traffic courts, juvenile courts, and courts
of domestic relations.

---

[30] Chisholm v. Georgia, 2 U.S. (2 Dall.) 419 (1793).

[31] A codification of the statutes governing the federal judicial system may be
found in Title 28 of the *United States Code*.

State supreme courts are the ultimate interpreters of their own constitution and laws. If, however, an unsuccessful litigant can persuade the judges of the United States Supreme Court that he has been deprived of some right or immunity granted by the federal Constitution, his case will be transferred to the high federal court, either by appeal or by writ of certiorari. This writ is an order from a superior to a lower court, requiring the transmittal of all documents of the case in question to the superior court for review. An appeal is granted if the litigant is entitled to a review of his case as a matter of right. A writ of certiorari may be granted or denied at the discretion of the superior court.

CHAPTER II

The College Corporation

THE majority of institutions of higher education in this country are private charitable corporations.[1] In the early days there was considerable uncertainty as to the corporate status of colleges, as illustrated by the controversy over the precise character of the charter granted to Dartmouth College by George III in 1769. The Legislature of New Hampshire in 1816, acting on the assumption that the charter granted by the British Crown had created a public institution, proceeded to reorganize the college in order to bring it under state control. The original Board of Trustees was made subservient to a Board of Overseers composed of public officials and appointees of the governor. The institution was renamed Dartmouth University.

The newly appointed board occupied the college buildings and took possession of the records of the college and its corporate seal. The college trustees brought an action in the state court to recover physical possession of the college property. The state court upheld the action of the legislature and the college trustees appealed on a writ of error to the Supreme Court of the United States. Daniel Webster, an alumnus of the college, served as their chief counsel. The opinion of Chief Justice Marshall in this case is one of the most famous in legal history. He declared:

From this review of the charter, it appears that Dartmouth College is an eleemosynary institution, incorporated for the purpose of perpetuating

---

[1] According to the U.S. Office of Education, *Education Directory, 1959–60: Part 3: Higher Education* (Washington: Government Printing Office, 1959), p. 11, institutions of higher education in this country may be classified by type of control as follows: federal, 8 institutions; state, 379; district or city, 311; private, 520; denominational, 793; total 2,011. For a discussion of the concept of the college, see Burns B. Young, "What Is a College?" *Educational Record*, XXX (October 1949), 385–406.

the application of the bounty of the donors . . . , that its trustees . . . are not public officers, nor is it a civil institution, participating in the administration of government.[2]

STATE SUPERVISION AND CONTROL OF
EDUCATIONAL CORPORATIONS

THE CORPORATE STATUS OF AMERICAN COLLEGES. According to the principle of law enunciated in this celebrated decision, a college or university founded by private enterprise and endowed or supported by private donations is a private eleemosynary institution, that is, a charitable corporation. Today, the converse is true: A college or university is deemed to be public in character if its primary support is derived from public funds.[3] And yet, as late as 1852, the Supreme

---

[2] Trustees of Dartmouth College v. Woodward, 17 U.S. (4 Wheat.) 518 (1819). In this celebrated case, Chief Justice Marshall established the doctrine that a corporate charter is a contract between the state and its incorporators, and, as such, it is protected by the tenth section of the first article of the federal Constitution which declares that "no state shall pass . . . any law impairing the obligation of contracts."

This aspect of the decision is the basis for the right of some colleges today to complete exemption from state and local property taxation on the grounds that their corporate charters conferred this right and that the charters were granted without the reservation of power by the state to amend them. As soon as the significance of the Dartmouth College case was realized, the states took appropriate steps to make certain that new corporate charters, when issued, and old charters, when amended for any reason, are subject to a reservation of power by the state to amend. See "Property Exemption by Charter Right," pp. 156–59.

The Dartmouth College case has another claim to fame. Chief Justice Marshall, in his opinion in that case, gave us what is probably the most frequently quoted definition of a corporation: "A corporation is an artificial being, invisible, intangible, and existing only in contemplation of law. Being a mere creature of law, it possesses only those properties which the charter of its creation confers upon it, either expressly or as incidental to its very existence. These are such as are supposed best calculated to effect the object for which it was created. Among the most important are immortality, and, if that expression may be allowed, individuality; properties, by which a perpetual succession of many persons are considered as the same, and may act as a single individual. They enable a corporation to manage its own affairs, and to hold property without the perplexing intricacies, the hazardous and endless necessity, of perpetual conveyances for the purpose of transmitting it from hand to hand. It is chiefly for the purpose of clothing bodies of men in succession with these qualities and capacities that corporations were invented and are in use. By these means a perpetual succession of individuals are capable of acting for the promotion of the particular object like one immortal being."

[3] For a discussion of the distinction between public and nonpublic institutions of higher education, see 5 *Am. Jur.: Universities and Colleges* § 3 (1946); 14 *C.J.S.: Colleges and Universities* § 2 (1939). In general, the chief factor in the

Court of the United States declared that Vincennes University, established by the territorial legislature of Indiana in 1806 and endowed by it with a grant of public lands received from the Federal Government, was not a public corporation, but private in character. Thus, the corporate status[4] of an institution of higher education in this country can only be determined by an analysis of its charter and the method of its establishment, support, and control, as interpreted by the courts.

CORPORATE STATUS OF CHURCH-RELATED COLLEGES. In a case involving the validity of the charter granted to Westminster College in 1857, Judge Valliant of the Supreme Court of Missouri said:

Appellant contends that this charter is in violation of section 5 art. 13 of the Constitution of 1820, which ordained that "no religious corporation can ever be established in this state." The sum of the argument is that, because the Synod of the Presbyterian Church in Missouri is given the care and control of the interests of the corporation and the appointment of the trustees, it is therefore a "religious" corporation. A corporation established for purely academic purposes, for education in literature and in the arts and sciences, is in no sense a religious corporation, even though it be given into the care and under the management of a religious body. Religious corporations, as they were known at common law, were not looked upon with favor by the early inhabitants of this country, in whose mind they were associated in a great degree with the idea of a union of church and state, and therefore the disposition was to give them no countenance in law.

But this has always been a Christian country, and there is nothing to be found in either the letter or the spirit of our law, or in the spirit of our republican institutions, that disapproves of educational institutions under the control of churches.[5]

---

determination of their status is their origin; if founded by private individuals, privately endowed and supported, the courts will consider it to be a private corporation, even though it may receive a substantial amount of public funds. If, on the other hand, it was organized and established by the legislature and if it is supported primarily by public funds, it is treated as a public corporation or as an agency of government.

If a majority of the members of its governing board are elected by the people, or appointed by the legislature, the governor, or other public official or public body, the institution is considered to be public in character. See Annot., 65 A.L.R. 1396 (1930).

[4] Trustees of Vincennes University v. State of Indiana, 55 U.S. 269 (1852). For further discussion of the distinction between a private and a public institution of higher education, see "Higher Education as a Function of Government," pp. 237–40.

[5] State v. Board of Trustees of Westminster College, 175 Mo. 52, 74 S.W. 990 (1903).

REQUIRED STANDARDS FOR INCORPORATION. By requiring those seeking incorporation to furnish evidence of their qualifications to conduct the proposed enterprise, the legislature is in a position to exert a degree of control over such ventures. At first, corporate charters were granted by a special act of the legislative body, after a review of the proposed charter and the qualifications of the incorporators. When the number of applications for charters became too great to be handled by the legislature, responsibility for review was delegated to an administrative officer or an administrative agency, in accordance with the provisions of statutes of general applicability. Since 1850 many states have amended their constitutions so as to prohibit the creation of corporations by special legislation.

Educators from abroad have expressed astonishment at the lack of adequate standards provided to guide state officials in their granting of charters to institutions of higher education.[6] Only one state has delegated the important governmental function of granting charters to an educational agency: the Regents of the University of the State of New York have sole authority[7] to grant college and university charters within that state. Those seeking such a charter must convince the Regents that

---

[6] According to Robert H. Reid, *American Degree Mills* (Washington: American Council on Education, 1959), pp. 7, 8, diploma mills, calling themselves colleges and universities, are taking in an estimated $75 million annually and are seriously injuring American prestige abroad. A major factor, the report says, is the fact that "The United States, unlike most other countries of the world, has no ministry of education. State laws chartering institutions are not uniform and are actually quite lax in controlling educational malpractice. . . . nationals of other countries . . . cannot appreciate that a country can have educational standards unless there is a federal agency controlling such matters."

The Council of State Governments, as part of its program for 1959, drafted a model act "to prevent deception of the public resulting from fraudulent or substandard degrees" for adoption by state legislatures. Copies of the proposed legislation may be obtained from the Council of State Governments, 36 West 44th St., New York, N.Y.

The American Council on Education at its Forty-second Annual Meeting in October 1959 adopted a resolution commending the Council of State Governments for its constructive action and urging its own member institutions and organizations to support this or similar legislation "designed to eliminate so-called educational institutions which defraud their students and the public by selling degrees without demanding legitimate academic achievement." See the bulletin of the American Council on Education, *Higher Education and National Affairs*, VIII (Oct. 15, 1959), 3.

[7] *N.Y. Educ. Law* § 216. The corporation known as "The Regents of the University of the State of New York" was created in 1784. Later its name was changed to "The University of the State of New York."

their "purposes are, in whole or in part, of educational or cultural value deemed worthy of recognition and encouragement."

In Arkansas,[8] Illinois,[9] Vermont,[10] West Virginia,[11] and in several other states, responsibility for review and approval of the applications of those seeking corporate status for institutions of higher education is delegated to the state departments of education, although the charter itself is issued by another state official, usually the secretary of state. Massachusetts[12] has delegated responsibility for review to its board of collegiate authority. In Pennsylvania,[13] no institution may designate itself as a "college" or "university" without the approval of the state council of education.

STATE SUPERVISION AND CONTROL OF NONPUBLIC EDUCATIONAL CORPORATIONS. Visitors from overseas have also expressed surprise at the lack of state supervision over the activities of our privately controlled institutions of higher education. New York[14] is almost alone in conferring broad powers of "visitation" and inspection of nonpublic schools upon its educational agency, the Regents of the University of the State of New York. Even the important function of accreditation has, by common consent rather than legislation, been delegated to nonpublic agencies and organizations.

All individuals, organizations, and associations are subject to the inherent police powers of the state, that is, those exercised for the protection of the lives and property of its citizens. Building codes, fire regulations, health and sanitation codes, and motor vehicle codes are expressions of the exercise of police power.

The state, in the exercise of this power, restricts the practice of certain professions, such as medicine, dentistry, and architecture, to those granted a license after a review of their qualifications by an administrative agency of government. The power to confer certain professional degrees by educational institutions has also been subjected to state regulation in the interest of the protection of the public.

In 1935 the New York Legislature prohibited[15] any individual or corporation from conferring degrees in law, medicine, dentistry, phar-

---

[8] *Ark. Stat.* § 64–1409 (1947).
[9] *Ill. Rev. Stat.* ch. 144, § 122 (1957).
[10] *Vt. Stat.* tit. 18, ch. 188, ¶ 4186 (1947).
[11] *W.Va. Code* ch. 18, art. 2, ¶ 1731 (1955).
[12] *Mass. Gen. Laws* ch. 69, § 30 (1952).
[13] *Penn. Stat.* tit. 24, ch. 3, § 2421 (1949).
[14] *N.Y. Educ. Law* § 215.
[15] *N.Y. Educ. Law* § 224.

macy, veterinary medicine, nursing, optometry, chiropody, architec
ture, or engineering "unless the right to do so shall have been granted
by the regents of the University of the State of New York in writing
under their seal."

The constitutionality of this delegation of power to an administrative
board was challenged[16] by the Institute of the Metropolis, Inc. In upholding the statute in question, Justice Schanck declared:

It is proper for a legislature to commit to an administrative board the determination of a standard of fitness when the subject necessarily involves
technical training and varying standards. The regulation of educational
institutions is peculiarly a matter affected with the public interest and involves the welfare and morals of citizens and even the safety of the state.
In general, it has been held that the state may require a license of a physician, surgeon, dentist, lawyer and school teacher.

This decision was upheld by the appellate division of the court.
There, Justice Hill stated:

In the exercise of the police power, the legislature must be reasonable.
There must be a tendency to promote the general welfare, and the act must
not be arbitrary or capricious. This legislation is not arbitrary or capricious.

Other states have delegated the responsibility for passing upon the
educational standards of colleges desiring to confer degrees in the
healing arts to state boards of medical examiners. The constitutionality
of this delegation of legislative authority has been upheld by the courts
of New Jersey[17] and Illinois.[18] The Legislature of Illinois, in 1903, delegated to its state university the responsibility of determining the qualifications of certified public accountants desiring to practice within
the state. The constitutionality of this act was upheld by the Supreme
Court of Illinois[19] and by the Supreme Court of the United States.

PUBLIC FUNDS FOR SUPPORT OF
EDUCATIONAL INSTITUTIONS

APPROPRIATION OF PUBLIC FUNDS FOR THE SUPPORT OF NONPUBLIC COL-
LEGES. Students of American history will recall that, for more than half
a century after the establishment of the national government, it was

---

[16] Institute of the Metropolis v. University of the State of N.Y., 159 Misc. 529,
289 N.Y. Supp. 660 (1936), aff'd, 249 App. Div. 33, 291 N.Y. Supp. 893 (1936).
[17] College of Mecca of Chiropractic v. State Board of Medical Examiners of
New Jersey, 113 N.J.L. 327, 174 Atl. 562 (Ct. Err. & App. 1934).
[18] People v. Apfelbaum, 251 Ill. 18, 95 N.E. 995 (1911).
[19] Elliott v. University of Illinois, 365 Ill. 338, 6 N.E.2d 647 (1936), rehearing
denied, 302 U.S. 774 (1937).

common practice for Congress and the state legislatures to grant direct
financial aid and credit to railroads and other business ventures in the
belief that, by promoting the growth and expansion of the nation, such
use of public funds was justified. Evidence of favoritism and corrup-
tion became so overwhelming that the people in many states demanded the adoption of constitutional amendments to restrain this
practice. At the present time, the constitutions of twenty-four states[20]
prohibit the appropriation of public funds to private persons or organizations. This general prohibition does not extend to educational
institutions in three of the states.

On the other hand, there are fourteen states that have constitutional
provisions explicitly prohibiting appropriation of money or property to
privately controlled schools or institutions, and there are eight states
with constitutional provisions specifically authorizing such action under certain conditions.

Public aid to privately controlled educational institutions was quite
customary during the colonial period of our history and for some years
thereafter. This was apparently due to the fact that the line of de-
marcation between the privately controlled and the publicly controlled
institutions of learning was not sharply drawn[21] during this early
period.

Furthermore, the idea that higher education should be undertaken
as a direct function of the state developed rather slowly in this country. Harvard College received appropriations of public funds from the
colonial government of Massachusetts and from various towns during
the seventeenth century and from the State of Massachusetts until
1823. The State of New Hampshire made regular grants of public
funds to Dartmouth College until 1920. Howard University, a privately

---

[20] For a summary and analysis, state by state, of the constitutional and statutory
provisions concerned with the privately controlled institutions of this country, see
Fred F. Beach and Robert F. Will, *The State and Nonpublic Schools*, U.S. Office
of Education Misc. No. 28 (Washington: Government Printing Office, 1958).

[21] The Problems and Policies Committee of the American Council on Education, in a statement entitled *The Need To Close Ranks in Higher Education*, released in February 1959, reminded the citizens of this country that "Private institutions no less than public institutions are by their charters dedicated to the
public service. Private institutions receive direct or indirect benefits from tax-
supported programs of student aid; many receive state and federal grants for
research and other purposes. Most public institutions have income from student
fees and individual donations; many receive substantial contributions from industry and philanthropic foundations. Institutions of both types enjoy tax-exemp-
tion because of their public purpose. Hence, in terms of financial support, no institution is strictly private or strictly public."

controlled, nondenominational institution, was founded in 1867. In 1931 the Federal Government undertook responsibility for developing it into a university of the first class, at a cost of approximately $15 million. The University of Pennsylvania, Temple University, and the University of Pittsburgh receive appropriations from the State of Pennsylvania as consideration for the awarding of scholarships. The recipients of these scholarships are designated by state senators and representatives.

THE "CONTRACT COLLEGES" OF THE STATE UNIVERSITY OF NEW YORK. New York, without a state university of its own for many years, has followed a unique pattern of providing financial support for schools and colleges administered by private universities under contract with the state. In accordance with specific statutory authority, state funds are appropriated for the support of an Agricultural and Technical Institute and a College of Ceramics at Alfred University; a College of Agriculture, a College of Home Economics, a Veterinary College, and a School of Industrial and Labor Relations at Cornell University; and a College of Forestry at Syracuse University. Although located at private universities, these educational activities are listed as divisions of the recently established State University of New York.

ALLOCATION OF FEDERAL LAND-GRANT FUNDS TO NONPUBLIC INSTITUTIONS. The famous Morrill Land-Grant Act of 1862 made public lands available to the several states for the endowment, support, and maintenance of colleges for instruction in "such branches of learning as are related to agriculture and the mechanic arts." The act did not limit the use of the proceeds from the sale of these public lands to publicly controlled institutions.

In 1863 the Legislature of Massachusetts granted to the Massachusetts Institute of Technology one-third of the income of its federal land-grant fund. This action was challenged by the Massachusetts Agricultural College in 1892, but the state supreme court upheld the legality of the allocation.[22]

The State of Connecticut received from the United States Government land scrip subsequently sold for $135,000 under the provisions of the Morrill Act. By contract with Yale University, the state agreed to pay the interest from the investment of these proceeds in consideration

---

[22] Massachusetts Agricultural College v. Marden, 156 Mass. 150, 30 N.E. 555 (1892).

of the university's agreement to fulfill the duties and obligations required by the act. The required instruction was given by the Sheffield Scientific School of Yale University. In 1893 the general assembly established Storrs Agricultural College as a state college and instructed the state treasurer to pay the interest on the land-grant fund to the newly established institution rather than to Yale University. The university brought suit against the state treasurer to prevent the threatened diversion of the income. The federal court was of the opinion that the university had a vested beneficial right to the income and that it was entitled to an injunction to restrain the state treasurer from paying the income from the land-scrip fund to any other institution, but that a state cannot be coerced or compelled by suit of one of its citizens to perform its contracts.[23] In view of this decision, the state set up a special commission to investigate the claim of Yale University. After long negotiations, the commission recommended that the legislature appropriate funds to compensate the university for the breach of contract, with an award of damages of approximately $155,000.

The State of Rhode Island followed a similar course of action. It negotiated a contract with Brown University in 1863 for the establishment of a college or department of agriculture to be financed by funds received by the state under the Morrill Act. In 1892 the general assembly established and incorporated the Rhode Island College of Agriculture and Mechanic Arts and designated it as the recipient of income from the land-grant funds and subsequent appropriations of Congress for similar purposes. A federal court declined to interfere with the discretion of the legislature in its allocation of these funds.[24] New Jersey allocated land-grant funds to Rutgers College,[25] and, as we have noted, New York designated Cornell University to conduct the educational program required by the Morrill Act.

However, this pattern was not followed by the states beyond the Atlantic seaboard. There, the state legislatures either established new educational institutions or designated existing institutions under direct public control to carry out the provisions of the act.

CONSTITUTIONAL LIMITATIONS ON THE USE OF PUBLIC FUNDS. As we have seen, the legislatures of twenty-one[26] of our American states are

---

[23] Yale College v. Sanger, 62 Fed. 177 (C.C.D. Conn. 1894).

[24] Brown University v. Rhode Island College of Agriculture and Mechanic Arts, 56 Fed. 55 (C.C.D.R.I. 1893).

[25] See chap. 8, "Additional Problems of Publicly Controlled Colleges," pp. 275–77.

[23] Beach and Will, op. cit. supra note 20, at 18.

forbidden by their constitutions to appropriate public funds for the support of educational institutions not owned or controlled by the state or political subdivision thereof.

The Board of Trustees of Straight University applied to a Louisiana district court for a writ of mandamus against the state auditor to compel him to issue to them warrants in the amount of $35,000, the amount appropriated by the state for the benefit of the university represented by them. The state auditor, in his reply, defended his refusal to issue the warrants on the ground that the act of the legislature was in violation of that article of the state constitution which forbids the legislature to make appropriations for the support of any private institution of learning. He asserted that Straight University was such an institution. The state supreme court[27] upheld the action of the state auditor in these words from the opinion of Judge Taliaferro, handed down in May 1873:

We conclude that the constitutional objection named in this case must prevail. The Straight University was incorporated under the general statutes of the state as a private corporation. . . . The state, through its officers or otherwise, exercises no control or direction over the university, nor has it any voice as to the manner in which it shall be conducted.

Even in the absence of a specific constitutional prohibition, the courts of Kansas and Wisconsin have declared that the use of public funds for the support of private educational institutions is unconstitutional.

In 1887 the city of Atchison subscribed the sum of $50,000 for the benefit of Midland College and a like sum for the benefit of St. Louis College. A taxpayer brought suit to recover taxes paid as the result of a tax levy to pay these subscriptions. The Supreme Court of Kansas[28] declared:

While it is argued that the public is benefited by the increase of schools and the spread of learning and knowledge, it is not contended that the colleges in question are under the supervision and control of the public, or that there is or could be any legislative authority to expend the public revenues for their support.

In 1867 the Wisconsin Legislature authorized the town of Jefferson to raise by taxes $5,000 to aid in the erection of the Jefferson Liberal Institute. A taxpayer refused to pay the tax assessed against his prop-

---

[27] State v. Graham, 25 La. Ann. 440 (1873).
[28] Atchison T. & S.F.Ry. v. City of Atchison, 47 Kan. 712, 28 Pac. 1000 (1892).

erty. The state supreme court[29] refused to uphold the validity of the assessment. The following is from the opinion of Chief Justice Dixon:

That there exists in the state no power to tax for such purpose, is a proposition too plain to admit of controversy. Such a power would be obviously incompatible with the genius and institutions of a free people; and the practice of all liberal governments, as well as all judicial authority, is against it.

CONSTITUTIONAL RESTRICTIONS ON THE USE OF PUBLIC FUNDS FOR THE SUPPORT OF CHURCH-RELATED COLLEGES. The First Amendment to the federal Constitution declares that "Congress shall make no law respecting an establishment of religion, or prohibiting the free exercise thereof." The restraint is laid upon Congress, not upon the states, but the Supreme Court of the United States has extended this prohibition to the states by its interpretation of the phrase "due process of law" in the Fourteenth Amendment. In a case[30] decided in 1925 involving freedom of speech, the court declared that the freedoms "protected by the First Amendment from abridgment by Congress are among the fundamental personal rights and 'liberties' protected by the due process clause in the Fourteenth Amendment from impairment by the states."

Two conflicting theories of what the makers of the Constitution and its first ten amendments had in mind when they used the phrase "an establishment of religion" in the First Amendment have been debated by legal scholars[31] and jurists.[32] According to one side of the argument, Congress is forbidden merely to grant *preferential* treatment to any particular religion, but religion, in the broader sense of the word, is to be encouraged by government. Those holding to this interpretation of

---

[29] Curtis' Administrator v. Whipple, 24 Wis. 350 (1869); see also Elsberry v. Seay, 83 Ala. 614, 3 So. 804 (1888).

[30] Gitlow v. New York, 268 U.S. 652 (1925).

[31] Edward S. Corwin, *The Constitution and What It Means Today* (12th ed.; Princeton, N.J.: Princeton University Press, 1958), pp. 188–204. See also Cagel, "Public Aid for Sectarian Schools," 2 *Baylor L. Rev.* 159 (1950); Scanlan, "Providing Publicly Financed Benefits to Private Schools," 11 *U. of Pitt. L. Rev.* 318 (1950); Moehlman, "Wall of Separation: The Law and the Facts," 38 *A.B.A.J.* 281, 343 (1952). One should bear in mind that the first eight amendments to the federal Constitution limit the powers of the national government and not those of the states. Our Fifth Amendment freedoms under due process are really Fourteenth Amendment freedoms when we are thinking of limitations on state action. Some, though not all, of the limitations found in the first eight amendments of the Bill of Rights are, by court interpretation, included in the Fourteenth.

[32] Murdock v. Pennsylvania, 319 U.S. 105 (1943); Everson v. Board of Education, 330 U.S. 1 (1947); McCollum v. Board of Education, 333 U.S. 203 (1948).

the phrase point to the third article in the Northwest Ordinance of 1787, drafted only a few years before the wording of the first amendment was under consideration: "Religion, morality, and knowledge being necessary to good government and the happiness of mankind, schools and the means of education shall forever be encouraged." The exponents of the other side of the argument call attention to the fact that Jefferson, in a letter which he wrote in 1802, expressed the conviction that it was the purpose of the First Amendment to build "a wall of separation between Church and State." In 1879, Chief Justice Waite characterized[33] this statement by Jefferson as "almost an authoritative declaration of the scope and effect of the amendment."

At the present time the constitutions of thirty-eight states[34] have provisions explicitly forbidding the use of public funds for the support of church-related schools or institutions or for the benefit of any sect or religious society. The New York constitution[35] has this to say on the subject:

Neither the state nor any subdivision thereof shall use its property or its credit or any public money, or authorize or permit either to be used, directly or indirectly, in aid or maintenance . . . of any school or institution of learning wholly or in part under the control of any religious denomination, or in which any denomination tenet or doctrine is taught.

Despite this inhibition upon the use of public funds, the New York courts[36] in 1958 declined to restrain the City of New York from consummating a contract with Fordham University, whereby Fordham was permitted to purchase land from the city at approximately 44 percent of its cost of acquisition by condemnation proceedings. The difference between cost and sales price was borne two-thirds by the Federal Government and one-third by the City of New York, in accordance with the provisions of Title I of the Federal Housing Act of 1949. The federal contribution to this slum clearance project in the Lincoln Square area of Manhattan was approximately $28 million. The following is from the opinion of Judge Desmond:

Plaintiffs say that, because the city arranged to sell this land at a price much below what the city will pay for it, this necessarily amounts to a subsidy or gift. But what the city is buying is not the same as what Fordham

---

[33] Reynolds v. United States, 98 U.S. 145, 164 (1879).

[34] Beach and Will, op. cit. supra note 20, at 15.

[35] N.Y. Const. art. XI, § 4.

[36] 64th St. Residences v. City of New York, 4 N.Y.2d 268, 150 N.E.2d 396, 174 N.Y.S.2d 1 (1958).

is buying. . . . What Fordham is paying for is the re-use value of the land.
. . . The city benefits by the achievement of its valid municipal purpose of
eliminating a slum.

Those initiating the injunction proceedings against the city petitioned the Supreme Court of the United States to review the decision
of the state court, but the petition was denied.[37] Mr. Justice Douglas,
however, was of the opinion that the petition for the writ of certiorari
should have been granted.

STATE SCHOLARSHIP PROGRAMS. A system of state scholarships has been
in successful operation in New York for many years.[38] In 1872 the legislature provided funds for free scholarships at Cornell University to
be awarded to "the best scholar from each academy and each public
school" in the state. A statute of 1913 established five state scholarships
in each assembly district, to be awarded annually. The scholarships
could be used in any college approved by the Regents of the University of the State of New York.

Where the state constitution prohibits the use of public funds for the
support of private or church-related institutions, state scholarship programs have been challenged in the courts. The New Jersey Legislature
in 1888 established a system of state scholarships to be used in the
College of Agriculture at Rutgers College. For ten years the state
auditor refused to pay the scholarship vouchers on the ground that
such payments would, in effect, represent a gift to a private corporation and hence be contrary to the provisions of the state constitution.
A commission was appointed to review the problem. The commissioners recommended that the state pay Rutgers only $80,000 instead
of the $133,100 billed for the education of the state scholars. The audi-
tor still refused to honor the voucher. The Supreme Court of New
Jersey ordered[39] payment on the grounds that, although Rutgers was
privately controlled, the state had been given a large measure of control over its College of Agriculture.

In this case, the court apparently assumed that an educational institution receives some financial benefit from the receipt of tuition and
that the payment of tuition by the state for its scholars was, in effect,
financial support of the institution and hence contrary to constitu-

---

[37] Harris v. City of New York, 357 U.S. 907 (1958).

[38] *N.Y. Educ. Law* § 601. For a survey of recent state scholarship programs,
see *The Book of the States, 1960–61* (Chicago: Council of State Governments,
1960), p. 300.

[39] Trustees of Rutgers College v. Morgan, 70 N.J.L. 460, 57 Atl. 250 (1904).

tional prohibitions unless the institution receiving it was controlled, at least in a degree, by the state. One method of avoiding this problem would be to limit the payment by the state to the demonstrated incremental cost of educating the state scholars.

This procedure was successfully employed by Wisconsin. Its legislature in 1919 provided for a system of state scholarships for World War I veterans to be used at any nonprofit high school or college approved by the state board of education. The statute provided for the payment, not of the customary tuition, but only of "the actual increased cost of operation in excess of the costs of the institution if such legislation had not been passed."

Despite a constitutional prohibition of state aid to church-related schools, the legislation was upheld. In his opinion, Justice Vinje made this statement:

> The contention that financial benefit accrues to religious schools from the act is untenable. Only actual increased cost to schools occasioned by the attendance of beneficiaries is to be reimbursed. They are not enriched by the service they render. Mere reimbursement is not aid.[40]

During 1956 attendance at the large institutions of higher education in this country reached a new high, whereas many of the small, privately controlled and church-related colleges were still seeking to enroll more students. With this fact in mind, a senator in the Nebraska Legislature drafted a bill for the establishment of a state scholarship system. His bill would have provided five hundred scholarships each year, permitting the recipients to attend the college or university of their own choice. He requested a ruling from the attorney general of the state on the constitutionality of the proposed legislation. The pertinent section of the Nebraska constitution reads as follows:

> Neither the state legislature nor any county, city, or other public corporation shall ever make any appropriation from any public fund, or grant any public land in aid of any sectarian or denominational institution, school or college, or any educational institution which is not exclusively owned or controlled by the state or a governmental subdivision thereof.[41]

The attorney general submitted his ruling to the senator in a letter dated January 12, 1957. He stated that the courts of Nebraska had not, as yet, been called upon to construe this section of the state constitution. In the absence of decided cases, he made use of a procedure

[40] State v. Johnson, 170 Wis. 251, 176 N.W. 224 (1920).
[41] *Neb. Const.* art. VII, § 11.

frequently employed by judges and other legal scholars. He turned to
the recorded proceedings of the constitutional convention[42] at which
the document in question was drafted to ascertain the intention of the
members of the convention. The attorney general summarized his
review of the proceedings thus:

It seems clear from reading the debates pertaining to this section of the
constitution that the members of the convention did not want aid extended
to private or sectarian schools under any guise.

CORPORATE POWERS AND THEIR EXERCISE

POWER OF VISITATION. Probably the leading case in this country involving the respective rights of (1) the religious body under whose
auspices a church-related college was established, (2) the donor of the
funds required for its construction and endowment, and (3) the governing board of the institution, is the one brought by the College of
Bishops of the Methodist Episcopal Church, South, against the Board
of Trust of Vanderbilt University, decided by the Supreme Court of
Tennessee in 1914.[43]

In 1872 committees appointed by the annual conferences of the
Methodist Episcopal Church, South, adopted resolutions calling for
the establishment of the Central University of the Church. Those
resolutions requested the bishops of the church "to act as a board of
supervision of the university and, jointly with the Board of Trust, to
elect officers and professors, and prescribe the course of study and plan
of government."

Mr. Cornelius Vanderbilt, in a letter dated March 17, 1873, to one
of the bishops, offered to contribute the sum of half a million dollars
as an endowment for the new university. His offer was accepted, and
the university was renamed Vanderbilt University. His contributions
and those of his family were approximately $2 million.

The general conference of the church, in 1906, appointed a commission of five laymen of the church "to inquire into and determine the
present relations of the Vanderbilt University to the Methodist Episcopal Church, South" and "to define the charter rights of the bishops."
The commission declared in its report that the university had been
founded by the conferences of the church, not by Mr. Vanderbilt;

---

[42] *Proceedings of the Nebraska Constitutional Convention of 1919–20*, II.

[43] State v. Board of Trust of Vanderbilt University, 129 Tenn. 279, 164 S.W.
1151 (1914).

that the general conference was "the sole member of the corporation of the university" and that the bishops "were visitors of the university, with common law visitatorial powers."

In 1910 the Board of Trust of the university declared that the general conference had no right to elect members of the Board of Trust. The college of bishops met as visitors of the university, vetoed this action of the Board of Trust, declaring it "null and void," and filed a petition for an injunction against the board to prevent it from seating its own appointees as members of the board.

The court ruled that Mr. Vanderbilt and not the original incorporators, or the church conferences they represented, was the founder of the university and, as such, was the only one entitled to the common law powers of visitation. The court further ruled that the provisions of the charter of the institution, as construed by the courts, determined the powers of the respective parties. On this basis, the court declared that:

the inherent power of the Board of Trust to fill vacancies in its own body authorizes it to elect and install members to fill such vacancies, and that such new members are entitled to their seats on the board ad interim, until such time as they may be rejected by the General Conference, or its General Board of Education . . .

The Court of Civil Appeals of Texas, in a case involving Baylor University, declared:

An individual who conveys property in trust for charitable purposes has, unless he should assign it to another, what is called the "visitatorial power," in the exercise of which he may prescribe rules for its management and for the administration of the trust, and may govern and control the trustees, inspect their proceedings, and correct abuses in their conduct. But this is a power which may be assigned, and the incorporation of trustees under a charter which confers upon them the full power of management of the property and of the institution, divests such rights of the founder, and vests it, as well as absolute title to the property conveyed, in the corporation.[44]

Phillips Academy was incorporated in 1780 as Trustees of Phillips Academy. In 1808 the Board of Trustees accepted a substantial gift of money for the establishment of a theological seminary, subject to the provisions of a deed of gift which read in part as follows:

We, the aforesaid founders, do hereby constitute a board of visitors, to be

---

[44] Trustees of the Union Baptist Association v. Huhn, 7 Tex. Civ. App. 314, 26 S.W. 754 (1894).

as in our place and stead the guardians, overseers, and protectors of this, our foundation.

A plan for a closer affiliation between the theological seminary and the divinity school of Harvard was adopted in 1922. The Board of Visitors of the seminary declared that the plan was inconsistent with the principles of its foundation and therefore void. The Supreme Judicial Court of Massachusetts, in a decision[45] upholding this declaration of the Board of Visitors, said:

> The principle generally recognized is that, in all cases where a visitor has given a decision within his powers, it is final and not subject to re-examination at law or in equity.

Harvard University is still administered under the charter of its college, granted in 1650. The corporation, known as the President and Fellows of Harvard College, is a self-perpetuating body, consisting of the president of the institution, the treasurer, and five fellows. The property of the university is held by, and all important business is transacted in the name of, the corporation, but a Board of Overseers performs functions similar to those of a Board of Visitors. It was originally composed of the ministers of the neighboring towns and the upper house of the Massachusetts Legislature, presided over by the governor of the commonwealth. After the state ceased appropriating funds for the support of the college, the composition of the Board of Overseers was gradually changed. Since the Civil War its members have been elected by the alumni.

POWER OF EMINENT DOMAIN. In view of the ever-increasing demand for higher education, colleges are, and will continue to be, faced with the need for an expansion of physical facilities. Few are fortunate enough to have sufficient land for this purpose. The purchase of a sufficiently large, contiguous tract for an enlarged campus usually presents serious difficulties. Owners of adjacent properties may refuse to sell or may feel justified in taking full advantage of their bargaining position. The acquisition of land for public purposes at a judicially determined valuation, despite the unwillingness of the owner to sell, is known as the exercise of the power of eminent domain. It is an inherent power of the state, but it may be delegated to others in the public interest. There seems to be no question as to the legitimacy of its

---

[45] Trustees of Andover Theological Seminary v. Visitors of the Theological Institution, 253 Mass. 256, 148 N.E. 900 (1925).

exercise for the acquisition of property to be used by a tax-supported college.[46] This is clearly a public use. The real point at issue today is the extent to which it may be exercised by privately controlled institutions of higher education.

The case usually cited as authority for the statement that they do not have such power, involved the attempt, by the Connecticut College for Women, to acquire, by condemnation, land needed for its original campus.

The college was incorporated in 1911 by a special act of the legislature. Later, in the same session of the legislature, another special act was passed containing the following language:

Whereas, the higher education of women of this state is a matter of great public concern, and, whereas, it is a matter of public concern that a suitable site be provided for the purpose of said Connecticut College for Women: Therefore, be it enacted: The Connecticut College for Women shall have power to take such real estate in the Town of New London and Waterford as its trustees shall find necessary for the purpose of said educational corporation, upon payment of just compensation therefor.

Despite the specific grant of the power of eminent domain by the legislature, the Supreme Court of Errors of Connecticut, in 1913, held that, in the absence of a showing that the public generally would, under the charter of the college, have the right to enjoy the benefit of the college without regard to religious, social, or other distinction, the act of delegation of this power by the legislature to a privately controlled corporation was unconstitutional and void.[47]

Justice Wheeler, in a strong dissenting opinion, declared:

In this case, the character of the college, a charity maintained at private cost and without profit, serving a great public need and relieving the state of a duty which it might well assume, renders it impossible for the court, of its own knowledge, to say that the resultant public welfare is not so great as to make it a public use, as the General Assembly declared it to be.

The Supreme Court of California, faced with this problem in 1934, came to the conclusion that Justice Wheeler's dissent reflected better reasoning than the majority opinion. The University of Southern California, after completing the erection of a library building, decided that it needed additional land for proper landscaping. Unable to purchase adjacent land at what it regarded as a reasonable price, it requested

---

[46] Russell v. Purdue University, 201 Ind. 367, 168 N.E. 529 (1929); Craddock v. University of Louisville, 303 S.W.2d 548 (Ky. 1957).

[47] Connecticut College for Women v. Calvert, 87 Conn. 421, 88 Atl. 633 (1913).

the power to seize the property at a judicially determined valuation. In its petition, the university called the attention of the court to the following paragraph in its articles of incorporation:

This university shall be open and equal privilege accorded alike to each and every resident of the state, whether male or female, and regardless of nationality, race or religious belief, who possesses the required qualifications for admission, and no person shall be denied admission who possesses such qualifications.

The court decided that the university, although not tax supported or publicly controlled, possessed the right of eminent domain.[48] The property owner carried the case to the Supreme Court of the United States on the grounds that he had been deprived of his property without due process of law. In refusing to hear the case,[49] the high court, in effect, affirmed the decision of the state court.

POWERS OF THE CORPORATE BOARD. In this country, the governing board of a nonpublic college or university has plenary authority, limited only by the provisions of its charter, the laws of the land, and public opinion. Much of this authority is usually delegated to the president, the chief executive officer of the institution. The president, in turn, delegates many of his duties and responsibilities to his administrative officers, deans, and faculty committees. However, the governing board remains the repository of power since it may, at its pleasure, withhold or withdraw its delegation of power.

We are so habituated to this pattern of centralization of power in an external board of laymen that it is interesting to remind ourselves that it is quite at variance with the form of self-government evolved by the medieval universities of continental Europe. At Salerno, Bologna, and Padua, the students as well as the faculty were represented in an all-powerful university council. At Paris, Oxford, and Cambridge, the students were somewhat younger and were granted little voice in administration.

The university chancellor was originally the representative of the Church, but by the latter part of the fourteenth century, the congregation or faculty of arts at Oxford had obtained full control over his selection and appointment. This power was lost by the faculty in 1484 when the chancellorship became an honorary position, filled by a nonresident

---

[48] University of Southern California v. Robbins, 1 Cal. App. 2d 523, 37 P.2d 163 (2d Dist. Ct. App. 1934).
[49] Robbins v. University of Southern California, 295 U.S. 738 (1935).

and selected now by the political group in power in England. The chancellor was given the right to appoint the vice-chancellor, who became the resident officer in charge of university administration. In 1569 the faculty of Oxford lost further control of administrative functions by the creation of an executive council composed of the vice-chancellor, heads of houses, and proctors.

When Harvard, the first American university, was established in 1636 and its form of government determined in 1642, all responsibility for the administration of the institution was placed in the hands of a body of laymen, neither selected by, nor responsible to, its faculty. According to Lindsay and Holland:

> The theory of university administration upon which Harvard was founded is the theory of the modern American university, though the form is not always the same. Not all have the Board of Overseers; not all have the Closed Corporation; but the principle of centralized administrative authority, responsible to powers outside the institution, obtains in practically all American institutions of higher learning today.[50]

A modern case, involving delegation of power to the president of a college by its governing board, came before the appellate division of the Supreme Court of New York in 1955.[51] Harry S. Kieval, an instructor at Brooklyn College, handed his letter of resignation to the president of the college. It was accepted at once. The next day Mr. Kieval informed the president that he had reconsidered his decision to resign and that he would like to withdraw his resignation. A few days later he addressed a formal written withdrawal of his resignation, requesting that it not be reported to the governing board. He was informed that it would be reported at the next meeting of the board.

Mr. Kieval filed an application with the commissioner of education for a review of his case and for an order to the Board of Higher Education of the City of New York to reinstate him, with payment of accrued salary. His petition was denied and he appealed the decision of the commissioner. The court upheld the decision on the following grounds:

> We think that the president had the power to accept the petitioner's resignation, and by acceptance, place it beyond the legal election of the petitioner thereafter to withdraw it. The by-laws of the Board delegated to the president certain administrative functions between meetings of the

---

[50] Ernest E. Lindsay and E. O. Holland, *College and University Administration* (New York: Macmillan Co., 1930), p. 14.

[51] Kieval v. Wilson, 285 App. Div. 1203, 140 N.Y.S.2d 756 (1955).

Board. He could fill temporary vacancies in the instructional staff of a grade to which the petitioner's position belonged and make "such administrative arrangements" as "cannot well await" the action of the Board. The acceptance of a resignation effective at once is within the frame of such a delegation. It is an administrative arrangement to be integrated with the operation of a college while the administrative board is not in session and is to be grouped with filling temporary vacancies arising between such meetings.

EXERCISE OF CORPORATE POWERS BY THE BOARD. In the exercise of corporate powers, the governing board of a nonpublic educational institution must look to the provisions of its charter, to the laws of the state of its incorporation, and to the general principles of corporation law.[52]

One of the most fundamental principles of the law of private corporations, and one that is overlooked at times by members of a corporate board, is that the board can act only as a body, not as individuals. A board member, even the chairman, has no authority over the affairs of the institution unless he acts pursuant to formal action of his board. The reason for this rule of law has been well expressed by a federal judge:

> It is fundamental that officers of boards can only act as such constituted boards when assembled as such, and by deliberate and concerted action dispose of the issue under consideration. They cannot act in an individual capacity outside a formal meeting. . . . The law believes that the greatest wisdom results from conference and exchange of individual views, and it is for this reason that the law requires the united wisdom of a majority of the several members of the board in determining the business of a corporation.[53]

CORPORATION MEETINGS. Since the powers of the corporate board can only be exercised by the board, duly assembled in meeting as a body, it becomes important to determine when it is thus assembled.

A meeting of directors or trustees must be called in accordance with the provisions of its certificate of incorporation and bylaws.[54] If the meeting is a regular or stated meeting, the time and place being fixed by charter or bylaw, notice of the meeting is not necessary unless expressly required,[55] nor is it necessary to give notice of an

---

[52] See William M. Fletcher, *Cyclopedia of the Law of Private Corporations* (20 vols.; Chicago: Callaghan & Co., 1954), Vol. II, chap. 11, "Directors, Other Officers and Agents."

[53] Ames v. Goldfield Merger Mines Co., 227 Fed. 292 (D.D.C. 1915).

[54] *In re* Allied Fruit & Extract Co., 243 App. Div. 52, 276 N.Y. Supp. 153 (1934).

[55] White v. Penelas Mining Co., 105 F.2d 726 (9th Cir. 1939).

adjourned meeting.[56] However, sound administrative policy would seem to dictate that the corporation bylaws should require notice of all meetings, stated, special, and adjourned, in ample time for busy men to arrange to be present.

The validity of a meeting is not affected by failure to give notice, even when notice is expressly required by the charter or bylaws, if all of the members were present and raised no objections. In other words, presence at a meeting waives the want of notice.[57]

In the absence of some provision to the contrary in the charter or bylaws, a majority of the directors or trustees is necessary, and is sufficient, to constitute a quorum and to transact business.[58]

A director or trustee with a personal interest in the matter or transaction before the board of which he is a member cannot be counted for the purpose of making a quorum, nor can his vote be counted for the purpose of determining whether a resolution has been passed by a majority vote.[59] Well-established custom calls for a director or trustee to disqualify himself voluntarily and perhaps to withdraw from the meeting while the subject in which he has a personal interest is under discussion. These rules of law and custom are merely applications of the elementary principle existing in every system of jurisprudence that a man may not sit as judge in his own case.[60]

REVISION OF BYLAWS AND CHARTER. Since the legality of corporate action is dependent upon compliance with the provisions of the corporate charter and bylaws, it is essential that their contents be reviewed at suitable intervals to make certain that they facilitate rather than impede good administration. If revision is indicated, the drafting should be done by legal counsel or under his direction. Clear, unambiguous language and logical arrangement of subject matter is important. Periodic revision of the bylaws is not difficult of accomplishment, but revision of the provisions of the corporate charter is quite another matter. However, it should be undertaken if the need therefor is deemed sufficiently urgent. The usual procedure is to file a petition with the appropriate court, setting forth the desired change in the charter and "praying" for a pro forma decree from the court. The

---

[56] Seal of Gold Mining Co. v. Slater, 161 Cal. 621, 120 Pac. 15 (1911).

[57] Clark v. Mutual Loan & Investment Co., 88 F.2d 202 (8th Cir. 1937).

[58] *In re* Lake Placid Co., 274 App. Div. 205, 81 N.Y.S.2d 36 (1948).

[59] Wishon-Watson Co. v. Commissioner of Internal Revenue, 66 F.2d 52 (C.C.A. 1933).

[60] Hinkley v. Sagemiller, 191 Wis. 512, 210 N.W. 839 (1926).

decree, when issued by the court, should be filed with the secretary of state of the state of incorporation for recording.

Many of the older colleges were chartered by special act of the state legislature. At the present time, some states by constitutional provision deny their legislators the power to enact legislation other than that which is general in its application. In states where this constitutional prohibition against special acts does not exist, a college may obtain a revision of its corporate charter by action of the legislature.

For example, in 1959, Wesleyan University obtained a revision of its charter, altering the number of the members of its governing board. The Connecticut College may now, by a recent revision of its charter, accept male students. The procedure used in these cases was substantially as follows: A bill providing for the proposed changes in the charter was introduced into either the house or senate of the General Assembly of Connecticut in the ordinary fashion. It was referred to the appropriate committee for hearing. Upon favorable action by the committee, the private bill was acted upon by both houses and signed into law by the governor.

THE CORPORATE SEAL. The legal significance of a seal on a document today is much less than it was in earlier times. When illiteracy was the rule rather than the exception, men were compelled to "make their mark," and this mark usually took the form of the impression of a seal on wax. The king and every individual of importance possessed a personal seal. This seal, or signet, usually bore his coat of arms, establishing his identity and status. Seals came into use in England after the Norman Conquest.

At common law, a formal agreement or covenant under seal was enforceable. The very formality of the method of its execution was deemed sufficient evidence of the intention of the parties to be bound by its terms. A mere gratuitous promise, not under seal, could not be enforced in a court of law. Something of value, some "consideration" had to pass from the promisee to the promisor to "bind the contract." However, the use of a seal on a document converted it from a simple or "parol" contract into what is known as a "specialty," that is, a sealed instrument, enforceable without proof of consideration. In general, deeds, mortgages, and bonds had to be authenticated by the use of a seal. Gradually, the importance of the seal became less, and the modern trend of decisions is to ignore the distinction between sealed and unsealed instruments. Some states have abolished the necessity for the use of a seal.[61]

Lacking a statutory requirement, a corporation need not adopt a special seal. In the execution of documents requiring a seal for authenticity, the corporation may make use of any legally sufficient indicia of a seal.[62]

According to Blackstone:

A corporation, being an invisible body, cannot manifest its intentions by any personal act or oral discourse; it therefore acts and speaks only by its common seal.[63]

This ancient doctrine has been discarded by the courts, and the modern and more sensible rule is that the impression of the seal of a corporation on a document performs no greater function than to provide prima-facie evidence of due execution of the document in question.[64] In some states, use of a seal is authorized, but failure of the corporation to affix the seal does not affect the validity of any instrument of the corporation. The seal is usually entrusted to the secretary of the corporation, and his function in this connection is to attest the fact that the document was executed in accordance with the powers delegated by the corporate board to its officers.

PROTECTION OF THE CORPORATE NAME. By the adoption and use of a name and seal, a corporation acquires property rights therein, rights which the courts will protect, in much the same manner and for the same purpose as a trade-mark. Priority of use in a particular field is essential.[65] This rule of common law, protecting against a wrongful or unfair use of a corporate name, is not limited to corporations conducted for pecuniary profit.

The proprietor of a business school in Philadelphia was forbidden by a state district court in 1900 to use the name and title of The University of Philadelphia on the grounds that "letters, intended for the provost and faculty of the University of Pennsylvania had been directed by persons residing in other states and countries to the University of Philadelphia." The court ruled that the similarity of names tended to

---

[61] 79 C.J.S.: Seals §§ 1–8 (1952).

[62] 18 C.J.S.: Corporations § 175 (1939).

[63] 1 Blackstone, Commentaries *475.

[64] Gottfried v. Miller, 104 U.S. 521 (1881).

[65] American Products Co. v. American Products Co., 42 F.2d 488 (E.D. Mich. 1930).

mislead the public and that the University of Pennsylvania, having been established for many years, was entitled to protection under the common law relating to trade-marks.[66]

In 1921 F. Arthur Clawson filed in the office of the clerk in the County of New York the customary trade-name certificate of his intention to conduct the business of a private school in New York City under the name of Columbia Preparatory School. Shortly after the opening of his school, he was notified by the Columbia Grammar School that, by adopting a similar name for his school, he had created the erroneous impression among intending students and others that there was some connection between the two schools. When he declined to change the name, the Columbia Grammar School petitioned for an injunction. According to evidence introduced, the Columbia Grammar School had been established as the "Grammar School of Columbia College" in 1764 and, although incorporated as an independent school in 1907, it had continued to maintain a close relationship with the College of Columbia University. The injunction was granted, and the following is an excerpt from the opinion of Justice Tierny:

> The evidence in this case shows that similarity of names is not only apt to be misleading, but has in fact misled to such an extent that it can be safely said that the defendant is unfairly competing with the plaintiff.[67]

Some years later, the courts of New York were again called upon to protect the use of the name "Columbia." According to Justice Townly:

> The conclusion is irresistible that the defendants, in adopting the name "Columbia Educational Institute," did so with the deliberate design of conveying to the public the impression that they were identical or associated with the plaintiff. The right of the plaintiff to its name "Columbia University" was expressly conferred by the Legislature in 1784 and has been in constant use since that time. It has built up a great name and standing among educational institutions of the country, which name cannot be appropriated by the device resorted to by the defendants.[68]

Although the courts have been prompt to protect an educational institution from unfair competition by another educational institution, they have not been so ready to protect the right of a college or uni-

---

[66] The Commonwealth of Pennsylvania v. Banks, 9 Pa. Dist. 436 (1900).

[67] Columbia Grammar School v. Clawson, 120 Misc. 841, 200 N.Y. Supp. 768 (Sup. Ct. 1923).

[68] Trustees of Columbia University v. Axenfeld, 136 Misc. 831, 241 N.Y. Supp. 4 (Sup. Ct. 1930).

vorrity to the exclusive use of its name as against commercial exploitation thereof.

Vassar College in 1912 attempted to restrain the Loose-Wiles Biscuit Company of Kansas City from marketing its candy under the trade name of Vassar Chocolates. In its petition for an injunction, the college made the following allegations:

the packages containing that candy and the advertisements thereof employ the name of Vassar, a likeness of a young lady in scholastic garb and wearing mortarboard hat, an imitation of the college pennant, a college yell, and an imitation of the college seal, with the words, "Vassar Chocolates" and "Always Fresh" substituted for the words "Vassar College" and "Purity and Wisdom," respectively. Complainant is thereby brought into public contempt and ridicule, and that, because thereof its business is injured and its graduates and students humiliated.

Judge Van Valkenburg justified his rejection of the petition of Vassar College for an injunction in the following words:

The injurious effects, if any, of the advertisement complained of, are speculative in the highest degree. They seem to me to be largely creations of fancy, due to supersensitiveness and apprehension. They are lodged rather in a feeling of distaste on the part of those interested in Vassar College for seeing its name and insignia, inferentially at least, linked with any commercial pursuit, rather than to any appreciable injury to its tangible property. . . . If the use of a name in a commercial publication, as in the case at bar, be deemed an unwarranted invasion of personal rights, it is within the province of the Legislature so to declare. The courts cannot create a right unknown to the common law, and not protected by statute.[69]

In 1946 Dr. Clive McCay, a member of the faculty of the College of Agriculture of Cornell University, developed a formula for a highly nutritious bread. This formula was published in various journals for the benefit of the general public. The Messing Bakeries, Inc., became interested in producing and marketing bread according to the new formula and conducted negotiations with the university in an endeavor to arrive at some mutually accceptable method and standard of advertising.

Without waiting for the consummation of an agreement, the baking company applied for and was granted the registration of the name "Cornell Bread" and "Cornell Loaf" as trade-marks in the State of New York. Upon the petition of the university, the registration of the trade-marks was canceled, and the baking company was restrained

---

[69] Vassar College v. Loose-Wiles Biscuit Co., 197 Fed. 982 (W.D. Mo. 1912).

from using the word "Cornell" in such a manner as to deceive the public. Justice Newman declared:

The manner of use is the objectionable feature of this case. The entire makeup of the defendant's bread wrappers and advertising is such as to present to the public the idea of Cornell University. The use of the name "Cornell" in white letters on a red pennant, and later on a red scroll is so designed as to necessarily impress upon the mind of the casual observer the idea of Cornell University. When one considers the vast number of people who are undoubtedly acquainted with Cornell and its reputation, either by having attended some of its colleges as a student, or having some close relative or friend who attended as a student, or has otherwise come in close contact with the university, the value of this type of advertising is apparent. As stated by the court in Tiffany & Co. v. Tiffany Productions, 147 Misc. 679, 264 N.Y.S. 459, 461: "From these facts the conclusion is inescapable that the sole reason for the defendant's choice of the name was to trade on plaintiff's reputation and to reap the benefit of the public belief that the plaintiff was connected with the defendant."[70]

The following year the baking company succeeded in persuading the court to permit it to use the designation "Cornell Recipe Bread" for its product, upon condition that it eliminate the use of a scroll on its wrapper and in its advertising. The following portion of the opinion of Justice Bergan is pertinent to a consideration of the issues involved:

Had Cornell firmly insisted that the baker should not use "Cornell" at all in selling this bread evolved at the University, we would have had no great difficulty in sustaining the injunction in full ambit. But the University left open, or seemed to be leaving open, to the baker a limited use of the name "Cornell" during the time when the baker was extensively investing in the commercial promotion of the product.[71]

ADMINISTRATION OF THE INSTITUTION

DUTIES AND RESPONSIBILITIES OF THE COLLEGE BOARD. Perhaps the most important functions of the governing board of a college are:
1. The determination and establishment of the fundamental policies of the institution;
2. The selection and appointment of a competent administrator, such as the college president, and the delegation to him of powers commensurate with his responsibilities;

---

[70] Cornell University v. Messing Bakeries, 135 N.Y.S.2d 101 (Sup. Ct. 1954).
[71] Cornell University v. Messing Bakeries, 285 App. Div. 490, 138 N.Y.S.2d 280 (1955).

3. The preservation of the capital assets[72] and financial integrity of the institution.

These are duties that cannot be delegated. Some courts[73] have declared that the directors of a corporation cannot delegate powers which involve the exercise of judgment and discretion and which should be exercised by them in person, but this language is much too broad. The better rule[74] is that they may delegate extensive powers to officers and agents, even in the matters involving a considerable degree of judgment.

It is not uncommon for the corporate by-laws to provide that the executive committee shall exercise the powers of the board in the intervals between meetings of the board, with perhaps certain exceptions. Despite this delegation of authority, good practice calls for ratification of all actions of the executive committee at the next meeting of the board.

THE COLLEGE PRESIDENT. Unlike the president of a commercial corporation, the president of a college is usually not a member of the corporate board. There is some difference of opinion as to whether it is desirable for him to be a voting member of the governing board. Perhaps the strongest argument against his actual membership on the board is the necessity of the board evaluating his competency as an administrator at appropriate intervals. If he attends meetings as a matter of right and not by invitation, such evaluation may be inhibited.

However, he should, as a general rule, be invited to attend board meetings, and this invitation, with his approval, should be extended to his major administrative officers. It is essential that there be the closest possible working relationship between the board and the major administrative officers of the college.

The president of a business corporation, by virtue of his office, has certain inherent powers. These are discussed at length in any text on corporation law. For instance, it is a general rule of common law that the president of a corporation has the inherent power to execute promissory notes in behalf of the corporation and that the corporation is thereby bound as against an innocent holder of the note. How-

---

[72] For a discussion of the problems incident to the investment of endowment and other restricted funds, see "The Investment of Restricted Funds," pp. 210–14.

[73] Royal Theatre Corp. v. United States, 66 F. Supp. 301 (D. Kan. 1946).

[74] Union Pac. R.R. v. Chicago R.I. & P.R.R., 163 U.S. 564 (1896).

ever, a federal court has held that this rule does not apply so as to make a college liable on notes executed by its president without the authorization of its governing board. The funds derived from the loan were used by the president for his own purposes.[75] An Illinois court handed down a similar decision in 1917.[76]

THE SECRETARY OF THE BOARD. It is highly desirable that the secretary of the governing board of a college be familiar with the general principles of corporation law. There is, therefore, merit in the practice of restricting the holder of this office to one trained as a lawyer. It is his duty to make and keep the minutes of the proceedings of the board. Since these minutes may be subjected to judicial scrutiny in the event of litigation, it is important that they be drafted by one familiar with legal usage. Resolutions with respect to the purchase and sale of land should be drawn with attention to the laws of property. If the one serving as secretary is not a lawyer, he should consult, at appropriate intervals, with the college counsel and seek his review of the minutes of important meetings of the board.

In the interest of good administration and to avoid the possibility of later legal complications, the call of each meeting should state, in as much detail as possible, the items to be presented for consideration and approval, in order that each board member may have an opportunity to obtain whatever information and advice he may deem essential for his decision.

The unapproved minutes of each meeting should be mailed to each member as promptly as possible after the meeting, as a reminder of actions taken, and to facilitate the approval of the minutes at the next meeting of the board.

A useful tool of administration is a cumulative index and cross index of all actions of the corporate board. It is extremely important that past actions be easily available for reference and for correlation with contemplated actions.

The secretary of the board or someone designated by him should undertake responsibility for the assembly and preservation of the basic

---

[75] St. Vincent College v. Hallett, 201 Fed. 471 (C.A. Ill. 1912).

[76] McNeil & Higgins Co. v. Greer College, 206 Ill. App. 533 (1917); see chap. 3, "The College Faculty and Staff," pp. 59–62 for a discussion of the implied powers of the president and other college officials to negotiate contracts of employment.

corporate records.[77] These include the original charter of the college or a verified copy of the legislative act creating the college, and all subsequent acts pertaining thereto. Copies of all judicial proceedings interpreting the corporate powers should also form part of the documentary files of the institution. These basic documents should be indexed, and the index correlated with the cumulative index of the proceedings of the board. When not in use, they should be in a fireproof safe or vault.

An apparently minor aspect of preserving these basic records is the quality of the paper on which they are typed. The commercial grades of paper today are manufactured from wood pulp and disintegrate within a comparatively few years. Corporate board proceedings and all other important documents should be typed on 100 percent rag content bond.

MANUALS OF PROCEDURES. An indication of good administration is the preparation and publication of current manuals of procedures for all major officers and administrators. The basic manual should be the one designed for the use of the members of the governing board. Such a manual will be found of especial value to newly elected or appointed members of the board. It should include verified copies of the basic corporate documents, the by-laws of the governing board, a summary, in logical order, of all important actions of the board, and a list of all board committees, with the names and addresses of members. The manual should contain a summary of the duties and responsibilities of the members of the board and a statement of the organization and administration of the college and of its major divisions and affiliated corporations and organizations.

This manual and all others of the college should be drafted under the general supervision of its legal counsel. For example, the manual of procedure for the director of purchasing and his staff should contain all the forms used for the procurement of equipment, supplies, and services. These forms should be drafted with advice of counsel, and those authorized to sign them on behalf of the college should be designated in the minutes of the governing board. Prevention of litigation being one of the principal objectives of a good lawyer, the legal

---

[77] For a discussion of the importance of the retention of records, see Robert B. Whelan, *Corporate Record Retention* (New York: Controllership Foundation, 1958); and Kenneth F. Martin, "Keeping Records—How Many and How Long?" *College and University Business*, XXVII (November 1959), 59–61.

counsel should make certain that the procedures set forth in the college manuals are in accord with sound legal principles, that the responsibilities and duties of every major executive are set forth with clarity and precision, that the delegation of authority to execute contracts on behalf of the institution is clearly stated and limited, and that appropriate safeguards are established to prevent the misappropriation and maladministration of funds entrusted to the administration of the college.

AUXILIARY CORPORATIONS. Because of statutory restrictions and external control of funds, many tax-supported colleges and universities have found it expedient to create auxiliary corporations to conduct certain activities and to collect and expend the revenue derived therefrom, such as intercollegiate athletics, bookstores, student housing, student unions, publication, sponsored research, and alumni activities.

From a legal standpoint, probably the most important question in this connection is the extent to which the courts will respect the fiction of separate corporate entity. When a nonprofit corporation, the Board of Control of Athletics of the University of Michigan, sought to obtain titles to land needed for a golf course by the use of the power of eminent domain, the Michigan court disregarded the fiction of separate legal entity and held that this corporation was merely an operating agency of the Board of Regents of the University of Michigan, subject at all times to its full control.[78] Hence, as an instrumentality of the state, it had the power to acquire titles to property by eminent domain. The courts of Florida have followed this same trend.[79]

Where the subsidiary corporation has failed to confine its activities to those directly related to those of the parent corporation, the courts have not hesitated to take a different stand. Thus, when it was shown that the Cardinal Publishing Company, a nonprofit corporation created for the purpose of printing the student newspaper of the University of Wisconsin, was deriving a substantial portion of its revenue from printing privately owned newspapers in Madison, the court upheld the assessment of taxes on its property.[80]

It is not difficult to understand why tax-supported colleges and

---

[78] People v. Pommerening, 250 Mich. 391, 230 N.W. 194 (1930).

[79] Boyd v. University Athletic Association, 117 Fla. 188, 157 So. 576 (1934).

[80] Cardinal Publishing Co. v. City of Madison, 205 Wis. 344, 243 N.W. 325 (1932). See also Westbrook v. University of Georgia Athletic Ass'n, 206 Ga. 667, 58 S.E.2d 428 (1950).

universities feel compelled to organize separate corporate entities to conduct subsidiary but related functions. The degree of administrative control exercised by the legislature and by state officials over the fiscal and educational policies of these institutions will be discussed in Chapter 8 [81]

However, it is somewhat surprising to see the number of research foundations and other auxiliary corporations established in recent years by nonpublic institutions of higher education. With complete freedom from external control and supervision, there would seem to be no legal reason why the parent corporation should not perform the functions thus delegated. Before approving the creation of separate corporations for research and other related activities, the governing boards of privately controlled universities would be well advised to consider the disadvantages as well as the advantages of a separate corporation. In order to maintain the fiction of separate legal entity, certain vexatious formalities must be observed. These could ripen into serious conflict of policy between the members of the board of the parent corporation and those of the subsidiary corporation. Moreover, the existence of an auxiliary corporation may raise certain tax questions.

DURATION OF CORPORATE LIFE

In general, unless restricted by law, a corporation has duration for the period stated in its charter, which is usually perpetual.[82] In the event of termination, some states provide, by general law, a procedure for renewal. In other states, such problems are met by special legislation.

VOLUNTARY DISSOLUTION OF THE CORPORATION. Some states provide statutory authorization for the voluntary dissolution of nonprofit educational corporations.[83] In the absence of statutory authority, an educa-

---

[81] See "Interference in the Internal Administration of Institutions of Higher Education," pp. 251–55.

[82] The Pritchett School Institute was granted a charter by the state of Missouri in 1868 containing the provision that "The trusteeship shall be perpetual . . ." In 1897 the institute requested authorization to change its name to Pritchett College. The secretary of state took the position that the corporation had been dissolved by operation of law, in accordance with a state statute limiting corporate life to twenty years unless otherwise stipulated in its charter. The court ruled that the secretary was in error; that the wording of the charter clearly implied that the corporation was to exist in perpetuity. State v. Lesueur, 141 Mo. 29, 41 S.W. 904 (1897).

[83] State v. U. S. Grant University, 115 Tenn. 238, 90 S.W. 294 (1905).

tional or charitable corporation may voluntarily surrender its charter
if it acts with the approval and under the supervision of an appropriate
court, sitting as a court of equity.[84]

INVOLUNTARY DISSOLUTION. The courts have held that the attorney
general, as representative of the public interest, may challenge the
power and right of a notorious "diploma mill" to continue to function.[85]
This is done by bringing an action in quo warranto—a legal procedure
by which an individual or corporation is brought into court and there
required to show by what right he is claiming to exercise a privilege,
franchise, or office. If flagrant abuse of the power to confer degrees
can be shown, the court will order the dissolution of the corporation.

FORFEITURE OF CHARTER BY NONUSER. If the charter powers of a corporation organized for profit are not exercised for a prolonged period,
courts have declared them forfeited. However, the courts have been
reluctant to apply this rule to educational and other nonprofit corporations. Even the death or departure from the state of all members of the
corporation may not be sufficient to justify the forfeiture of the
charter.[86]

LOSS OF CHARTER BY ULTRA VIRES ACTION. A corporation possesses only
those powers conferred upon it by its charter, expressly or by necessary
implication. Consequently, if it attempts to exercise powers in excess
of those thus granted, the attorney general of the state of its incorporation may bring a quo warranto proceeding to question its use
of these powers. If the court should find that the corporation has
exceeded its charter powers, it may penalize the act of ultra vires by
the imposition of a fine or by the cancellation of its corporate charter.

In 1955, the governing board of Washington University requested
the appropriate court to determine whether its implied charter powers
included the right to conduct extension courses in states other than
Missouri, the state of its incorporation. Its charter was of unusual
value, since it conferred upon the institution complete exemption from

---

[84] In re Washington Monument Fund, 154 Pa. St. 621, 26 Atl. 647 (1893); for
a discussion of the legal problems incident to the merger or consolidation of colleges, see Adams v. Flora Macdonald College, 111 S.E. 2d 859 (N.C. 1960).

[85] Illinois Health University v. People, 166 Ill. 171, 46 N.E. 737 (1897); Independent Medical College v. People, 182 Ill. 274, 55 N.E. 345 (1899).

[86] Trustees of Vincennes University v. State of Indiana, 55 U.S. 269 (1852);
Murphy v. Luttrell, 56 Tex. Civ. App. 149, 120 S.W. 905 (1909).

property taxation.[87] Consequently, in order to avoid the possibility of the loss of this valuable privilege, the board sought the advice of a court of equity.

The attorney general, made a party to the proceedings, asserted in his brief that, should the university offer extension courses outside the State of Missouri, he would regard the act as ultra viros and would therefore be compelled to institute proceedings for the forfeiture of its charter. He cited a case[88] involving the charter powers of the University of Colorado as support for his position.

Counsel for the university called the attention of the court to a more recent case, decided in 1925 by the Supreme Court of Pennsylvania.[89] Based upon this decision, the Circuit Court of the County of St. Louis declared that the implied charter powers of Washington University included the right to conduct courses of study outside the state of its incorporation.[90]

THE CONTROL OF HIGHER EDUCATION BY
ACCREDITING ORGANIZATIONS

In 1938 the State of North Dakota, at the instigation of its governor, brought suit in a federal district court to enjoin the North Central Association of Colleges and Secondary Schools from removing the University and State Agricultural College of North Dakota from its list of accredited colleges, or "from interfering with or obstructing the administration, operation and maintenance of the public school system of the State of North Dakota."

THE NORTH DAKOTA CASE. The Board of Administration of North Dakota had dismissed the president and six members of the faculty of the agricultural college. In lieu of the customary notice, those dismissed were given an extra month's salary. The Committee of Inquiry of the North Central Association made an investigation of the college and of its administration. After reviewing the evidence, the committee recommended that the college be removed from the list of accredited institutions of the North Central Association because:

---

[87] See "The Tax Status of College Property," pp. 155–56, and "Property Exemption by Charter Right," pp. 156–59.

[88] People v. Regents of University of Colorado, 24 Colo. 175, 49 Pac. 286 (1897).

[89] Hemstead v. Meadville Theological School, 284 Pa. 147, 130 Atl. 421 (1925).

[90] The Washington University v. Dalton, Equity No. 209,617, Cir. Ct. Co. St. Louis, Sept. 14, 1955.

1. The evidence indicated undue interference by the Board of Administration in the internal administration of the college.

2. The morale of the faculty had declined to the point where the quality of instruction was seriously jeopardized.

3. There was no convincing assurance that the legal structure and organization for the administration of the North Dakota Agricultural College and other institutions of higher education in the state would provide a sufficient degree of autonomy to the individual institutions to guarantee a satisfactory level of performance.

The federal district court declined to grant the injunction requested by the state and its governor. The following is an excerpt from the opinion:

> Voluntary associations have the right to make their own regulations as to admission or expulsion of members and one who becomes a member, by his membership, assents to the constitution and rules of procedure adopted by such an association. The constitution, by-laws and rules, knowingly assented to, become, in effect, a civil contract between the parties, whereby their rights are fixed and measured. Consequently, in the absence of fraud, collusion, arbitrariness or breach of contract, such as to give rise to a civil action, the decisions of such voluntary associations must be accepted in litigation before the court as conclusive, for the members of the organization have made them binding by contract.[91]

The state appealed the decision, but the federal circuit court of appeals upheld the decision of the district court.[92]

ACCREDITATION IN HIGHER EDUCATION. According to Lawrence G. Derthick, then U.S. Commissioner of Education:

> One of the features of higher education in the United States is the practice of accreditation, which consists of setting standards and according recognition to those institutions which conform to the standards. Accreditation in higher education is carried on almost entirely by nongovernmental associations and agencies. These voluntary agencies have no inherent legal power to control the operations of institutions of higher education. In practice, however, they have come to exercise a most significant influence upon: (1) the choices of students in selecting the colleges and universities they will attend; (2) determination of the acceptability of the product of institutions (for transfer to another recognized college or university, for entering the occupation for which he has been prepared, for membership in a professional organization in his chosen field of activity); (3) eligibility for participa-

---

[91] State v. North Central Association of Colleges and Secondary Schools, 23 F. Supp. 694 (E.D. Ill. 1938).
[92] *Ibid.*, 99 F.2d 697 (7th Cir. 1938).

tion in programs sponsored by the Federal Government (research contracts, loans under the College Housing Program, distribution of surplus property, etc.) and by philanthropic organizations and foundations.[93]

This extralegal influence of accrediting agencies was questioned by Samuel P. Capen in a paper read at the 1927 meeting of the Association of Urban Universities. Dr. Capen pointed out that, in addition to the regional accrediting agencies, such as the North Central Association of Colleges and Secondary Schools, many professional organizations were beginning to bring pressure upon the colleges and universities to meet standards which, in the opinion of some educators, were unrealistic. Increasing friction between accrediting organizations and institutions prompted the American Council on Education to hold conferences to discuss the need for coordination of accrediting agencies in 1939, 1940, and again in 1949. In 1950 the National Commission on Accrediting adopted its present form of organization. In a further effort to clarify the appropriate functions of accrediting agencies, the national commission, in cooperation with the United States Office of Education, sponsored a workshop conference which was held in Washington, D.C., June 25–26, 1957. The published report of this conference is an excellent summary of the issues involved.[94]

[93] Lloyd E. Blauch (ed.), *Accreditation in Higher Education*. U.S. Office of Education (Washington: Government Printing Office, 1959), pp. v, 22–28.

[94] *Report on Workshop Conference on Accrediting, June 25–26, 1957* (Washington: National Commission on Accrediting, 1957).

CHAPTER **III**

The College Faculty and Staff

MANY of the legal problems to be considered in this chapter are of primary concern to the individual faculty members rather than to the college. However, in view of the close relationship that must always exist between faculty and administration on the campus, and of the fact that faculty members traditionally turn to their college administration for advice in such matters, it is considered advisable to include many of the legal and tax problems of individuals in this chapter. This line of reasoning also justifies the inclusion of the legal problems of individual students in Chapter 4.

TENURE

A faculty member's security against dismissal may be for a fixed term or for the professional life of the individual. In the former case, his tenure is said to be "limited"; in the latter it is "indefinite," "continuous," or "permanent." Status of tenure may depend upon the specific terms of the contract of employment, or it may rest upon principles of employment and tenure adopted and approved by the governing body of the institution. The following statement of academic tenure, formulated by the American Association of Colleges and the American Association of University Professors, has been endorsed by a number of scholarly organizations and adopted by many institutions of higher education:

After the expiration of a probationary period, teachers or investigators should have permanent or continuous tenure, and their services should be terminated only for adequate cause, except in the case of retirement for age or, under extraordinary circumstances, because of financial exigencies.[1]

THE CONTRACT OF EMPLOYMENT. If one may judge from the number of recent cases, status of tenure is the question most frequently liti-

---

[1] "1940 Statement of Principles on Academic Freedom and Tenure," *AAUP Bulletin,* XLIV (1958), 290, 291–92.

gated by members of the faculty. Since avoidance of litigation is one of the primary objectives of all good lawyers, the college attorney should be consulted during the development of procedures for the guidance of administrators in the negotiation, drafting, and execution of the contract of employment of both faculty and staff. These procedures should be carefully outlined and exemplified in the manuals to be used by those responsible for the recruitment and employment of faculty and staff.

DELEGATION OF CONTRACTUAL AUTHORITY. One of the more frequent causes of litigation is the lack of precision in the delegation of the important function of the negotiation and execution of contracts. Who has the power to bind the corporation by contract? There should be no doubt on this point. If the bylaws and regulations of the institution are vague on this question; if manuals of procedure are non-existent or inadequate; if individuals not formally authorized to contract in the name of the institution are permitted to exercise this power and agreements consummated by them are accepted and adopted by the institution, the probability of costly litigation is increased.

IMPLIED POWER TO CONTRACT. Those who may exercise the power to execute contracts in the name of the corporation should be designated by title in its bylaws, ordinances, regulations, and manuals of procedure, under the guidance of legal advice and review. However, from the standpoint of the outsider desiring to enter into contractual relations with the college, it is not a question of who has the formal power but of who has the ostensible power. It is a well-established principle of the law of agency[2] that one is not required to demand documentary proof of an individual's authority to consummate contracts on behalf of another. It is enough if the principal has clothed the one asserting the right to act as his agent with sufficient indicia of authority. For instance, if an individual is given a title that usually implies the power to contract, the principal may be bound by the actions of his agent, despite the fact that he may have expressly forbidden the agent to execute the contract in his name.

EQUITABLE ESTOPPEL. Furthermore, if the principal permits one claiming to be his agent with power to contract in his name to exercise such powers openly and if a third person, in reasonable reliance upon

---

[2] 2 *C.J.S.: Agency* § 29 (1936).

such apparent authority, enters into a contract in good faith, the principal is bound. This is what is known as the doctrine of "equitable estoppel." Although the old common law courts would not recognize such an agreement as a contract binding on the principal, if the power of the chancellor's court (a court of equity) was invoked, the chancellor would say that, in good conscience, the principal should not be permitted to deny, that is, he should be estopped to deny, that he had delegated the contractual authority, since he had, by his own failure to act before the agreement was consummated, misled the one relying on the apparent authority.

EMPLOYMENT NEGOTIATIONS. In litigation involving members of the faculty, this question of implied authority is frequently the point at issue. Preliminary negotiations for the recruitment of faculty are, in many institutions, conducted by the head of a department or by a dean. An examination of the correspondence may reveal that the departmental chairman or dean has gone considerably beyond his actual authority, as stated in the corporation bylaws. He would probably hesitate to affix his signature to a formal contract, but an exchange of correspondence may have all the binding effect of such a contract. However, an essential element of the doctrine of equitable estoppel is the question of whether one is justified in relying upon the apparent or asserted authority of the agent to contract. Only if the claim of authority has been exercised over a sufficiently long period of time so that a reasonably prudent individual would be justified in assuming that the principal had, in fact, delegated such power to him, does it serve as the basis of equitable estoppel.

According to a recent survey,[3] the majority of our colleges and universities have not, as yet, adopted the practice, almost universal in the public schools, of requiring faculty members to execute formal, legally phrased contracts of employment. Two institutions reported that the only written statement that goes to a new teacher is an engraved or printed card announcing the candidate's appointment as a member of the faculty.

IMPLIED POWER TO CONTRACT IN STATE COLLEGES. The courts have been reluctant to apply the doctrine of equitable estoppel against the state.

[3] Tyrus Hillway, "When Hiring Professors, Hasn't the Time Arrived To Supplant the 'Gentleman's Agreement' with a Legal Contract?" *College and University Business,* XXVI (February 1959), 27.

One is presumed to know the extent and limitation of contractual power of officers of the state.

On September 12, 1949, Professor B. B. Bennett, head of the department of languages at the Michigan College of Mining and Technology, wrote to Dr. Edward V. Sittler as follows:

This letter will confirm our telephone conversation of September 10. The position you have accepted is an assistant professorship of German, with a salary of $4000 for the three-term year of approximately nine months. . . . I believe it was our understanding that the appointment is for a one-year period but will become permanent if both you and the administration of the college are quite satisfied at the close of the first year.

Dr. Sittler performed his duties as assistant professor of German from September 19, 1949, to November 10, 1949. On that date he was informed that his services were no longer required. He immediately filed suit for recovery of his salary for the remainder of the academic year, relying on his letter of September 12 as constituting a valid contract of employment. The board of control of the college pointed out in its plea that, by terms of the statute which established the institution and its governing board, authority to enter into contracts of employment of the faculty was vested in the board.

Dr. Sittler, in reply, offered to prove that, on other occasions, heads of departments of the college had been permitted to negotiate and to consummate contracts of employment and thus, by well-established custom, the board of control had delegated its contractual powers to departmental chairmen.

The Supreme Court of Michigan, in affirming the trial court's judgment against Dr. Sittler, stated the rule of law as follows:

Public officers have and can exercise only such powers as are conferred on them by law and a state is not bound by contracts made in its behalf by its officers or agents without previous authority conferred by statute or the constitution.

The powers of state officers being fixed by law, all persons dealing with such officers are charged with knowledge of the extent of their authority or power to bind the state, and are bound, at their peril, to ascertain whether the contemplated power was conferred.

Because of an absolute lack of power vested in Professor Bennett to consummate a contract which would be binding upon defendants, nothing in this record would or could constitute ratification of an alleged contract as asserted by appellant.[4]

---

[4] Sittler v. Board of Control, 33 Mich. 681, 53 N.W.2d 681 (1952).

IMPLIED POWER TO CONTRACT IN NONPUBLIC COLLEGES. In the case of a privately endowed college, if it could be shown that the governing board and the president have permitted, over a period of years, chairmen of departments to negotiate and consummate contracts of employment on behalf of the institution, such established custom would be deemed to constitute an equitable estoppel, that is, the institution would not be permitted to deny that power to contract had, in fact, been delegated, despite institutional regulations to the contrary.

However, a prospective employee must use due care in relying upon the assumption of authority by institutional officers. According to evidence presented at the trial in the case of *Braden v. Trustees of Phillips Academy,* the controller of Phillips Academy, a man named Hooper, offered George D. Braden, business manager of St. Mark's School, a position for life, in order to persuade him to resign his position and accept the position of assistant controller at Phillips Academy. The offer was made in the course of conversation, and there was never a written confirmation of the terms and conditions of his contract of employment. In 1941, Hooper discharged him, and Braden brought suit against the trustees for breach of his alleged life contract. The trustees offered no evidence to refute the oral offer of permanent tenure, and thus the sole question before the court was whether a reasonably prudent man would be justified in assuming that a controller of a preparatory school had actual authority to make such an offer. The court ruled that, in view of the usual limitations upon the responsibility of a controller, the burden of proof was upon the plaintiff and that he had failed to sustain his claim by sufficient evidence.[5]

PERMANENT TENURE. It is a matter of common knowledge in academic circles that, as a general rule, permanent tenure can be conferred only by formal action of the governing board of the institution. Hence, the courts have uniformly held that a faculty member is not justified in relying upon the assumed power, even of the president, to confer tenure rights.

Louis R. Trilling, a teacher in the Townsend Harris High School, the preparatory school of the City College of New York, acquired full tenure rights in the high school in 1931. The high school was abolished by statute in 1942, terminating his position. He was employed on a temporary basis as an instructor in the City College and later received a letter from the president of the college assuring him that, for the

---

[5] Braden v. Trustees of Phillips Academy, 321 Mass. 53, 71 N.E.2d 765 (1947).

purpose of voting in his department of English, he would be regarded as having tenure from the date of his transfer from the high school to the college.

In March 1945 Trilling, still employed on a temporary basis, wrote to the Board of Higher Education of the City of New York, outlining his teaching career and stating that, since September 1944, he had been denied status as a member of the permanent teaching staff of the day session of the City College and asking that he be restored to his "rightful status." He was instructed by the board to make his request through the president of the college. He did so but received no reply. In April 1946 he instituted proceedings to obtain a declaratory judgment to the effect that "he is a regular member of the English Department of the day session faculty of the College of Liberal Arts and Sciences of City College, with full tenure rights as of May 20, 1931."

The court declared that the degree to which City College and Townsend Harris High School had been administered as a unit was not clear from the record. Hence, tenure rights earned in one might not carry over to the other. Moreover, it ruled that the president of the college had no power to confer tenure and that his action could not estop the Board of Higher Education from denying that Trilling had acquired tenure thereby.[6]

THE KENTUCKY WESLEYAN COLLEGE CASE. After four years of service in the department of English at Kentucky Wesleyan College, an associate professor was not re-employed. She brought suit for damages, alleging in her petition that, at the beginning of her fourth year of work, the governing board of the college had promised her that she would be granted permanent tenure if she served satisfactorily during her fourth year. Her counsel, in his brief, declared that his client was a member of the American Association of University Professors and that, in the association's statement of principles with respect to academic tenure, a college teacher is entitled to permanent or continuous tenure after a three-year probationary period.[7] The Court of Appeals of Kentucky in 1953 held that she was not entitled to damages, since she had failed to prove a specific contractual promise of the board to give her tenure or to rehire her for the year in question. More-

---

[6] Trilling v. Board of Higher Education of the City of New York, 190 Misc. 52, 67 N.Y.S.2d 572 (Sup. Ct., 1946).

[7] The "1940 Statement of Principles on Academic Freedom and Tenure," *supra* note 1, at 292, provides for a seven-year probationary period, not a three-year period, as asserted by the counsel for the plaintiff in this case.

over, no evidence had been introduced to prove that the governing board had accepted the statement of principles of the A.A.U.P. as a binding part of its contract of employment of members of its faculty.[8]

THE EFFECT OF LOYALTY OATHS UPON TENURE

Much of the litigation during the last decade with reference to tenure involved the validity and necessity of the various oaths of loyalty demanded of state employees.

THE UNIVERSITY OF CALIFORNIA CASE. One of the first cases of this nature involved the University of California.[9] In April 1949 the Board of Regents decided that all members of the faculty should be required to sign the following statement:

Having taken the constitutional oath of office required of public officials of the state of California, I hereby formally acknowledge my acceptance of the position and salary named, and also state that I am not a member of the Communist party or of any other organization which advocates the overthrow of the government by force or violence, and that I have no commitment in conflict with my responsibilities with respect to impartial scholarship and free pursuit of truth. I understand that the foregoing statement is a condition of my employment and a consideration of payment of my salary.

Thirty-nine members of the faculty who refused to sign this affirmation were granted hearings before the Committee on Privileges and Tenure and were cleared. The president of the university recommended that they be reappointed, but the Board of Regents declined to do so. Upon failure to receive notification of appointment for the academic year 1950–51, eighteen nonsigning members of the faculty requested the district court of appeals to issue a writ of mandamus to compel the secretary of the board to issue their letters of appointment. The court ordered the secretary to issue the letters forthwith, and, in its opinion, declared that

if the faculty of the university can be subjected to any more narrow test of loyalty than the constitutional oath, our great institution now dedicated to learning and the search for truth would be reduced to an organ for the propagation of the ephemeral political, religious, social and economic philos-

---

[8] Scott v. Joint Board of Education, 258 S.W.2d 449 (Ky. Ct. App. 1953).

[9] For the background of the controversy, see George Stewart, *The Year of the Oath* (Garden City, N.Y.: Doubleday & Co., 1950). The Board of Trustees of the Ohio State University, in 1948, instituted an oath requirement applicable to all members of the faculty and staff. The oath was very similar to the one adopted by the Board of Regents of the University of California in 1949. See "Academic Freedom and Tenure in the Quest for National Security," *AAUP Bulletin*, XLII (Spring 1956), 49–107, especially 83.

ophies, whatever they may be, of the majority of the board of regents at that moment.[10]

The Board of Regents, by an 11 to 10 vote, decided to accept this decision of the district court as final. However, a minority group of the Regents instructed its special counsel to file an appeal, and on October 17, 1952, the Supreme Court of California affirmed the decision of the lower court.[11]

THE LEVERING, THE FEINBERG, AND THE OBER ACTS. The Supreme Court of the United States has upheld[12] the constitutionality of loyalty oaths of the character of those required under the Levering Act of California,[13] the Feinberg law of New York,[14] and the Ober law of Maryland.[15]

However, an Oklahoma loyalty oath statute was declared to be unconstitutional on the grounds that mere membership in an organization, declared to be subversive, without actual knowledge of its character, would, under the provisions of the law, disqualify one for employment by the state.[16] Mr. Justice Clark, speaking for the court, declared:

Indiscriminate classification of innocent with knowing activity must fall as an assertion of arbitrary power. An oath so broad, one covering associations which were well meant as well as others that might be intentionally subversive, offends due process.

LOYALTY OATHS DURING THE CIVIL WAR. Many have mistakenly assumed that the loyalty oath controversy is of recent origin. On the contrary, public school teachers were required by statute to take oaths of loyalty during the critical period of the War between the States. From 1862 to 1867, Arkansas, California, Kentucky, Missouri, Nevada, Oregon, and West Virginia attempted, by legislation, to weed out instructors of doubtful loyalty to the Federal Government.[17]

---

[10] Tolman v. Underhill, 229 P.2d 447 (3d D. Cal. 1951).

[11] Tolman v. Underhill, 39 Cal. App. 2d 708, 249 P.2d 280 (Cal. Sup. Ct. 1952).

[12] Garner v. Board of Public Works of Los Angeles, 341 U.S. 716 (1951).

[13] *Cal. Gov. Code* §§ 3100–109.

[14] Adler v. Board of Education, 343 U.S. 485 (1952); *N.Y. Educ. Code* § 3022.

[15] Gerende v. Board of Supervisors, 341 U.S. 56 (1951); *Md. Code* art. 85A, § 13 (1957).

[16] *Okla. Stat.* tit. 51, §§ 37.1–.8 (1952 Supp.); Wieman v. Updegraf, 344 U.S. 183, 191 (1952).

[17] E. Edmund Reutter, Jr., *The School Administrator and Subversive Activities* (New York: Bureau of Publications, Teachers College, Columbia University, 1951).

THE LUSK LAWS OF 1921. After the Russian Revolution of 1918, the question of disloyalty of members of the teaching staff of the public schools of the City of New York began to make headlines in the public press. In 1919 the New York Legislature organized the Lusk Committee, and in 1921 the widely publicized "Lusk laws" were enacted over the veto of the governor. Since the end of World War II, when the conspiratorial nature of the Russian menace has been more clearly recognized, public demand for protection against the disloyal public servant has greatly increased. Almost all states, as well as the Federal Government, have enacted legislation to meet this demand.

ACADEMIC FREEDOM AND THE FIFTH AMENDMENT

One of the most critical problems confronting college administrators and the members of their governing boards is the formulation of institutional policy with reference to the college professor who, in the name of academic freedom, invokes the protection of the Fifth Amendment when questioned by a congressional committee as to his Communist affiliations. This amendment, a fundamental bulwark of our rights as free men, an integral part of our Bill of Rights in the federal Constitution, declares that no person "shall be compelled, in any criminal case, to be a witness against himself." The origin of this protection of the individual against self-incrimination has been traced as far back as the twelfth century in English history.[18] It grew out of a natural repugnance against requiring people to provide evidence against themselves and their associates. The ecclesiastical courts of the period, seeking to uncover heresy and other violations of Church law, frequently compelled unwilling witnesses to answer questions about their own intimate personal affairs and about their friends. Those who came to America knew, from bitter experience, the importance of this protection against Church and Crown. Consequently, the first bill of rights, drafted in 1776 after the opening of the Revolutionary War, became a part of the Virginia state constitution and included a guarantee against self-incrimination.

THE BROOKLYN COLLEGE CASE. In 1952 an associate professor at Brooklyn College, a tax-supported institution, refused to testify before a congressional committee as to his membership in the Communist party

---

[18] Erwin N. Griswold, *The Fifth Amendment Today* (Cambridge, Mass.: Harvard University Press, 1955), p. 2.

during 1940 and 1941 on the grounds that his answers might tend to incriminate him. He was discharged by the college in accordance with the provisions of Section 903 of the charter of the City of New York, which declares that whenever an employee of the city uses the privilege against self-incrimination to avoid answering a question relating to his official conduct, "his term or tenure of office or employment shall terminate."

He brought suit for reinstatement and the case reached the Supreme Court of the United States on the narrow issue of the constitutionality of that portion of the charter of the City of New York which permits discharge without the formality of notice and a hearing. Mr. Justice Clark delivered the opinion[19] of the majority of the court, of which the following is an excerpt:

The State has broad powers in the selection and discharge of its employees, and it may be that proper inquiry would show Slochower's continued employment to be inconsistent with the real interest of the State. But there has been no such inquiry here. We hold that summary dismissal of the appellant violates due process of law.

In a strong dissenting opinion, Mr. Justice Reed had this to say:

We assert the contrary—the city does have reasonable ground to require its employees either to give evidence regarding the facts of official conduct within their knowledge or to give up the position they hold. . . . Such conclusion is reinforced when the claimant for the position is the instructor of youth.

Mr. Justice Reed then quotes the following excerpt from "The Rights and Responsibilities of Universities and Their Faculties," published by the Association of American Universities, March 24, 1953:

In all acts of association, the professor accepts conventions which become morally binding. Above all, he owes his colleagues in the university complete

---

19 Slochower v. Board of Higher Education of New York City, 350 U.S. 551, 559, 561, 562, 564 (1956); see also Application of Hughes, 286 App. Div. 180, 141 N.Y.S.2d 392 (1955), aff'd, 309 N.Y. 319, 130 N.E.2d 638 (1955); Beilan v. Board of Public Education, School District of Philadelphia, 357 U.S. 399 (1958); Byse, "Teachers and the Fifth Amendment," 102 U. Pa. L. Rev. 871 (1954); Claflin, "The Self-Incriminating Clause of the Fifth Amendment: Its Interpretation, Use and Misuse," 42 A.B.A.J. 935 (1956); Pittman, "The Fifth Amendment: Yesterday, Today and Tomorrow," 42 A.B.A.J. 509 (1956); for a discussion of the adequacy of the federal Immunity Act as a condition for the denial of the privilege against self-incrimination, see Annot. 53 A.L.R.2d 1030 (1957); a recent decision of the United States Supreme Court, i.e., Nelson v. County of Los Angeles, 362 U.S. 1 (1960), reduces, to some extent, the importance of the Slochower case.

candor and perfect integrity, precluding any kind of clandestine or conspiratorial activities. He owes equal candor to the public. If he is called upon
to answer for his convictions, it is his duty as a citizen to speak out. It is
even more definitely his duty as a professor. Refusal to do so, on whatever
legal grounds, cannot fail to reflect upon a profession that claims for itself
the fullest freedom to speak and the maximum protection of that freedom
available in our society. In this respect, invocation of the Fifth Amendment
places upon a professor a heavy burden of proof of his fitness to hold a teaching position and lays upon his university an obligation to re-examine his
qualifications for membership in its society.

However, Erwin N. Griswold, dean of the Harvard Law School, re-
minds us:

We may better understand the importance of the Fifth Amendment by
considering what not having it would mean. We usually think of the privilege
against self-incrimination either in historical terms, in the light of past
tyrannies, or in terms of the embarrassment that a witness may experience as
a result of the exposure of political mistakes. Let us look, though, at the
reverse of the coin in terms of the standard operating procedures of the
police state which have brought the medieval techniques up to date. If we
are not willing to let the amendment be invoked, where, over time, are we
going to stop when police, prosecutors, or chairmen want to get people to
talk? Lurking in the background here are really ugly dangers which may
transform our whole system of free government. In this light, the frustrations
caused by the amendment are a small price to pay for the fundamental
protection it provides.[20]

TENURE IN TAX-SUPPORTED COLLEGES

The power of the administration in many of the tax-supported institutions to employ, promote, and discharge is restricted by provisions of
state civil service legislation.[21] Those responsible for personnel administration in those institutions should have available in their manuals of
procedures pertinent excerpts from statutes, rulings, and court decisions
concerning this matter.

THE PROFESSOR AS A PUBLIC OFFICER. One question on which the courts
have divided is that of whether a member of the faculty in a public
institution is a public officer or an employee. This distinction becomes
of importance in the issue of tenure where the state statutes give the
governing board the power to appoint, suspend, remove, or discharge
members of the faculty. If they are public officers, then, according to

[20] Griswold, op. cit. supra note 18, at 27.
[21] See the discussion of "State Civil Service Regulations Limit Local Autonomy,"
p. 254, in chap. 8.

the usual court interpretation of such statutory powers, they may be dismissed by the board at its pleasure, whereas if they are held to be employees and if their contract of employment is for a certain fixed time, they cannot be lawfully discharged before the expiration of their term of employment without due cause. Moreover, "due cause" or "cause" has a special connotation in the language of the law; it means that a court reserves to itself the right to review the question of whether, in fact, there was cause or justification for the action at issue and to substitute its judgment for that of the parties directly concerned.

The following is from the opinion of the Court of Appeals of Georgia on this question of the legal status of a public school teacher:

> It will be seen from the foregoing that the great weight of authority in other states, and in the textbooks, is that a teacher is a mere "employee" and not an "officer," and that, where a board of education has made a contract with a teacher for a fixed period of time, the teacher can be discharged before the contract has expired, only for cause.[22]

If members of the faculty of endowed colleges, as well as those in the tax-supported institutions, desire the right of a court review of their tenure rights, the words "may be dismissed only for cause" should form a part of their contract of employment or of the tenure statement approved by the governing board of their institution.

THE PHELPS CASE. The significance of contractual tenure rights as contrasted with statutory rights was emphasized in the Phelps case, which came before the Supreme Court of New Jersey in 1935. Certain public school teachers in that state had acquired the status of indefinite tenure under the New Jersey Tenure Act of 1909. In 1933, due to the great economic depression of that period, the state legislature authorized local boards of education to readjust the annual compensation of public school teachers. Acting under the authority of this statute, the West New York school board reduced the salaries of its employees. According to the provisions of the state tenure act, no teacher with tenure could be dismissed or subjected to a reduction of salary except for cause, after due process of a hearing.

Jay B. Phelps and others with tenure rights challenged the constitu-

---

[22] Board of Education v. Bacon, 22 Ga. App. 72, 95 S.E. 753 (1918); see also Annot. 75 A.L.R. 1352 (1931); Elwood v. State ex rel. Griffin, 203 Ind. 626, 180 N.E. 471 (1932); for another example of the extent to which a court will substitute its judgment for that of a university governing board if the question of "cause" is involved, see State ex rel. Richardson v. Board of Regents of University of Nevada, 70 Nev. 347, 269 P.2d 265 (1954).

tionality of the action of the school board as in violation of their vested contractual rights. The state supreme court rejected this contention in the following words:

> The status of tenure teachers, while in one sense perhaps contractual, is, in essence, dependent upon a statute, like the incumbent of a statutory office, which the Legislature, at will, may abolish, or whose emoluments it may change.[23]

This decision was unanimously approved by the state court of errors and appeals[24] and by the Supreme Court of the United States.[25]

THE ANDERSON CASE. The high federal court reached a different conclusion the following year in its interpretation of the Indiana Tenure Act of 1927. Mary Anderson, a teacher in the Chester School Township, acquired tenure rights under the act which provided that a person who has served for five or more successive years as a teacher and shall thereafter enter into a contract for future service shall become a permanent teacher. In 1933 the state legislature amended the tenure act, removing the employees of township school boards from its protection. Upon her discharge, Miss Anderson sought a writ of mandamus to compel the board to continue her as a teacher. The state supreme court refused to grant the writ and the following is an excerpt from the opinion of the court:

> The tenure statute was only intended as a limitation upon the plenary power of the local school officials to cancel contracts. It was not intended as, and cannot be, a limitation upon the power of future Legislators to change the law respecting teachers and their tenure. These are matters of public policy, of purely governmental concern, in which the legislative power cannot be exhausted or consumed, or contracted away, so as to limit the discretion of future General Assemblies.[26]

The case reached the United States Supreme Court in 1938, and Mr. Justice Roberts delivered the majority opinion, which read in part as follows:

> we are of the opinion that the petitioner had a valid contract with the respondent, the obligation of which would be impaired by the termination of her employment. . . . Until its decision in the present case, the Supreme

---

[23] Phelps v. State Board of Education, 115 N.J.L. 310, 314, 180 Atl. 220, 222 (N.J. Sup. Ct. 1935).

[24] 116 N.J.L. 412, 185 Atl. 8 (N.J. Ct. Err. & App. 1936).

[25] 300 U.S. 319 (1937).

[26] State ex rel. Anderson v. Brand, 214 Ind. 347, 352, 5 N.E.2d 531, 533 (1937), aff'd on rehearing, 214 Ind. 352, 7 NE.2d 779 (1937).

Court of the State has uniformly held that the teacher's right to continued employment by virtue of the indefinite contract created pursuant to the Act was contractual.[27]

The opinion rejected the contention of the school board that every contract of any agency of the state is subject to the police power of the state and, that, in repealing the teachers' tenure act, the legislature had validly exercised that reserved power of the state.

The following is from the dissenting opinion of Mr. Justice Black:

I cannot agree that the constitutional prohibition against impairment of contracts was intended to—or does—transfer the determination of the educational policy of Indiana from the legislature of the State to this Court.

Indiana's highest court has said that the State *did not* and has strongly indicated that the legislature *could not*, make contracts with a *few citizens* that would take away from *all the citizens*, the continuing power to alter the educational policy for the best interest of Indiana school children.

The Indiana Supreme Court had the last word on the case. The high federal court had remanded the case to the state court for further proceedings not inconsistent with its opinion. The following is from the opinion of the state court with reference to the ruling of the United States Supreme Court:

That court held the repeal of the statute to be ineffective to strike down the teachers' contractual tenure rights. We conclude that the repeal of the statute is otherwise valid in all respects, and therefore there is no longer any statutory duty to continue the teachers in employment. . . . We must still conclude therefore that the complaint in the name of the State for mandate does not state a cause of action.[28]

THE WORZELLA CASE. The Worzella case, decided by the Supreme Court of South Dakota in 1958, involved the constitutional question: Can the governing board of a state college, charged by the state constitution and by statute with responsibility for the government and control of that institution, lawfully delegate that power or any portion thereof to a faculty tenure committee?

Dr. W. W. Worzella was discharged by the State Board of Regents of Education from his position as professor of agronomy at the South Dakota State College of Agriculture and Mechanic Arts in 1958. He peti-

---

[27] Indiana *ex rel.* Anderson v. Brand, 303 U.S. 95, 104, 105, 117 (1938).

[28] Indiana *ex rel.* Anderson v. Brand, 214 Ind. 356, 359, 13 N.E.2d 955, 957 (1938), supplemental opinion on mandate of the United States Supreme Court; see also Annot. 110 A.L.R. 791 (1937), 113 A.L.R. 1495 (1938), 127 A.L.R. 1298 (1940); for a summary of the history and rationale of teachers' tenure statutes, see McSherry v. St. Paul, 202 Minn. 102, 277 N.W. 541 (1938).

tioned the court for a writ of mandamus to compel the board to reinstate him, contending that he had acquired permanent tenure under a
faculty tenure policy approved by the board. The board maintained
that the tenure policy did not, and could not, abrogate its constitutional
and statutory power to dismiss all officers, instructors, and other employees under its control. The court declined to grant the writ, and the
following is from the opinion of the court:

> The exact meaning of this so-called tenure policy eludes us. . . . Appar-
> ently the Board could not discharge or remove a faculty member with tenure
> for any reason if the President failed to, or refused to file a complaint, or if
> the Tenure Committee and President failed or refused to recommend dis-
> missal. We believe this to be an unlawful abdication of the Board's exclusive
> prerogative and power.[29]

THE KEENEY CASE. This Montana case in 1939 enunciated the interesting doctrine that tenure rules, adopted by the governing board of a
publicly controlled college or university, become, by a process of sublegislation, a law of the state, with the force and effect of an act duly
adopted by the legislature. Consequently, a member of the faculty had
the protection of the tenure rule, despite the fact that the board, in
tendering him his contract, had deleted that portion of the tenure clause
which stated that "re-appointment after three years service shall be
deemed a permanent appointment."

The court declared:

> Striking the regulations from the contract could have no more effect than
> the striking of a provision of a statute, and petitioner's acceptance of the
> contract would no more constitute a waiver of the regulation than it would
> constitute a waiver of the statute.[30]

Justice Morris, in his dissenting opinion, took judicial notice of the
fact, legally irrelevant, that Professor Keeney had apparently been the
leader in organizing the instructors of the Montana State University
into an affiliate of the American Federation of Labor and that an attorney, with the permission of the court, had filed a brief "on behalf of
the American Civil Liberties Union."

---

[29] Worzella v. Board of Regents of Education, 93 N.W.2d 411, 412, 413 (S.D.
1958); see Clark Byse, "Academic Freedom, Tenure, and the Law: A Comment on
Worzella v. Board of Regents," 73 *Harv. L. Rev.* 304 (1959).

[30] State *ex rel.* Keeney v. Ayers, 108 Mont. 547, 556, 92 P.2d 306, 310 (1939);
see also State *ex rel.* Richardson v. Board of Regents of University of Nevada,
70 Nev. 144, 261 P.2d 515 (1953).

THE AMERICAN ACADEMIC FREEDOM PROJECT AT COLUMBIA UNIVERSITY. Clark Byse and Louis Joughin, as part of the American Academic Freedom project at Columbia University, prepared a report[31] on tenure in American higher education, financed by a grant from the Fund for the Republic. The report, published in 1959, is based upon an analysis of the tenure plans supplied by eighty institutions in response to a questionnaire. The following is an excerpt from a summary:

The stated plans and practices which have been reviewed yield a picture of mixed deficiency and completeness, clarity and confusion. If the eighty institutions are at all typical of American colleges and universities, tenure systems in higher education present a wide range in degree of perfection, and the poorest of them are notably deficient in providing a sound relationship between the teacher and the institution.

In the chapter entitled "Tenure and the Law," the distinction is made between the legal enforcement of tenure in a state-financed and in a "private" college or university. In the public institutions of higher education, the teacher who has been dismissed in violation of the tenure plan in force at his institution is advised, in effect, to present the argument that, since the tenure plan promulgated by the governing board as an instrumentality of a state is a form of sublegislation, which has the force and effect of law, the court should uphold and enforce the law by ordering the board to reinstate the teacher.

In Chapter 4 of the report, the authors give their conclusions and recommendations. They are summarized in the following excerpt:

The recommendations that follow do not propose action by state or federal legislative bodies. Nor do they call for the use of outside arbitrators to resolve differences. The prime need is not for extra-mural intervention, but for each institution of higher learning to engage in systematic discussion and analysis and to take appropriate action to make tenure as positive a force as possible for the good of education.

---

[31] Clark Byse and Louis Joughin, *Tenure in American Higher Education* (Ithaca, N.Y.: Cornell University Press, 1959); passages quoted here are from pp. 68 and 132. The Appendix reprints the "1940 Statement of Principles . . ." drafted as the result of a series of joint conferences between representatives of the American Association of University Professors and the Association of American Colleges; "Recommended Institutional Regulations on Academic Freedom and Tenure," from a memorandum issued in 1957 by the A.A.U.P.; and "Statement on Procedural Standards in Faculty Dismissal Proceedings," prepared by a joint committee representing the Association of American Colleges and the American Association of University Professors. See also "Academic Freedom and Tenure in the Quest for National Security," *AAUP Bulletin*, XLII (Spring 1956), 49–107.

DISCRIMINATION BECAUSE OF RACE, COLOR, OR CREED
IN THE APPOINTMENT OF FACULTY
IN PUBLIC INSTITUTIONS

Apparently, the first time the constitutional question of discrimination based upon race or color in the appointment, pay, and promotion of public school teachers reached a federal court was in 1939.

THE MARYLAND CASE. A school teacher brought an action against the State Department of Education of Maryland to enjoin the enforcement of Maryland law and practice thereunder of paying Negro teachers substantially less than white teachers having equal professional qualifications. The following is from the opinion of the court:

The right of the State to prescribe the qualifications for, and the salary annexed to, a public office of employment is ordinarily free from restriction; and it would not seem that a state employee who has accepted employment at a stated salary could complain that he had been denied a *civil* right under the equal protection clause of the Fourteenth Amendment. However, it is not necessary in this case to decide this precise question because, in my opinion, there is another aspect of the plaintiff's situation which entitles him to attack the legislation in its practical application. The plaintiff is a qualified school teacher and has the civil right, as such, to pursue his occupation without discriminatory legislation on account of his race or color. While the State may freely select its employees and determine their compensation, it would, in my opinion, be clearly unconstitutional for a state to pass legislation which imposed discriminatory burdens upon the colored race with respect to their qualifications for office or prescribe a rate of pay less than for other classes solely on account of race or color.[32]

THE ALABAMA CASE. However, in 1955, when a Negro teacher in Alabama attempted to persuade a federal district court to impose a fine of $2,970 against the school board of Jefferson County to compensate her for salary lost as a result of the board's disobedience to an injunction restraining it from discriminating against her because of her color or race, the court refused. The following is an excerpt from the reasoning of the court:

To hold that the Board, as a corporate entity, would be liable in pecuniary damage, to be satisfied out of public funds, for the tortious conduct of its

---

[32] Mills v. Lowndes, 26 F. Supp. 792, 801 (D. Md. 1939); see also Mills v. Board of Education, 30 F. Supp. 245 (D. Md. 1939); Alston v. School Board, 112 F.2d 992 (4th Cir. 1940); *cert. denied*, 311 U.S. 693 (1940); Annot. 130 A.L.R. 1512 (1940); Davis v. Cook, 80 F. Supp. 443 (N.D. Ga. 1948); West v. Board of Education of Prince Georges County, 165 F. Supp. 382 (D. Md. 1958).

individual members in wilfully and arbitrarily discriminating against any class of teachers in establishing and paying their salaries in violation of the Fourteenth Amendment, a discrimination unauthorized under the laws of the State and powers conferred upon the Board, would be to authorize a suit against the State of Alabama without its consent, proscribed by the Eleventh Amendment.[33]

DISCRIMINATION BECAUSE OF CREED. In 1956 the Court of Appeals of Kentucky ruled that, if members of a religious order were prevented from teaching in the public schools of the state because of their religious beliefs or because they wore the dress and emblems of their order in the classroom, such action would constitute a violation of their right of equal protection under the law, guaranteed to them by the Fourteenth Amendment.[34]

LABOR LEGISLATION

As we have seen, the Fourteenth Amendment has been interpreted by the courts to prohibit the states from enacting legislation or indulging in administrative procedures that tend to discriminate against individuals seeking employment by the state or by instrumentalities of the state. The first attempt, on a national scale, to protect the rights of individuals against such discrimination by private employers was the establishment in 1941 of the Fair Employment Practices Committee by order of the President.[35] Stimulated by this action of the Federal Government, state and municipal governments entered the field. By 1952 Connecticut, Massachusetts, New Jersey, New Mexico, New York, Oregon, Rhode Island, and Washington had passed legislation barring discrimination in employment procedures. A long list of cities have enacted ordinances to the same effect.[36] In general, educational, social, and other nonprofit organizations are excluded from the provisions of these acts.

FEDERAL LABOR LEGISLATION. The National Labor Relations Act of 1935 declared it to be the policy of the Federal Government to encour-

---

[33] Gainer v. School Board of Jefferson County, 135 F. Supp. 559, 570 (N.D. Ala. 1955).

[34] Rawlings v. Butta, 290 S.W.2d 801 (Ky. Ct. App. 1956).

[35] Elson and Schanfield, "Local Discriminatory Employment Practices," 56 Yale L.J. 431, 434 (1947).

[36] Morris D. Forkosch, A Treatise on Labor Law (Indianapolis, Ind.: Bobbs-Merrill Co., 1953), § 83; see also Note, "The New York State Commission against Discrimination: A New Technique for an Old Problem," 56 Yale L.J. 837 (1947).

age the practice and procedure of collective bargaining and to protect the rights of workers to organize for the purpose of negotiating the terms and conditions of their employment. Employers were prohibited from indulging in what were designated as "unfair labor practices." A semijudicial board was created to implement the provisions of the act.[37] The constitutional basis for this legislation is the power granted to Congress "to regulate commerce . . . among the several states."[38]

This commerce clause of the Constitution has been interpreted and expanded by decisions of the United States Supreme Court so that Congress may regulate not only commerce among the several states, that is, interstate commerce in the strict sense of the term, but also almost any activity within a state if, in the opinion of the Court, it "substantially affects" interstate commerce.[39] On this basis, the National Labor Relations Board has not hesitated to take jurisdiction over labor disputes involving the employees of colleges and universities where the activity in which they are engaged is deemed to have a substantial effect upon the stream of interstate commerce.

By provisions of the National Labor Relations Act, the only nonprofit organizations specifically exempted from the jurisdiction of the NLRB are hospitals.[40] The United States Supreme Court has ruled that the jurisdiction of the Board is not affected by the nonprofit character of the employer.[41] By a series of unanimous decisions issued in October 1950, the NLRB set forth its own concept of intrastate activities which affect the flow of interstate commerce. In general, the Board will take jurisdiction if the activity produces goods destined to flow into interstate commerce or if the service is rendered outside the state or if the annual volume is valued at $50,000 or more or if the enterprise has an indirect inflow of goods or materials valued at $1 million or more. In the case of nonprofit educational institutions, the Board has decided that it will accept jurisdiction only in connection with what it considers the "commercial" activities of such institutions.

THE ILLINOIS INSTITUTE OF TECHNOLOGY CASE. In 1949 a union claimed the right to represent machinists employed in shops of two research foundations affiliated with the Illinois Institute of Technology and lo-

---

[37] 29 U.S.C. §§ 141–51 (1956), 49 Stat. 448; 61 Stat. 136.
[38] U.S. Const. art. I, § 8, cl. 3.
[39] NLRB v. Jones & Laughlin Steel Corp., 301 U.S. 1 (1937).
[40] 29 U.S.C. § 152(2) (1956).
[41] The Associated Press v. NLRB, 301 U.S. 103 (1937).

cated on the campus of the Institute. The NLRB accepted jurisdiction of the labor dispute on the following grounds:

The employer and the intervenor contend that the employer is not subject to the Board's jurisdiction because (1) it is an educational institution operating without profit and (2) it uses the channels of interstate commerce to transmit scientific ideas and information and not any commercial product. Whatever its general purposes may be, there can be little doubt that the research features of the employer's activities as carried out by the Foundation and Gas Technology are operated on a commercial or business basis. These two divisions of the employer furnish research services to industrial concerns and the federal government which have, as their purpose, the improvement of manufacturing processes. Moreover, their sponsors reimburse them for all cost engendered in connection with these services. . . . The facts herein established that the employer's sponsored research projects are of a business nature. We are of the opinion and find that the employer is engaged in commerce within the meaning of the Act. This finding is unaffected by the fact that the employer does not operate for profit or that its activities in interstate commerce involve the communication of information rather than the transmission of specific products.[42]

THE PORT ARTHUR COLLEGE CASE. A union petitioned for the right to represent the employees of the radio station of Port Arthur College in 1950. The NLRB found, upon investigation, that the radio station was not used for instructional purposes, that it accepted commercial advertising, and that it was a member of a national radio network. The Board therefore held[43] that, by the operation of the station, the college was engaged in interstate commerce, within the meaning of the act.

THE COLUMBIA UNIVERSITY CASE. The Board declined to accept jurisdiction in a labor dispute in 1951 involving the clerical employees of the libraries of Columbia University. The following is from the opinion of the Board:

Although the activities of Columbia University affect commerce sufficiently to satisfy the requirements of the statute and the standards established by the Board for the normal exercise of its jurisdiction, we do not believe that it would effectuate the policies of the Act for the Board to assert jurisdiction here.[44]

THE CALIFORNIA INSTITUTE OF TECHNOLOGY CASE. The Board asserted jurisdiction over the employees on an experimental wind tunnel op-

---

[42] Illinois Institute of Technology, 81 NLRB 201, 204 (1949).
[43] Port Arthur College, 92 NLRB 152 (1950).
[44] The Trustees of Columbia University, 97 NLRB 424, 427 (1951).

erated by the California Institute of Technology as one of its research projects. The tunnel was owned by five aircraft companies and operated by the institute under a management contract. Students participated in the project, and classroom discussions resulted from tests made. The following is from the majority opinion of the Board:

The Board has had occasion in the past to review the question as to whether it would assert its jurisdiction over non-profit, educational, charitable, and religious organizations. It has refused to exempt such non-profit organizations from the operation of the Act when the particular activities involved were commercial in nature. Conversely, where the activities involved were *noncommercial* in nature and intimately connected with the educational activities of the institution, the Board has refused to assert its jurisdiction.

Although we are cognizant of the educational benefits to be derived from the Institute's operation of the Cooperative Wind Tunnel, it is nevertheless apparent that the Institute's extensive research services performed for industrial users have, as their purpose, the improvement of the products of the aircraft industry. Moreover, the Institute operated the project under a management agreement on a commercial cost-reimbursement basis.[45]

Two members of the Board joined in the following dissent:

Unlike the majority, we do not believe that the commercial aspects of the research activities of the Institute's cooperative wind tunnel project are sufficient to warrant our asserting jurisdiction, in the light of what we consider the intimate relation between these activities and the admitted educational purposes of the Institute itself.

THE CARNEGIE INSTITUTE OF TECHNOLOGY CASE. In a brief administrative decision, the NLRB declined jurisdiction in a dispute in 1953 involving the employees of the nuclear research center of the Carnegie Institute of Technology. The following is from the opinion:

The center was financed in 1951 by grants from the Office of Naval Research, the Atomic Energy Commission, and the employer. The center is engaged in continuing and furthering the scientific study of physics, chemistry, metallurgy, and mathematics involved in atomic nuclear research. There is no direct monetary contribution made to the center by any company, nor is any work done for commercial organizations.[46]

THE SECOND ILLINOIS INSTITUTE OF TECHNOLOGY CASE. By 1954 the Board was ready to revise its views with reference to the work done in

---

[45] The California Institute of Technology, 102 NLRB 1402, 1404, 1405 (1953).
[46] Carnegie Institute of Technology, Case No. 6–RC–1092, 32 L.R.R.M. 1310 (June 1, 1953).

the Armour Research Foundation of the Illinois Institute of Technology. The change in point of view was justified on the grounds that

the foundation is physically located on the campus of the institute. Some
students are employed by the foundation in aid of the alternating study-
work program of the institute. Others are given fellowships in the institute
by the foundation. Only 27% of the foundation's work is commercially sponsored.

One member dissented:

In view of the majority's admission that 27% of the work of the Foundation, which is separately incorporated, is commercially sponsored, I cannot
comprehend the ultimate conclusion that the Foundation's activities are "noncommercial in nature." Surely 27%, amounting to 2½ million dollars a year,
cannot be deemed *de minimis* or an incidental aspect of the Foundation's
work.[47]

STATE WORKMEN'S COMPENSATION ACTS

In earlier times under the common law, an employee injured in line
of duty could obtain compensation therefor only if it could be proven
that the accident was caused by the negligence of his employer or that
of his agents. Moreover, the employer could plead that the employee
had assumed the known risks of the job, that the employee's own
negligence or that of a fellow employee had been a contributing cause
of the accident. Strong agitation began during the nineteenth century to
remedy the evils resulting from the application of these harsh doctrines
of the common law.[48]

By 1897 England had adopted a somewhat limited workmen's compensation law, and in 1911 ten American states enacted similar laws.
Mississippi in 1948 became the last state to follow this trend. Under the
theory of this legislation, injured employees are paid compensation,
and their dependents are compensated for their accidental death, irrespective of the question of negligence. The justification for this is that
it is impossible to reduce industrial accidents below a certain minimum, even with the best safety precautions. Since they are an inevitable part of our industrial society, their costs should be borne by society

---

[47] Armour Research Foundation of the Illinois Institute of Technology, 107
NLRB No. 228, 33 L.R.R.M. 1311 (1954). Howard H. Moore, legal counsel of
the University of Chicago, furnished the above NLRB citations.

[48] Bruce Alden Greene, *State Workmen's Compensation Laws as of September
1950*, U.S. Bureau of Labor Standards Bulletin No. 125 (Washington: Government
Printing Office, 1952). For a discussion of state workmen's compensation legislation
from the standpoint of the employer, see chap. 5, pp. 153–55.

as a whole in the form of increased prices for commodities and services, rather than by the individual workers and their families.

No state law covers all employers. In general, agriculture, domestic service, and casual employment are exempted. Some states permit employers to reject the provisions of the law. The legislation is administered by a state commission or board. In order that the employee may be compensated promptly after the commission has made its award, employers are required to obtain insurance or to give proof of their qualifications to carry their own risk. Some states administer a form of state insurance fund.

THE TORT LIABILITY OF FACULTY AND STAFF

An individual may be compelled to reimburse another for injury or destruction of life or property caused by his wrongful or negligent acts. This personal liability is, of course, in addition to that of the employer or principal of the one guilty of such acts of commission or omission.[49] Many professional men, especially physicians, surgeons, and psychiatrists, have found it advisable to obtain insurance protecting them against financial loss resulting from charges of malpractice and negligent care and treatment of patients. Institutions employing such individuals should consider the desirability of obtaining insurance protecting both employer and employee.

THE STOUT STATE COLLEGE CASE. A student enrolled at Stout State College committed suicide. Her parents brought an action against the director of student personnel service. In their bill of complaint, the parents alleged:

That said defendant negligently and carelessly failed to perform his duties as such Director in the following: (a) That he failed to secure or attempt to secure emergency psychiatric treatment after he was aware or should have been aware of her inability to care for the safety of herself. (b) That he failed at all times to advise the said parents of Jeannie Bogust or contact them concerning the true mental and emotional state of their said daughter, thus preventing them from securing proper medical care for her. (c) That he failed to provide proper student guidance.

The National Education Association was permitted to file a brief as amicus curiae, that is, a friend of the court. The following is from the brief:

The implications of this case for the future of guidance programs in the

---

[49] See chap. 5, p. 147.

schools and colleges of this country become clearer with the realization that, at the present time, there are approximately 25,000 full- or part-time counselors employed by the schools and colleges in the fifty states. Any one of them might have been the defendant in this case. To establish a precedent that a cause of action is stated by the facts pleaded here would create an occupational hazard of indeterminate proportions for each of these individuals and would, in effect, undermine the effectiveness of a part of the public educational program that needs to be greatly strengthened at the present time.

The court found in favor of the defendant[50] on the ground that the complaint filed by the parents did not state facts sufficient to create a cause of action. The following is from the opinion of the court:

Defendant is not a person qualified as a medical doctor or a specialist in medical disorders. It is alleged that he is an "educator by profession," a professor of education with a doctor of philosophy degree. . . . Granting that he had some knowledge of Jeannie's emotional and other difficulties as the result of his meeting with her during a period of five months, as a teacher he cannot be charged with the same degree of care based upon such knowledge as a person trained in medicine or psychiatry could exercise.

FEDERAL IMMIGRATION LEGISLATION

In recent years, colleges and universities, as employers of personnel from abroad, have become increasingly concerned with restrictions imposed by the Federal Government on the admission and employment of aliens. The current basic law on this subject is known as the Immigration and Nationality Act of 1952.[51] It retained the quota system, under which the number of immigrants to be admitted to the United States annually from any foreign country is limited to one-sixth of 1 percent of the number of persons of that national origin already living in this country as shown by the 1920 census. It introduced a system of selective immigration by giving a special preference to skilled workers urgently needed. Its provisions may be summarized as follows:

An alien coming to this country first applies for a visa. He may not take passage to this country unless a visa is issued. On his arrival, he is examined by an officer of the Immigration and Naturalization Service and a final decision as to his admissibility is made. If he does not intend to make his home in this country, he is classified as a nonimmigrant. There are ten classes of nonimmigrants. The three classes of interest to

---

[50] Bogust v. Inverson, 102 N.W. 2d 228 (Wis. 1960).

[51] 66 *Stat.* 166 ch. 477, tit. I, §§ 101–407 (1953). 8 *U.S.C.* §§ 1101–1503. Much of the material on federal immigration legislation and regulations in this chapter is based upon suggestions from Alban Weber, counsel for Northwestern University.

college officials are: Class 6, students who seek to enter solely to pursue a full course of study at an established college or university; Class 8, aliens of distinguished merit and ability coming temporarily to perform temporary services of exceptional nature or other services where unemployed persons capable of performing such services cannot be found in this country; and Class 10, exchange visitors.

Nonimmigrants of these various classes are admitted for designated periods appropriate to accomplish the intended purpose of their stay; but in no case, in excess of time limits fixed by the regulations relating to their particular class. They must post bond of at least $500 insuring their departure on time.

An alien seeking admission who is not a member of a classified nonimmigrant group is classified as an "immigrant." Immigrants are subject to the restrictions of their particular quota area. Among quota immigrants, the first 50 percent of each quota is allocated to aliens whose services are urgently needed because of technical training, specialized experience, or exceptional ability and to the accompanying spouse and children of such an alien. "Nonquota immigrants" includes spouses and children under twenty-one of U.S. citizens and a number of other special groups.

The problems arising at universities with respect to immigration have usually been in connection with Public Law 555, Eighty-fourth Congress,[52] passed in June 1956 as an amendment to the U.S. Information and Educational Exchange Act (Public Law 402, Eightieth Congress). In general, this amendment provides that no exchange visitor can apply for an immigrant or nonimmigrant visa under Section 101(a) (15) (H) of the Immigration and Naturalization Act or for adjustment of status to that of an alien lawfully admitted to permanent residence, unless it is established that he has resided and has been physically present in a cooperating country or countries for two years following departure from the United States. Waivers of this period of foreign residence may be granted, but only in the most exceptional cases. They are generally only granted (1) when political changes have occurred in the immigrant's home country which would impose hardship on the applicant if he were required to return, (2) if illness or misfortune has occurred justifying postponement of departure, (3) in case of marriage or other family situations which justify special consideration, or (4) if the applicant's departure would be clearly detrimental to a program or activity of official interest to an agency of the Federal Government.

---

[52] The regulations under this act may be found under 8 *C.F.R.* § 214 j (1958).

The original purpose of Public Law 402 was to encourage the interchange of students and teachers between cooperating countries and to give an opportunity to foreign professors to teach for one or two years in American institutions, in the belief that there would be advantage to both participating countries and that students and professors, studying and teaching here, would bring back added experience and new ideas to their home countries. In practice, however, it was found, in the early experience under Public Law 402, that a large proportion of the students and educators, coming to this country for a year or two, decided that they would like to remain, if possible, and thus destroyed, in effect, the fundamental objectives of the interchange aspects of the program. This resulted in many protests from foreign educational institutions through diplomatic channels. Under the provisions of the amendment of June 4, 1956, exchange visitors are required to sign certificates before applying for admission to this country in which they agree to return to their own country following their stay here. They must also agree that they will not reapply for admission to this country as permanent residents within a two-year period.

Cases have arisen in which foreign professors who have been admitted under the Educational Exchange Act either were not fully aware of their obligation to return to their home country or felt, through subsequent discussions, that a waiver might be granted. The State Department has been reluctant to grant such waivers. Colleges are advised to deal directly with the Immigration and Naturalization Service.

GARNISHMENT

One of the minor irritations of life for the average college business officer is the legal process known as "garnishment." With the great increase in installment purchasing, it is not unusual for a college employee, especially one in the lower wage bracket, to default on his purchase agreement. This normally results in a prompt garnishment of his salary or wages by his creditor.

The term itself is derived from the Norman-French word *garnir,* meaning "to warn." It is not one of the ancient common law procedures, and, in the absence of a statute conferring this right upon a creditor, it would not exist. One must therefore look to the current statutes in force in any given jurisdiction in order to ascertain the duties and obligations of the garnishee, that is, the College. In some states, garnishment is termed a "trustee process." In Connecticut and Vermont, it is described as "factorizing," and in a few states the more general term "attachment" is employed. The garnishee becomes, in effect, the trustee of the funds or property he may hold belonging to the debtor, that is, the college employee. The garnishee may not pay it to the employee but must, in strict accordance with the provisions of the statute, hold it and pay it as directed.

Some creditors serve what purports to be a notice of garnishment without going to the time and expense of complying in full with the provisions of the statute. The legal counsel of the college should furnish the college business office a simple but explicit memorandum explaining the process, just what steps should be taken in order to ascertain whether or not the process has been properly served, and the respective rights and duties of the parties to the proceedings. The statute usually prohibits the garnishment of the entire salary of individuals with dependents.

In general, public institutions of higher education are not subject to the process of garnishment.[53] In 1907 a federal circuit court held that the "Regents of the University of Idaho," was a public corporation and, as such, could not be garnished. The following is an excerpt from the opinion:

The prevailing, though not universal rule is, that, in the absence of a statute clearly expressing the intention of the legislature to the contrary, the state, its officers, and its agencies . . . are not subject to the garnishment process. The rule is based upon considerations of public policy.[54]

THE FEDERAL TAX STATUS OF RETIREMENT BENEFITS

College administrators are called upon frequently to advise faculty and other employees as to the tax status of pensions and income to be received from annuity contracts after retirement. In the absence of specific legislation or a contractual agreement, an employer is under no legal obligation to pay retirement benefits. Since the Sixteenth Amendment permits Congress to levy a tax only upon income, if a pension is a gift, it is not income, and hence it cannot be made subject to the federal income tax. However, the Internal Revenue Service has been reluctant to admit that an employer can make a true gift to an employee: it takes the position that all payments from an employer to an employee are based upon service rendered or to be rendered, unless there is convincing evidence to the contrary.

THE CARNEGIE INSTITUTE CASE. In June 1922 the members of the Board of Trustees of the Carnegie Institute retired Dr. John W. Beatty from

---

[53] For an example of statutory authorization for the garnishment of state agencies and state officers, see *Okla. Stat. Ann.* tit. 12, § 1192–94 (1951).

[54] Moscow Hardware Co. v. Colson, 158 Fed. 199, 201 (C.C.D. Idaho 1907).

active service as director of their department of fine arts with an annual pension of $6,000. When the Treasury Department attempted to collect a tax on these payments, his widow contended that they represented a gift or gratuity and hence were not taxable to the recipient. The U.S. Board of Tax Appeals held[55] that, in order to qualify as a gift, there must be complete absence of consideration for the payments. The Board found that prior services rendered by Dr. Beatty constituted sufficient consideration to classify these payments as additional salary, although the institution was under no contractual obligation to pay it.

THE BOGARDUS CASE. In 1937 a pension case reached the Supreme Court of the United States. Mr. Justice Brandeis laid down the following test to determine the tax status of a pension:

Has it been made with the intention that services rendered in the past shall be requited more completely? . . . If so, it bears a tax. Has it been made to show good will, esteem or kindliness toward persons who happened to have served, but who are paid without thought to make requital for the service? If so, it is exempt.[56]

It is a test difficult of application to specific situations, since intention and motivation do not lend themselves to ready analysis and measurement. As a result of the decision in the Bogardus case, the federal courts have held[57] that a pension paid to a clergyman is a gift and not income if it was awarded, not on the basis of an established plan which might have furnished some incentive to the employee during his term of service, but made after his retirement with expressions of good will and esteem. A federal district court has ruled[58] that it is the function of a jury, not of the court, to ascertain the intention of the employer and to apply the test established in the Bogardus case.

THE PRESENT TAX REGULATION. The Code of Federal Regulations declares:

Pensions and retirement allowances paid either by the government or by private persons constitute gross income unless excluded by law. Usually, where the tax payer did not contribute to the cost of a pension and was not taxed on his employer's contribution, the full amount of the pension is to be included in his gross income.[59]

---

55 Cora B. Beatty, 7 B.T.A. 726 (1927).

56 Bogardus v. Commissioner, 302 U.S. 34 (1937).

57 Schall v. Commissioner, 174 F.2d 892 (5th Cir. 1949); Kavanagh v. Herman, 210 F.2d 654 (6th. Cir. 1954); Abernethy v. Commissioner, 211 F.2d 651 (D.D.C. 1954). *Contra*, Wallace v. Commissioner, 219 F.2d 855 (5th Cir. 1955).

58 Peters v. Smith, 221 F.2d 721 (3rd Cir. 1955).

59 26 C.F.R. § 1.61–11 (pensions) (a) (1958).

CARNEGIE FOUNDATION PENSIONS ARE NOT TAXABLE. The following is from a law opinion of the Treasury Department published in 1920:

When one enters the services of an employer who has inaugurated a pension system, such system is one of the inducements for entering the employment, and, in such circumstances, the fact that the pension is part of the compensation received, and not a gift, is very clear.

When, however, the pension is awarded by one to whom no services have been rendered and who has received no direct benefit from the services rendered, it seems impossible to regard them as additional compensation. They seem to become mere gifts or gratuities. . . . Retirement allowances made to teachers or to widows of teachers by the Carnegie Foundation for the Advancement of Teaching do not constitute taxable income.[60]

WIDOWS' PENSIONS. Many institutions have adopted the plan of making substantial payments to the widow of an employee dying in service. In the beginning these plans were usually quite informal. The widow was paid perhaps all or a portion of the employee's salary for the remainder of the academic year. In the interest of equity of treatment, these plans were gradually formalized and made known to prospective and present employees.

In 1939 the Commissioner of Internal Revenue ruled that these payments were gifts and not income if the employer was under no legally enforceable obligation to make them.[61] However, under the present code, payments made to the widow of a deceased employee by his employer are considered to be made in recognition of past services rendered and hence are taxable income to the recipient.[62] The code specifically exempts from taxation payments to the widow up to $5,000 in amount.[63]

RETIREMENT ANNUITY CONTRACTS PURCHASED BY THE EMPLOYER. The following are excerpts from Senate Report No. 1938 with reference to Section 23 of the Technical Amendments Act of 1958:

---

[60] L.O. 1040, 3 *Cum. Bull.* 120, 121, 122 (1920).

[61] I.T. 3329, 1939–2 *Cum. Bull.* 153.

[62] Mr. Grant Nickerson, of counsel for Yale University, read this guide in manuscript. The following is one of his helpful comments: "In chapter 3 the categorical statement is made that, under the present income tax law, payments made to the widow of a deceased employee by the employer are taxable income to the recipient. This is undoubtedly the position of the Treasury Department, but, in my opinion, it is by no means settled law. Litigation is presently in progress in the courts which should decide whether all such payments are taxable or whether they are wholly exempt (not merely under Code Section 101 (b)) if and to the extent they are found to constitute gifts."

[63] 26 *U.S.C.* § 101(9b).

Under the present law (sec. 103), an annuity purchased by an employer for an employee, under a qualified nondiscriminatory type of plan, is taxable at the time the employee receives the annuity payment rather than in the year the payments are made for the annuity by the employer. However, where the employer is a tax exempt educational, charitable, or religious organization, described in section 501(c) (3), this deferment of tax, in the case of the employee, is available with respect to annuities whether or not they are paid under a qualified nondiscriminatory type of plan.

It is understood that certain of these organizations are paying selected employees all, or almost all, of their compensation in the form of annuities. Usually these are part-time employees of the organization who derive their principal income from other employment, and desire to be compensated by the organization in the form of an annuity rather than money, as a means of deferring income tax on funds they, in any case, intend to save.

Your Committee agrees with the House that these organizations should not be permitted to trade on this tax-deferment for their employees. . . . This new subsection [26 U.S.C. § 403(b)] provides that, in the case of annuity contracts purchased for employees by educational, charitable, or religious organizations exempt under section 501(c) (3), if the annuity contract does not come under a qualified nondiscriminatory plan and the employee's rights to the contract are nonforfeitable, the amount contributed by the employer is to be excluded from the gross income of the employee in the taxable year of the contribution only to the extent the contribution does not exceed an "exclusion allowance" for the year. The "exclusion allowance" is 20% of the employee's compensation for the last 12 months period, multiplied by the employee's years of service, reduced by the amounts contributed by the employer for annuity contracts which were excluded from the gross income of the employer in prior tax years.[64]

This "exclusion allowance" will be of little concern to the typical full-time college employee. Comparatively few colleges and universities are contributing more than 10 percent of the annual salary of their employees to their retirement annuity contracts. The new law will permit colleges to make more generous provision for their older employees. The Technical Amendments Act of 1958 also corrected certain inequities with respect to the exclusion of annuity payments from the gross estate of the employee.[65]

---

[64] 3 *U.S. Code Cong. and Ad. News* 4824, 4825 (1958); see also Arthur L. Nims III, "Deferred Compensation Agreements," 45 *A.B.A.J.* 1204 (1959).

[65] P.L. 85–866, 72 *Stat.* 1606, § 23 (1958). For a discussion of the effect of this legislation upon the retirement plans of colleges and universities making use of annuity contracts, see the November 1960 Memorandum of the Teachers Insurance and Annuity Association of America, "Use of a Salary-or-Annuity Option under the Technical Amendments Act of 1958." Address: 730 Third Ave., New York 17, N.Y.

RETIREMENT ANNUITY CONTRACTS PURCHASED BY THE EMPLOYEE. As stated in the preceding paragraphs, all income received by an individual from an annuity contract purchased for him by his employer is taxable, whereas only a portion of the income received from an annuity contract that he has himself purchased is taxable, namely, that amount which represents interest on his investment. Consequently, if a retirement annuity contract is purchased jointly by the employer and the employee, it is necessary, as of the date of the maturing of the contract, to ascertain what percentage of the premium payments was made by the employer and what portion was paid by the employee, usually by deductions from his salary.

Having ascertained the individual's own investment in the contract and the annual payments to be received from the contract as the result of his own investment, it is necessary to compute his expected return. This amount is found by multiplying the annual income anticipated from that portion of the annuity contract purchased with his own funds by the number of years of his anticipated life as disclosed in the actuarial table adopted for use by the Internal Revenue Service. With these three amounts ascertained—the individual's own investment in the contract (I), his annual payments to be received therefrom (P), and his anticipated return (R)—it is possible to compute the amount which may be excluded from his taxable income each year by the use of the formula:

$$\frac{I}{R} \times P = E$$

or the exclusion amount. The net effect of the application of this formula is the exclusion from taxation of that portion of the annuity income which represents, in theory, the return of the principal amount invested in the contract. Once computed, this exclusion amount need not be recomputed, unless the amounts received under the contract change.

The Internal Revenue Service published, in 1956, regulations[66] governing the computation of taxable income from annuity contracts. Section 1.72–5(a) states the procedure to be used in computing the expected return from a contract under which the annuitant is to receive a fixed income for life. Instructions in Section 1.72–5(b)(1) are to be followed in the case of a joint and survivor annuity contract involving two an-

---

[66] 26 *C.F.R.* § 1.72 (1958).

nultants, which provides the first annuitant with a fixed monthly income for life, and, after the death of the first annuitant, provides an identical monthly income for life to the second annuitant. Section 1.72–5(b)(2) is to be used if the second annuitant is to receive a different rather than an identical monthly income.

FEDERAL SOCIAL SECURITY

The Social Security Act of 1935[67] initiated the most comprehensive program of social welfare ever undertaken by the Federal Government. The statute imposed two different types of tax, a so-called income tax on employees and an excise tax on employers. The constitutionality of the tax on employers was sustained by the Supreme Court of the United States in May of 1937.[68] The act of 1935 excluded from its provisions agricultural laborers; domestic servants; sailors; employees of federal, state, and local governments and their instrumentalities; and the employees of religious, charitable, and educational institutions not conducted for profit. The 1939 amendments extended coverage to those serving on American ships and the employees of national banks and building and loan associations.

THE 1950 AMENDMENTS. For the first time, Social Security protection, on a voluntary basis, was made available to the employees of educational institutions by the Social Security Act Amendments of 1950.[69] The privately controlled institutions obtained coverage for their employees by conducting a referendum of their employees on the question and by appropriate action by their governing boards.[70] The employees of public institutions of education could also obtain coverage under the provisions of the 1950 amendments if they were not under a state or local government retirement system.

The 1954 amendments made it possible for protection to be extended to public employees already in a retirement plan, and the amendments of 1956 and 1957 extended the scope of this coverage. The technical difficulties of integrating federal and state retirement benefits have been the chief retarding factor. To secure Social Security coverage for state employees, the legislature must authorize the execution of an

---

[67] 49 *Stat.* 620, 42 *U.S.C.* §§ 301–425 (1957).

[68] Steward Machine Co. v. Davis, 301 U.S. 548 (1937); Helvering v. Davis, 301 U.S. 619 (1937).

[69] P.L. 734, ch. 809 (1950).

[70] See 26 *U.S.C.* § 3121(k) (1955).

agreement with the Federal Government and a majority of eligible employees in each group must have voted in favor of coverage.[71]

Those responsible for advising members of the faculty and staff of the college should maintain as complete a file as possible of the published material on the Social Security system of protection. Many valuable benefits are lost by failure of individuals concerned to understand the full scope of the program.

SOCIAL SECURITY BENEFITS NOT TAXABLE INCOME. Insurance benefit payments received by individuals under the Social Security Act do not represent taxable income to the recipient.[72] These include the primary monthly benefit payments to the employee himself, wife's income benefits, child's insurance benefits, parents' insurance benefits, and the lump sum death benefit.

OTHER TAX PROBLEMS OF FACULTY AND STAFF

Almost every college provides living accommodations and meals for a few members of its faculty and staff. Unless the nature of the employee's duties is such as to require him to live in the quarters provided and to accept the meals served to him by his employer, the cash value of the facilities provided is taxable income to the recipient.

MEALS AND HOUSING FURNISHED FOR THE CONVENIENCE OF THE EMPLOYER. Until 1954 the statutes were silent on this question, and the tax status of meals and housing furnished for the convenience of the employer, that is, in order that the employee might more efficiently perform his assigned duties, depended upon administrative rulings and court decisions. Since the Commissioner of Internal Revenue was reluctant to accept the decisions of the lower federal courts as definitive, this question was a source of confusion and conflict for many years. This was especially true in situations where, under state statute or regulations, the cash value of the meals and lodgings furnished to employees of the state was considered to be part of their total compensation in computing deductions for retirement and other bene-

---

[71] Statutory provisions of the Social Security Act may be found in 42 *U.S.C.* §§ 401–1368 (1955); see also *Complete Social Security Law, 1956* (Chicago: Commerce Clearing House, 1956); the law with reference to taxes on employer and employee, with which the benefits of the program are financed, may be found in 26 *U.S.C.* §§ 3101–21 (1955).

[72] I.T. 3447, 1941–1 *Cum. Bull.* 191.

fits, even though the employees were required by the nature of their employment to live on the institutional premises.[73]

In view of this conflict, Congress decided to settle the question in 1954. The statutory language[74] is clear and unambiguous:

There shall be excluded from the gross income of an employee the value of any meals or lodgings furnished to him for the convenience of the employer . . .

In determining whether meals or lodgings are furnished for the convenience of the employer, the provisions of an employment contract or a state statute fixing the terms of employment shall not be determinative of whether meals or lodgings are intended as compensation.

In this connection, it is important to note that, under the provisions of the Social Security Act,[75] the cash value of meals and lodgings furnished to an employee for the convenience of his employer must be included as compensation in computing the Social Security tax of both the employer and the employee, despite the fact that this amount must be excluded in computing his federal income tax.

EMPLOYEE'S MOVING EXPENSES. In order to induce a good man to accept appointment as a member of its faculty, a college may pay his entire moving expenses. Does this payment or reimbursement represent taxable income to the recipient? The answer has been given by the U.S. Supreme Court in a case involving the Sandia Corporation, engaged in important research work for agencies of the Federal Government at Albuquerque, New Mexico. In order to secure engineers and other technically trained personnel, it conducts extensive recruiting programs at various universities. In April 1954 Sherrill Woodall accepted employment with the corporation, and the terms of his contract of employment provided that he would be reimbursed for certain expenses incurred in

---

[73] I.R. Mim. 38, 1952–2 *Cum. Bull.* 70; Gordon v. United States, 152 F. Supp. 427 (D.N.J. 1957).

[74] 26 *U.S.C.* § 119 (1955); 26 *C.F.R.* § 1.119.1 (1958). Note that the provisions of the code and the regulations thereunder refer to meals or lodgings, furnished in kind, on the premises of the employer. Therefore, any cash allowance for meals or lodgings received by an employee is taxable as income; Gunner Van Rosen, 17 T.C. 834 (1951). However, it is probable that "supper money" given to employees who work after regular hours would not be considered taxable, either on the grounds that it represents reimbursed expense rather than compensation or because it is usually an item of relatively small value. See 1 *P-H Fed. Taxes,* ¶ 3676 (1959).

[75] 26 *U.S.C.* § 3121(a) (1955); Pacific American Fisheries v. United States, 138 F.2d 464 (9th Cir. 1943).

moving himself and his family from Dallas to Albuquerque. He received the sum of $592.28 as reimbursement for these expenses, but he did not report the amount in his taxable income for the year.

The Commissioner of Internal Revenue ruled that the item was taxable and the tax thereon was paid under protest. Mr. Woodall filed a claim for refund, and the trial court ruled that his attorney had been correct in his assumption that such payments are not taxable. The appellate court reversed the holding of the trial court, and the Supreme Court of the United States declined to review the holding.[76] The following are excerpts from the opinion of the appellate court:

> We agree with the contention of the United States that payments such as those received in these cases are income within the meaning of the Internal Revenue Code, and that the expenses incurred here are not expenditures for which deductions may be made in computing income taxes.
>
> . . . .
>
> While it is true that there was no gain or profit from the payments to the taxpayers, it cannot be denied that they received an economic and beneficial gain. . . . The payment was in the nature of a cash bonus as an inducement to accept employment.
>
> . . . .
>
> Before one can deduct travel expense, it must be shown that the expense was reasonable and necessary, incurred away from home, and in the pursuit of business.

TRANSFER OF RESIDENCE FOR THE CONVENIENCE OF THE EMPLOYER. If an employer requires an employee to move from one location to another as a condition of continued employment, that is, for the convenience of the employer rather than as an inducement to obtain the services of a new employee, the Internal Revenue Service has held that the allowance or reimbursement to cover the cost of the move does not represent taxable income, provided the entire amount of the allowance or reimbursement is expended for this purpose. Any excess must be reported and the tax paid thereon. If the employee finds it necessary to pay more than the amount agreed upon with his employer, he is not permitted by the Internal Revenue Service to claim the excess as a deduction from gross income. Moreover, if it can be shown that the transfer was made primarily for the benefit or convenience of the employee himself, even though the cost thereof is paid by the employer, the reimbursement or allowance for such a move constitutes taxable income to the recipient.[77]

---

[76] United States v. Woodall, 255 F.2d 370, 372 (10th Cir.), *cert. denied,* 358 U.S. 824 (1958).

[77] 26 *C.F.R.* §§ 39.23(a)–15(f) (1954); Rev. Rul. 429, 1954–2 *Cum. Bull.* 53.

COST OF EDUCATION NECESSARY TO MAINTAIN PROFESSIONAL COMPETENCE. For years, members of the teaching profession have been attempting to convince the Commissioner of Internal Revenue and the courts that the costs of their continuing education, necessary to keep abreast of the growth of knowledge disclosed by research, should be considered as a legitimate expense of their profession, deductible from gross income for tax purposes, on exactly the same basis that lawyers and physicians are permitted to deduct their professional expenses.

The Commissioner had issued the following regulation in 1921:

The expenses incurred by school teachers in attending summer school are in the nature of personal expenses incurred in advancing their education and are not deductible in computing net income.[78]

The justification for this discrimination against members of the teaching profession was said to be that only those self-employed were permitted to deduct the costs of conducting their business or profession. Since teachers are employees and not self-employed, they cannot have or incur professional expenses. This reasoning was not always sufficient to convince the courts, as illustrated by the Hill case, decided in 1950.[79]

In 1945 a Virginia school teacher was required to obtain additional college credit in order to renew her teaching certificate. She elected to attend the Columbia University summer school and, when preparing her tax return, she deducted the cost of attending the session. The deduction was disallowed and the Commissioner's ruling was sustained by the federal Tax Court.

A federal circuit court of appeals reversed the Tax Court decision on the grounds that such expenses were not personal in nature but were necessary in carrying on her profession. The judge pointed out that, in other tax cases, motion picture actors had been permitted to deduct the cost of maintaining their physical fitness and opera singers were permitted to deduct sums paid to voice coaches. The following is from his opinion:

This taxpayer went to Columbia, prompted by the necessity of renewing her certificate as a prerequisite to continuing her work as a teacher. . . . The commissioner has specifically ruled . . . that the initiation fee required to be paid to a labor union in order to obtain employment . . . may be deducted from gross income. . . . How much stronger in favor of deductibility and more persuasive are the facts in the case of this taxpayer?

[78] O.D. 892, 4 *Cum. Bull.* 209 (1921).
[79] Hill v. Commissioner, 181 F.2d 906, 909 (4th Cir. 1950).

Although this decision made it impossible for the Commissioner of Internal Revenue to collect the specific tax involved in the case, the court decision did not establish a precedent which he was compelled to respect and to follow in the future. The Commissioner and his staff are not bound by precedents established by the lower federal courts. They are required to respect and to follow only those established by the Supreme Court of the United States and the statutes enacted by Congress. Since the Commissioner did not acquiesce in the decision under discussion, the Internal Revenue Service continued to enforce the 1921 regulation, as illustrated by the following case.[80]

An instructor, employed by Queens University (*sic*) on a temporary basis for one year, was informed by his dean that substantial progress toward the attainment of the doctoral degree was a prerequisite for continued employment and promotion. The Internal Revenue Service refused to permit the deduction of the cost of his graduate studies as a professional expense. This ruling was sustained by the Tax Court, with three judges dissenting. The court of appeals reversed the Tax Court in January 1958.

By this time members of Congress had begun to take an active interest in the problem. Stimulated by letters and the testimony of members of the teaching profession and by magazine articles stressing the need to give all possible encouragement to those desiring to increase their efficiency as teachers, more than sixty senators and congressmen introduced bills during the Eighty-fifth Congress designed to grant more equitable tax treatment for teachers.

Rather than wait for congressional action, the Commissioner of Internal Revenue authorized the publication on April 5, 1958, of a new regulation[81] which, in effect, abrogates the 1921 ruling and accepts the decisions of the federal courts in the Hill and Marlor cases. It does not permit the deduction of the costs of educational work undertaken to qualify for admission to a profession, but only those incurred after one has begun his professional career and those necessary for maintaining or increasing his professional competency.

OTHER PROFESSIONAL EXPENSE OF COLLEGE FACULTY. According to present regulations:

A professional man may claim as deductions the cost of supplies used by him in the practice of his profession, expenses paid or accrued in the opera-

---

[80] Marlor v. Commissioner, 251 F.2d 615 (2d Cir. 1958).
[81] T.D. 6291, 1958–1 *Cum. Bull.* 63; 26 C.F.R. § 1.162–5 (1958).

tion and repair of an automobile used in making professional calls, dues to professional societies and subscriptions to professional journals, the rent paid or accrued for office rooms, the cost of fuel, light, water, telephone, etc., used in such offices and the hire of office assistance. Amounts currently paid or accrued for books, furniture, and professional instruments and equipment, the useful life of which is short, may be deducted.[82]

Presumably, to the extent not furnished or paid by his college, a member of the faculty may claim these items as deductions from his gross income for tax purposes.

LIFE INSURANCE PREMIUMS PAID BY THE EMPLOYER. As a general rule, life insurance premiums paid by an employer on the lives of his employees, where the proceeds are payable to the beneficiaries of such employees, are part of the gross income of the employees. However, in the case of group term life insurance, the premiums paid by the employer do not constitute taxable income to his employees.[83]

CONTRIBUTIONS OF AN EMPLOYER TO ACCIDENT AND HEALTH PLANS. Contributions by an employer to health and accident plans for his employees, whether made as insurance premiums or otherwise, do not constitute taxable income to his employees.[84] However, when benefit payments are received as a result of such payments by the employer, such payments constitute taxable income to the recipients.[85]

If the employer has not paid the cost of health or accident protection plans or insurance, benefits received thereunder are not taxable. In general, amounts received under workmen's compensation acts as compensation for personal injuries or sickness and amounts received on account of personal injuries or sickness, whether by suit or by agreement, do not constitute taxable income.[86]

PRIZE AWARDS AND POSTDOCTORAL FELLOWSHIPS. The tax status of scholarships, fellowships, and prize awards is usually considered to be of interest only to students.[87] However, members of the faculty are not infrequently the recipients of prize awards and postdoctoral fellowship stipends. Until 1954 the Internal Revenue Code was silent as to the tax-

---

[82] T.D. 6291, 1958–1 *Cum. Bull.* 63; 26 C.F.R. § 1.162–6 (1958).
[83] 26 *C.F.R.* § 161–2(d)(2) (1958).
[84] 26 *U.S.C.* § 106 (1955).
[85] 26 *U.S.C.* § 105 (1955).
[86] 26 *U.S.C.* § 104 (1955).
[87] See "Tax Problems of Students," pp. 127–30, in chap. 4.

ability of such payments, and the Commissioner of Internal Revenue and the courts could not agree on where to draw the line between compensation for service rendered and a gift.

In 1950 a professor of English literature at George Washington University received a Guggenheim Foundation fellowship to enable him to spend a year on a research project of his own choosing. The Commissioner ruled that it was not the intention of the Guggenheim Foundation to make a real gift to the professor but to pay him for the accomplishment of a project in which he and the foundation had a mutual interest. In other words, the foundation has many worthy tasks to perform, and it selects persons qualified to perform them, paying them for service rendered.

Fortunately for higher education, the majority of the judges of the Tax Court disagreed with the point of view of the Commissioner and ruled that the Guggenheim fellowship awards are gifts and not salary.[88] There was a vigorous dissent by one member of the court, of which the following is an excerpt:

> However strong the feeling or desire may be that the doing of such work as herein described be fostered and promoted, we must leave to Congress the prerogative of saying that the compensation for service rendered in doing such work is to be free from taxation.

Eventually, Congress did take cognizance of the problem. The provisions of the 1954 amendments to the code are quite specific.[89] In establishing yardsticks to measure the difference between salary paid to a research worker for service rendered and a gift to permit an individual to add to the sum total of human knowledge, the congressional committee members were concerned with two aspects of the problem: (1) the source of the fund from which the stipend is to be paid and (2) the amount of the stipend.

If the source is a commercial organization, the members of Congress were of the opinion[90] that a stipend paid to a mature individual, that is, one who had completed his formal education and hence was not a candidate for a degree, would, in every instance, represent payment for service rendered, even though designated as a fellowship. Consequently, the code provides that a postdoctoral fellowship stipend, to be tax free, must be paid from a fund received from an organization or foundation exempt from taxation or from a governmental agency.

---

[88] Stone v. Commissioner, 23 T.C. 254 (1954).

[89] 26 U.S.C. § 117 (b)(2) (1955).

[90] 3 U.S. Code Cong. and Ad. News 4173, 4823, 5285 (1954).

The amount of the stipend was considered by the congressional committee to be indicative of its character. If it was as large or larger than the normal earning capacity of the recipient or of others of the same age and training, the presumption was strong that he had entered upon his professional career and that the payments to him represented salary, not gifts. In the House version of Section 117(b)(2) of the code, the lawmakers declared that a postdoctoral fellowship stipend, to be tax free, must not exceed 75 percent of the recipient's earned income during the prior twelve-month period. The Senate's version established a ceiling of $300 per month for thirty-six months, and the House committee accepted the Senate's revision on the grounds that it would be easier to administer and yet accomplish the same purpose.

In other words, the stipend must not exceed an amount equal to $300 times the number of months during which the recipient receives payments under the fellowship grant, and for a total period not to exceed thirty-six months, whether or not consecutive. For example, the maximum amount of tax-free postdoctoral fellowship stipends payable to an individual during his entire lifetime under the present code would be $10,800, that is, $300 × 36.[91] However, if the individual received, for instance, only $100 per month for the first thirty months, he would be entitled to receive only $1,800 additional tax free, that is, $300 × 6, or a total of only $4,800 during the thirty-six-month period, tax free.

The tax status of prize awards, based upon scholarly and scientific achievements, has also been the subject of disagreement between the Internal Revenue Service and the courts. In 1928, Erskin M. Ross, a retired federal judge, bequeathed the sum of $100,000 to the American Bar Association to endow an annual prize award "for the best discussion of a subject, to be by it suggested." In 1939 an award of $3,000 was made to Malcolm McDermott, a professor of law at Duke University. The federal Tax Court held that the award was not a gift but payment for service rendered and hence taxable. The appellate court apparently found this conclusion almost ludicrous.[92] The following is from the opinion of the court:

---

[91] The following is another helpful comment of Mr. Grant Nickerson: "It is stated that the maximum amount of tax-free postdoctoral fellowship stipends which can be exempt to an individual during his entire lifetime is $10,800. Again, this is undoubtedly the position of the Treasury Department, as reflected in its regulations, but it is my own opinion that this position is not necessarily correct. So far as I know, the issue has not, as yet, been raised in cases or rulings (other than as provided in the Regulations), but I think that Section 117 is at least susceptible to the interpretation that the maximum of $300 for thirty-six months refers to each award or grant separately and is not necessarily a lifetime maximum."

[92] McDermott v. Commissioner, 150 F.2d 585, 587, 588 (D.C. Cir. 1945).

No one not talking law would be likely to say that the Bar Association paid the petitioner $3,000 for writing an essay. In plain English, the association gave the petitioner a prize. . . . It is safe to say that the dominant motive for a normal contestant for this prize is not the hope of immediate gain. He does not regard himself as exchanging his services for money. To one whose life is devoted to scholarship . . . , the publication of an outstanding essay is its own reward. Finally, requiring winners of scholarly awards to pay tax on them would conflict with the wise and settled policy of encouraging scholarly work.

Despite this clear decision of the court, the Commissioner of Internal Revenue served notice on the public that he did not intend to regard it as a precedent and that he would continue to levy a tax on the Ross Prize Awards and similar prizes.[93]

Congress took due notice of this and declared that it was in the public interest that such awards should be tax free.[94] The code states that prizes and awards made primarily in recognition of religious, charitable, scientific, educational, artistic, literary, or civic achievements are to be tax free, but only if (1) the recipient was selected without any action on his part to enter the contest or proceedings and (2) the recipient is not required to render substantial future services as a condition to receiving the prize award.

Since this section of the code set no upper limit to the monetary value of such awards, it is obviously to the advantage of an individual receiving an award in excess of the ceiling imposed upon postdoctoral fellowship stipends to have his case considered under Section 74(b) rather than under Section 117(b)(2).

THE UNIVERSITY OF CHICAGO RULING. The Ford Foundation made a grant to the University of Chicago for the establishment of an Inter-University Visiting Scholars Program for the purpose of advancing intellectual understanding between nations. The program was particularly directed toward countries in Southeast Asia and the Near East. Selected citizens of those countries were invited to make extended visits to the United States as guests of the participating universities, including the University of California, Columbia University, Harvard University, and the University of Chicago.

Each invitee was selected by the participating universities without any action or knowledge on his part, and applications for an invitation were not accepted. Selection was based on outstanding quality

---

[93] I.T. 3960, 1949–2 *Cum. Bull.* 13.
[94] 26 *U.S.C.* § 74 (a), (b) (1955).

of past work of the invitee and the prospect that he would influence intellectual development in the future. Each recipient of an invitation was offered: (1) an allowance not to exceed $5,000 to pay for foreign travel and incidental expenses; (2) an allowance not to exceed $1,237 to pay for travel in this country related to his professional program, for books, and other professional expenses; and (3) an honorarium of $900 per month for the six to nine months of the visit.

The University of Chicago, as coordinator of the program, requested a ruling as to the tax status of the honorarium of $900 per month to be paid to the recipients of the awards. The university representative urged that the question be considered under the provisions of Section 74(b) of the code. However, the ruling of the Commissioner declared that it was the intention of Congress, in enacting Section 17 of the code, to subject to taxation grants such as those made under the program in question, to the extent that they exceed the limitations of exclusions which are provided in that section.[95] In other words, only $300 of the $900 designated as an honorarium would be exempt from the federal income tax.

PRIZE AWARDS FROM A COLLEGE TO MEMBERS OF ITS OWN FACULTY ARE TAXABLE. The Commissioner has ruled that prize awards represent taxable income if there is evidence that the award was motivated by an employer-employee relationship. The following ruling is evidence of this trend:

An educational institution received a substantial gift from an individual, with the stipulation that it be used solely to supplement one-year's existing compensation of the institute's faculty and related staff on the basis of individual merit and special service as distinguished from the general level of performance. It was further stipulated that this be done through the granting of a limited number of awards for outstanding performance.[96]

The Commissioner held that such awards were taxable under Section 1.74–1(b) of the current income tax regulations because they were granted by an employer to an employee in recognition of some achievement in connection with his employment. As an achievement in connection with his employment would be the normal and usual basis of an award by an educational institution to a member of its faculty, even though the achievement itself represented an outstanding contribution

---

[95] Letter ruling to the University of Chicago dated Aug. 6, 1957, reference symbol: T.R.I., ROS–1.

[96] Rev. Rul. 460, 1957–2 *Cum. Bull.* 69; see also 26 C.F.R. 1.74–1(b) (1958).

to human knowledge, this section would seem to render it difficult for any educational institution to make a tax-free prize award to a member of its own faculty.

THE WITHHOLDING TAX. The Federal Government, faced with the task of financing World War II and the problem of collecting vastly increased personal income taxes, resorted to the device of transforming employers into unremunerated tax collectors. They were required to withhold from the salary or wage of each employee a given percentage thereof and pay over such sums to the government. This withholding tax was continued after the war emergency and was embodied, as part of our permanent tax structure, in the 1954 Internal Revenue Code.[97]

In general, the following forms of remuneration are not subject to withholding: (1) for active service as a member of the Armed Forces; (2) for agricultural labor; (3) for domestic service in a private home, local college club, or local chapter of a college fraternity or sorority; (4) for casual labor; (5) for services performed for a foreign government; (6) for services performed as a minister of a church; (7) for services performed as a newspaper vendor.

---

[97] 26 *U.S.C.A.* §§ 3401–4 (1955). In this book, attention has been directed primarily to federal tax problems. However, in view of the trend to impose a state tax upon income, college administrators should accumulate a file of state tax legislation, regulations, and rulings.

CHAPTER IV

The College Student

T RADITIONALLY, colleges looked to the parent rather than to the student for the payment of tuition and other charges. To an increasing degree, colleges today expect the student to make his own arrangements for enrollment and for payment of fees. This is in accord with modern educational theory and practice. The college student has been given and has accepted a larger burden of responsibility for his own development and self-government.

MINORS AND THE CONTRACT OF ENROLLMENT

It should be remembered, however, that, in the eyes of the law, he is still an infant until he reaches the age of majority. At common law, an infant becomes of age the first instant of the day preceding the twenty-first anniversary day of his birth. By statute in many states, a female reaches her majority at the age of eighteen.[1]

Some colleges have been faced with the demand of a student for a refund of tuition on the ground that he was a minor at the time of enrollment. Due to the natural reluctance of the colleges to litigate this issue, there have been comparatively few court decisions of record on this question.

The basic problem is simple and well known. In general, an infant may, at his pleasure, repudiate and disaffirm some of his contracts. This rule of protection has very few exceptions. In some jurisdictions, an infant need not even return the goods purchased or restore the amount paid as a condition of disaffirmance.[2]

The major exception to the rule that an infant may disaffirm his contracts is the well-established principle that an infant may make himself liable for goods and services that are necessary, considering his position and station in life. Even for what the law has held to

---

[1] 43 *C.J.S.: Infants* §§ 2–3 (1945).
[2] *Ibid.* § 47 (3)(d).

be "necessaries," an infant is merely liable for the reasonable, not the contractual, price for such goods or services. It depends upon the facts in each case whether goods or services contracted for by an infant are necessary.

Sir Edward Coke, the greatest common lawyer of all time, in the first volume of his *Institutes* (1628) stated that an infant binds himself to pay "for his teaching and instruction." The early cases restricted this dictum to rudimentary education[3] and to training for a trade.

Apparently, the first American case on the legal status of a college education was decided by the Supreme Court of Vermont in 1844.[4] The defendant enrolled in August 1836, at the age of fifteen, in Middlebury College. After the death of his father in 1837, the college attempted to collect tuition, room, and board from the student himself. The court, in its opinion, held that

A good common school education, at least, is now fully recognized as one of the necessaries for an infant. . . . But it is obvious that the more extensive attainments in literature and science must be viewed in a light somewhat different. . . . The mass of our citizens pass through life without them. . . . We therefore consider that such an education should not be ranked among those necessaries, for which he could, as an infant, render himself . . . liable by contract.

In 1926 the Supreme Court of Washington held that a college education was a necessary for a daughter who had displayed remarkable aptitude for classical studies, although her father was a railroad conductor with an annual salary of about $3,000. The reasoning of the court is of interest to us:

The rule in Middlebury College v. Chandler was clearly based upon conditions which existed at that time. An opportunity at that early date for a common school education was small, for a high school education less, and for a college education, was almost impossible to the average family. . . . But conditions have changed greatly in almost a century that has elapsed since that time. Where the college graduate of that day was the exception, today such a person may almost be said to be the rule. . . . It cannot be doubted that the minor who is unable to secure a college education is generally handicapped in pursuing most of the trades or professions of life.[5]

However, in 1930, when the courts of Indiana[6] and Massachusetts[7] were faced with this same problem, both of them declined to follow

---

[3] *Ibid.* § 78 (3).
[4] Middlebury College v. Chandler, 16 Vt. 683 (1844).
[5] Esteb v. Esteb, 138 Wash. 174, 244 Pac. 264 (1926).
[6] Morris v. Morris, 92 Ind. App. 65, 171 N.E. 386 (1930).
[7] Moskow v. Marshall, 271 Mass. 302, 171 N.E. 477 (1930).

the lead of the Washington court. In the Massachusetts case, the two defendants had signed a lease for a suite of rooms in a privately owned dormitory used exclusively for students at Harvard University. The court held that

As a matter of law, . . . a college education is not such a necessary to either defendant as to take the contract out of the rule relating to infants.

In 1938 a Massachusetts court permitted the plaintiff to recover the full tuition, with interest, paid for courses of instruction in aviation, on the ground that the contract of enrollment had been signed while the plaintiff was still a minor. The judge ruled that the courses of instruction were not necessaries, and, hence, the minor could disaffirm the contract, even though he took no action by way of disaffirmance for almost a year after attaining his majority.[8]

The defendant contended that there could be no disaffirmance because the plaintiff could not return the instruction he had received by virtue of the contract. In reply, the court held that "a minor who had lost or squandered what he has received under the contract may nevertheless disaffirm it and recover what he paid."

A case on this subject came before a New York city court in 1948. Here, a young girl, at the age of sixteen, paid $250 for a course of instruction in voice. After receiving fourteen of the thirty-six lessons of the course, she disaffirmed the contract, and the court permitted her to recover the full tuition paid. The court felt it necessary to apologize for the verdict:

The result which must be reached here may seem to be unjust, but whatever may be individual opinion respecting its soundness in a modern day and age, the law still guards the interests of minors against their own assumed improvidence and want of judgment.[9]

It is obvious that the common law in this area has not kept pace with modern educational concepts and procedures. In view of the many millions of dollars involved in the tuitions paid by minors each year to our American colleges and universities, this "cultural lag" presents potential hazards of some magnitude.[10]

---

[8] Adamowski v. Curtiss-Wright Flying Service, Inc., 300 Mass. 281, 15 N.E.2d 467 (1938).

[9] Icovinco v. Haymes, 191 Misc. 311, 77 N.Y.S.2d 316 (Munic. Ct. 1948).

[10] In order to correct this failure of the common law to keep in step with public opinion, the Legislature of Illinois in July 1959 enacted the following statute relating to student loans to minors:

"Section 1. Any student who has been accepted for admission to an institution in the State of Illinois approved by the State Superintendent of Public Instruction

COLLEGE RESTRICTIONS AND THE RIGHTS
OF STUDENTS

The power which the officers of a college may lawfully exert to restrict and to control the actions of its students is based upon the fact that, in law, the college stands in the same position to its students as that of a parent—in loco parentis—and it can therefore direct and control their conduct to the same extent that a parent can.

THE LOCO PARENTIS RULE. This principle of law was well stated by the court in a case involving Berea College in 1913. The college issued a regulation prohibiting its students from entering public eating houses in the community. The owners of a nearby restaurant, dependent chiefly on student patronage, sought an injunction to compel the college official to rescind this regulation. The court refused the petition for an injunction and sustained the right of the college to control its students in the following words:

College authorities stand *in loco parentis* concerning the physical and moral welfare and mental training of pupils. For the purposes of this case, the school, its officers and students are a legal entity, as much so as any family, and, like a father may direct his children, those in charge of boarding schools are well within their rights and powers when they direct their students what to eat and where they may get it; where they may go and what forms of amusement are forbidden.[11]

REQUIRED RESIDENCE IN COLLEGE DORMITORIES. In 1947 the Board of Regents of the University of Oklahoma adopted a resolution requiring all students, with certain exceptions, to live in university-operated dormitories to the extent such facilities were available. The owner of an approved private rooming house near the campus, finding it no longer possible to fill her rooms with students, sought equitable relief from a federal district court on the grounds that

the rules pertaining to the housing of students deprive the plaintiff of her liberty to contract and of her property without due process of law, contrary to the Fourteenth Amendment to the Constitution of the United States.

---

as an institution of higher education on either the graduate or undergraduate level shall be permitted to execute a legally binding promissory note for a loan necessary to attend or to continue in attendance at an institution of higher education, subject to approval by the institution attended." *Ill. Rev. Stat.* ch. 29, § 43 (1959).

Similar legislation was enacted by the Oklahoma Legislature: *S.L. 1959* tit. 15, ch. 1, p. 81.

[11] Gott v. Berea College, 156 Ky. 376, 161 S.W. 204 (1913).

The court, in declining to grant the relief requested, had this to say:

When a state, acting in a proper sphere, passes regulations which are valid and suitable to attain a desired end, the mere fact that such legislation or regulatory measures have an incidental effect upon a few individuals does not make the regulations invalid or abridge the constitutional rights of the individual. . . . The state has a decided interest in the education, well-being, morals, health, safety and convenience of its youth. When a situation arises where it becomes necessary to expend great sums for buildings to house students . . . and when it becomes necessary for rules to be passed to provide payment for such buildings, . . . such rules will be valid as a means of accomplishing the over-all policy of furnishing the needed facilities.[12]

COMPULSORY MILITARY TRAINING. In 1933 several students of the University of California were suspended for refusal to take the required military training courses. The students, in their petition for readmission, claimed that compulsory military instruction was a violation of their right to religious liberty under the Fourteenth Amendment. They declared that their church, at its general conference of 1928, had

renounced war as an instrument of national policy and petitioned the United States government to grant exemption from military service to such citizens who, as members of the Methodist Episcopal Church, conscientiously believe that participation in war is a denial of their supreme allegiance to Jesus Christ.

Mr. Justice Cardozo dismissed this objection in the following words:

Instruction in military science, unaccompanied here by any pledge of military service, is not an interference by the state with the free exercise of religion when the liberties of the Constitution are read in the light of a century and a half of history during days of peace and war.[13]

COMPULSORY VACCINATION. The statute requiring all students attending public schools in California to be vaccinated was amended in 1911 to permit parents to withhold their consent to such treatment for their children.[14] The Board of Regents of the University of California declined to be governed by this statute on the ground that the university had been created by the state constitution and its Regents had been

---

[12] Pyeatte v. Board of Regents, 102 F. Supp. 407 (W.D. Okla. 1951), aff'd, 342 U.S. 936 (1952).

[13] Hamilton v. Regents of the University of California, 293 U.S. 245 (1934).

[14] Cal. Stat. at 295 (1911). See also Cal. Educ. Code §§ 16, 401.

given therein full control over the adminstration of the university. The court upheld[15] the position of the board with the statement that the university was a constitutionally independent division of the state government and that the only controls the legislature retained over it were those of fiscal appropriation and the plenary police powers of the state, that is, those necessary for the protection of the life and property of its citizens.[16] Since the 1911 amendment was not, in itself, a positive health regulation, it was not the exercise of police power and hence could not prevail over the compulsory vaccination rule enacted and enforced by the Board of Regents.

THE RIGHT TO JOIN FRATERNITIES. Apparently, the first wave of opposition to the existence of Greek-letter fraternities on the college campus came in 1880. The Trustees of Purdue University made membership in such organizations a basis for dismissal. In 1882 the Indiana Supreme Court issued a writ of mandamus to compel the admission of a student who had been rejected solely because he had declined to sign a promise to resign as an active member of the Sigma Chi fraternity during his stay at the university. The court justified its action as follows:

> The admission of students into a public educational institution is one thing, and the government and control of students after they are admitted, and have become subject to the jurisdiction of the institution is quite another thing. . . . The possession of this great power over a student after he has entered the university does not justify the imposition of either degrading or extraordinary terms and conditions of admission into it . . .[17]

Several decades later the Legislature of Mississippi enacted a statute prohibiting the existence of secret societies in its tax-supported institutions of higher education. In 1913 the state supreme court sustained[18] the action of the Trustees of the University of Mississippi requiring all matriculants to sign a promise to obey the antifraternity statute while enrolled as students. The issue was carried to the Supreme Court of

---

[15] Williams v. Wheeler, 23 Cal. App. 619, 138 Pac. 937 (1st Dist. Ct. App. 1913); see also State *ex rel.* Holcomb, 39 Wash. 2d 860, 239 P.2d 860 (1952).

[16] The University of California shares this favored status of a constitutionally independent corporation with several other public colleges and universities. For more details, see "The Constitutionally Independent Corporations," pp. 242–50.

[17] State v. White, 82 Ind. 278 (1882).

[18] Board of Trustees of the University of Mississippi v. Waugh, 105 Miss. 623, 62 So. 827 (1913).

the United States, and the action of the state court was affirmed. In his opinion, Mr. Justice McKenna declared:

It is trite to say that the right to pursue happiness and exercise rights and liberty are subject in some degree to the limitations of the law, and the condition upon which the state of Mississippi offers the complainant free instruction in its University, that while a student there he renounce affiliation with a society which the state considers inimical to discipline, finds no prohibition in the 14th Amendment . . .[19]

NATIONAL FRATERNITIES FORBIDDEN AT THE STATE UNIVERSITY OF NEW YORK. During the fall of 1953 a comprehensive survey of the practices of the national fraternities and sororities at the tax-supported institutions of higher education in the State of New York was conducted. The following is from the report of the president of the State University of New York to his board:

The university must always be in a position to exercise sufficient supervision over students and their social organizations to assure compliance with university policies. So long as such organizations are local in character, the situation is manageable. But when they involve ties outside the university, over which the university can exercise no control, serious conflicts may arise. This is something no university can tolerate.

On October 8, 1953, the university board adopted the following resolutions:

Resolved that no social organization shall be permitted in any state-operated unit of the State University which has any direct or indirect affiliation or connection with any national or other organization outside the particular unit; and be it further

Resolved that no such social organization, in policy or practice, shall operate under any rule which bars students on account of race, color, religion, creed, national origin or other artificial criteria, . . .

On November 25, 1953, Earl Webb, as president of Sigma Tau Gamma, supported by six fraternities and sororities as intervenors, filed a petition in the federal district court to void these resolutions on the grounds that they deprived them of their civil rights guaranteed to all citizens under the Bill of Rights of the federal Constitution. Specifically, the petitioners charged that the resolutions were adopted without due process of law, that they encroached upon their constitutional freedom of assembly, denied them equal protection of the law, and adversely affected their existing contractual and property rights. Judge

---

[19] Waugh v. Board of Trustees of the University of Mississippi, 237 U.S. 589 (1915).

Hand ruled that the petitioners had failed to show that they had been deprived of any civil rights.[20] From this decision, an appeal was taken to the Supreme Court of the United States.

The following is from the brief filed by counsel for the fraternities:

Appellants seriously urge that the national fraternity system, which has existed in American colleges for over one hundred and twenty-five years, and has included in its membership many of the finest minds in the country, among whom are several presidents of the United States, should not be arbitrarily thrown out without an opportunity to be heard by the highest court in our land.

Notwithstanding this plea, the United States Supreme Court declined to review the ruling of the federal district court.[21] According to the 1954 *Britannica Book of the Year*,[22] in May 1953 Columbia University announced that it would withdraw recognition by 1960 from all student organizations—except those of a religious type—which discriminate against applicants because of race, color, or religion.

RIGHT OF A NONPUBLIC COLLEGE TO FORBID FRATERNITY MEMBERSHIP. The cases thus far considered have involved the legal right of tax-supported institutions to control the actions of students with respect to social fraternities. The case usually cited to show the power of a nonpublic college in this matter involved Wheaton College. In 1866 the Supreme Court of Illinois declared:

Wheaton College is an incorporated institution, resting upon private endowments, deriving no aid whatever from the state or from taxation. Its charter gives the trustees and faculty power to adopt and enforce such rules as may be deemed expedient in the government of the institution, a power which they would have possessed without such express grant, because it is incident to the very object of their incorporation and indispensable to the successful management of the college. Among the rules they have deemed it expedient to adopt is one forbidding students to become a member of a secret society. . . . Whether the rule be judicious or not, it violates neither good morals nor the laws of the land and is clearly within the power of the college authorities to make and enforce. So long as the rules violate neither divine nor human law, we have no more authority to interfere than we have to control the domestic discipline of a father in his family.[23]

---

[20] Webb v. State University of New York, 120 F. Supp. 554, 125 F. Supp. 910 (N.D.N.Y. 1954).

[21] Webb v. State University of New York, 348 U.S. 867 (1954).

[22] *Britannica Book of the Year, 1954* (Chicago: Encyclopaedia Britannica, 1954), p. 238.

[23] People v. Wheaton College, 40 Ill. 186 (1866).

RIGHT OF ADMISSION TO A NONPUBLIC COLLEGE. A high school graduate applied for admission to Northwestern University and was refused, on the grounds that, being only fourteen years of age, he was too young for enrollment. He filed a mandamus action, seeking to compel the university to admit him. The proceeding was dismissed "with the understanding" that he would be admitted the following year, 1945. He was again denied admission, this time on the grounds that he had filed suit against the university. The appellate court of Illinois refused[24] to compel the institution to admit him. The following is from the opinion of the court:

The University is a private charitable corporation and its charter is a contract. . . . The state, through the legislature, has no power to take from or interfere with the power of the trustees of the University to make such rules as are necessary to conduct the University business. The state, through its courts, has not the power. . . . It is our view that . . . the University is not required to give a reason for denying Tinkoff, Jr. admission; and that it could refuse for any reason it considered adequate.

RACIAL DISCRIMINATION IN THE ADMISSION OF STUDENTS

Upon the termination of the so-called carpetbagger regimes, which followed in the wake of military conquest and occupation of the states of the Southern Confederacy after the end of the Civil War, the people of the South re-enacted legislation requiring rigid segregation of the Negro and white races in educational institutions, theatres, hotels, and public service facilities. Until declared unconstitutional by the United States Supreme Court, such statutes were enforced in seventeen states[25] and in the District of Columbia. Segregation was optional in four more states[26] by constitutional provisions.

At first, the federal courts were inclined to hold that segregation deprived a citizen of his "equal protection of the laws" guaranteed to him by the Fourteenth Amendment. In 1873 the United States Supreme Court ruled that Catherine Brown, a Negro woman ejected from a railroad car reserved for members of the white race, had been unlawfully deprived of her rights as a citizen, even though the car reserved

---

[24] People v. Northwestern University, 303 Ill. App. 224, 77 N.E.2d 345 (1947).

[25] Alabama, Arkansas, Delaware, Florida, Georgia, Kentucky, Louisiana, Maryland, Mississippi, Missouri, North Carolina, Oklahoma, South Carolina, Tennessee, Texas, Virginia, and West Virginia.

[26] Arizona, Kansas, New Mexico, and Wyoming.

for the use of Negroes was equal, in every respect, to those for members of the white race.[27]

THE "SEPARATE BUT EQUAL" DOCTRINE. However, the famous "separate but equal" doctrine was accepted by the high court in 1899 in the case of Homer Plessy, also ejected from a railroad car reserved for white persons.[28] In that same year the United States Supreme Court held that public school authorities may even suspend, temporarily, the operation of a Negro high school for reasons of economy, while supporting a high school for white children. Mr. Justice Harlan, in delivering the opinion of the unanimous court, had this to say:

> While all admit that the benefits and burdens of public taxation must be shared by citizens without discrimination against any class on account of their race, the education of the people in the schools maintained by state taxation is a matter belonging to the respective states, and any interference on the part of federal authority with the management of such schools cannot be justified, except in the case of a clear and unmistakable disregard of rights secured by the supreme law of the land.[29]

As a matter of fact, the "separate but equal" doctrine in public education was first promulgated in Massachusetts in 1849.[30] In the city of Boston, a Negro child applied for admission to a "white" school much closer to her home than the "colored" school of the district. Her application was rejected, and her parents brought an action in her behalf against the city on the grounds that her rejection was contrary to the bill of rights of the State of Massachusetts. The court rejected the argument that segregation by race in the public school system constituted discrimination.

Segregation and the "separate but equal" doctrine continued to be the law of the land in the South for over half a century. In 1908, the high federal court upheld[31] a Kentucky statute which prohibited endowed, privately controlled colleges and universities from giving instruction to classes composed of both white and Negro students.

Gradually, the yardstick with which the equality of the separate educational facilities offered to students of the Negro race was measured was applied with greater precision. For instance, in 1938 the United

---

[27] Railroad Co. v. Brown, 84 U.S. 445 (1873).

[28] Plessy v. Ferguson, 163 U.S. 537 (1899).

[29] Cumming v. Richmond County Board of Education, 175 U.S. 528 (1899).

[30] Roberts v. City of Boston, 59 Mass. (5 Cush.) 198 (1849).

[31] Berea College v. Commonwealth of Kentucky, 211 U.S. 45 (1908)

States Supreme Court declared[32] that equal opportunity for a legal education must be provided by a state for its Negro citizens within its own borders. Missouri could not, by offering to pay the tuition of qualified Negro students at law schools outside the state, fulfill its constitutional obligations to afford equal educational facilities for all its citizens.

THE SWEATT CASE. By 1950 the United States Supreme Court, although continuing to pay lip service to the "separate but equal" doctrine, had abandoned it for all practical purposes. An examination of the opinion in the Sweatt case will show that it would have been physically impossible for the State of Texas to have made its law school for Negroes comply with the standard of equality therein defined, no matter how much money it had been willing to appropriate. Here is the yardstick adopted by the court:

Moreover, although the law is a highly learned profession, we are well aware that it is an intensely practical one. The law school, the proving ground for legal learning and practice, cannot be effective in isolation from individuals and institutions with which the law interacts. Few students and no one who has practiced law would choose to study in an academic vacuum, removed from the interplay of ideas and the exchange of views with which the law is concerned. The law school to which Texas is willing to admit petitioner excludes from its student body members of the racial groups which number 85% of the population of the state and include most of the lawyers, witnesses, jurors, judges and other officials with whom petitioner will inevitably be dealing when he becomes a member of the Texas Bar. With such a substantial and significant segment of society excluded, we cannot conclude that the education offered petitioner is substantially equal to that which he would receive if admitted to the University of Texas Law School.[33]

---

[32] Missouri v. Canada, 305 U.S. 337 (1938).

[33] Sweatt v. Painter, 339 U.S. 629 (1950). In this same year of 1950, the high federal court held that the State of Oklahoma could not meet the "separate but equal" standard by admitting a Negro student to courses of study in the University of Oklahoma which were not available in Negro schools, while requiring that instruction be given on a segregated basis. G. W. McLaurin had been admitted to the Graduate College of the university but had been required to sit apart at a designated desk in an anteroom adjoining the classroom. He was not permitted to use the regular reading room in the library but was required to sit at a designated desk on the mezzanine floor of the library. He was permitted to take his meals in the school cafeteria but was required to sit at a designated table and at a different time from the other students. Mr. Chief Justice Vinson, speaking for the unanimous Court, said, in part: "We conclude that the conditions under which this appellant is required to receive his education deprive him of his personal and present right to the equal protection of the laws." McLaurin v. Oklahoma State Regents for Higher Education, 339 U.S. 637 (1950).

THE REJECTION OF THE "SEPARATE BUT EQUAL" DOCTRINE. The final blow to the "separate but equal" doctrine was delivered by the court in the historic case of *Brown v. Board of Education of Topeka.*[34] Negro parents, conceding the physical equality of the separate schools provided by the local board of education, charged that segregation was, itself, socially and psychologically injurious to young children and hence a denial of their constitutional right to "equal protection of the laws."

The judges of the high federal court agreed that this contention was "amply supported by modern authority" and "that in the field of public education, the doctrine of 'separate but equal' has no place. Separate educational facilities are inherently unequal."

However, the court recognized the fact that full implementation of this new policy, in all areas and at all levels of public education, would probably take time. It held open for reargument the questions of whether Negroes shall "forthwith be admitted to schools of their choice," or whether the courts may "permit an effective gradual adjustment." On May 31, 1955, a brief ruling[35] was read by Chief Justice Warren on how integration shall be carried out. The order imposed no deadline for implementation, and the somewhat ambiguous term "all deliberate speed" was the key phrase.

How much time will federal judges give the people of the South in which to effectuate this revolution in their social mores? Those basing their hopes upon the word "deliberate" could point to the following excerpt from the order of the court in support of their view:

Full implementation of these constitutional principles may require solution of various local school problems. School authorities have the primary responsibility for elucidating, assessing and solving these problems; courts will have to consider whether the action of school authorities constitutes good faith implementation of the governing constitutional questions. Because of their proximity to local conditions and the possible need for future hearings, the courts which originally heard these cases can best perform their judicial appraisal.

Others, less optimistic about the time that would be granted, could cite the following statement from the same order:

---

[34] Actually, there were five cases argued together before the Court in December 1952: Brown v. Board of Education of Topeka, 347 U.S. 483 (1954); Gebhart v. Belton, 347 U.S. 483 (1954); Briggs v. Elliott, 347 U.S. 483 (1954); Davis v. County School Board, 347 U.S. 483 (1954); Bolling v. Sharpe, 347 U.S. 497 (1954).

[35] Brown v. Board of Education, 349 U.S. 294, 299, 300, 301 (1955).

While giving weight to these public and private conditions, the courts will require that the defendants make a prompt and reasonable start toward full compliance with our May 17, 1954 ruling.

The first case to reach the high federal court after its rejection of the "separate but equal" doctrine in 1954 was that of Autherine J. Lucy, a young Negro woman. Refused admission to the University of Alabama in 1952, she applied to the courts for relief.[36] After three years of litigation, the Supreme Court of the United States issued an order to admit her, and the dean of admissions was enjoined from denying the right of enrollment to anyone solely on account of his race or color.

On February 1, 1956, Miss Lucy was enrolled and attended her first classes the following day. Serious public disturbances resulted. They received world-wide publicity. After three days the Board of Trustees required her to withdraw, on the grounds that her continued presence on the campus would endanger her safety and that of others.

She immediately filed a motion with the federal district court asking that the members of the board and the president of the university be punished for contempt of court. In her petition she alleged that concern for her safety was not the real motivation for her suspension but that it was part of a "cunning stratagem for denying her right to attend and pursue courses of study at the University of Alabama."

These allegations were not sustained. In the opinion of the federal district court, "the action which the Trustees and officials took to protect her and others from bodily harm was not taken in defiance of the court's injunction, but was taken in good faith." On March 1, 1956, the university board adopted the following resolution:

Now therefore, be it resolved by the Board of Trustees of the University of Alabama, in meeting assembled, that, in view of said false, defamatory, impertinent and scandalous charges made by said Autherine J. Lucy against university authorities and trustees, she is hereby permanently expelled from the University of Alabama.

THE FRASIER AND HAWKINS CASES. The next case on this issue to reach the United States Supreme Court was that of Leroy B. Frasier and two other Negro youths seeking admission to the undergraduate schools of the University of North Carolina. On April 27, 1955, these three young men received identical letters from the director of admissions in which they were told that the trustees of the university would admit

---

[36] Lucy v. Adams, 134 F. Supp. 235 (N.D. Ala. 1955), aff'd, 228 F.2d 619 (3d Cir. 1955), cert. denied, 351 U.S. 931 (1956).

properly qualified Negroes to graduate and professional courses of study not offered at a Negro college in the state but that Negroes would not be admitted to the undergraduate courses.

On September 16, 1955, a federal district court ordered[37] the university to admit them. The decision was appealed and the university, in its brief filed with the United States Supreme Court, had this to say:

Second, even if the Brown decision is assumed, for purposes of argument, to be correct, it does not apply to the facts of this case. The modern psychological authority relied on by this court dealt with segregation of children, of the "tendency to retard the educational and mental development of Negro children," not of adults attending institutions of higher learning. For these reasons, the Brown decision does not apply to institutions of higher learning and the education of adults, in the absence of a finding, based on competent evidence, that there is, in fact, an inequality imposed upon the Negro citizens involved.

Despite this argument, the decision of the lower federal court was affirmed on March 5, 1956.[38]

The third case in this series of decisions in 1956 was that of Virgil D. Hawkins, refused admission to the College of Law of the University of Florida in 1952. The issue reached the Supreme Court and on March 12, 1956, the following brusque order was issued: "As this case involves the admission of a Negro to a graduate professional school, there is no reason for delay."[39]

Counsel for the university, in his brief filed with the court requesting a rehearing, had this to say:

Petitioner is prepared to submit competent and conclusive evidence, if permitted by the court, to show that valid, sufficient and urgent reasons do exist in Florida for delay in admitting negroes to the graduate professional schools; that if such evidence is ignored, the public safety in Florida will be endangered and the administration and operation of institutions of higher education in Florida will be disrupted.

The petition for rehearing was denied without opinion.

---

[37] Frasier v. Board of Trustees, 134 F. Supp. 589 (M.D.N.C. 1955).

[38] Board of Trustees v. Frasier, 350 U.S. 979 (1956).

[39] Florida v. Board of Control, 350 U.S. 413 (1956), *rehearing denied,* 351 U.S. 915 (1956). See also Hawkins v. Board of Control, 162 F. Supp. 851 (N.D. Fla. 1958). After six years of litigation, Mr. Hawkins again failed to gain admission to the College of Law of the University of Florida. In the opinion of the Court, he had not presented evidence of his educational qualifications to undertake the study of law.

THE "DECLARATION OF CONSTITUTIONAL PRINCIPLES." On the same day the Hawkins decision was handed down by the United States Supreme Court, one hundred members of Congress—nineteen senators and eighty-one representatives—joined in issuing a "Declaration of Constitutional Principles," sometimes referred to as the "Southern Manifesto":

We regard the decision of the Supreme Court in the school cases as a clear abuse of judicial power. It climaxes a trend in the federal judiciary, undertaking to legislate in derogation of the authority of Congress, and to encroach upon the reserved rights of the states and the people.

The original Constitution does not mention education. Neither does the Fourteenth Amendment nor any other amendment. The debates preceding the submission of the Fourteenth Amendment clearly show that there was no intent that it should affect the systems of education maintained by the states.
. . . .
We appeal to the states and people who are not directly affected by these decisions to consider the constitutional principles involved, against the time when they too, on issues vital to them, may be the victims of judicial encroachment.

THE MEMPHIS STATE UNIVERSITY CASE. The Tennessee State Board of Education, after long consultation with interested groups, drew up a program for the gradual integration of the races in the six tax-supported institutions of higher education under its control. Five Negro students, unwilling to wait until they could be admitted under the program of gradual integration, applied for immediate admission to Memphis State College, now Memphis State University. Refused, they applied to a federal district court for an injunction. The judge found that there was no effort or intention on the part of the state board to evade or to circumvent the decision of the court; that it had devised the proposed plan, in good faith; and that time was absolutely necessary to carry out, in an effectual manner, the ruling of the United States Supreme Court.

Despite this judicial determination of facts by the local federal court and its plea for more time for the social adjustments required, the United States Court of Appeals reversed the lower court's decision and declared the program of gradual admission of Negro students to be in violation of the Fourteenth Amendment to the federal Constitution.[40]

---

[40] Booker v. State of Tennessee Board of Education, 240 F.2d 689 (6th Cir. 1957).

Judge Miller declined to agree with the majority of the court. In his dissenting opinion he declared:

Unless the district judge abused his discretion in approving the plan proposed to meet the problems presented by the factual background, we are not authorized to reject the plan in order to substitute a different plan of our own. That there are problems, practical as well as physical and financial, can hardly be denied. The district judge, a long-time resident of Memphis, Tennessee, and closely in touch with the local situation, is much better situated to understand, analyze and evaluate the problem than we are. . . . I am of the opinion that there was no abuse of discretion on the part of the district judge and that the judgment should be affirmed.

THE GIRARD COLLEGE CASE. On April 29, 1957, the Supreme Court of the United States ordered Girard College, supported entirely by income derived from an endowment fund created by the will of Stephen Girard, to admit two Negroes. Until this decision, students of the subject had assumed that the court would apply the non-discriminatory provisions of the Fourteenth Amendment only to institutions supported by public funds.

That portion of the Girard estate designated for the establishment of his college was left in trust to "The Mayor, Aldermen, and Citizens of Philadelphia," their successors and assigns. In 1869 the state legislature provided that all funds left in trust to the city would be administered by a Board of Directors of City Trusts.

In his will, Stephen Girard had declared that his college should admit as students only "poor male white orphan children." In February 1954 William A. Foust and Robert Felder applied for admission. Their applications were refused on the ground that, as Negroes, they were not eligible under the terms of the Girard will. A suit was filed in their behalf to compel the trustees to admit them. By a unanimous decision of the Philadelphia Orphans' Court and by a five to one decision of the Supreme Court of Pennsylvania, the provision of the will was upheld. The following is from the majority opinion:

While it may seem unfortunate that the court is obliged to sanction the exclusion of any child from even a *private* school or orphanage because of race, creed or color, if otherwise entitled to admission, the court is clearly of the opinion that . . . the beneficiaries of the charity of Stephen Girard are not being determined by the state of Pennsylvania, nor by the city of Philadelphia, nor by this court, but solely by Girard himself in the exercise of his undoubted right to dispose of his property by will, and, in so doing, to say, within the bounds of law, who shall enjoy its benefits.

No right of a citizen is more valued than the power to dispose of his property by will. No right is more solemnly assured to him by law.

If the present contention of the city is correct, its effects will be catastrophic on church and charitable bequests as well as on the law of wills in Pennsylvania. The constitutional prohibition against discrimination in the Fourteenth Amendment . . . is not confined to color. It prohibits the states from making any discrimination because of race, creed or color. It follows, logically and necessarily, that an individual . . . cannot constitutionally leave his money to a Catholic, or Episcopal, or Baptist, or Methodist, or Lutheran or Presbyterian Church. . . . That would shock the people of Pennsylvania and the people of the United States more than a terrible earthquake or a large atomic bomb.[41]

Despite this strong language of the Pennsylvania Supreme Court, the Supreme Court of the United States, in a brief and unsigned opinion, declared:

The board which operates Girard College is an agency of the state of Pennsylvania. Therefore, even though the board was acting as a trustee, its refusal to admit Foust and Felder to the college because they were Negroes was discrimination by the state. Such discrimination is forbidden by the Fourteenth Amendment.[42]

In compliance with this decision, the state supreme court vacated the decree of the Philadelphia Orphans' Court that had upheld the exclusion of Negro students as in conformity with the provisions of the Girard will and remanded the case to that court. The Orphans' Court, construing the decision of the federal Supreme Court to mean no more than that the Board of Directors of City Trusts, as an instrumentality of the State of Pennsylvania, was constitutionally incapable of administering Girard College in accordance with the testamentary requirements of its founder, exercised its equitable jurisdiction over charitable trusts by removing the municipal board as trustee and appointing thirteen private citizens to act as a new Board of Trustees of the college. As private citizens, their actions would not be those of the state and hence would not be subject to the restrictions upon state action imposed by the Fourteenth Amendment.

Counsel for the Negro applicants for admission to the college contested this action, but the supreme court of the state upheld[43] the change of trusteeship and the United States Supreme Court declined[44] to review the issue.

---

[41] In re Girard's Estate, 386 Pa. 548, 127 A.2d 287 (1956).

[42] Pennsylvania v. Board of Directors of City Trusts, 353 U.S. 230 (1957).

[43] In re Girard College Trusteeship, 391 Pa. 434, 138 A.2d 844 (1958).

[44] Pennsylvania v. Board of Directors, 357 U.S. 570 (1958), appeal dismissed and cert. denied.

CONSTITUTIONALITY OF RACIALLY RESTRICTED SCHOLARSHIPS. Since the United States Supreme Court has declared that, if the trustee of a charitable trust is a state or one of its instrumentalities, restrictions upon its use based upon race are unconstitutional, the status of racially restricted scholarships and prize funds administered by tax-supported colleges has been placed in doubt. In view of the possible implications of the Girard College case, the *New York University Law Review*,[45] in 1958 sent a questionnaire to four hundred and fifty state-supported colleges, requesting information about the extent of restrictions imposed by the donors upon the use of scholarships administered by them. Two hundred and thirty-nine colleges replied. Twenty-three institutions reported racially restricted scholarships, ten reported scholarships for the benefit of individuals of a designated religious group, and sixteen declared that they held scholarships restricted with respect to nationality.

RACIAL DISCRIMINATION IN PRIVATE SCHOOLS. In 1948 the New York Legislature declared[46] that, after September 15, 1948:

It shall be an unfair educational practice for an educational institution . . . to exclude or limit or otherwise discriminate against any person or persons seeking admission as students to such institutions because of race, religion, creed, color or national origin.

It should be noted that this legislation does not exclude or exempt nonpublic educational institutions from the provisions of the act. Similar legislation is in effect in Massachusetts and New Jersey.[47]

Arthur S. Miller, associate professor of law at Emory University, has made a careful analysis[48] of this problem. The research for his study was made possible by a grant from the Fund for the Republic. He reviewed the legal status of nonpublic education in this country and the degree of control by the state. The following is an excerpt from his appraisal and evaluation of the problem:

The law itself can be viewed as a group of concepts which have stopped short of extremes. Much of law, as in all of politics, is a balancing of diverse

---

[45] Patricia P. Shad, "Constitutionality of Restricted Scholarships," 33 *N.Y.U.L. Rev.* 604 (1958).

[46] *N.Y. Educ. Law* § 313(3)(a).

[47] *Mass. Ann. Laws* ch. 151(c), §§ 1–5 (Michie 1957). *N.J. Stat. Ann.* § 18:25 (West Supp. 1957).

[48] Arthur S. Miller, "Racial Discrimination and Private Schools," 41 *Minn. L. Rev.* 145–86, 245–86 (1957).

interests. It is seldom indeed that any concept is of such overriding importance that it will be carried out without regard for countervailing interests. This is particularly true of the "great generalities" of the Constitution.

. . . .

In addition, extending the concept of state action to true private education would tend to jeopardize all types of private group activity. Only the most compelling reasons would lead the court to open that "Pandora's Box," and much of the virtues of private education are extant because it is private and not controlled, except in a tenuous manner, by the state.

THE AMHERST COLLEGE LOAN FUND CASE. In 1957 a graduate of Amherst College bequeathed $50,000 to his alma mater for the establishment of a scholarship loan fund. His will stipulated that those receiving the benefit of the trust fund must be Americans by birth, that they should not smoke, drink, or gamble and that they must be Protestant and gentile.

Amherst College declined the legacy on the grounds that its acceptance with the last two restrictions would violate one of its charter provisions. The executor of the estate filed an action with the Chancery Division of the Essex County Superior Court of New Jersey, requesting instructions as to the disposition of the trust fund.

The court came to the conclusion that the primary desire of the testator had been that the fund should go to his college, since he was a devoted alumnus. In view of the fact that the college could not accept the bequest subject to religious limitations as to its use, the court, in the exercise of its cy pres power, deleted the words "Protestant" and "gentile" from that portion of the will on the grounds that these religious limitations on the use of his fund had not been of paramount importance to the testator. In other words, had he known of the provisions of the charter of his college, he would probably have omitted the religious restrictions on the use of his fund.[49] The executor has stated that the decision of the trial court will be appealed.

DISCRIMINATION ON THE BASIS OF SEX. Two young women applied for admission as students to the Agricultural and Mechanical College of Texas. Their applications were refused solely on the grounds of their female sex. The office of admissions reminded them of the fact that the governing board of the college had, as a matter of policy, excluded female students from the college since its establishment in 1876.

---

[49] Howard Savings Institution v. Trustees of Amherst College, 61 N.J. Super. 119, 160 A.2d 177 (1960). For a discussion of the power of cy pres, see chap. 7, n. 2, p. 191.

Their petition for a writ to compel the college to admit them was granted by the trial court. The following is from the opinion of the district court:

As a matter of law, separate but equal facilities are inherently unequal as applied to males and females, and, as a matter of law, any attempt at classification of males and females for educational purposes at the Agricultural and Mechanical College of Texas is irrational and immaterial to the educational objectives sought, and does violence to Article I of Section 3 of the Texas Constitution, and is contrary thereto, and is in clear violation of the equal protection clause of the Fourteenth Amendment to the United States Constitution, and denies the relators the equal protection of the laws.

This decision of the district court was reversed by the state court of appeals. The following is from the opinion of Judge Tirey:

The Texas system of higher education, as it exists today, is composed of 18 institutions fully supported by state funds. . . . There are 16 coeducational institutions. . . . There is one institution which offers an all-male environment, and one which offers an all-female environment. The legislature, in its wisdom, has seen fit to afford the individual the widest possible choice in the selection of a college or university. . . . We think the foregoing shows conclusively that appellants' exclusion from the college was not in violation of their constitutional rights.[50]

EDUCATIONAL RIGHTS OF STUDENTS

The courts have been reluctant to interfere with the broad area of discretion inherent in the relationship of professor and student and to substitute the judgment of the court for that of the faculty on the questions of the issuance of certificates of academic credit and the granting of diplomas. However, if the evidence presented shows that the student has fulfilled all the published requirements of the institution and that its action in refusing to issue the certificate or diploma is clearly capricious or arbitrary, the courts have granted writs of mandamus compelling the institution to act in good faith.

THE RIGHT TO EARNED ACADEMIC CREDITS. A student, after having successfully completed the work prescribed for the first two years of a

[50] Heaton v. Bristol, 317 S.W.2d 86 (Tex. 1958), *appeal dismissed and cert. denied*, 359 U.S. 230 (1959). Dean Stanley Samad of the College of Law, University of Akron, read this guide in manuscript. Following is one of his helpful comments: "The reader may probably infer from reading and comparing the excerpts of the cases that the Fourteenth Amendment (especially the 'equal protection' clause) is a limit on discrimination without rational foundation by the state or those acting under the color of state authority, but not discrimination by private individuals. You may wish to point this out in the text or footnote to orient the reader."

course in nursing, was dismissed in her third and final year of training because she had broken a rule of the school. The published catalogue of the institution stated that an infraction of any rule would automatically cause the dismissal of a student nurse and that no transfer of credits would be given.

The student brought an action against the hospital and its director of nursing to compel them to issue her credits for the two years of work she had completed so that she might secure advanced standing in another nursing school. Her case reached the Supreme Court of Pennsylvania in 1954. It ruled that since the hospital in question was a privately conducted institution, without support from public funds, the court could not issue a writ of mandamus compelling its officers to issue credits to a student.[51] In other words, since the duty of the hospital to issue the credits was not one imposed by law but one that rested solely on contract, a court of common pleas did not have jurisdiction to grant equitable relief by issuing a writ of mandamus to compel the hospital to issue them.

The student and her attorney continued their efforts to obtain a favorable decision. Finally, in November 1955 the Supreme Court of Pennsylvania ruled that a court of common pleas had the power of a court of equity to afford specific relief where recovery in damages would be an inadequate remedy. The hospital was ordered to issue the earned academic credits to the student. Chief Justice Stern, in his opinion, stated that such courts

have jurisdiction not only for the prevention of acts contrary to law and prejudicial to the rights of individuals, but also for the enforcement of obligations, whether arising under express contracts, including those in which a duty may have resulted from long recognized and established customs and usages, as in this case, perhaps, between an educational institution and its students.

It is unfortunate that a case which involves merely the claimed right of a student nurse to be given credit for her two years work . . . should be enveloped in a veritable maze of pleadings, arguments, decisions and appeals now protracted over a course of three years . . .[52]

THE RIGHT TO AN ACADEMIC DEGREE. A graduate student, Richard Edde, enrolled as a candidate for the degree of doctor of philosophy at Columbia University, submitted his dissertation to the appropriate faculty committee for review. The committee rejected the dissertation

---

[51] Strank v. Mercy Hospital of Johnstown, 376 Pa. 305, 102 A.2d 170 (1954).
[52] Strank v. Mercy Hospital of Johnstown, 383 Pa. 54, 117 A.2d 697 (1955).

in the form submitted but granted the candidate the opportunity of revising it and continuing his candidacy for the degree.

Mr. Edde refused to make any revision in his dissertation and filed an application for a court order directing the university to reinstate him

as a certified candidate for the degree of doctor of philosophy at Columbia University in the City of New York and to have him finally examined for that degree on the basis of his dissertation as it now stands.

The case reached the New York Supreme Court and, on December 2, 1957, Justice Gold delivered the following opinion:

For the purpose of this opinion, it will be assumed that, in a proper case, a proceeding of this nature may be maintained against a private university. . . . Even on this asumption, the application must be denied.

It was within the discretion of the university's proper authorities to reject the petitioner's doctoral dissertation. There is ample evidence to support the refusal of the dissertation, and it is not established that the rejection was arbitrary, capricious or unreasonable. The court will not substitute its own opinion as to the merits of a doctoral dissertation for that of the faculty members whom the university has selected to make a determination as to the quality of the dissertation.[53]

Justice Gold, in support of his opinion in this Columbia University case, cited several early New York cases. In one of these, a medical student applied for a writ of mandamus to compel the dean and faculty of the college to issue a diploma to him. The court, in refusing his petition, said this:

The relator charges bad faith and ill will upon the part of some of the officials of the college, but these allegations do not alter the fundamental principles of law. . . . The court will not and cannot reexamine the relator as to his qualifications to practice medicine . . .[54]

On the other hand, a New York court had held that a college of medicine can be compelled to examine a student for graduation where the college makes no explanation of its refusal to do so. The court explained this point thus:

It may be true that this court will not review the discretion of the corporation in the refusal, for any reason, to permit a student to be examined and to receive a degree; but where there is an absolute and arbitrary refusal,

---

[53] Edde v. Columbia University, 8 Misc. 2d 795, 168 N.Y.S.2d 643 (Sup. Ct. 1957), aff'd, 175 N.Y.S.2d 556 (App. Div. 1958).

[54] People v. New York Homeopathic Medical College, 47 N.Y. St. R. 395, 20 N.Y. Supp. 379 (Super. Ct. 1892).

there is no exercise of discretion. It is nothing but a wilful violation of the duties which they have assumed.[55]

An interesting case arose in New York after World War I, involving a senior law school student, refused his degree because of his alleged "unpatriotic and revolutionary" views.[56] According to his petition for a court order to compel the faculty to issue his diploma, the student had been summoned before a committee of the faculty. There, the dean of the faculty had said to him:

Goldenkoff, it has come to our attention that you are in sympathy with the doctrines of the Socialist party and that you are disseminating offensive propaganda about the school, converting students to the cause.

The student's petition further alleged that the dean and faculty were very bitter against the Socialist members of the New York Legislature who had just been expelled from the legislature, and the fact that the petitioner did not express approval of this expulsion was the only and real cause for his own expulsion from the law school. The student further asserted that he was "one hundred percent American" in his views and that his opinion in regard to the Socialists and their expulsion was the same as that of Charles Evans Hughes, then governor of the state.

The court, in refusing to grant his petition for a writ of mandamus, said: "Clearly, therefore, the faculty acted within the scope of its discretion, to such purpose that no review may be made by a court."

Another case involved the refusal of a law school to confer a degree upon a student who had passed all his final examinations. On the day before commencement he became involved in a heated argument with the dean. The court, in declining to order the school to confer the degree, declared:

Where a student is guilty of contumacious conduct, it is within the discretion of the faculty to refuse him his degree, and the fact that the objectionable conduct occurred between the final examinations and the day of graduation is immaterial.[57]

THE RIGHT TO "DUE PROCESS" BEFORE DISMISSAL. A young woman enrolled in the medical school of the University of Illinois in 1949. She was suspended in May 1953. According to her statement, she was not

[55] People v. Bellevue Hospital Medical College, 38 St.R. 418, aff'd, 128 N.Y. 621, 28 N.E. 253 (Sup. Ct. 1891).

[56] People v. Albany Law School, 198 App. Div. 460, 191 N.Y. Supp. 349 (1921).

[57] People v. New York Law School, 68 Hun. 118, 22 N.Y. 663 (1893).

informed of the reason for her suspension until her attorney demanded a hearing on her behalf.

A year after her dismissal, she and her attorney appeared before the university committee on policy and discipline. There, she was informed by the attorney for the university that she had been suspended for submitting as her own, two examination papers written by another individual. No witnesses were produced at the meeting to support these charges.

Despite her vigorous denial of this accusation, the committee recommended her expulsion. After expulsion, she petitioned the circuit court for a writ of mandamus to compel the trustees of the university to re-admit her. She claimed that she had a constitutional right to due process of law, that is, the right to a formal hearing at which she would have an opportunity to confront the accusing witnesses and to cross-examine them under oath. The circuit court declined to grant the writ, and she appealed to the state supreme court. Three years after her suspension the highest state court issued[58] its decision.

Judge Niemeyer, in confirming the refusal of the circuit court to grant the writ of mandamus, quoted with approval the following opinion of another Illinois court:

> In order to carry out the powers and duties of school directors, . . . no form of trial or hearing is prescribed. . . . The board of education is authorized, in a reasonable and parliamentary way, to investigate charges of disobedience and misconduct and to suspend or expel one whom they may find guilty of violation of their reasonable and valid rules.[59]

A young woman registered as a student in Syracuse University in 1923. Three years later she was peremptorily dismissed. No statement of the grounds of dismissal was made, and no opportunity to answer charges was given. In this action, the university relied upon the following statement, published in its catalogue and specifically referred to in its registration form, signed by every student:

> The university, in order to safeguard its scholarship and its moral atmosphere, reserves the right to request the withdrawal of any student whose presence is deemed detrimental. Specific charges may or may not accompany a request for withdrawal.[60]

---

[58] People v. Board of Trustees of University of Illinois, 10 Ill. App. 2d 207, 134 N.E.2d 635 (1956).

[59] Smith v. Board of Education, 182 Ill. App. 342 (1913).

[60] College catalogues should be reviewed by legal counsel since some of their provisions may be construed by the courts as forming part of the contract of enrollment. Care should be taken to reserve the right to revise tuition and other charges.

The student brought an action in the New York Supreme Court for a judgment directing the university to reinstate her. In granting the order, Judge Smith had this to say:

The right to one's life, to develop one's character, to have one's reputation free from smirching by the acts of others, is inherent and one of the most valuable of rights; no institution, by its own act, can endow itself with the power to impair, by indirection, by innuendo, or by implication, the reputation of an individual. . . . The regulation, as operative in the instant case, creates an intolerable and unconscionable situation, and the action of the university is arbitrary, unreasonable, and, in a high degree, contrary to a true conception of sound public policy.[61]

Despite this ringing declaration by Judge Smith, his decision in favor of the student was reversed on appeal. Judge Sears justified his reversal on the following grounds:

The university need not accept as a student one desiring to become such. It may, therefore, limit the effect of such acceptance by express agreement, and thus, retain the position of contractual freedom in which it stood before the student's course was entered upon. I can discover no reason why a student may not agree to grant to the institution an optional right to terminate the relations between them.[62]

Probably the leading case on this subject came before the Supreme Court of Montana in 1927. A young woman was dismissed from the University of Montana without having been granted a hearing and the opportunity to defend herself. The court, after a review of virtually all the important cases on this issue, rejected her petition for reinstatement on the following grounds:

The president of the university has no authority to compel the attendance of witnesses at a hearing or to compel them to testify if they were present. To hold that the power of suspension could only be exercised after a hearing had been held . . . would be to hold that the power was practically ineffective.[63]

The student, through her counsel, requested the Supreme Court of the United States to review the question of her constitutional right to due process of law. The request was denied.[64]

---

[61] Anthony v. Syracuse University, 130 Misc. 249, 223 N.Y. Supp. 796 (Sup. Ct. 1927).

[62] Anthony v. Syracuse University, 224 App. Div. 487, 231 N.Y. Supp. 435 (1928).

[63] State *ex rel.* Ingersoll v. Clapp, 81 Mont. 200, 263 Pac. 433 (1927).

[64] State of Montana *ex rel.* Ingersoll v. Clapp, *cert. denied,* 277 U.S. 591, *appeal dismissed,* 278 U.S. 661 (1928).

The courts of Florida[65] and Kentucky[66] have said, in effect, that an educational institution, supported in whole or in part by appropriations from the public treasury, has somewhat less arbitrary power over its students in the matter of discipline and that its rules will be reviewed somewhat more critically by the courts than those of a privately controlled institution.

Committees on student discipline might well ponder the following comments of Mr. Justice Galen, in his dissenting opinion in the University of Montana case:

> A case of this character should never be before the courts, and would not therein be given serious consideration, were administrative officers disposed to perform their simple duty in the premises. Their determination, made upon facts presented, ordinarily should never be disturbed by the courts, but where, as here, they acted arbitrarily, it presents a proper case for judicial interference. . . . The relatrix should not have been suspended without a hearing.[67]

A statement from an Ohio court opinion has frequently been cited as providing an outline of the proper procedure to be followed by disciplinary committees:

> It is not necessary that the professors should go through the formality of a trial. They should give the student whose conduct is being investigated every fair opportunity of showing his innocence. They should be careful in receiving evidence against him, they should weigh it; determine whether it comes from a source freighted with prejudice; determine the likelihood, by all surrounding circumstances, as to who is right, and then act upon it as jurors with calmness, consideration and fair minds. When they have done this and reached a conclusion, they have done all that the law requires them to do.[68]

RIGHTS OF A COLLEGE STUDENT UNDER A FEDERAL CIVIL RIGHTS STATUTE. In 1948 the Congress authorized the federal district courts

> To redress the deprivation, under color of any state law, statute, ordinance, regulation, custom or usage, of any right, privilege or immunity secured by the Constitution of the United States or by any Act of Congress providing for equal rights of citizens or of all persons within the jurisdiction of the United States.[69]

---

65 John B. Stetson University v. Hunt, 88 Fla. 510, 102 So. 637 (1925).

66 Gott v. Berea College, 156 Ky. 376, 161 S.W. 204 (1913). See also 14 *C.J.S.: Colleges and Universities* § 26 (1939); Annot. 50 *A.L.R.* 1497 (1927).

67 State *ex rel.* Ingersoll v. Clapp, 81 Mont. 200, 263 Pac. 433 (1927) at 439.

68 Koblitz v. Western Reserve University, 21 Ohio C.C.R. 144, 11 Ohio C.C. Dec. 515 (1901).

69 28 *U.S.C.A.* § 1343 (3) (1950).

Arthur Steier entered Brooklyn College, a unit of the public school system of the State of New York, in the fall of 1952. Apparently, he became convinced that certain of the student organizations were too much dominated by the college administration. He assumed the role of a reformer. After much controversy, he was dismissed in December 1956. He appealed for readmission to the Board of Higher Education and to the state commissioner of education. Failing to obtain reinstatement, he filed an action in the federal district court under the provisions of the federal civil rights statute quoted above. In his complaint, he alleged that he had been deprived, without due process of law, of his right to freedom of speech and equal protection of law. The trial court dismissed his complaint and he appealed.

The following is from the majority opinion of the court of appeals:

Education is a field reserved to the individual states. The only restriction the Federal government imposes is that, in their educational program, no state may discriminate against an individual because of race, color or creed. . . . To expand the Civil Rights Statute so as to embrace every constitutional claim such as here made would, in fact, bring within the jurisdiction of the United States District Courts that vast array of controversies which heretofore have been raised in the state tribunals by challenges founded upon the 14th Amendment to the United States Constitution. . . . Conceivably, every State College student, upon dismissal from such college, could rush to a Federal Judge seeking review of the dismissal.[70]

The judgment dismissing the complaint is affirmed on the grounds that the United States district court lacked jurisdiction over this matter.

Circuit Judge Moore and Chief Judge Clark, dissenting, held that federal courts have jurisdiction over such issues. The following is from Judge Clark's opinion:

Surely, the City's public education system has failed in its purpose when, for its assumed self-protection, it must deny all its benefits to one whose only apparent transgression is a persistent and even irritating spirit of independence.[71]

TAX PROBLEMS OF STUDENTS

Until 1954 the Internal Revenue Code was completely silent about the tax status of scholarships, fellowships, and prize awards. In the absence of statutory language, the Internal Revenue Service was free to issue its own regulations and rulings on the subject, limited only by

---

[70] Steier v. New York State Education Commission, 271 F.2d 13 (2d Cir. 1959) at 18.

[71] *Ibid.* at 22.

the basic legal concept that true gifts are not subject to taxation to the recipient as income.

TAX STATUS OF SCHOLARSHIPS AND FELLOWSHIPS. A scholarship or fellowship award covering merely tuition has rarely been questioned, if no service or duty of any kind is required of the recipient in return for the award. However, prior to 1954 the Treasury Department took the position that the cash stipend of a fellowship was taxable unless the recipient could show that the payment to him was intended as a gift and not as compensation for service rendered.

FELLOWSHIP STIPENDS. Since many institutions expect their graduate students to carry an appreciable portion of the undergraduate teaching load, it has not been easy for members of the staff of the Internal Revenue Service to draw the line of distinction between fellowship stipends and instructional salary. The task has been rendered more difficult by the fact that some institutions use the euphemistic designation of "fellowship" for what is, in reality, the appointment of a part-time assistant instructor.

In the case of a candidate for a degree, there has been little difficulty in establishing the tax-free status of his stipend if (1) the recipient rendered no service of any kind to the institution making the award; (2) the recipient is free to select his field of study and research; and (3) no restrictions are placed upon the publication of his thesis or dissertation.

However, postdoctoral fellowship stipends were almost always questioned by the Internal Revenue Service under the 1939 code. Because of the fact that these stipends were usually much larger than predoctoral fellowships, it was difficult for the tax officers to convince themselves that the recipient had not begun his professional career as a full-time research worker.[72]

Subsection (b)(1) of Section 117 of the 1954 Internal Revenue Code declares that fellowship stipends of those who are candidates for a degree at an educational institution shall be taxable to the recipient if they represent "payment for teaching, research, or other services in the nature of part-time employment required as a condition of receiving the scholarship or fellowship grant."

---

[72] For a discussion of the tax status of postdoctoral fellowship stipends and prize awards with reference to members of the faculty, see chap. 3, "The College Faculty and Staff," pp. 95–100.

On the other hand, the same section of tho oodo states that "if teaching, research, or othor oorvices are required of all candidates (whether or not recipients of scholarship or fellowship grants) for a particular degree as a condition to receiving such degree, such teaching, research, or othor services shall not be regarded as part-time employment within the meaning of this paragraph."

It is in the interpretation and administration of this portion of Section 117 of the 1954 Internal Revenue Code that most of the apparent inconsistencies and ambiguities of current tax rulings on fellowship stipends are to be found.

Despite the fact that the code declares unequivocally that fellowship stipends are not to be taxed if they represent payment for services required of all candidates for the particular degree in question, the Commissioner of Internal Revenue has established the following important qualification or limitation to this statutory exemption, as follows:

> With regard to stipends paid to interns, it is the position of the National Office that, where a trainee performs services which are of material benefit to the trainer, such as those performed by interns and assistant residents, and he receives substantially the same amount therefor as is paid to an individual performing similar services, the payment made to him by the trainer constitutes compensation for labor or personal service rendered.[73]

The interns referred to in the foregoing ruling were all candidates for a graduate degree, that is, M.S. or Ph.D. in their specialty, and the service as intern was a condition required of all candidates for these special medical degrees. They are known as medical fellows. A similar ruling was received with reference to stipends paid to interns serving as a requirement for the degree of Master of Hospital Administration.

Since much of the service rendered by graduate students in the form of teaching, research, and as interns is of "material benefit" to their institutions, it has become almost impossible to determine in advance whether a particular fellowship stipend is or is not taxable if service of any character is rendered by the recipient. Consequently, it has become the practice in several large universities to withhold the estimated tax on all fellowship stipends paid to research and teaching assistants, even though the rendering of such service may be a condition to the awarding of degrees, leaving it up to the individual to apply for a tax refund if he feels that he is entitled to one.

---

[73] Letter ruling dated Oct. 3, 1955, from the District Director of the Internal Revenue Service at St. Paul, Minn. See also Rev. Rul. 57–522, 1957–2 *Cum. Bull.* 50. Check index of all *Internal Revenue Bulletins* under "Scholarships."

ACADEMIC PRIZE AWARDS. The 1954 Internal Revenue Code states that prizes and awards made primarily in recognition of religious, charitable, scientific, educational, artistic, literary, or civic achievements are to be free of taxation, but only if (1) the recipient was selected without any action on his part to enter the contest or proceedings and (2) the recipient is not required to render substantial further services as a condition to receiving the prize or award.[74]

In 1957 the Internal Revenue Service was asked for a ruling on the following situation: A prize had been offered, and the award was to be based upon past academic record and citizenship achievements. The young contestants were required to fill out a form and present themselves for a personal interview. Despite the language of Section 74(a) of the code, it was held that these actions on the part of the contestants did not make the awards taxable.[75]

FEDERAL FELLOWSHIPS AND LOANS

Although the National Defense Education Act of 1958[76] did not make available federal scholarships for undergraduates, it did make it possible for undergraduates as well as graduates to borrow up to $1,000 each year, with interest at 3 percent, to start one year after graduation. Repayment may be spread over a ten-year period. Half of the amount of the loans will be cancelled if the student enters the teaching profession and continues for five years therein.

Graduate fellowship stipends of $2,000 for the first year, increasing to $2,400 the fourth year, are also made available. Additional amounts are granted to those with dependents.

The institution which a National Defense fellow attends will be paid that portion of the cost of the new graduate program, or of the expansion of the existing program, in which the fellow is pursuing his course of study, which is reasonably attributable to him—but not more than $2,500 per year per fellow.

Institutions participating in the National Defense Student Loan Program assume responsibility for the following: (1) the establishment and maintenance of an adequate student loan record system and the

---

[74] *Int. Rev. Code of 1954,* §§ 74(a),(b).

[75] Rev. Rul. 57–67, 1957–1 *Cum. Bull.* 33.

[76] For the full text of the act see National Defense Education Act of 1958, 72 Stat. 1580, 20 *U.S.C.* § 401. For the legislative history of the act, a statement of its purposes, and a summary of its provisions, see *U.S. Code Cong. and Ad. News* at 6303 (1958).

submission of required reports; (2) the award of loans in accordance with the standards of financial need and the other requirements of the act, including the execution of the required oath and affidavit forms; (3) the development of an approved repayment program at the time the borrower concludes full-time study or leaves the college; and (4) the collection of the loan principal and interest, including the determination of the full-time teacher status and permanent and total disability of the borrowers who request partial or total cancellation of their obligations under the provisions of the act.

Those responsible for the administration of these fellowship and loan programs should have in their files the manuals of general information and instructions, obtainable from the Financial Aid Branch, Division of Higher Education, Office of Education, Department of Health, Education, and Welfare, Washington 25, D.C.

THE DISCLAIMER AFFIDAVIT REQUIREMENT OF THE NATIONAL DEFENSE EDUCATION ACT. Congress included the following requirement in the National Defense Education Act of 1958:

No part of any funds appropriated under this act shall be used to make payments or loans to any individual unless such individual (1) has executed and filed with the Commissioner an affidavit that he does not believe in, and is not a member of and does not support any organization that believes in or teaches, the overthrow of the United States government by force or violence, or by any illegal or unconstitutional methods and (2) has taken and subscribed to an oath or affirmation in the following form: "I do solemnly swear (or affirm) that I will bear true faith and allegiance to the United States of America and will support and defend the Constitution and laws of the United States against all its enemies, foreign and domestic.[77]

This disclaimer affidavit has become a matter of controversy and current developments should be watched.

---

[77] 72 Stat. 1580, 20 U.S.C. § 581(f).

CHAPTER V

College Property and
Related Problems

THE maintenance of law and order on the college campus is an ancient problem. In the early days, college officials exercising the rights and duties of a foster parent, enforced their regulations by the use of corporal punishment. Since this is no longer the custom, the implementation and enforcement of college rules have become more difficult.

THE COLLEGE CAMPUS

TRAFFIC REGULATION. With the introduction of the motor car to the campus, traffic regulation and the control of parking have been added to the burdens of the college business officer and the members of his staff.

Threat of dismissal is a potent weapon, but it is too drastic a penalty to invoke for minor offenses. The imposition of fines upon both faculty and students can probably be justified as a means of enforcement of reasonable campus regulations, but the legality of the procedure, apparently, has never been tested in a modern court of record. Temporary suspension of the right to park or to drive on the campus is one means of enforcement.

CAMPUS POLICE. Publicly controlled institutions can, to some extent, invoke the general police powers of the state itself, but this right is not available to the privately controlled colleges. Many have found a partial solution to the problem of law and order by requesting that the members of the campus police force and night watchmen be deputized by the county sheriff and by maintaining a close and friendly relationship with the local police.[1]

---

[1] At the organizational meeting of the National Association of Traffic and Security Directors of Colleges and Universities, held in Houston, Texas, in April

The authority of a sheriff to appoint deputies is an ancient common law right, and, in the absence of constitutional and legislative restrictions, a sheriff has absolute discretion to determine what deputies shall be employed and the length of their service.[2] Even without this grant of official status, an officer or an employee of a college, as a private citizen, may make arrests. At common law, any private person may arrest, without a warrant, one who commits a breach of the peace in his presence,[3] or where it is reasonably suspected that a person is threatening to commit a breach of the peace.[4]

However, if the offense is a mere misdemeanor, not sufficient to constitute a breach of the peace, a private person does not, at common law, have the right to arrest without a warrant.[5] If the offense is a felony, a private person has both the right and the duty, according to the common law, to apprehend the felon, if the felony was committed in his presence. The arrest may be made without waiting for the issuance of a warrant and at any subsequent time as well as at the time of the commission of the felony.[6] The manual of procedures for the campus police and night watchmen should be reviewed by the college counsel. The penalties for wrongful arrest can be rather severe.[7]

PROPERTY DEEDS AND THEIR CUSTODY. One evidence of good administration is the care with which basic documents are preserved and filed. An inspection of the documentary files of a college should be

---

1959, an informal report was drafted concerning the source of authority exercised by institutional traffic and security policemen. The following is an excerpt from that report:

"*Baylor University*—employs off-duty city police as its total security force. *University of Houston*—campus police commissioned by the City of Houston. They have no authority over anyone on the campus except students. *Arizona State College*—campus police commissioned by the City of Tempe. They have full authority of city police. *University of Arizona*—campus police commissioned as state police officers by the governor. *New Mexico State University*—commissioned as deputy sheriffs. A new state statute, effective July 1, 1959, created a traffic court within a specific framework for the institution. *College of the Pacific*—commissioned by the City of Stockton. *University of Colorado*—commissioned by both the city and county. *University of Oklahoma*—commissioned by the city and county and given state-wide authority over students by the board of regents. *Brigham Young University*—commissioned by the city police department. *Oklahoma State University*—not commissioned and have no authority to make 'citizens' arrests."

[2] State v. Griffin, 80 Ohio App. 447, 76 N.E.2d 294 (1947).

[3] Mallery v. Lane, 97 Conn. 133, 115 Atl. 694 (1921).

[4] Sloan v. Schomacker, 136 Pa. 382, 20 Atl. 525 (1890).

[5] 6 *C.J.S.: Arrest* § 8d (1937).

[6] *Ibid.* § 8b.

[7] *Ibid.* § 8c.

included in any general management survey of the institution. Good procedure demands that all deeds to property owned by the institution be preserved in a fireproof safe and adequately filed and indexed to provide prompt availability.

A MASTER PLAT OF THE CAMPUS. An effective aid to administration is the maintenance of a master plat of the campus, on which the exact location of property boundary lines is indicated with relation to boundary markers and physical improvements, including underground service lines and tunnels. If title to college land is represented by more than one deed, the property conveyed by each deed should be clearly indicated on the master plat, together with the deed recorder's notation for identification with the public records. The plats and description in each deed should be reconciled with the public records and with the master plat by a licensed surveyor. His survey certificate should be noted on the plat.

Every encumbrance, servitude, easement, license, or other right granted to or obtained by others should be indicated on the master plat, with a reference symbol to the official records or documents pertaining thereto. These grants should be cross-referenced on the master plat, in the index of the proceedings of the governing board authorizing the purchase or sale of land and the granting of rights therein to others, and in the general or subsidiary ledger sheets showing the dates and the amounts involved. This master plat and the notations thereon will prove of great value in avoiding future controversy and litigation.

EASEMENTS. "Easement" is the general term used to designate rights in the land of another. They include the right of way across the land and the right to construct and maintain utility service lines, such as telephone, telegraph, power, water, sewer, and gas lines.[8]

Easements should be granted only after due deliberation and advice of counsel. The easement agreement should be drafted by the attorney for the college or reviewed by him before execution to make certain that the rights therein granted are only those essential for the accomplishment of the purposes desired by the college.

College employees should be instructed to observe and to report any unauthorized encroachments upon college property. Unauthorized structures should be removed, and short cuts and other public use across college land should be blocked and posted, under advice of

---

[8] See 28 C.J.S.: Easements §§ 1–115 (1941).

counsel, to prevent the users from acquiring vested rights without the express consent of the college corporation. However, maintenance of good public relations should always be given consideration when the question of granting or denying an easement is under consideration.

The fact that an easement, once granted, continues to burden and encumber the use and enjoyment of the land in perpetuity, even in the hands of a subsequent purchaser, unless appropriately restricted by its terms, is illustrated by a case which came before a Missouri court in 1956.

In 1921 Park College granted an easement to the Kansas City Power and Light Company to "erect, construct and maintain" one of its transmission lines "over, along and across" a certain portion of its property. The rights granted by the easement were exercised by the power company for more than thirty years. In 1954 the college sold the tract of land to Richard R. Riss. The new purchaser proceeded to increase the size of a large lake on the property, submerging the base of some of the transmission poles of the power company. The power company went to court to enforce its rights, and the judgment of a circuit court, enjoining Mr. Riss from taking any action that would interfere with or endanger the power company's right of way, was affirmed by the appellate court.[9]

EVIDENCE OF TITLE. Before acquiring new property, a prudent purchaser will obtain satisfactory evidence that the seller has good title to the land under consideration. Evidence of title may consist of (1) an abstract of title and opinion, (2) a certificate of title, (3) title insurance, or (4) a Torrens certificate.

The usual evidence of title is an abstract. A complete abstract of title consists of a summary of the significant portions of every recorded instrument affecting the title of the tract of land in question. An abstractor may be a public official, a lawyer, or an abstract company. The work requires great skill, and, in many communities, the abstractor's records are more accurate than the public records. However, he does not guarantee the validity of the titles examined. His duty is merely to use due care in the preparation of his abstract.

After an abstract has been prepared by a reliable abstractor and certified, it should be examined by a competent attorney. His opinion should state the name of the titleholder and all defects and encum-

---

[9] Kansas City Power & Light Co. v. Riss, 319 S.W.2d 262 (Mo. Ct. App. 1958).

brances disclosed by the abstract. In some areas, no abstract is prepared; the attorney merely examines the public records and issues his certificate or opinion. An attorney or a title company issuing a certificate of title is liable only for damages occasioned by negligence.[10]

However, some certificates of title include a guarantee against loss occasioned by defects in the title not mentioned in the certificate. Such a document is more than a certificate of title; it is, in fact, a policy of title insurance. An adequate policy of title insurance guarantees the holder against any loss occasioned by defects in title.

In some states the Torrens system of land registration may be used. It was developed by Sir Robert Torrens and was first used in South Australia in 1858. The initial registration of land under this system is, in effect, a court proceeding to determine the titleholder of the tract to be registered. As a result of this proceeding, the court orders a public official to register the title of the tract of land, including mortgages, liens, easements, and other restrictions to which the title is subject. Once a tract has been registered under the Torrens system, subsequent transactions with respect thereto are not valid until they have also been registered. Thus, the Torrens certificate purports to be conclusive evidence that the title is as therein stated. However, the property owner must defend his title at his own expense.

CAMPUS BUILDINGS

As a general rule of law, the officer of a corporation, unless authorized by appropriate action of his corporate board, has no power to borrow money in its name or to execute a mortgage on corporate property. In some jurisdictions, however, if the loan is incurred apparently for corporate purposes, in the ordinary course of business, there is a legal presumption that the officer has acted within the scope of his authority.[11]

If the mortgage or the bond is regular in form and if it bears the corporate seal and the signatures of the proper corporate officers, some courts have held that these facts constitute prima facie evidence that the officers had been authorized to act on behalf of the corporation.[12]

---

[10] Robert Kratovil, *Real Estate Law* (3d ed.; Englewood Cliffs, N.J.: Prentice-Hall, 1958), pp. 211–13.

[11] Weaver v. Henderson, 206 Ala. 529, 91 So. 313 (1921).

[12] San Ramon Valley Bank v. Walden Co., 53 Cal. App. 534, 200 Pac. 662 (S.D. Cal. 1921).

THE POWER OF COLLEGE OFFICERS TO BORROW FUNDS FOR NEW BUILD-INGS. The courts have shown a tendency to protect the funds of educational and other charitable corporations from loss due to unauthorized actions of their officers.[13] A Texas court refused to enforce the promissory note of Thorp Springs Christian College, executed by its president in payment of an invoice for lumber and other material for the construction of one of the college buildings, on the grounds that the college charter vested the management and control of the institution in its board of trustees and the board had not authorized the execution of the note.[14] A similar ruling was made by a federal court in a case involving St. Vincent College.[15] One of the judges dissented, and the following is an excerpt from his opinion:

> Why should the rule of liability be modified in the case of a charitable or educational corporation where it engages in a business act? It is said in argument that it should have immunity because its officers are dealing with trust funds. . . . To give the immunity contended for would invite every variety of fraud and deception. The commercial world would distrust such institutions because it would be practically impossible for one to know when the inquiry as to legal compliance had been pursued far enough.

Investors and those who advise them are well aware of the fact that the legal review of a proposed bond issue requires specialized knowledge and experience. Even a minor defect in the bond indenture may reduce substantially the marketability of the bonds and thereby increase the net cost of the loan to the borrower. Consequently, colleges planning to raise funds by the sale of bonds to private investors should seek the advice of qualified experts in this field.

FEDERAL FUNDS FOR CAMPUS BUILDINGS. Many nonpublic institutions of higher education were able, for the first time, to obtain federal funds for construction purposes under the provisions of the Lanham Act of 1941. This act states that:

> Whenever the President finds that, in any area or locality, an acute shortage of public works . . . necessary to the health, safety or welfare of persons engaged in national defense activities . . . exists or impends . . . the Housing and Home Finance Administration is authorized . . . to make loans

---

[13] Peoples National Bank v. New England Home, 209 Mass. 48, 95 N.E. 77 (1911); McNeil & Higgins Co. v. Greer College, 206 Ill. App. 533 (1917); Credit Alliance Corp. v. Centenary College, 17 La. App. 365, 136 So. 130 (1931).

[14] R. B. Spencer & Co. v. Thorp Springs Christian College, 41 S.W.2d 482 (Tex. Civ. App. 1931).

[15] St. Vincent College v. Hallett, 201 Fed. 471 (7th Cir. 1912).

or grants to public or private agencies. . . . As used in this paragraph, the term, "private agency" means any private agency, no part of the net earnings of which inures to the benefit of any private shareholder or individual.[16]

Title IV of the Housing Act of 1950 made available a revolving fund of $750 million for federal loans for permanent housing and related service facilities for college students and faculty. Dr. Goodrich C. White, president of Emory University at that time and a member of the Committee on Relationships of Higher Education to the Federal Government of the American Council on Education, presented the following arguments to a congressional committee in 1949:

> Present housing conditions of college students are grossly inadequate. . . . Most of the temporary structures which were made available to institutions of higher education through congressional appropriations under the Lanham Act are rapidly deteriorating and repairs and increased maintenance are adding unduly to the cost of operation.
> Colleges and universities have long been proud of their self-sufficiency in terms of finances. . . . But the present situation is nothing short of desperate. Permanently increased enrollment, deterioration of temporary housing, high building costs, and tuition already increased to the point of diminishing return make it mandatory for them to ask for assistance now from the federal government.[17]

Title VI of the Housing Act of 1957 increased the revolving fund available for college housing loans by $200 million. Section 601 of the act amended the definition of an "educational institution" so as to remove any doubt concerning the eligibility for loans to accredited schools whose sole function is the training of ministers, priests, rabbis, and other divinity students. Another change permitted certain state agencies to qualify as eligible borrowers under the college housing program. The definition of "educational institution" now includes any hospital operating a school of nursing beyond the level of high school, approved by the appropriate state agency or any hospital approved for internships by recognized authority, if such hospital is either a public hospital or a private hospital, "no part of the net earnings of which inures to the benefit of any private shareholder or individual."[18]

The federal Housing and Home Finance Administrator is charged with responsibility for making loans to educational institutions. The act provides that:

---

[16] 42 *U.S.C.A.* § 1532 (1957).

[17] 2 *U.S. Code Cong. Serv.*, 81st Cong., Special Sess. 2124–25 (1950).

[18] 2 *U.S. Code Cong. & Ad. News,* 85th Cong., 1st Sess. 1347–48 (1957).

(1) No such loan shall be made unless the educational institution shows that it is unable to secure the necessary funds for such construction from other sources upon terms and conditions equally as favorable as the terms and conditions applicable to loans under this subsection, and

(2) No such loan shall be made unless the Administrator finds that the construction will be undertaken in an economical manner, and that it will not be of elaborate or extravagant design or materials.[19]

The loan must be repaid within fifty years, but, as a matter of policy, the Housing and Home Finance Agency requires that the loan be repaid within a forty-year period "unless it is impossible to develop a sound loan without a longer maturity period, or unless special justification exists for such longer period." Preliminary loan applications should be submitted to the regional office of the HHFA.[20]

THE FEDERAL URBAN RENEWAL PROGRAM. The Housing Act of 1959 established new procedures whereby land-locked urban universities may obtain help in combating the encroachment of slums and blight in university neighborhoods. Normally, a local urban renewal program is carried out by a local public agency which is either a department of the municipal government or an independent local authority. An institution of higher learning which desires to take advantage of the provisions of the Housing Act of 1959 should consult its city administration or other local governing body about the existence of an urban renewal program and the proper local official with whom to deal.

The American Council on Education appointed a special committee on urban renewal. Subcommittees were asked to draft suggestions for amendments to the basic federal legislation on the subject and to

---

[19] See 12 *U.S.C.A.* § 1749 (1957) for the full text of current legislation on "Housing for Educational Institutions."

[20] Regional offices of the Housing and Home Finance Agency: *Region I:* 346 Broadway, New York 13, N.Y., serving Maine, New Hampshire, Vermont, Massachusetts, Connecticut, Rhode Island, New York; *Region II:* 1004 Widener Bldg., Chestnut & Juniper Sts., Philadelphia 7, Pa., serving Pennsylvania, New Jersey, Maryland, Delaware, District of Columbia, West Virginia, Virginia; *Region III:* 645 Peachtree St., Seventh Bldg., N.E., Atlanta 23, Ga., serving Kentucky, Tennessee, North Carolina, South Carolina, Georgia, Alabama, Mississippi, Florida; *Region IV:* Bankers Building, 105 W. Adams St., Chicago 3, Ill., serving Michigan, Ohio, Indiana, Illinois, Wisconsin, Iowa, Minnesota, North Dakota, South Dakota, Nebraska; *Region V:* Federal Center, 300 W. Vickery Blvd., Fort Worth 4, Tex., serving Kansas, Missouri, Arkansas, Louisiana, Oklahoma, Texas, Colorado, New Mexico; *Region VI:* 989 Market St., San Francisco 3, Calif., serving California, Washington, Oregon, Arizona, Idaho, Nevada, Utah, Montana, Wyoming, Alaska, Hawaii, Guam; *Region VII:* 1608 Ponce de Leon Ave., P.O. Box 9093, Santurce 17, Puerto Rico, serving Puerto Rico and the Virgin Islands.

draft a model act for adoption by the various state legislatures to permit the creation of public bodies eligible to act as planning agencies under existing federal law.

The March 7, 1960, issue of the Council's bulletin *Higher Education and National Affairs* published in full federal regulations to govern urban renewal projects involving colleges or universities under Section 112 of Title I of the Housing Act of 1949, as amended.

STATE AID FOR COLLEGE BUILDINGS. Although many state constitutions forbid the legislature to appropriate public funds or to make the credit of the state available to nonpublic educational institutions, this is not true in all jurisdictions. Along the Atlantic seaboard, there has been a long-established pattern of the use of public funds in aid of so-called "private" institutions of higher education. In 1951 the Legislature of Maryland authorized the use of the credit of the state to provide funds for the construction of a new building for the School of Engineering at Johns Hopkins University, and again in 1954, for a gymnasium and field house at Washington College and a men's dormitory at Western Maryland College.[21]

The New York Dormitory Authority Act of 1944 created a public benefit corporation, authorized to "maintain, construct and operate dormitories and appurtenant facilities at state colleges and universities."[22] In 1957 the authority was given the power "to finance, plan, construct and operate dormitories and attendant facilities at private colleges in the state."[23]

CONSTRUCTION CONTRACTS

In view of the magnitude of the sums involved, all major construction contracts should be negotiated in consultation with the college attorney. College administrative officers charged with responsibility for the supervision of construction projects should become familiar

---

[21] Fred F. Beach and Robert F. Will, *The State and Nonpublic Schools*, U.S. Office of Education Misc. No. 28 (Washington: Government Printing Office, 1958), pp. 12–13. Twelve nonpublic educational institutions in Maryland receive regular appropriations of public funds. These include Johns Hopkins University, St. John's College, Washington College, Western Maryland College, and Hood College. For example, Johns Hopkins received an appropriation of $210,000 in 1958. In return, the university provided 150 state scholarships. (*Laws of Md. 1958* § 1304.10.05.)

[22] *N.Y. Pub. Authorities Laws* §§ 1430–43.

[23] *Ibid.* §§ 1675–90.

with the rules of law governing the relationships of architects, engineers, and contractors with their clients.[24]

THE CONTRACT FOR ARCHITECTURAL SERVICES. The professional competency of the architect to be employed is of paramount importance. In this connection, it should be noted that some states permit unlicensed individuals to practice the profession of architecture. In the interest of public safety, however, the majority of states have enacted statutes restricting the practice of architecture and engineering to those able to convince the members of a state examining board of their educational qualifications and experience. A few states still permit unlicensed individuals to design buildings and other structures if they do not call themselves an architect or use the word "architect" on their letterheads, professional cards, or in their contracts for services.

THE ARCHITECT AS AGENT. Judgment and discretion as well as professional ability are essential qualities in an architect since it is one of his duties to serve as the representative or agent of his client during the course of construction. His powers and authority as an agent are restricted to those expressly conferred by the provisions of his contract with his client or reasonably implied from the nature of his undertaking. It is his duty to make a full disclosure of all matters upon which he has information which it is desirable or important for his principal to know. He should not have a financial interest in the performance of the building contract or receive compensation from the contractor or from those who supply material for construction without the knowledge and consent of his principal.

THE ARCHITECT AS ARBITER. In many building contracts, the contractor and the owner agree that the certification of the architect that each portion of the construction project has been completed in accordance with the plans, specifications, stipulations, and conditions of the contract shall be conclusive and binding upon both parties. Courts have sustained such agreements and have accepted as final the certification

---

[24] Clarence W. Dunham and Robert D. Young, *Contracts, Specifications, and Law for Engineers* (New York: McGraw-Hill Book Co., 1958); Melvin Nord, *Legal Problems in Engineering* (New York: John Wiley & Sons, 1956); Laurence P. Simpson and Essel R. Dillavon, *Law for Engineers and Architects* (4th ed.; St. Paul, Minn.: West Publishing Co., 1958); Bernard Tomson, *Architectural and Engineering Law* (New York: Reinhold Publishing Corp., 1951); I. Vernon Werbin, *Legal Guide for Contractors, Architects, and Engineers* (1st ed.; New York: McGraw-Hill Book Co., 1952).

of the architect about questions of fact in the absence of fraud, caprice, or gross mistake.[25] The Indiana courts, however, have held[26] that an agreement to permit a third party to act as arbiter is void since this is the function and responsibility of a court of law and that it is contrary to public policy to oust the court of its jurisdiction.

Until the decision of the United States Supreme Court in 1950 in the Mooreman case,[27] courts were in general agreement that it was contrary to public policy to permit the parties to a contract to agree, in advance of disagreement, that the decision of a designated arbiter shall be conclusive on points of law involved in the contract as well as on questions of fact. However, in the Mooreman case, the court held that, since the parties had by the terms of the contract intended to authorize final determination by the Secretary of War, he was clearly empowered to make the determination, whether or not his decision was one of fact or of law.

THE GENERAL CONTRACTOR AND HIS BONDS. In order to protect the owner against loss due to the inability or unwillingness of the general contractor to complete the building in accordance with the plans and specifications and to pay for all labor and materials utilized for its construction, it is considered good practice to require the contractor to execute and deliver a performance bond. The form of the bond and the adequacy of the resources of the surety should receive close attention. The American Institute of Architects has drafted a form for a performance bond which may be found useful as a guide. Normally, two bonds are required: a performance bond assuring completion of the project and a payment bond as protection against nonpayment by the contractor for labor and materials. The two bonds are frequently combined in one document. A bid bond, sometimes required, obligates the surety to compensate the owner within the face of the bond for loss occasioned, should the successful bidder fail to sign the construction contract.

MECHANICS' LIENS. At common law, one who is given physical possession of the personal property of another, under an agreement with the owner to expend labor and materials thereon, is entitled to retain

---

[25] Central Nebraska Public Power & Irrigation Dist. v. Tobin Quarries, 157 F.2d 482 (8th Cir. 1946).

[26] Wacker v. Essex, 67 Ind. App. 584, 119 N.E. 466 (1918); Maitland v. Reed, 37 Ind. App. 469, 77 N.E. 290 (1906).

[27] United States v. Mooreman, 338 U.S. 457 (1950).

possession of the property until he is paid for his labor and materials. Thus, if a watch is left for repair, the watchmaker is entitled to retain the watch until he is paid. This common law lien is not available to those who erect or repair buildings and other improvements to land, but by statute their rights have been given a high degree of protection.

A mechanic's lien has been defined as a right, created by statute, to secure priority of payment of the price or value of work performed and materials furnished in the improvement of land.[28] This means that the land itself and the improvements thereon are chargeable with the payment and that they may be sold to satisfy the lienholder's claims. In the majority of states, a mechanic's lien takes priority over an existing first mortgage.

In all jurisdictions, those who are directly employed on the construction project and those who supply material thereto are given the protection of a mechanic's lien. In many states, contractors, subcontractors, engineers, and architects are also given a lien against the property to ensure the payment of their fees.

In general, public property devoted to public use is not subject to a mechanic's lien unless it is expressly made subject to the lien statute. A Pennsylvania court ruled that a hospital building used for public purposes was exempt from mechanic's liens, even though the hospital was administered by a charitable corporation under regulations and control of the state.[29]

In order to be able to enforce the lien, the statutes generally require that notice of the claim be filed in an office of public record within a specified period. Thus, the owner may protect himself by stipulating in his agreement with the general contractor that he may withhold final payment until after the last possible date for the filing of liens. The right to a lien may be waived by a prior agreement based upon a consideration, and the owner may therefore protect himself by requiring all parties who might become entitled to file a lien to execute a waiver. However, the majority of owners prefer to require the general contractor to furnish a payment bond, with adequate surety.

INSURANCE

The law of insurance has many ramifications, and it is impossible in this volume to do more than to suggest some of its problems as

[28] 57 *C.J.S.: Mechanics' Liens* §§ 1–354 (1948).

[29] Pennsylvania Electric Equipment Co. v. Phoenixville Hospital, 37 Pa. County Ct. 671 (1910).

they relate to the interests of the insured. An insurance survey of a college will usually reveal many conditions demanding attention and correction. If such a survey is conducted by experts, it may be the means of saving the institution large sums. The college administrator responsible for the procurement of insurance for his institution should acquire as much technical information on the subject as possible.[30] Few areas of administration offer greater opportunities for the conservation of resources.

INSURANCE SURVEYS. An insurance survey includes the following: (1) An analysis of the hazards and how they may be reduced or eliminated, (2) an analysis of present insurance coverage—its adequacy and cost, and (3) recommendations for adequate insurance protection at minimum cost.

Insurance premiums are based upon the hazards as appraised by rating experts. An analysis of the insurance rates of your college buildings will frequently suggest corrective measures, resulting in substantial savings. It may be to the financial advantage of an institution to become self-insured in some areas, if adequate insurance reserves have been accumulated. These are problems requiring the advice of disinterested experts and the careful study of management.

PROPERTY INSURANCE. It is considered good practice to have one property insurance contract form, with scheduled coverage of individual buildings and their contents, providing protection against loss by fire, windstorm, cyclone, tornado, hail, explosion, riot, smoke, aircraft, vehicle, vandalism, and malicious mischief. By having one standard contract form, the possibility of gaps in the wall of protection is reduced, even though the actual insurance may be written by a number of companies.

INSURABLE INTEREST. It is basic to the law of insurance that one must have an insurable interest in property in order to obtain insurance on it. This means that you cannot insure the property of another unless you have some responsibility for its care or protection.

---

[30] Erwin W. Patterson, *Essentials of Insurance Law* (2d ed.; New York: McGraw-Hill Book Co., 1957); John H. Magee, *Property Insurance* (3d ed.; Homewood, Ill.: Richard D. Irwin, 1955); Albert H. Mowbray and Ralph H. Blanchard, *Insurance, Its Theory and Practice in the United States* (4th ed.; New York: McGraw-Hill Book Co., 1955); William H. Rodda, *Fire and Property Insurance* (Englewood Cliffs, N.J.: Prentice-Hall, 1956).

This rule of law also means that, in general, one cannot insure property for more than its cash value at the time of loss, or, perhaps better stated, one cannot collect insurance in excess of the actual cash value of the property destroyed or lost. The rationale for this legal principle is that insurance cannot be converted into a mere gamble or wager, that it is contrary to public policy to permit one to be benefited, rather than merely compensated, for loss, and that the "moral hazard" is too great if one were permitted to collect more than the value of the property lost or destroyed.

THE "VALUED" POLICY. Despite this general principle of the common law of insurance, by statute insurance companies in some states are permitted to write what is termed a "valued" policy, wherein the amount to be paid in the event of total loss is stipulated, without reference to the actual value of the property at the time of loss.[31] Under such a contract, it is possible to obtain coverage for the total cost of replacement of a building, at present construction costs. Some colleges have found this a very valuable feature.

THE COINSURANCE CLAUSE. Probably the greatest concealed hazard in the typical property insurance contract is what is known as the "coinsurance clause." This is an agreement between the insurer and the insured that, in consideration of a reduced premium, the insured will maintain insurance on his property at an amount not less than a stipulated percentage of its cash value.

Since it is a matter of common knowledge that the great majority of fire losses are partial rather than total, there is a tendency to underinsure property. In order to encourage higher coverage, insurance companies offer a substantial reduction in insurance rates if one will agree to carry 80, 90, or 100 percent of the full insurable value of the property. In order to protect themselves against failure on the part of the insured to keep his side of the bargain, the insurance companies stipulate that, in the event of loss, if it should be found

---

[31] Valued policies may be written in twenty-two states: Arkansas, California, Delaware, Florida, Iowa, Kansas, Kentucky, Louisiana, Minnesota, Mississippi, Missouri, Montana, Nebraska, New Hampshire, North Dakota, Ohio, South Carolina, South Dakota, Tennessee, Texas, West Virginia, and Wisconsin. They apply only in the event of a total loss. A building is considered to be a total loss, even though some part of it remains standing, if a prudent builder would tear down the structure to the foundation before rebuilding. See 49 *Colum. L. Rev.* 818 (1949).

that the insurance in force was less than the agreed percentage, the owner of the property becomes a coinsurer with the company to the extent of the underinsurance. This means that the owner is unable to collect the full amount of his loss, even if the loss is substantially less than the amount of the insurance carried. The possible magnitude of this penalty for underinsurance may be emphasized by an example.

If we assume that the actual insurable value of the property at the time of the loss was $500,000, that the insurance contract contained an 80 percent coinsurance clause, that the insurance in force was only $300,000, and that the loss was $300,000, the insurance company would be required to pay only $225,000, not $300,000. The calculation is simple. The amount of insurance that should have been carried, that is, 80 percent of $500,000, is $400,000. The actual amount carried, $300,000, is three-fourths the required amount. Therefore, the owner is deemed to be a coinsurer to the extent of the underinsurance, that is, one-fourth. He must therefore assume one-fourth of the loss, or $75,000, and he can collect only $225,000 from the insurance company for a $300,000 loss.

Due to inflation, the insurable value of a building may increase more rapidly than it is reduced by depreciation. Unless its present value is determined periodically by accepted appraisal methods and this value is checked against the insurance in force, the owner may be exposed to potential loss of some magnitude.

OBJECTS OF ART AND RARE BOOKS. An exhibition of objects of art belonging to others may subject the institution to unusual hazard unless the terms of the loan agreement are scrutinized before execution and arrangements made for adequate insurance coverage while en route and on exhibition. Objects of art received as gifts may not require replacement if lost or destroyed. This question may require a review of the terms and conditions of the gift by counsel.

The insurance of art objects and other property of the college presenting difficulties of realistic appraisal, such as rare books, should be given careful consideration. If such items are included under an insurance policy subject to a coinsurance covenant, the difficulty of appraisal may give rise to disagreement and possible litigation in the event of loss. If they need not be replaced if lost or destroyed, the insurance premiums paid for their protection may represent an unnecessary expense to the college. Self-insurance may be the answer to the problem.

OTHER FORMS OF PROPERTY INSURANCE. In addition to the risks protected by the standard fire, windstorm, and extended coverage policy, the college administrator should give consideration to the other hazards to which the property in his care may be exposed.

Boiler and machinery insurance offers reimbursement for losses resulting from the rupture, bursting, fracture, or cracking of boilers, air tanks, and other pressure vessels and the burnout or breaking of motors, pumps, and other machinery. Periodic inspection by competent engineers is one of the most valuable features of this form of insurance.

Since risk of loss is on the owner during process of construction, provision for builder's risk insurance should be made at the time the construction contract is executed. Other forms of property insurance may be needed under special circumstances, such as sprinkler risk and plate glass, use and occupancy, earthquake, flood, and aviation insurance.

FIDELITY AND THEFT INSURANCE. It is good practice to require that all employees responsible for the collection or custody of cash or negotiable securities be placed under bond. The by-laws of some institutions demand this coverage and impose upon the independent auditors the responsibility of verifying the adequacy of this coverage in their report to the members of the governing board. Positions, not individuals, should be specified in the fidelity insurance contract, so that anyone delegated to perform the functions of the position will be covered.

In addition to fidelity bond protection, the hazards of forgery, burglary, and robbery should be covered by insurance. One comprehensive insurance contract can give protection against all these risks, and, in borderline cases, eliminate the problem of proof as to just how the loss was incurred.

LIABILITY INSURANCE. As a general rule of common law, one is responsible for loss or injury suffered by others as the result of his own negligence and that of his agents and employees. By statute, an employer is held responsible for injuries to his employees arising out of and incurred in the course of their employment, regardless of any question of negligence.[32] To protect themselves, property owners and employers

---

[32] No state workmen's compensation act covers all employees. In general, agricultural, domestic service, and casual employment are exempted. See "State Workmen's Compensation Acts," pp. 153–55; for a discussion of the tort liability of employees, see "Tort Liability of Faculty and Staff," pp. 80–81.

may obtain various types of liability insurance. These include owner's, landlord's, and tenant's liability insurance; workmen's compensation insurance; and automobile, elevator, boiler explosion, malpractice, and contingent liability insurance. A comprehensive form may be obtained in some states, giving protection against a multiplicity of hazards.

SELF-INSURANCE. Liability insurance policies, as well as property insurance policies, may include a deductible provision whereby the insured assumes responsibility for losses and penalties up to a stipulated total. Since the majority of insurance claims are small, a major fraction of insurance premiums may represent the administrative cost of adjusting minor claims. By reducing the number of claims, a deductible clause in the policy may permit a substantial reduction in premium cost. It may also permit the insured to become, to an increasing degree, self-insured. By the accumulation of an insurance reserve, as a result of reduced premiums, the extent of self-insurance may be increased from year to year.

Because of the wide geographical distribution of risks, a state may, with some degree of safety, assume the burden of self-insurance of its properties.

THE TORT IMMUNITY OF EDUCATIONAL INSTITUTIONS

To what extent are colleges and universities liable for the negligence of their officers, employees, and agents? Any attempt to answer this question necessarily must be incomplete because the courts of the different states are not in agreement, and there is a strong trend to adopt new doctrines as social conditions evolve. Although the publicly controlled as well as the privately controlled colleges and universities may within a given jurisdiction enjoy practically the same degree of tort immunity, their immunity rests upon quite different legal concepts.

THE TORT IMMUNITY OF STATE COLLEGES. The state college or university, as an instrumentality of the sovereign power of government, exercising and conducting a necessary function of government (in contradistinction to the so-called proprietary functions of government) is usually immune from suit. This immunity is based upon the medieval philosophy of English common law, carried over into our American jurisdictions without adequate rationalization, and expressed in the legal maxim, "The King can do no wrong."

In the absence of statutory permission, no one may bring suit against a sovereign state or an instrumentality thereof for injuries inflicted in the exercise of its sovereign functions. Education is recognized as a primary or sovereign function of government. Hence, it follows that a public institution of higher education is immune from suit unless the state has seen fit, by statute, to set up administrative or judicial machinery to hear and adjudicate claims.[33]

THE IMMUNITY OF CHARITABLE CORPORATIONS. The tort immunity of the privately controlled and endowed university or college may be traced through the English law of charities, with the doctrine first clearly stated in a case before the House of Lords in 1846, *Feoffees of Heriot's Hospital v. Ross*.[34] This case, subsequently criticized and repudiated in part by the same English court,[35] did not even involve a tort claim. However, a mere dictum of the court has been relied upon by many American courts for the basis of what is termed the "trust fund doctrine" of immunity of charities; that is, to permit a recovery of damages from the trust property would result in a diversion of charitable trust funds from the purpose for which they were given.[36]

In some jurisdictions, an attempt is made to classify the issues by making a distinction between the situation wherein the claimant is one who has been benefited directly by the charitable funds (a student in a college, a patient in a hospital), as contrasted with a stranger to the charity (a member of the general public). Other distinctions drawn include a patient who had paid something for his services in the hospital, as against one who has paid nothing. Other courts make a distinction between the administration of the educational plant or hospital building and the supervision of property owned by the charity but used for commercial purposes for the production of endowment income, such as a downtown office building.[37] Only a careful analysis of all important cases on the subject within a given jurisdiction will indicate the degree and scope of the liability of charities in that state.

THE TRUST FUND THEORY. If the trust fund theory is adopted by the courts of a state, it follows necessarily that a charitable institution is

---

[33] For a more detailed discussion of this question of state immunity, see "The Constitutional Immunities of Public Institutions of Higher Education," p. 267.

[34] 12 Cl. & Fin. 507, 8 Eng. Rep. 1508 (H. L. 1846).

[35] Mercy Docks Trustee v. Gibb, 11 H. L. Cas. 686, 11 Eng. Rep. 1500 (1866).

[36] See Annot. 14 *A.L.R.* 572 (1921); Comment, 34 *Yale L.J.* 316 (1925); 72 *U. Pa. L. Rev.* 443 (1924).

[37] Gambel v. Vanderbilt University, 138 Tenn. 616, 200 S.W. 510 (1917).

under no liability either to a recipient of benefits, to an employee, or to a stranger, and it is immaterial whether the injury was the fault of an employee or of his employer. Such a sweeping exemption has been granted by few jurisdictions.

RESPONDEAT SUPERIOR. Another and less sweeping doctrine is that of *respondeat superior*. A master is held responsible for the negligence of his servant, a principal for his agent, on the ground that he derives a profit or benefit from the acts of his servants, and must, therefore, accept the burden of those acts with the benefits. This rationalization of vicarious liability of an employer obviously breaks down if no profit is derived by the principal, and under this theory the charitable institution is not liable for the negligence of the trustee, either in his conduct of the charity or in the selection and retention of improper or incompetent employees. A variation of this *respondeat superior* theory has been termed "the New York doctrine," which exempts hospitals from liability for the negligence of doctors and nurses on the theory that they are, in effect, in the service of the patient and not of the hospital and that the hospital has performed its full duty in exercising due care in their selection and retention.[38]

THE WAIVER THEORY. Other courts, in search of abstract justice in the situations presented to them, have evolved what might be called the "waiver theory" of immunity. Courts have been reluctant to refuse recovery for injuries to employees and strangers but have felt that it would be unjust to permit one who was a direct recipient of the charity, such as a student in a college or a patient in a hospital, to deplete further the funds available for charitable use by claims for compensation. This theory was stated first with clarity in 1901 when a federal court declared that an individual, by his very act of accepting the benefit of a charity, waived any right to hold it liable in damages for injuries.[39] Recovery by a charity patient would thus be barred but would be permitted if it were shown that the patient or student paid his full cost of service rendered.

THE DOCTRINE OF PUBLIC POLICY. Other courts, recognizing the futility of rationalization, have fallen back on the broad, if ambiguous, doctrine of public policy. In the last analysis, it is public policy, or at

[38] Schloendorff v. New York Hospital, 211 N.Y. 125, 105 N.E. 92 (1914); Note, "Damage Liability of Charitable Institutions," 19 *Mich. L. Rev.* 395 (1921).

[39] Powers v. Mass. Homeopathic Hospital, 109 Fed. 294 (1st Cir. 1901).

least a judge's concept thereof, that is the real support for whatever exemption from tort liability charities now enjoy. Some have questioned the soundness of a public policy that would permit the loss to fall upon the individual rather than shift it to the charity.

RECENT TRENDS. In 1942 Wiley Blount Rutledge, trained as a professor of law, delivered a devastating opinion against this rule of charitable immunity. At the time, he was serving as an associate justice in the U.S. Court of Appeals for the District of Columbia, but a year later he was appointed a member of the Supreme Court of the United States. The decision,[40] involving Georgetown University, has had a profound effect upon the law of torts in this country. It was the first case to come before his court involving the liability of a charitable corporation for the injury of an employee negligently inflicted by another employee in the course of duty. It afforded Mr. Justice Rutledge an opportunity to review the entire doctrine of charitable immunity. The following are excerpts from his opinion:

> Paradoxes of principle, fictional assumptions of fact, and confused results characterize judicial disposition of these claims. From full immunity, through varied but inconsistent qualifications to general responsibility is the gamut of decision. The cases are almost riotous with dissent. Reasons are more varied than results. These are the earmarks of law in flux. They indicate something wrong in the beginning or that something has become wrong since then.
> . . . .
> In taking this view, we are not unmindful that charitable institutions perform a high service in the community. In days when the state was less mindful of individual need, they gave a helping hand not otherwise held out to a large number of people. They still do.
> For reasons already stated, we do not believe the survival of charities will turn on whether or not they must answer for their wrongs to persons they are formed to help. . . . The incorporated charity should respond as do private individuals, business corporations and others, when they do good the wrong way.

By 1955 the courts of only twelve states—Arkansas, Idaho, Kentucky, Maine, Massachusetts, Missouri, Oregon, Pennsylvania, South Carolina, West Virginia, Wisconsin, and Wyoming—were still recognizing the doctrine of complete immunity for charities.[41] Later in 1955, Mis-

---

[40] President & Directors of Georgetown College [*sic*] v. Hughes, 76 U.S. App. D.C. 123, 130 F.2d 810 (1942).

[41] William L. Prosser, *Handbook of the Law of Torts* (2d ed.; St. Paul, Minn.: West Publishing Co., 1955), p. 786.

souri[42] abandoned its rule of long standing and held that a charitable corporation was liable for negligence in the maintenance of its income-producing or rental properties, and in 1957 Kentucky[43] followed Missouri in adopting this same rule of law.

Thus, it is clear that this historic wall of defense, erected by the courts to protect charitable and educational institutions, is in ruins, and it would seem a reasonably safe prediction that, by another decade, there will be little left of it to remind us of the principle first stated more than one hundred years ago.[44]

RETROACTIVE EFFECT OF JUDICIAL DECISIONS. On April 28, 1958, the New Jersey Supreme Court, in a series of three decisions, swept away the last vestige of the wall of immunity in that jurisdiction.[45] Members of the New Jersey Legislature, evidently unwilling to expose charitable corporations to the full impact of these decisions, on July 22, 1958, adopted legislation which nullified, in part, their effect. By the provisions of the act,[46] only nonprofit hospitals were made liable for the negligence of their employees and agents, and they, to the extent of only $10,000, to which interest and the cost of suit are added.

The legislation was made retroactive to January 1, 1956. However, a New Jersey court, on January 19, 1959, ruled that the legislature could not give effect to its will retroactively in this matter.[47] To do so, declared the court, would destroy a vested property right of an individual injured in the interval between the date of the 1958 decisions and the date of the remedial legislation. To a layman, it may seem strange that a court of law would deny to the legislature the power to extend protection, retroactively, to charitable corporations exposed to the hazard of litigation by a judicial decision which was, in its effects, retroactive.[48] The act in question expired by its own terms on

---

[42] Blatt v. Geo. H. Nettleton Home for Aged Women, 365 Mo. 30, 275 S.W.2d 344 (1955).

[43] Roland v. Catholic Archdiocese of Louisville, 301 S.W.2d 574 (Ky. Ct. App. 1957).

[44] See 62 Temp. L.Q. 96 (1958).

[45] Dalton v. St. Luke Catholic Church, 27 N.J. 22, 141 A.2d 273 (1958); Collopy v. Newark Eye & Ear Infirmary, 27 N.J. 29, 141 A.2d 276 (1958); Benton v. Y.M.C.A., 27 N.J. 67, 141 A.2d 298 (1958).

[46] N.J. Stat. Ann. § 16: 1–49 (Supp. 1958).

[47] Terracciona v. Magee, 53 N.J. Super. 557, 148 A.2d 68 (1959).

[48] See 60 Harv. L. Rev. 437 (1947); Dean Stanley Samad, of the College of Law of the University of Akron, suggested the following comment: "Ohio appeared to be on its way in joining the trend in Avellone v. St. John's Hospital, 165 Ohio St. 467, 135 N.E.2d 410 (1956) but that decision was emasculated by Gibbon v. Y.M.C.A., 170 Ohio St. 280 (1960)."

June 30, 1959, but the legislature, after public hearings, decided to enact permanent legislation containing the same provisions.[49] However, the legislature did not again attempt to give retroactive effect to the act.

LEGAL REVISION THE DUTY OF THE LEGISLATURE. A 1958 Pennsylvania decision is authority for the doctrine that the legislature, rather than a judge on the bench, should be the agency for so radical a change in the law of torts.[50] In a sweeping decision, upholding the Pennsylvania rule of complete charitable immunity, the court was of the opinion that, since the rule, although judge-made, had become so firmly established as part of the common law of the state, it should be abrogated, not by a court ruling upon the effect of acts already committed, but by the legislature, after full public debate of the issues involved. Thus, fair warning to all concerned could be given before the law is changed.

GOOD PUBLIC RELATIONS. Even though educational institutions in some jurisdictions still enjoy complete tort immunity, it may be good public relations to carry liability insurance.[51] If such insurance is purchased, a clause should be inserted in the policy prohibiting the insurance company from pleading the immunity of its insured as a defense without the written consent of the institution.

WORKMEN'S COMPENSATION ACTS

Workmen's compensation legislation has been enacted by all of the states and Puerto Rico.[52] Such legislation is designed to assure prompt payment of benefits to injured employees or to the dependents of those

---

[49] *Laws of 1959,* ch. 90; *N.J. Stat. Ann.* 2A: 53A–7 (1959 Supp.).

[50] Knecht v. St. Mary's Hospital, 392 Pa. 75, 140 A.2d 30 (1958).

[51] Mr. B. E. Morrison, assistant counsel for Oklahoma State University, read this handbook in manuscript. The following is his comment: "It may be well to point out that the purchase of liability insurance by a state agency or public educational corporation in some states may be prohibited by constitutional or other prohibitions against the making of gifts of public funds. It would appear that the premium paid to protect the State against liability which cannot legally attach would be a gift of public funds to the insurer. In this connection it might be mentioned that personal liability insurance protecting the employee could be obtained without violation of gift prohibitions by considering the premiums as additional compensation to the covered employee." See the discussion of liability insurance, "Liability Insurance" and "The New Mexico College Case," pp. 269 and 270.

[52] Bruce Alden Greene, *State Workmen's Compensation Laws as of September 1950,* U.S. Bureau of Labor Standards, Bulletin No. 125 (Washington: Government Printing Office, 1952); see also the discussion in chap. 3 of "State Workmen's Compensation Acts," p. 79.

killed in industry, regardless of who was at fault in the accident. Under the common law, if an injured worker sued his employer for damages, he had to prove that the employer had been negligent. Furthermore, the employer was entitled to all the customary common law defenses —that is, that the employee, by his act of accepting employment, had assumed the normal risks of the industry and that the accident had been caused by the negligence of "fellow servants" or by the contributory negligence of the employee himself. Under a workmen's compensation act, the question of fault or blame for the accident is not raised[53] since, under the rationale of this type of legislation, industrial accidents are considered part of the expense of production, to be borne by the public, not the burden of the injured worker or his family.

In twenty-eight states, the workmen's compensation acts are compulsory, that is, they require every employer within the scope of the act to accept the act and pay the compensation specified. However, in twenty-six of these states, the employer has the option of either accepting or rejecting the act, but, in case he rejects it, he loses his customary common law defenses.

To make certain that benefit payments will be made when due, the legislation requires that the covered employer shall either obtain insurance or shall give proof of his financial qualifications to carry his own risk. Seven states and Puerto Rico require employers to insure their risks in a state fund. In eleven states, employers may choose whether they will insure their risks in the state fund, with private insurance companies, or qualify as self-insurers.

THE UNIVERSITY OF DENVER CASE. In 1950, a student at the University of Denver was employed by the university to perform certain work in and about the tennis courts and to take care of the furnace at the faculty club. While engaged in football practice, he received an injury to his back. Fifteen months after his injury he filed claim with the Industrial Commission of Colorado for compensation, contending

---

[53] The following is the comment of Dean Stanley Samad: "With regard to workmen's compensation acts, 'fault' is ordinarily not at issue. However, there is proscribed conduct which either denies or reduces compensation if the injury or death was caused by conduct of the employee falling within the proscribed category (intoxication, intentional self-infliction of injury, etc.). See Riesenfeld & Maxwell, *Modern Social Legislation* (1950), pp. 290–91. Failure to comply with workmen's compensation laws often results in the imposition of (unlimited) common law liability."

that he had been employed to play football and that his injury arose out of and was incurred in the course of his employment. His claim was allowed by the commission, and the ruling was sustained by the Supreme Court of Colorado.[54]

THE FORT LEWIS COLLEGE CASE. A similar case arose, also in Colorado, in 1955. A student at Fort Lewis Agricultural and Mechanical College was fatally injured in a football game. His widow filed a claim under the state workmen's compensation act. Her claim was granted by the commission, but this time the state supreme court did not sustain the commission. The court was of the opinion that, since continuation of his employment by the college had not been made contingent upon his playing football, he had not been injured in line of duty.[55]

THE TAX STATUS OF COLLEGE PROPERTY

Exemption from taxation is not an inherent right of educational institutions. It is a privilege granted or withheld by the state as a matter of public policy. Either by constitutional provision, by statute or by court interpretation, every state in this country has granted this privilege to nonprofit institutions of higher education incorporated therein.[56] Most of the litigation in this area is concerned with the legal status of property used for noninstructional purposes.

THE PROPERTY OF TAX-SUPPORTED COLLEGES. Logically, there is no reason for the state to tax the property of its own institutions.[57] However, the legal status of publicly controlled institutions of higher education was not as clear-cut during the eighteenth and nineteenth cen-

---

[54] University of Denver v. Nemeth, 127 Colo. 385, 257 P.2d 423 (1953).

[55] State Compensation Insurance Fund v. Industrial Commission, 137 Colo. 570, 314 P.2d 288 (1957).

[56] See Appendix, pp. 279–304, for a state-by-state summary of the constitutional and statutory provisions granting exemption to the property of nonpublic institutions of higher education.

[57] The following is an excerpt from 24 So. Cal. L. Rev. 252, 268–69 (1951): "Although there is no true 'exemption' involved in freeing publicly owned property from taxation, assuming the same amount of public expenditures in each case, the practical effect of freeing mathematically increases the tax rate on the remaining subject property to the same extent as would follow for a true 'exemption' of private property of the same value. When publicly owned property of a subordinate state agency is located within its own boundary, no practical detriment to the private citizen results from its omission from the tax base.

. . . .

"But this does not hold true if the publicly owned property is owned by a dif-

turies as it is today, and there has been considerable litigation of record[58] on the question of the taxability of their property. The courts have ruled that if the state institution holds full title to the property, it is exempt from taxation, but if the title is less than that of complete ownership, the property is not exempt. Thus, property held by the University of Illinois as trustee, with income from the trust to be used for scholarships and agricultural research, was held to be subject to taxation.[59]

PROPERTY EXEMPTION BY CHARTER RIGHT. The majority of institutions of higher education in America enjoy exemption from property taxation as the result of general statutory or constitutional provisions applicable to all charitable and educational institutions within the state of incorporation. A fortunate few, however, have been granted complete exemption from taxation on all their property, even that held as investment of endowment funds. Since their grant of tax immunity was received as the result of a special act of legislation, without a reservation of the power to amend the charter rights thus granted, the courts have held that it constitutes an irrevocable contract between the state and the incorporators which cannot be impaired without violating the federal Constitution. This is the doctrine of the famous Dartmouth College case,[60] enunciated by the Supreme Court of the United States

---

ferent entity. In such case, the result of omission to tax the property of the foreign identity is identically the same as would occur from the exemption of privately owned property in the same amount, with the consequent increase of burden on the private taxpayer. First exemplified in the acquisition by San Francisco of watersheds located in other counties, and soon followed by the development of Los Angeles water system situated, in large part, hundreds of miles from its municipal boundaries, omission of publicly owned property from the tax base in certain counties, by the end of the first decade of the Twentieth Century, had raised certain fiscal problems. This resulted in the amendment to the state constitution expressly to require continued taxation of publicly owned property, acquired by an entity outside its boundaries, to the extent it had been taxable in prior private ownership."

[58] Board of Trustees of Illinois Industrial University v. Board of Supervisors of Champaign County, 76 Ill. 184 (1875); Auditor General v. Regents of the University, 83 Mich. 467, 47 N.W. 440 (1890); City of Detroit v. George, 214 Mich. 664, 183 N.W. 789 (1921); Board of Regents of Kansas State Agricultural College v. Hamilton, 28 Kan. 376 (1882); Oswalt v. Hallowell, 15 Kan. 154 (1875); Dickinson County v. Baldwin, 29 Kan. 538 (1883); *In re* Macky, 46 Colo. 79, 102 Pac. 1075 (1909).

[59] People v. University of Illinois, 328 Ill. 377, 159 N.E. 811 (1927), People v. University of Illinois, 357 Ill. 369, 192 N.E. 243 (1934).

[60] Trustees of Dartmouth College v. Woodward, 17 U.S. (4 Wheat.) 518 (1819). See Joseph H. Zumbalen, "The Federal Constitution and Contract Exemption from

in 1819. Although it did not involve a question of taxation, the Dartmouth College case established the contractual character of charters of incorporation granted by special legislative action, and, according to Section 10 of Article I of the federal Constitution: "No state shall . . . pass any . . . law impairing the obligation of contracts."

During the period of internal expansion and development of this country just preceding and following the Civil War, the legislatures of many of our states granted special charters of incorporation on generous terms to banks, railroads, and canal companies to encourage the rapid exploitation of our natural resources. Within a few years, the taxpayers realized that this tendency of the legislature to relinquish its sovereign power to tax should be curbed. As a result, state constitutions were amended, prohibiting such action. However, once issued without reserved power to amend, these special charters could not be recalled.

Four institutions of higher education holding these valuable charters are located in the State of Missouri: Lindenwood College,[61] Westminster College,[62] William Jewell College,[63] and Washington University.[64] Other states were also generous. Northwestern University[65] in Illinois, Sheffield Scientific School[66] of Yale University in Connecticut, Hamline University[67] in Minnesota, Brown University[68] in Rhode Island, Whitman College[69] in Washington, Colorado Seminary[70] (University of Denver) in Colorado, and the University of the South[71] in Tennessee were granted similar charter exemption.

Taxation," 17 *St. Louis L. Rev.* 191 (1932). Robert Eugene Cushman, *Leading Constitutional Decisions* (9th ed.; New York: Appleton-Century-Crofts, 1950), p. 215.

[61] No litigation of record.

[62] State v. Board of Trustees of Westminster College, 175 Mo. 52, 74 S.W. 990 (1903).

[63] State v. Trustees of William Jewell College, 234 Mo. 299, 136 S.W. 397 (1911); Trustees of William Jewell College v. Beavers, 351 Mo. 87, 171 S.W.2d 604 (1943).

[64] Washington University v. Rouse, 75 U.S. (8 Wall.) 439 (1869); Washington University v. Bauman, 341 Mo. 708, 108 S.W.2d 403 (1937).

[65] Northwestern University v. Illinois, 99 U.S. 309 (1879).

[66] New Haven v. Sheffield Scientific School, 59 Conn. 163, 22 Atl. 156 (1890).

[67] County of Nobles v. Hamline University, 46 Minn. 316, 48 N.W. 1119 (1891).

[68] Brown University v. Granger, 19 R.I. 704, 36 Atl. 720 (1897).

[69] Berryman v. Board of Trustees of Whitman College, 222 U.S. 334 (1912).

[70] County Commissioners v. Colorado Seminary, 12 Colo. 497, 21 Pac. 490 (1889); Colorado Seminary v. Arapahoe County, 30 Colo. 507, 71 Pac. 410 (1903); City and County of Denver v. Colorado Seminary, 96 Colo. 109, 41 P.2d 1109 (1934).

[71] Fetton v. University of the South, 208 U.S. 489 (1908).

THE WILLIAM JEWELL COLLEGE CASE. These valuable charters have been under almost continual legal assault since they were granted. In 1953, the Supreme Court of Missouri again sustained the validity of the charter exemption granted to William Jewell College in 1849.[72] The case arose as the result of the purchase by the college, in 1943, of a foundry, owned and operated by the Century Electric Company. Immediately after the purchase, the college leased the property back to the company for a term of twenty-five years, with provision for renewal. The Collector of Revenue for the City of St. Louis assessed real estate taxes against this property for the years 1945, 1946, and 1947, and in December 1949 he filed suit for the payment of these tax bills.

Attorneys for the college, in defending the suit, called the attention of the court to the many decisions upholding the validity of such charter exemption from taxation. In view of this weight of precedent, the court, by a unanimous decision, en banc, ordered the cancellation of the tax bills in question and granted an injunction restraining the further assessment of the property as long as it is owned by the college. In his opinion, Judge Tipton stated:

> there can be no doubt that the trustees had a right to purchase the tract of land on which the foundry is located, and as long as the rents therefrom are used for the benefit of education, the tract is exempt from all taxes. The tax exemptions granted to William Jewell College are not limited to real estate actually occupied and directly used to support the educational establishments.

CRITICISM AND JUSTIFICATION OF THE DOCTRINE. Some students of constitutional law have been critical of the courts' steadfast determination to uphold the validity of these charter rights. Hugh E. Willis has this to say:

> Undoubtedly, it should be held that, even if a charter of a corporation is a contract, it should be subject to the exercise of all these sovereign powers: taxation, police, and eminent domain. The Supreme Court has corrected the original mistake of the Dartmouth College Case except for taxation and the rate and franchises of public utilities. It should finish the work which it has begun and make contracts subject to every form of the exercise of all of these sovereign powers.[73]

On the other hand, Thomas M. Cooley asserts that there is strong social justification for the continuation of these grants of tax immunity.

---

[72] State v. Trustees of William Jewell College, 364 Mo. 199, 260 S.W.2d 479 (1953).

[73] Willis, *Constitutional Law in the United States* (Bloomington, Ind.: Principia Press, 1936), p. 620.

If the tax cases are to be regarded as an exception . . . the exception is perhaps to be considered as a nominal rather than a real one, since taxation is for the purpose of providing the state a revenue, and the state laws which have been enforced as contracts in these cases have been supposed to be based upon consideration, by which the state receives the benefit which would have accrued from an exercise of the relinquished power in the ordinary mode.[74]

RECENT TRENDS. All direct legal assaults upon tax exemption by charter right have failed. An indirect impairment of this privilege may result from a decision of the United States Supreme Court in 1958.[75] Federal property had long enjoyed immunity from state and local taxation even when loaned or leased to private corporations under contract with the Federal Government to supply needed commodities or services. Much to the surprise of some constitutional authorities, the high federal court upheld the validity of a Michigan statute imposing a use tax on federal property in the hands of private contractors. The state tax was measured by the value of the property itself, not by the value of the leasehold interest of the private contractor. Courts have, for many years, held that the exemption of a property owner from taxation does not prevent the taxation of the value of the leasehold.[76]

However, this 1958 decision of the high federal court went much further. It permitted a state to levy a tax computed upon the full value of exempt property used for private gain, not merely upon the value of the leasehold interest therein.

Encouraged by this trend, legislators in many states hastened to revise their tax laws in order to obtain much-needed additional revenue from property formerly exempt. Unless these statutes specifically exempt the income-producing property of charitable and educational corporations, tax exemption by charter right may become merely an episode in the history of taxation.

THE EFFECT OF PROFIT ON TAX EXEMPTION. In 1908 the Superior Court of Pennsylvania denied property exemption to Mercersburg College on the grounds that, for a period of five years, its receipts from students' fees were in excess of its operating expenses.[77] The court refused to

---

[74] Cooley, *Constitutional Limitations* (8th ed.; Boston: Little, Brown & Co., 1927), p. 579.

[75] United States v. City of Detroit, 355 U.S. 466 (1958); *see also* United States v. Township of Muskegon, 355 U.S. 466 (1958); and City of Detroit v. Murray Corp., 355 U.S. 489 (1958); 13 *Wyo. L.J.* 229 (1959).

[76] See Annot. 23 *A.L.R.* 248 (1923).

[77] Mercersburg College v. Poffenberger, 36 Pa. Super. 100 (1908).

recognize the validity of a journal entry, charging operating expense with the estimated rental value of the college physical plant. The court admitted that the college had been chartered and conducted as a non-profit charitable corporation, but it held that, in order to claim exemption under Pennsylvania statutes as a public charity, the institution must be barely self-supporting, that is, the income from student fees alone must not exceed the amount necessary to maintain the institution. This decision, of course, is not typical, but it shows how narrowly some courts have interpreted tax exemption legislation.

COLLEGE RESIDENCE HALLS EXEMPT FROM TAXATION. The first recorded case in this country to deal with the problem of the tax status of college residence halls involved the attempt, in 1899, of the town of New Haven to assess the dining halls and dormitories of Yale University. The court, in its opinion upholding[78] the freedom from taxation of such facilities, traced the history of the English college and university from the year 1200 and emphasized the importance of student housing as an essential element in the total educative process. This ruling was followed by the courts of Massachusetts,[79] Illinois,[80] and New York.[81] It remains the general rule today.

THE PRESIDENT'S RESIDENCE. By long-established tradition, a college president is granted the use of one of the college buildings as a residence. This is well recognized as one of the perquisites of his office. The courts have recognized this and granted tax exemption. One of the first cases in this country involved the president's house at Lafayette College in 1889. Although temporarily rented to one not associated with the college, it was held to be tax exempt.[82]

The presidents' residences at Amherst,[83] Harvard,[84] Kenyon,[85] Syra-

---

[78] Yale University v. Town of New Haven, 71 Conn. 316, 42 Atl. 87 (1899).

[79] President & Fellows of Harvard College v. Assessors of Cambridge, 175 Mass. 145, 55 N.E. 844 (1900).

[80] City of Chicago v. University of Chicago, 228 Ill. 605, 81 N.E. 1138 (1907).

[81] In re Syracuse University, 124 Misc. 788, 209 N.Y. Supp. 329 (Sup. Ct. 1925).

[82] Northampton County v. Lafayette College, 128 Pa. 132, 18 Atl. 516 (1889).

[83] Amherst College v. Assessors, 173 Mass. 232, 53 N.E. 815 (1899); Amherst College v. Assessors, 193 Mass. 168, 79 N.E. 248 (1906).

[84] President & Fellows of Harvard College v. Assessors of Cambridge, 175 Mass. 145, 55 N.E. 844 (1900).

[85] Kenyon College v. Schnebly, 12 Ohio C.C.R. (n.s.) 1, 21 Ohio C.C. Dec. 150 (1909); aff'd without opinion, 81 Ohio St. 513 (1909).

cuse University,[86] and Kansas Wesleyan University[87] have also been declared to be exempt property by the courts, despite the efforts of local tax authorities to assess them. Although the president's house at Syracuse University was located at some distance from the campus, and, in the opinion of the assessors, was more elaborate than necessary for a university president, the court disregarded the question thus raised.

FACULTY HOUSING. In 1837 an Ohio court was not willing to grant tax-exempt status to residences owned by Kenyon College and used as professors' residences,[88] but by 1909, in interpreting a more recent act of the legislature, the court ruled[89] that they should not be assessed. Faculty housing at Harvard,[90] Princeton,[91] Lafayette College,[92] Lehigh University,[93] and Griswold College[94] has been granted exemption. Houses owned by Williams College and occupied by professors, the registrar, the librarian, and the superintendent of buildings were denied exemption in 1897.[95] As late as 1947, a New Jersey court held[96] that faculty housing was not exempt from taxation in the absence of evidence that charges therefor were such as to return no profit to the college, in this case Stevens Institute of Technology.

HOUSING FOR MARRIED STUDENTS. The presence of married students in significant numbers on the college campus is a postwar phenomenon. In 1956 the taxing authorities of Berkeley, California, assessed two residence halls of the Pacific School of Religion housing married students. In its brief filed with the district court of appeals contesting the assessment, the school contended that the housing of married students and their families is now just as much a proper educational function as the housing of single students. The brief declared:

---

[86] *In re* Syracuse University, 124 Misc. 788, 209 N.Y. Supp. 329 (Sup. Ct. 1925).

[87] Kansas Wesleyan University v. Saline County Commissioners, 120 Kan. 496, 243 Pac. 1055 (1926).

[88] Kendrick v. Farquhar, 8 Ohio 189 (1837).

[89] Kenyon College v. Schnebly, 12 Ohio C.C.R. (n.s.) 1, 21 Ohio C.C. Dec. (1909); *aff'd without opinion*, 81 Ohio St. 513 (1909).

[90] President & Fellows of Harvard College v. Assessors of Cambridge, 175 Mass. 145, 55 N.E. 844 (1900).

[91] State v. Ross, 4 N.J. 497, 24 N.J.L. 497 (1854).

[92] Northampton County v. Lafayette College, 128 Pa. 132, 18 Atl. 516 (1889).

[93] Northampton County v. Lehigh University, 13 Pa. County Ct. 659 (1893).

[94] Trustees of Griswold College v. Iowa, 46 Iowa 275, 26 Am. Rep. 138 (1877).

[95] Williams College v. Assessors, 167 Mass. 505, 46 N.E. 394 (1897).

[96] City of Hoboken v. Division of Tax Appeals, 136 N.J.L. 328, 55 A.2d 291 (1947).

Before the influx of married veterans to campuses in recent years, colleges and universities did not feel they had much responsibility for housing married students. Recently, however, practically all the large institutions in this country, and many of the small ones as well, have been forced to provide some form of housing for this group of married students; . . .

The court agreed with the arguments in the brief and granted this exemption. Two divinity schools also contested the taxation of their housing for married students. The case of the Church Divinity School of the Pacific reached the appellate court and became the basis for the precedent upholding the tax-exempt character of this type of educational property in California.[97]

ATHLETIC FIELDS. In some states it has been difficult to persuade tax assessors and judges that athletic fields and football stadiums are sufficiently related to education to come within the scope of the tax exemption statutes. The athletic fields of Adelphi College[98] were subjected to taxation in 1905 and those of the Stevens Institute of Technology[99] in 1909 and again[100] in 1926.

In 1946 a New Jersey court declined to grant exemption to the million dollar stadium of Rutgers University.[101] The judge conceded that physical education is a proper subject of instruction, but he questioned the necessity of "stands to accommodate 20,000 spectators when the enrollment of the university is under 1,700." In the same year, the same court granted tax exemption to the athletic fields of the Stevens Institute of Technology.[102]

SERVICE FACILITIES. Apparently, the first case of record on this question involved the machine shop, pumping station, and icehouse of Haverford College in 1897. A Pennsylvania court ruled[103] that they were tax exempt. A Kentucky court, in a similar ruling,[104] sustained the tax ex-

---

97 Church Divinity School of the Pacific v. Alameda County, 152 Cal. App. 2d 496, 314 P.2d 209 (S.D. Cal. 1957).

98 People v. Wells, 98 App. Div. 237, 90 N.Y. Supp. 488, *aff'd without opinion,* 180 N.Y. 534, 72 N.E. 1147 (1905).

99 Trustees of Stevens Institute of Technology v. Bowes, collector, 78 N.J.L. 205, 73 Atl. 38 (Sup. Ct. 1909).

100 Stevens Institute of Technology v. State Board of Taxes & Assessments, 3 N.J. Misc. 1094, 130 Atl. 925 (Sup. Ct.), *aff'd,* 102 N.J.L. 727 (Sup. Ct. 1926).

101 Trustees of Rutgers University v. Piscataway Township, 134 N.J.L. 85, 46 A.2d 56 (1946).

102 City of Hoboken v. Division of Tax Appeals, 134 N.J.L. 594, 49 A.2d 587 (Sup. Ct. 1946).

103 Haverford College v. Rhoads, 6 Pa. Super. 71 (1897).

104 Commonwealth v. Berea College, 149 Ky. 95, 147 S.W. 929 (1912).

emption of the laundry, waterworks, printing plant, supply store, and hotel of Berea College, despite the protests of local businessmen that these facilities were patronized, to some extent, by the general public.

However, a pumping station, owned and operated by Kenyon College,[105] which supplied water to outsiders at a profit, and an electrical power plant of the Smallwood Memorial Institute,[106] also serving the public, were refused tax exemption.

COLLEGE FARMS. Farm land, if used by a college for instruction or research in agriculture, is usually exempted without question when the acreage held is not in excess of the limitation imposed by statute. A Texas court denied tax exemption to land used to supply food for the faculty and students of St. Edward's College.[107] If operated or leased to provide revenue for the college, farm land is generally held to be taxable property[108] unless the statute is sufficiently broad to exempt all property "used exclusively for school purposes."[109]

PROPERTY USED FOR RESEARCH. Since property used for research may, as a rule, be employed for purposes of instruction, the question of its taxability has rarely come before a court of record. In 1946 a New Jersey court ruled that a towing tank research laboratory, owned by the Stevens Institute of Technology, was exempt from taxation. The opinion of the court declared emphatically that research is an inherent function of institutions of higher education.[110]

PROPERTY HELD AS AN INVESTMENT. In general, real estate held by a college as an investment is not exempt from taxation. In 1943 the city of Louisville attempted to assess all income-producing property held therein by educational and other charitable institutions, despite a chain of court decisions extending back to 1896 which held that such property was not subject to taxation. The Kentucky court, in adhering to prior decisions thus construing the tax exemption statute, declared:

---

[105] Kenyon College v. Schnebly, 12 Ohio C.C.R. (n.s.) 1, 21 Ohio C.C. Dec. 150 (1909); *aff'd without opinion*, 81 Ohio St. 513 (1909).

[106] Commonwealth v. Smallwood Memorial Institute, 124 Va. 142, 97 S.E. 85 (1919).

[107] St. Edward's College v. Morris, 82 Tex. 1, 18 S.W. 512 (1891); *but see* State v. Fisk University, 87 Tenn. 233, 10 S.W. 284 (1889).

[108] Willamette University v. Knight, 35 Ore. 33, 56 Pac. 124 (1899); State v. Carleton College, 154 Minn. 280, 191 N.W. 400 (1923).

[109] Central Union Conference Association of College View v. Lancaster County, 109 Neb. 106, 189 N.W. 982 (1922).

[110] City of Hoboken v. Division of Tax Appeals, 134 N.J.L. 594, 49 A.2d 587 (N.J. Sup. Ct. 1946).

Property rights have vested on the faith of that construction. . . . To make it subject to taxation would materially impair its value and, in many instances, adversely affect the activities of the institution.[111]

EFFECT OF ADMISSION RESTRICTIONS ON TAX EXEMPTION. For years, the courts of Ohio, in their interpretation of a statute restricting tax exemption to property owned by "a public college or academy or a public institution of learning," had ruled that any restriction on the admission of students, other than those based upon educational qualifications, would deprive an institution of tax exemption.

In 1949 these decisions were disregarded as precedents in a case involving the property of the Cleveland Bible College. Admission of students was restricted to those of the Christian faith. The majority of the court was of the opinion that this limitation should not deprive the college of the privilege of tax exemption, but the decision was close, four to three.[112] The minority opinion declared that an institution must be open to all if it is to be considered "a public institution of learning."

COLLEGE FRATERNITY AND SORORITY HOUSES. In general, courts have held[113] that college fraternity and sorority houses are subject to taxation, just as any other private boarding house. However, a Kansas court in 1914 granted exemption[114] to a sorority house, and in the same year the Indiana legislature granted specific exemption to Greek-letter college fraternity houses. The exemption statute is still in force.[115] In 1920 an Indiana court ruled[116] that the word "fraternity" in the statute included organizations of either or both sexes. The Delaware[117] Legislature has extended the privilege of tax exemption to incorporated college fraternities, with a limit of $10,000 for each fraternity house. Fraternity houses at the University of Nevada are exempt by statute[118]

---

[111] City of Louisville v. Presbyterian Orphans Home Society, 299 Ky. 566, 186 S.W.2d 194 (1945).

[112] Cleveland Bible College v. Board of Appeals, 151 Ohio St. 258, 85 N.E.2d 284 (1949).

[113] Orono v. Sigma Alpha Epsilon Society, 105 Me. 214, 74 Atl. 19 (1909); Phi Beta Epsilon Corp. v. Boston, 182 Mass. 457, 65 N.E. 824 (1903); People v. Lawler, 74 App. Div. 553, 77 N.Y. Supp. 840 (1901), *aff'd*, 179 N.Y. 535, 71 N.E. 1136 (1904); Knox College v. Board of Review, 308 Ill. 160, 139 N.E. 56 (1923).

[114] Kappa Kappa Gamma House Ass'n v. Pearcy, 92 Kan. 1020, 142 Pac. 294 (1914).

[115] *Ind. Stat.* ch. 2, § 64–201 (1951).

[116] State v. Allen, 189 Ind. 369, 127 N.E. 145 (1920).

[117] *Del. Code Ann.* tit. 9, § 8105 (1953).

[118] *Nev. Rev. Stat.* § 361.100 (1957).

with a $5,000 limitation. North Dakota[119] and Vermont[120] have also followed this trend. However, the citizens of Georgia, on November 4, 1958, defeated by a 31,516 to 72,044 vote a proposed constitutional amendment that would have granted exemption to college fraternity and sorority houses.[121]

THE TAXATION OF UNRELATED BUSINESS INCOME

The Revenue Act of 1950, enacted into law at the second session of the Eighty-first Congress and approved by the President on September 23, 1950, marked a major milestone in the history of the tax problems of the colleges. For the first time, the general income of nonprofit educational and other charitable corporations was made subject, under certain conditions, to the federal income tax.

During the decade preceding the passage of this legislation, friends of certain educational institutions were tempted to take advantage of what appeared to be a loophole in the tax laws by purchasing large commercial enterprises and dedicating their entire net income to the support of education. Some institutions purchased large business properties with borrowed funds and leased the properties back to the original owners.

Congress closed this gap by levying a tax on the "unrelated business income" of charitable and educational institutions. The lawmakers were concerned only with income derived from activities unrelated to the primary objectives of tax-free organizations. In the case of income from the ownership of real estate, the act imposed a tax only if the property was acquired with borrowed capital and leased for a comparatively long term.[122]

EXEMPTION FROM FEDERAL EXCISE TAXES

In 1958 Congress granted to all nonprofit educational institutions the same exemption from federal excise taxes as that enjoyed by the public

---

[119] *N.D. Code* tit. 57, § 0208(11) (1943).

[120] *Vt. Stat. Ann.* tit. 32, § 3802(5) (1959).

[121] Letter to the author dated May 15, 1959, from the Office of the Attorney General for the State of Georgia; see 35 *A.L.R.* 1045 (1925), and 54 *A.L.R.* 1381 (1928).

[122] See 26 *U.S.C.* §§ 511–14 (1955) for the text of the code relating to "Imposition of Tax on Unrelated Business Income of Certain Exempt Organizations," "Unrelated Business Taxable Income," "Unrelated Trade or Business," and "Business Leases." See also 35 *Cornell L.Q.* 922 (1950); 60 *Yale L.J.* 851 (1951); Fikelstein, "Tax Exempt Charitable Corporations: Revenue Act of 1950," 50 *Mich. L. Rev.* 427 (1952).

institutions under their constitutional immunity. For years, privately controlled colleges were compelled to pay federal taxes levied on the purchase price of many of their items of equipment and on the cost of communication and transportation services. This discrimination was removed by the passage of the Excise Tax Technical Changes Act of 1958, effective January 1, 1959.[123] However, in order to claim the benefit of this exemption, the institution must execute and submit to the seller of the goods or services a properly executed exemption certificate.

FEDERAL PROPERTY AVAILABLE FOR EDUCATIONAL INSTITUTIONS

During and after World War II, institutions of higher education received much valuable property and equipment no longer required by the armed services and other federal agencies. The Federal Property and Administrative Services Act of 1949, as amended,[124] authorizes the Secretary of Health, Education, and Welfare to allocate federal surplus property to state agencies, which in turn distribute such property to eligible health and educational institutions. The act also provides for the transfer of federal surplus real property at a price that takes into consideration any benefit which may accrue to the United States because of its use. To be eligible to obtain this surplus federal property, privately controlled educational institutions must have qualified for exemption from the federal income tax under Section 501(c)(3) of the 1954 Internal Revenue Code.

Under the terms of the National Defense Education Act of 1958, public and privately controlled institutions of higher education are eligible to receive federal aid in the acquisition of scientific equipment.

---

[123] Temporary rules relating to the registration and exemption of nonprofit educational organizations were issued by the Internal Revenue Service by Tax Decision 6344, dated December 25, 1958: 23 Fed. Reg. 10344 (1959); see also *Federal Tax Regulations* 1959 at 1591–1601.

[124] Pub. L. No. 152, 81st Cong., 1st Sess. §§ 2–505 (1949), 63 *Stat.* 377.

CHAPTER VI

Research and Publication

ALTHOUGH research, the quest for new truths, and publication, their dissemination, have always been recognized as major functions of institutions of higher education, the great expansion of these functions in recent years has multiplied and emphasized their inherent legal problems. The growing burden of their administration[1] has prompted the establishment of separate divisions and of separate but related corporations. University research foundations and university presses demand the attention of competent legal counsel. However, even the smaller colleges have not escaped the pressure of events.

RESEARCH

Both government and industry have made increasing demands upon the colleges and their faculty during the past two decades. The negotiation of contracts for sponsored research has made it necessary for college administrators to consult more frequently with legal counsel. In negotiations with industry there is usually greater flexibility in the drafting of the terms of the agreement. With agencies of the Federal Government, one is usually compelled to accept many provisions of the standard contract form or reject the contract in its entirety.

THE "FINALITY CLAUSE" IN GOVERNMENT CONTRACTS. The call of patriotic duty to serve the government during the war and the cold war has induced many institutions to accept contracts with potentially burdensome provisions. One such standard provision is termed the "finality clause." The following is an excerpt from a typical government contract:

Article 15. Disputes—Except as otherwise specifically provided in this contract, all disputes concerning questions of fact arising under this contract

---

[1] See *College and University Business Administration* (2 vols.; Washington: American Council on Education, 1952 and 1955), II, 70–71, 129–50, for a discussion of the administrative problems raised by research and publication.

shall be decided by the contracting officer subject to written appeal by the contractor within 30 days to the head of the department concerned or his duly authorized representative, whose decision shall be final and conclusive upon the parties thereto.

THE WUNDERLICH CASE. Even at face value, this is a most one-sided arrangement, whereby one of the parties to a contract is given full and conclusive power to interpret all its provisions. As expanded in meaning by a decision of a federal court, this finality clause became even more burdensome.

In 1938 the Martin Wunderlich Company was awarded a contract by the Bureau of Reclamation to construct the Vallecito Dam in southern Colorado. The contract contained the standard clause in question. The dam was completed on schedule time, but the contracting officer refused to approve vouchers in the amount of $172,302.23. The construction company filed an appeal with the Secretary of the Interior, as required by the finality clause. The Secretary confirmed the decision of his contracting officer in all respects.

The company filed its claim with the Court of Claims. The court, by a unanimous decision,[2] held that the ruling of the Secretary of the Interior was "arbitrary," "capricious," and "grossly erroneous" and awarded the plaintiff the sum of $155,748. The Department of the Interior appealed to the United States Supreme Court. The following is from the majority opinion of the court:

> This court is again called upon to determine the meaning of the "finality clause" of a standard government contract. . . . This court has consistently upheld the finality of the department head's decision unless it was founded on fraud, alleged and proved. . . . By fraud we mean conscious wrongdoing, an intention to cheat or be dishonest. The decision of the department head, absent fraudulent conduct, must stand under the plain meaning of the contract.[3]

Mr. Justice Douglas delivered a dissenting opinion, in which he was joined by Mr. Justice Reed:

> Where discretion is absolute, man has always suffered. . . . Absolute discretion is a ruthless master. The instant case reveals only a minor facet in the age-long struggle. . . . It may be that, in this case, the equities are with the Government, not with the contractor. But the rule we announce has a wide application and a devastating effect. It makes a tyrant out of every contracting officer.

---

[2] Wunderlich v. United States, 117 Ct. Cl. 92 (1950).

[3] United States v. Wunderlich, 342 U.S. 98 (1951).

Mr. Justice Jackson also filed a dissenting opinion:

Men are more often bribed by their loyalties and ambitions than by money. I still believe that one should have a judicial hearing before his business can be destroyed by administrative action.

It would be difficult to add much to these vigorous protests of the three dissenting justices. The decision clearly called for legislative action. In 1954 Congress declared[4] that those under contract with the Federal Government are entitled to a review by a court of any decision of an administrative officer if the court finds that it was fraudulent, arbitrary, capricious, or so grossly erroneous as necessarily to imply bad faith or that it was not supported by substantial evidence.

GROUP DISCUSSION OF FEDERAL CONTRACT PROVISIONS. Contract negotiation between an agency of the Federal Government and an individual college or university is a misnomer. Because of their obvious lack of equality in bargaining power, college business officers initiated discussions with representatives of the armed services and other federal agencies on a group basis. In March 1949 the Armed Services Procurement Regulations were revised to include a section summarizing the results of these group discussions. Some federal agencies declined to accept the procedures thus developed. The Bureau of the Budget, on September 10, 1959, issued Circular No. A-21, entitled "Principles for Costing Research and Development under Grants and Contracts with Educational Institutions." Discussion seems fated to continue indefinitely on this subject.

THE LAW OF PATENTS

The etymological meaning of the word "patent" is "open," "obvious." Until the last year of the reign of James I, it was customary for the English monarch to grant royal favors, including lands, titles of nobility, and other privileges by issuing "letters patent," that is, open letters to all concerned. In order to reward faithful service to the crown, the king might grant to an individual or a guild the exclusive right to produce or sell a commodity or product throughout the realm.

Such royal patents creating monopolies were, of course, resented by those compelled to pay the resulting higher prices. Francis Bacon, in the House of Commons, led the attack upon these royal grants to court

---

4 Pub. L. No. 356, 83d Cong., 2d Sess. (May 11, 1954). For the text of the statute, see 68 *Stat.* 81 (1954). See 2 *U.S. Code Cong. & Ad. News* 2191 (1954) for the legislative history.

favorites. He declared that a monopoly should be granted only to one who had first developed a "new manufacture." Bacon's proposal became the law of the land in 1623 by the enactment of the Statute of Monopolies.[5] It voided all monopolies and letters patent "of or for the Sole Buying, Selling, Making, Working, or Using of anything within this Realm." However, Section 6 of this act became the basis of all modern patent law. It granted the privilege of the

sole working of any manner of new manufactures within the realm to the true and first inventor and inventors of such manufactures which others, at the time of making such letters patent and grants shall not use, so as also they be not contrary to the law or mischievous to the state by raising the prices of commodities at home or the hurt of trade or generally inconvenient.

THE DEVELOPMENT OF AMERICAN PATENT LAW. Charles Pinckney, at the Constitutional Convention in Philadelphia in 1787, drafted the following paragraph, which became Article I, Section 8, Clause 8 of the federal Constitution:

The Congress shall have power to promote the progress of science and useful arts by securing for limited times to authors and inventors the exclusive rights to their respective writings and discoveries.

Congress, under this grant of power, by a series of acts, has created the patent system in use today. George Washington signed the first patent act in 1790. It declared that one might obtain a patent on "any useful art, manufacture, engine, machine, or device, or any improvement thereon not before known or used."

To be patentable, a device must actually work, and to prove this, the Patent Act of 1836 required the applicant to file a model of his invention as well as a drawing and specifications. Under the act of 1870, it became unnecessary to submit a model unless requested to do so by the Commissioner of Patents. Today, models are rarely demanded by the Commissioner. Patent legislation in force, as well as current rules and regulations issued by the Patent Office, will be found in the United States Code[6] and in the Code of Federal Regulations.[7]

REQUIREMENTS FOR PATENTABILITY. To be patentable, an idea must be "new and useful" and it must pertain to a "process, machine, manufacture, or composition of matter, or any new and useful improvement

---

[5] 21 Jac. 1, c. 3, § 1.
[6] 35 *U.S.C.* §§ 1–293.
[7] 37 *C.F.R.* §§ 1.1–1.352 (1949).

thereof."[8] A federal judge has stated the requirements for patentability as follows:

One may not patent a mere idea, although novel and useful, but idea must be reduced to practice; and a practical method of making and using it must be described so as to enable the public to use the invention after the patent expires.[9]

Before the patent can be issued, the staff of examiners of the Patent Office must determine, from the application and other evidence presented to them, whether the conception therein set forth meets the statutory requirements for a patent.

PLANT AND DESIGN PATENTS. One may also obtain a patent on a plant or a design. The current patent code declares that

whoever invents or discovers and asexually reproduces any distinct and new variety of plant, including cultivated sports, mutants, hybrids, and newly found seedlings, other than a tuber-propagated plant or a plant found in an uncultivated state, may obtain a patent therefor.[10]

The inventor of a "new, original and ornamental design for an article of manufacture" may also obtain a patent therefor.[11]

THE LAWS OF NATURE CANNOT BE PATENTED. If an invention or discovery is too basic and fundamental or if it does not come within any of the categories of inventions enumerated by Congress, as interpreted by the courts, it cannot be patented. In 1846 William T. Morton, a dentist, and Charles T. Jackson, a professor of chemistry, discovered that the pain of surgical and dental operations could be relieved by the inhalation of sulphuric ether. Despite the value of this discovery, a federal court in 1862 declared that they were not entitled to the protection of the patent law. Judge Shipman declared:

Its discoverer is entitled to be classed among the greatest benefactors of mankind. But the beneficent and imposing character of the discovery can not change the legal principles upon which the law of patents is founded, nor abrogate the rules by which judicial construction must be governed.[12]

Samuel F. B. Morse, in addition to claiming patent rights on the telegraph instrument itself, attempted to claim the right to patent the use

[8] 35 *U.S.C.* § 101.

[9] Wayne v. Humble Oil & Refining Co., 175 F.2d 230 (Tex. Ct. App. 1949).

[10] 35 *U.S.C.* § 161.

[11] 35 *U.S.C.* § 171.

[12] Morton v. New York Eye Infirmary, 17 Fed. Cas. 879, 883 (No. 9865) (C.C.S.D.N.Y. 1862).

of the electric current to produce "intelligible characters, letters or signs at any distance." The Supreme Court of the United States declared[13] that this power of nature could not be the subject of patent rights. Mr. Justice Grier dissented. He declared:

The great art of printing, which has changed the face of human society and civilization, consisted in nothing but a new application of principles known to the world for thousands of years. . . . Yet if the inventor of printing had, under this narrow construction of our patent law, claimed his art as something distinct from his machinery, the doctrine now advanced would have declared it unpatentable to its full extent as an art, . . .

THE "SUNSHINE VITAMIN" CASE. Harry Steenbock, a member of the faculty of the University of Wisconsin, obtained three patents for the development of a method for the production of Vitamin D by activating ergosterol and yeast with ultraviolet rays. He assigned his patents to the Wisconsin Alumni Research Foundation.

By 1940 the foundation had received over $7 million from food processors licensed to use the patented procedures. In an action for infringement,[14] the court ruled that the patents were invalid, basing its decision on the following arguments:

Ultra-violet light is a natural form of energy. Like the sun, which is the source of that energy, and like the air we breathe, ultra-violet rays are the property of all mankind. Men may devise or improve machines for their more effective utilization and may obtain patents upon the machine or the improvement. But it would be a monstrous thing if the energy itself could be made the subject of a monopoly.

THE "FLASH OF GENIUS" REQUIREMENT FOR PATENTABILITY. In general, a device, to be patentable, must be more than new and useful; it must represent a real invention or discovery, that is, more than the work of a mechanic skilled in the art.[15] However, in the Cuno case, the Supreme Court of the United States established a much higher standard for patentability. The court ruled that a

new device, however useful it may be, must reveal the flash of creative genius, not merely the skill of the calling. If it fails, it has not established its right to a private grant on the public domain.[16]

---

[13] O'Reilly v. Morse, 56 U.S. (15 How.) 62, 129, 133 (1853).
[14] Vitamin Technologists v. Wisconsin Alumni Research Foundation, 146 F.2d 941, 954 (9th Cir. 1944).
[15] Spring-Air Co. v. Regains, 96 F. Supp. 79 (Dist. Ct. Mich. 1951).
[16] Cuno Engineering Corp. v. Automatic Devices Corp., 314 U.S. 84, 91 (1941).

CORPORATE RESEARCH UNDER JUDICIAL HANDICAP. A federal court in 1944 apparently set a higher standard of patentability for those working in a corporate research organization than for others working independently. The rule of law was stated as follows:

patents are not intended as a reward for a highly skilled scientist who completes the final step in a technique, standing on the shoulders of others who have gone before him. By the same token, they are not intended as a reward for the collective achievement of a corporate research organization.
. . . .
To give patents for such routine experimentation on a vast scale is to use the patent law to reward capital investment, and to create monopolies for corporate organizers instead of men of creative genius.[17]

Great dissatisfaction with these decisions was expressed in the press and in Congress. The members of Congress came to the conclusion that the courts had set the standard for patentability too high and that it was inequitable to impose a handicap upon the great research laboratories of industry. When the patent laws were revised and recodified in 1952, Congress established for the first time its own standard of patentability. In Section 103 of the new act, it declared that "patentability shall not be negatived by the manner in which the invention was made,"[18] that is, the test must be objective, not subjective.

As stated by Arthur H. Seidel:

On the grounds of logic as well as practicability, the determination of patentability based upon the presence of a "flash of genius" is an impossibility. For there is no standard for measuring "genius," which, by definition, is transcendent ability, much less a "flash" of it.

The second doctrine outlawed by the last sentence of 103 is the one imposing a standard of patentability based upon the origin of the invention, or what amounted to a judicially administered handicap system. Under this doctrine, the level of patentability was to be varied in proportion to the research facilities available to the inventors, e.g., the director of research of a corporation having extensive research facilities had to effect a higher standard of advance over the art before achieving a patentable advance than an individual not having such facilities available to him. The inequity of discrimination by the method is obvious.[19]

---

[17] Potts v. Coe, 78 U.S. App. D.C. 297 (1944), 140 F.2d 470, 474.
[18] 66 *Stat.* 798, 35 *U.S.C.* § 103 (1954).
[19] Seidel, *What the General Practitioner Should Know about Patent Law and Practice* (Philadelphia, Pa.: Committee on Continuing Legal Education of the American Law Institute, 1956), p. 19. See also "Symposium: Intellectual Property," 9 *Clev. Mar. L. Rev.* (1960).

STEPS TO BE TAKEN TO PRESERVE PATENT RIGHTS. Since priority of conception of the basic idea for an invention, rather than priority of filing the application for the patent thereon, is essential to ownership of the resulting patent, faculty members should be advised to maintain detailed notebooks and records of their developing concepts. In order to prove priority of conception, the idea should be reduced to writing, with a diagram, sketch, or any other graphic presentation to enable someone else to understand clearly its proposed operation or purpose.

These disclosure records should be reviewed and signed by one or more individuals capable of understanding the invention and of giving testimony, if necessary, as to the actual date of its conception and disclosure. It is considered good practice to have laboratory notebooks and diaries witnessed and dated, page by page, in order to increase their value as evidence of priority of conception.

THE WORK OF A PATENT ATTORNEY. The work of a patent attorney is highly specialized. Unless one has followed step by step the arduous task of searching the files of existing records required for the proper presentation of a patent application, it is difficult to appreciate the skill and patience demanded. Almost three million patents have been issued in this country. The Patent Office search room is the only place in which they are arranged both numerically and by subject matter. These records must be searched to determine, first, whether the idea can be patented under existing statutes; second, if the patent is granted, whether its use will constitute an infringement upon existing patents; third, the probability of the courts sustaining the patent if its validity is questioned; and, last but probably most important, to what extent it represents an improvement over present technology in competition with articles or commodities now available, that is, what its commercial possibilities are.

THE BOARD OF PATENT INTERFERENCE. On the average, it takes three years from the date the application for the patent is filed until the final patent papers are issued. The life of a patent is seventeen years, not from the date of filing, but from the date of issue. Roughly, one patent in twenty is challenged by one or more inventors claiming the same invention. In the field of electronics and the other more active areas, the number of conflicting claims is much greater. It is here that the value of the services of a really competent patent attorney becomes evident. The adjudication of conflicting claims prior to the issuance of the patent is termed an "interference." Congress has established[20] the Board of Patent Interference to hear and decide these conflicting claims, with appropriate provision for appeal.

THE SELECTION OF A PATENT ATTORNEY. Only those who have been admitted to practice before the Patent Office may represent clients in hearings conducted by the examining division of the Office. Few general practitioners of the law feel qualified to cope with the technicalities of patent law, but it is important that there be a close working relationship between the regular attorney representing the college and the patent attorney. Those requiring the services of a surgeon or any other specialist in the healing arts are well advised to make their selection in close consultation with their family physician. For many of the same reasons, a patent attorney should be selected by or with the advice of a reputable general practitioner of the law. Consultation with an experienced patent attorney at an early stage in the development of a patent is advisable in order to make certain that the disclosure records are properly preserved.

THE ADMINISTRATION OF FACULTY PATENTS

Apparently, many faculty members have assigned their patent rights to the institutions which employ them, or have executed agreements to do so, on the assumption that all patents developed by an employee in the course of his employment belong to his employer. This is not the law. Courts have gone to great lengths to protect the rights of employees in their own inventions.

THE OWNERSHIP OF FACULTY PATENTS. Colleges and universities have engaged in very little patent litigation of record, but if we may draw upon the experience of industry in this field, the general rule seems to be well established that, in the absence of a prior agreement, an invention conceived by an employee in the course of his employment is his own property and not that of his employer.[21] There are two major exceptions to this general rule, as follows:

1. When an employee is assigned the task of invention or the im-

---

[20] 35 *U.S.C.* § 135.

[21] United States v. Dubilier Condenser Corp., 289 U.S. 178 (1933); Dalzell v. Dueber Mfg. Co., 149 U.S. 315 (1893); Hapgood v. Hewitt, 119 U.S. 226 (1886); Heywood-Wakefield Co. v. Small, 87 F.2d 716 (1st Cir. 1937); McNamara v. Powell, 256 App. Div. 554, 11 N.Y.S.2d 491 (1939), *modifying same at* 168 Misc. 806, 7 N.Y.S.2d 141 (1938), *reargument denied,* 12 N.Y.S.2d (1939).

provement of a specific process and in the course of his employment he succeeds in his assigned task, his employer is entitled to full patent rights in his invention.[22]

2. The second major exception to the general rule is what has been termed "shop rights." This principle was concisely stated by Judge Sparks in the Pure Oil Company case:

> We are in accord with the principle relied upon by appellant that if an employee in the course of his employment makes an invention, using his employer's time and materials, the employer has a free indefeasible license and shop right under the invention and any patent covering the invention which shop right is co-extensive with the business requirements of the employer.[23]

LIMITATIONS OF A "SHOP RIGHT." Note that this "shop right" is far from complete ownership of the patent itself. It is merely a nonexclusive license to the employer to make use of the invention in his own business. Unless the device can be used in the regular course of the employer's normal area of activity, shop rights therein have no value.

Moreover, the concept is based upon the equitable doctrine of estoppel, that is, a bar to one's alleging or denying a fact because of one's own previous action, by which the contrary has been admitted, implied, or determined. Because of the equitable character of shop rights, other equitable doctrines, such as unjust enrichment, have been invoked by the courts to limit the rights of the employer and to protect the rights of the employee.

Employment itself does not import a license to use the employee's inventions. One must find in the conduct of the employee an implied consent to the use of his invention by his employer. If by his actions he implicitly consents, he is said to be estopped from later denying that assent was, in fact, given.

THE EVERGLADES EXPERIMENT STATION CASE. An example of the extent to which the courts have gone in protecting the rights of an employee in his own inventions is that of the Everglades Experiment Station case, decided by the Supreme Court of Florida in 1942.[24] The Board of Edu-

---

[22] Standard Parts Co. v. Peck, 264 U.S. 52 (1924); Houghton v. United States, 23 F.2d 386 (4th Cir. 1928); Goodyear Tire & Rubber Co. v. Miller, 22 F.2d 353 (9th Cir. 1927), *reversing* 14 F.2d 776 (S.D. Cal. 196); Wireless Spec. Apparatus Co. v. Mica Condenser Co., 239 Mass. 158, 131 N.E. 307 (1921); Quaker State Oil Ref. Co. v. Talbot, 315 Pa. 517, 174 Atl. 99 (1934).

[23] Pure Oil Co. v. Hyman, 95 F.2d 22, 25 (7th Cir. 1938).

[24] State Board of Education v. Bourne, 150 Fla. 232, 7 So. 2d 838 (1942).

cation of the State of Florida brought an action to compel Dr. Benjamin A. Bourne to assign to the state certain plant patents he had obtained while employed by the Everglades Experiment Station. The following is from the opinion of the court:

The record shows that the appellee was employed annually as plant pathologist or physiologist and was assigned to project 171, having to do with cane breeding experiments. He contends that project 171 was limited to the breeding of syrup cane as distinguished from sugar cane. . . . There is no evidence that any specific varieties of cane were in mind when the contract with the appellee was made nor was he instructed as to any. All we get from the contract and project statement is that he was employed, among other duties, to develop cane varieties which was to be done by research and experimentation that may or may not lead to invention. . . . An employment to design, devise or construct methods of manufacture is not the equivalent of an employment to invent.

The court permitted Dr. Bourne to retain full rights to his plant patent. Here we have a very close analogy to a state college or university laboratory. Dr. Bourne was employed with state funds to conduct research for the benefit of the citizens of Florida and for the public in general. And yet he was permitted to retain full patent rights in his new variety of sugar cane and to assign his rights to the United States Sugar Corporation, apparently on the very narrow issue that he had been assigned to a project calling for the development of syrup canes rather than sugar canes. The court concluded its opinion with the following rule of law:

Where an employer undertakes to establish a claim to a patent or patentable object as against his employee who is the inventor, he must show beyond question that the employment was for the specific purpose of making the invention. If the employment was general and the invention was an incident to that, the employer cannot claim the patent.

THE ADOPTION OF A COLLEGE PATENT POLICY. The reluctance of the courts to grant an employer even shop rights in the inventions of his employees would seem to be a compelling reason for the adoption of a clear, unambiguous patent policy by colleges and universities. If the institution desires to retain patent rights, the retained rights should be set forth in agreements drafted with the advice of counsel and signed prior to employment by faculty and employees engaged in research.

The patent policy should be formulated in consultation with representative members of the faculty and adopted by the governing board. Such a policy may involve the leaving of patent rights to the staff member, the retention and exploitation of patents by the institution itself, or the assignment of patent rights to an affiliated corporation or to an outside nonprofit organization such as the Research Corporation.

PATENT ASSIGNMENT TERMS MUST BE REASONABLE. In order to compel an employee to execute an assignment of patent rights in accordance with the terms of a prior agreement, an employer must invoke the equitable remedy of specific performance. It is an ancient rule or maxim of equity that one who seeks equitable relief must conduct himself with equity. Consequently, a court will take into consideration the reasonableness of the provisions of a contract it is petitioned to enforce.

This rule is illustrated in a case[25] involving the Minnesota Mining and Manufacturing Company, sometimes known as the "3M" Company. The company petitioned a court for a writ of specific performance to compel a former employee to assign the patent rights to his invention, in accordance with his contract with the company. The contract was without limit in time and in subject matter of invention and the court refused to enforce it. The court ruled that an agreement of this character must be limited in time to include only patents developed by the employee during the period of his employment, and, in subject matter, it must be restricted to inventions related to the business of the employer at the time of the employment.

In the absence of a decision in point, one can only speculate as to how a court would apply the rule of the 3M case to a patent assignment contract between a college and a member of its faculty. If the faculty member had agreed to assign all inventions developed during the period of his employment, would the court refuse to enforce it as being too broad in scope as to subject matter of invention? How can one restrict the subject matter of an invention to those related to the business of the employer if the employer is not engaged in business?

PATENT ASSIGNMENT AGREEMENTS BY FACULTY MEMBERS WITH PERMANENT TENURE. Another problem confronting the college attorney in the drafting of an agreement to assign patent rights is the question of adequacy of consideration. According to the criteria of common law, even a peppercorn has been held sufficient to bind a contract, but equity must be satisfied that the consideration bears some reasonable relationship to the probable benefits to be derived from the contract. In a busi-

---

[25] Guth v. Minnesota Mining & Mfg. Co., 72 F.2d 385 (7th Cir. 1934), *cert. denied,* 294 U.S. 711 (1935).

ness corporation, it is considered sufficient for the patent assignment contract to recite a nominal consideration and the expectation of continued employment. In an educational institution many members of the faculty are on a permanent tenure basis. Consequently, the agreement by the college to continue to employ them would not, so far as they are concerned, constitute consideration.

A SURVEY OF UNIVERSITY PATENT POLICIES. As a service to American higher education, the National Research Council initiated, in 1946 under the direction of Archie M. Palmer, the compilation and dissemination of information concerning the policies, practices, and procedures of colleges and universities in the handling of patentable results of scientific and technological research.[26] Dr. Palmer was also requested to prepare a report on patents and nonprofit research as part of a study of the United States patent system by the Subcommittee on Patents, Trademarks, and Copyrights of the Senate Committee on the Judiciary. The following are excerpts from that report:

There is a wide diversity of practice among educational institutions, and often in the various divisions of the same institution, in the handling of these patentable discoveries and inventions. Existing practices vary from strictly drawn research and patent policy to laissez-faire attitudes, and even an unwillingness to become concerned with patents. At a considerable number of institutions little or no serious official consideration has been given to the patent problem. . . . Frequently the failure on the part of an institution to establish such a policy is the result of limited experience or no experience at all with patent problems.

. . . .

General research and patent policies have been adopted, as a definite course of action formulated and expressed in a systematic statement, by boards of control, state legislatures, or other governing bodies of the following 85 universities, colleges, technological institutes, and professional schools [list omitted].

Most universities and other nonprofit research organizations endeavor to

---

[26] The following monographs on nonprofit research and patent management by Dr. Archie M. Palmer have been published by the National Academy of Sciences—National Research Council, 2101 Constitution Ave., N.W., Washington 25, D.C.: *Nonprofit Research and Patent Management in the United States* (1956); *Nonprofit Research and Patent Management Organization* (1955); *Nonprofit Research Institutes* (1959); *Nonprofit Patent Management* (1961); *University Patent Policies and Practices* (1952); *Supplement to University Patent Policies and Practices* (1955); *Medical Patents* (1949); *Administration of Medical and Pharmaceutical Patents* (1955).

avoid becoming involved in the intricate technical and commercial aspects of patent management, mainly because they do not have the personnel with the requisite specialized knowledge and experience. . . . Frequently these functions are performed in behalf of an educational institution by a separately incorporated nonprofit management foundation affiliated with the institution. . . . At present more than 50 of these separately incorporated organizations are performing, or are authorized to perform, patent management functions for the institutions with which they are affiliated. . . . The following 69 colleges have, directly or through affiliated patent management organizations, entered into patent development agreements with the Research Corporation [list omitted] . . . , established in 1912 by Frederick Gardner Cottrell, with a gift of his patent rights in the field of electrical precipitation as a nonprofit organization. . . . The corporation's charter requires that its net earnings be contributed to such scientific and educational institutions and societies as its board of directors may from time to time select, to enable such institutions and societies to conduct technical and scientific investigations, research, and experimentation.[27]

PUBLICATION

The leading publishers of London in 1556 were granted a royal monopoly in their field but were placed under the supervision of the Star Chamber. The real reason for this action by the Crown was neither the encouragement of literature nor the protection of the rights of publishers but more effective censorship. The publishers were members of the Stationers' Company, and, by registering his publications in the office of the company, a publisher acquired the sole right to publish and print them for a term of years.

THE STATUTE OF ANNE. By 1694 the last of the royal censorship acts had expired and a number of independent printers began to contest the monopoly of the Stationer's Company. In order to clarify the respective rights of the public, the authors, and their publishers, the English Parliament in 1710 enacted the first copyright legislation in the world, known as the Statute of Anne. This act granted to the author of any book and to his assigns exclusive rights of publication for a term of fourteen years. The right could be extended for a further term of fourteen years if the author was still living at the expiration of the first term.[28]

---

[27] Staff of Senate Committee on the Judiciary, 85th Cong., 1st Sess., *Patents and Nonprofit Research* 6 (Comm. Print 1957), 2, 3, 37.

[28] Leon H. Amdur, *Copyright Law and Practice* (New York: Clark, Boardman & Co., 1936); Horace G. Ball, *The Law of Copyright and Literary Property* (New York: Matthew Bender & Co., 1944); Herbert A. Howell, *The Copyright Law*

AMERICAN COPYRIGHT LAW. The same section[29] of the federal Constitution that authorized Congress "to promote the progress of science and the useful arts of securing for a limited time to . . . inventors the exclusive right to their . . . discoveries" also gives it the power to grant the same right to authors to their writings. In 1790 Noah Webster, seeking protection for his famous and very popular "Blue-backed Speller," persuaded Congress to make use of this permissive clause in the Constitution. This first federal copyright statute extended protection only to books, maps, and charts. In 1802 prints and pictorial illustrations were added, musical compositions in 1831, dramatic compositions in 1856, photographs in 1865, paintings, drawings, sculpture, models, and designs in 1870, and motion picture photoplays in 1912. The present law[30] is based upon the Copyright Act of 1909,[31] with only minor amendments.

In order to obtain a copyright, an author, or the one to whom he assigns his rights, must see that the word "copyright" followed by the year and name of the copyright owner appears either on the title page or on the reverse side of the title page of every copy of his book. Two copies of the work, together with an application and fee for registration, must be sent promptly to the Register of Copyrights, Washington, D.C. A copyright assures exclusive rights in the publication or other reproductions of the work for a period of twenty-eight years, with the right to renew the copyright for the same period.

Patents are granted only after the Patent Office has made a thorough search of the "prior art" and determined, as far as possible, that the invention is both novel and useful and that it complies with all the other statutory requirements for patentability, whereas a copyright is obtained merely by the act of publication, with notice of the claim of copyright in the form and position as required by statute. The Copyright Office merely registers the claim to the copyright, it does not grant it. However, it is highly desirable to comply with all the provisions of the act, since this is essential to provide evidence in the event of litigation and infringement.

Before the Copyright Act of 1909, it was necessary to publish in order

---

(3d ed.; Washington: Bureau of National Affairs, 1952); Margaret Nicholson, *A Manual of Copyright Practice for Writers, Publishers, and Agents* (2d ed.; New York: Oxford University Press, 1956); Philip Wittenberg, *The Law of Literary Property* (Cleveland, Ohio: World Publishing Co., 1957).

[29] *U.S. Const.* art. I, § 8.

[30] 17 *U.S.C.* § 1 (1952).

[31] 61 *Stat.* 652 (1947).

to obtain the protection of the copyright statute, but the new act made provision, for the first time, for a statutory copyright of certain types of unpublished works, such as lectures; dramatic works; music and musical dramas; plastic works, drawings, and other works of art; and photographs and motion picture films.[32]

COPYRIGHT UNDER THE COMMON LAW. The common law has always recognized the inherent right of an individual to control his own property, and the property rights of authors in their own literary creations were protected by the courts[33] long before the passage of the Statute of Anne, even though such protection was not considered sufficient by the publishers after the expiration of the licensing acts.

After Parliament had provided statutory protection, the question arose as to whether the statute had extinguished the common law protection to literary property. In 1774 the judicial members of the House of Lords, sitting as a supreme court, ruled that an author retains the full protection of the common law as long as his work is unpublished.[34] After publication, however, his common law rights are gone forever, and he must henceforth look to the provisions of the copyright statute for his sole protection.

THE DANGER OF PUBLICATION WITHOUT CLAIM OF COPYRIGHT. A manuscript may be mimeographed or otherwise duplicated without loss of copyright if distribution is merely for the purpose of obtaining comment and criticism or for submission to publishers. However, if copies are sold or even given away, for use similar in character to eventual use after formal publication—for example, a textbook for use by students—this may constitute publication.

This is the common law in America,[35] and it should be called to the attention of college faculty members. They should be made aware of the hazard of publication in any form without compliance with the provisions of the copyright statutes. What constitutes publication?[36] A professor may mimeograph his new textbook or other teaching material for trial use in his own classes before formal publication. Under the common law, this preliminary multiplication and distribution may con-

---

[32] 17 *U.S.C.* § 12 (1952).

[33] Moore v. Ford Motor Co., 28 F.2d 529 (S.D.N.Y. 1928), *aff'd,* 43 F.2d 685 (2d Cir. 1930).

[34] Donaldson v. Beckett, 4 Burr. 2408, 98 Eng. Rep. 257 (H.L. 1774).

[35] Holms v. Hurst, 174 U.S. 82 (1899).

[36] See 18 *C.J.S.: Copyright and Literary Property* § 13 (1939).

stitute publication, and if done without claim of copyright by compliance with statutory requirements, all protection of the copyright act may be lost beyond recall. Once published without copyright, a literary work becomes part of the public domain.

COMMON LAW PROTECTION OF UNPUBLISHED MANUSCRIPTS. As we have seen, publication extinguishes the protection of the common law, and one must thereafter look to the provisions of the Copyright Act. Even if copyright is obtained, an author loses control over his literary creation after twenty-eight years, or fifty-six if the right of renewal is exercised. However, if one does not publish his manuscript, he, his heirs, and assigns may retain the rights therein and thus be in a position to restrain, in perpetuity, its unauthorized publication, despite public demand for the opportunity to read it. This fact became of public interest in 1949 when the trustees under the will of Samuel L. Clemens were successful[37] in their efforts to prevent the publication of one of his unpublished manuscripts.

A commentator[38] on this case suggested that "it may be contrary to sound public policy to keep meritorious literary achievement out of the public domain for so long a time."

INFRINGEMENT OF COPYRIGHT. With the development of educational television and the increasing participation of college professors in radio and television programs, college administrators should review carefully the legal restrictions on the unauthorized reproduction or publication of literary property. Moreover, many institutions have acquired modern equipment for sound recording and for the photographic reproduction of manuscripts and typed and published documents. Accordingly, the hazard of inadvertent reproduction of such material without the consent of the owner of the document or of the copyright has increased substantially. A survey of current procedures on the typical college campus probably would reveal many unintentional violations of literary property rights.

THE FAIR USE DOCTRINE. Many people are under the impression that they may quote freely from copyrighted material if they merely indicate the extent of the quotation and give due credit. Here, the legal doctrine of fair use must be one's guide. Some even assume that

---

[37] Chamberlain v. Feldman, 300 N.Y. 135, 89 N.E.2d 863 (1949).
[38] 62 *Harv. L. Rev.* 1406, 1407 (1949).

they may mimeograph generous excerpts from such works for distribution to students without the consent of the owner of the copyright if they do not sell the material and if they indicate the source of the quotation. Even the gratuitous distribution of an unauthorized abridgment of copyrighted material has been held to be an infringement.[39]

In the absence of any statutory definition of infringement, the courts have repeatedly held that copyright infringement consists of actual copying, whether intentional or unintentional, of some substantial and material part of that which is protected by statute. . . . The copying or printing of a copyrighted work is an infringement irrespective of the fact that no copies have been sold, or that no profits have been made from the sale of copies.[40]

The courts have long recognized what is known as the doctrine of fair use. This doctrine was evolved in early litigation in which irate authors attempted to bring legal pressure upon those publishing unfavorable reviews of their books. These cases held that, in the public interest, a reviewer might include reasonable excerpts from the work under discussion without violation of the copyright statute.

Fair Use may be defined as a privilege in others than the owner of a copyright to use copyright material in a reasonable manner without his consent, notwithstanding the monopoly granted to the owner by the copyright. Although the copyright law makes no provision for "fair use" of another work, the author's consent to a reasonable use of his copyrighted works has always been implied by the courts as a necessary incident of the constitutional policy of promoting the progress of science and useful arts.[41]

A federal judge has more recently given a definition of the doctrine of fair use:

The monopoly which a copyright holder does enjoy is not without its limitations. Since the Copyright Act is intended to afford encouragement to the production of literary works, reward to the owner is a secondary consideration. Accordingly, subsequent authors, publishers and the general public may use a copyrighted work in a reasonable manner without the consent of the copyright owner on the theory that such use constitutes a "fair use" of the copyrighted material.[42]

Another federal judge has suggested that

with reference to works in regard to the arts and sciences, using those words in the broadest sense . . . authors are sometimes entitled, indeed even re-

---

[39] Macmillan Co. v. King, 223 Fed. 862 (Mass. Dist. Ct. 1914).

[40] Horace G. Ball, *op. cit. supra* note 28, at 323–24.

[41] *Ibid.*, p. 260.

[42] Greenbie v. Noble, 151 F. Supp. 45, 67 (S.D.N.Y. 1957).

quired to make use of what precedes them in the precise form in which last exhibited.[43]

The freedom to quote from scholarly works for scholarly purposes has not been granted to those using such material for commercial purposes. Although a tobacco company quoted only three sentences from a scientific treatise in one of its advertising pamphlets, such use was held to constitute an infringement of the author's copyright.[44]

PROCEDURES TO BE FOLLOWED BY COLLEGE LIBRARIES. In the light of the following opinion by Mr. Justice Storey, it is difficult for an attorney to draft an entirely safe set of working rules to guide photocopiers in a college library:

> It is certainly not necessary to constitute an invasion of copyright that the whole of a work should be copied, or even a large portion of it, in form or substance. If so much is taken that the value of the original is sensibly diminished, or the labors of the original author are substantially to an injurious extent appropriated by another, that is sufficient, in point of law, to constitute a piracy *pro tanto*.[45]

Louis Charles Smith, senior attorney for the Copyright Office of the Library of Congress, has this to say on the subject:

> The safest procedure, of course, would be to require that the copyright owner's consent be obtained in each instance. But this would not meet the need of scholars; it would simply ignore the problem. Requests for the copyright owner's consent would frequently mean long delay; some copyright owners would refuse permission arbitrarily; others would fail to respond; and in some cases the copyright owner cannot be found or the identity of successor owners is difficult to determine. It should be possible, instead, for representatives of the several groups concerned—libraries, scholars, publishers, and authors—to agree on a general basis, consistent with their various interests, on which photocopying for scholarly research will be permitted.[46]

The so-called "Gentlemen's Agreement,"[47] entered into by the Joint Committee on Materials for Research of the American Council of

---

[43] Sampson & Murdock Co. v. Seaver Radford Co., 140 Fed. 539, 541 (1st Cir. 1905).

[44] Henry Holt & Co. v. Liggett & Myers Tobacco Co., 23 F. Supp. 302 (E.D. Pa. 1938).

[45] Folsom v. Marsh, 9 Fed. Cas. 342 (No. 4, 901) (C.C.D. Mass. 1841).

[46] Louis Charles Smith, "The Copying of Literary Property in Library Collections," 47 *L. Library J.* 204 (1954).

[47] "The Gentlemen's Agreement and the Problem of Copyright," 2 *Journal of Documentary Reproduction*, No. 1 (1939), at 31–33.

Learned Societies and the Social Science Research Council with the National Association of Book Publishers, represents an attempt of this character. The agreement was drafted in May 1935, but, unfortunately, it was not subscribed to by all publishers. Mr. Smith has proposed the following procedures to be followed by a library in the making of photocopies of literary property:

1. The scholar would be required to give some assurance (*a*) that the photocopy requested by him is desired for the sole purpose of his private study and (*b*) that he will not reproduce or distribute the photocopy, or copy any substantial part of it in his own work without the permission of the copyright owner.

2. Not more than one photocopy would be made for any one scholar.

3. Each photocopy would bear notations showing the source of the material and stating that it is copyrighted.

4. The scholar would be required to pay the full cost of making the photocopy in any event. Where the work to be photocopied is believed to be available for purchase from trade sources, the charge for the photocopy should be greater than the price of a trade copy.[48]

According to Mr. Smith, the Library of Congress, of which the Copyright Office is a department, attaches the following conditions, among others, to photocopying done by it:

1. The Library will make photoduplicates of materials in its collections available for research use. It performs such service solely for research and in lieu of loan of the material in question or in place of manual transcription.

2. All responsibility in the use made of the photoduplicates is assumed by the applicant.

3. Copyright material will ordinarily not be copied without the signed authorization of the copyright owner. Exceptions to this rule may be made in particular cases.[49]

PROPOSED STATUTORY RECOGNITION OF THE FAIR USE DOCTRINE. In order to reduce the uncertainty surrounding the legal right of scholars and libraries to make reasonable use of copyrighted material, it has been suggested that Congress write its own definition of this concept of the common law. Under Congressional authorization, the Copyright Office of the Library of Congress has undertaken a program of studies looking toward a general revision of the copyright law. In August 1958 it published one of these studies, by Alan Latman, on the question of fair use. After discussing the silence of the present code on the subject, the theoretical basis of the doctrine, various bills submitted for

---

[48] Smith, *op. cit. supra* note 46, at 206, 207.
[49] 46 *L. Library J.* 197, 206, 207 (1953).

Congressional action since 1909 and the laws of foreign countries on the subject, he submitted the following as possibilities for treatment of fair use in a new statute:

(1) Follow the approach of the Senate Committee in 1907 and maintain the present statutory silence on the question.
(2) Recognize the doctrine and grant it statutory status in broad terms, without clarifying the meaning accorded fair use by the courts.
(3) Specify general criteria. This would represent the boldest attempt to treat the problem. It could take the shape of codifying the common law.
(4) Cover specific situations.[50]

INTERNATIONAL COPYRIGHT PROTECTION. The International Copyright Union was created at the Berne Convention in 1887. The Union abolished all formalities in securing copyright protection in other countries. A book published in any member nation obtained a copyright in all member nations. This country did not become a member of the Union. American authors could obtain indirect protection by publication of their works in Canada, England, or any other member nation within thirty days of the date of publication in this country. By a series of treaties and presidential proclamations, American writers gradually obtained an increasing degree of copyright protection abroad.

Under the auspices of the United Nations Educational, Scientific, and Cultural Organization, a universal copyright convention was drafted and approved by the International Copyright Conference at Geneva in 1952. It became effective in this country on September 16, 1955.[51] Under the provisions of this international agreement, the published and unpublished works of "nationals of each contracting state shall enjoy in each other contracting state the same protection as that other state accords to the works of its own nationals."

THE LITERARY PROPERTY RIGHTS OF EMPLOYEES. Although faculty members are rarely under administrative pressure to assign their copyrights to their college, they should be advised that their employer has no legal claim to their literary creations. This is true, even if a textbook is written during regular office hours and tested in college class-

---

[50] Alan Latman, "Fair Use of Copyrighted Works," General Revision of the Copyright Law, Study No. 10 (Multilithed; Washington: Copyright Office, 1958), pp. 37–38.

[51] Theodore R. Kupferman and Mathew Foner (eds.), *Universal Copyright Convention Analyzed* (New York: Federal Legal Publications, 1955), pp. vii, 13, 15, 83–106. See also H. L. Pinner, *World Copyright: An Encyclopedia* (Leyden, Holland: A. W. Sijthoff, 1958).

rooms before formal publication. An employer has no more right to an assignment of the copyrights of his employees than he has to an assignment of their patent rights, unless he obtained this right by agreement, based upon adequate consideration, or unless the employee was engaged specifically for the purpose of writing or producing the work in question.[52]

Unlike a patent, which must be issued in the name of the inventor, a copyright may be issued in the name of the corporation or partnership to which the author may have assigned his rights. A federal court has ruled that a corporation is entitled to copyright a production by one it has employed to produce it, even though the corporation itself obviously is "incapable of exercising intellect."[53]

PROPERTY RIGHTS OF FACULTY IN EDUCATIONAL FILMS AND KINESCOPES. The use of educational tape recordings, films, television, and kinescopes has raised a number of new legal questions. If a faculty member has been paid for his time in making such recordings, has he any right to claim additional compensation when these recordings are used for instructional purposes? The residual rights of faculty in such productions, if they exist, would seem to be similar in character to the residual rights claimed by motion picture actors and writers in old films to be shown again on television.

A federal court has held that, if a motion picture actor has contractually relinquished all rights in films in which he appeared, he cannot thereafter contend that the use of such motion pictures in competition with him on television would constitute unfair competition.[54] Residual rights in films produced after 1948 were the basis of a prolonged strike in 1960 by the Screen Actors Guild against a number of the major producers. The Association of Motion Picture Producers refused to yield, contending that the actors had been fully compensated when the films were produced and that to pay them again when the old films are released on television would constitute double pay for one job. Furthermore, to yield to the demands of the actors would open the door to similar demands from studio technicians and craft unions.

---

[52] Dielman v. White, 102 Fed. 892 (C.C.D. Mass. 1900); Yardley v. Houghton Mifflin Co., 108 F.2d 28 (2d Cir. 1939), *cert. denied,* 309 U.S. 686 (1940); Grant v. Kellogg Co., 58 F. Supp. 48 (S.D.N.Y. 1944).

[53] Vitaphone Corp. v. Hutchinson Amusement Co., 28 F. Supp. 526, 529 (D. Mass. 1939).

[54] Republic Productions v. Rogers, 213 F.2d 667 (9th Cir. 1954).

The following are excerpts from an article by the general secretary of the American Association of University Professors:

The residual rights of faculty members in kinescopic reproductions pose questions seldom encountered before in contractual relations between a faculty member and his institution. It is not possible under present Federal laws to copyright kinescopes.

By analogy with printed materials, one would suppose that the "artist" chiefly responsible for a filmed teaching performance should have some kind of legal protection similar to copyright. Several experienced ETV teachers have expressed the view that a written contract with one's institution is a satisfactory method of protecting the rights of faculty talent.

One administrator recently informed the author that a teacher has no right to royalty claims incident to the making and use of kinescopes. He argued that an institution contracts for the teacher's time on the basis of a yearly salary, and for this reason the institution should own all rights in kinescopic reproductions, just as it has title to all the books in the college library. The administrator was reminded that teachers have traditionally written books and retained the royalties from them . . .

The issue of residual rights in kinescopes and similar considerations are relatively minor problems in higher education, but the philosophy used in settling these problems is fundamental to the health of the academic profession.[55]

THE HAZARD OF LIBEL. The publisher of a libelous statement may be required to respond in damages to injured parties. College administrators responsible for publications of the institution in any form—printing, tape recordings, films, kinescopes, radio, and television—should be aware of this hazard when reviewing material to be disseminated. Procedures to be followed in this matter should be reviewed by counsel and set forth in manuals to guide those concerned.

Separate incorporation of the publication division of the college may provide some protection, but there is always uncertainty as to the extent to which the court will respect the legal fiction of separate corporate identity in the event of suit, if the parent corporation continues to exercise any substantial degree of control over the subsidiary.

According to Paul P. Ashley:

Libel may be defined as any false statement, written or broadcast, which tends to (1) bring any person into public hatred, contempt or ridicule; (2) cause him to be shunned or avoided; or (3) injure him in his business or occupation.

. . . .

The publisher or broadcaster may be liable even though (1) the writer

---

[55] William P. Fidler, "Educational Television: A Faculty Point of View," *Quarterly Journal of Speech*, XLV (1959), 121, 125–26.

carefully gathered data and believed them true; (2) he did not intend the story to be read in a defamatory sense; (3) he did not realize that it could be so understood; and (4) no copyreader, continuity editor, proofreader, or anyone else suspected defamation. If the words are susceptible of a defamatory meaning, the copy or script may be defamatory, despite the most innocent of motives.[56]

---

[56] Paul P. Ashley, *Say It Safely: Legal Limits in Journalism and Broadcasting* (Seattle: University of Washington Press, 1956), pp. 27–28; see also Samuel Spring, *Risks and Rights in Publishing, Television, Radio, Motion Pictures, Advertising and the Theatre* (2d rev. ed.; New York: W. W. Norton & Co., 1956), pp. 41–70.

CHAPTER VII

The Solicitation and Administration of Funds

T H E procedures employed in the solicitation and acceptance of funds should receive the same careful scrutiny of legal counsel as those used in their administration. The significance of this statement will be appreciated when it is realized that the acceptance of a gift, grant, or bequest by a college, subject to restrictions imposed by the donor, creates a charitable trust.[1] Since the terms and conditions of a charitable trust cannot be modified by the trustee, even with the consent and approval of the donor, it is obvious that these terms and conditions should be reviewed with care before the gift is accepted for administration. If the restrictions would impose undue burdens upon the college, out of proportion to the benefits to be derived from the proposed gift, modification should be sought before the gift is accepted. After it is accepted, only a court, exercising the equitable power of cy pres, can grant relief therefrom.[2]

---

[1] See discussion under the heading, "The Final Repudiation of the New York Doctrine," p. 196.

[2] "Cy pres" came into the language of the law from Anglo-French, the tongue spoken by the dominant classes of Britain for several centuries after the Norman Conquest in 1066. The two words mean, literally, "as near [as possible]." The following is the modern interpretation of the term, taken from the wording of the Model Act Concerning the Administration of Charitable Trusts, Devises and Bequests, recommended by the National Conference of Commissioners on Uniform State Laws in 1944:

"If a trust for charity is or becomes illegal, or impossible or impracticable of fulfillment, and if the settlor, or testator, manifested a general intention to devote the property to charity, [a court of equity] may, on application of any trustee, or any interested party or the Attorney General of the state, order an administration of the trust, devise or bequest as nearly as possible to fulfill the general charitable intention of the settlor or testator."

In the majority of states, the cy pres doctrine has been accepted as part of the general body of the common law. A few states, at one time, rejected it, but they have subsequently authorized its use by statute.

The reasons for the rejection of the cy pres doctrine by some state courts are

THE DEVELOPMENT OF THE LAW OF CHARITABLE
TRUSTS IN THE UNITED STATES

Due to a peculiar quirk in the development of the law of charitable trusts in this country, it was possible for Austin Wakeman Scott, editor of the first restatement of the law of trusts in 1935, to make the following comment in his Introductory Note:

Where property is given to a charitable corporation, a charitable trust is not created, even though, by the terms of the gift, the corporation is directed to hold the principal forever and to devote the income only to the accomplishment of the purposes of the corporation, and even though, by the terms of the gift, the corporation is directed to use the property only for a particular one of its purposes.[3]

In other words, gifts, grants, and bequests to a charitable corporation, subject to restrictions imposed by the donor, do not create charitable trusts. Although this statement undoubtedly reflected the weight of judicial opinion in this country at that time, it was based largely upon the decisions of the courts of New York and of the other states following the trend of decisions in that jurisdiction. It failed to reflect a very substantial number of decisions directly contra.[4] Due to the large volume of trust fund litigation in New York, the numerical weight of opinion firmly supported the comment in the restatement.

---

based upon the historical evolution of the doctrine in the courts of chancery in England. During colonial times, cy pres was looked upon in this country as a rule of arbitrary disposition, giving the chancellor power to rewrite and mould charitable trusts and bequests according to his own social or religious views. The doctrine became associated, in the minds of many people, with royalty and monarchial privileges and hence unsuited to the usages of a democratic society. Courts, reluctant to accept the doctrine of cy pres, evolved what is termed the doctrine of approximation or deviation. It is a general principle of equitable procedures and permits a court to vary the details of the administration of a trust to meet changed conditions. It is more firmly established and more widely recognized than the cy pres doctrine.

See 2A Bogert, *The Law of Trusts and Trustees* §§ 431–50 (1935) [hereinafter cited as Bogert]; 4 Scott, *The Law of Trusts* §§ 395–401 (2d. ed. 1956) [hereinafter cited as Scott].

[3] *Restatement, Trusts* § 349 (1935). Professor Scott, in the Introductory Note, qualifies his comment as follows: "Although a gift to a charitable corporation for one or any of its purposes does not create a charitable trust, the rules of law which are applicable are, to a large extent, those which are applicable to charitable trusts, since the ends to be served are the same." Unfortunately, those seeking authoritative justification for a proposed diversion of charitable trust funds from the purposes for which they were given have been inclined to read and to quote the comment itself, and to omit all reference to its important qualification.

[4] 2A Bogert § 322.

Unfortunately, as we shall see, the opinions upholding it were premised upon a misconception of the true basis of the law of charitable trusts.

In his text[5] on the law of trusts, published in 1956, Professor Scott informs us that:

> The real mistake made by the courts in those states was in holding that the law of charitable trusts had its origin in and was dependent upon the enactment of the Statute of Charitable Uses. The mistake was at first excusable in view of the paucity of available historical material. The records which were available did not clearly show that charitable trusts were enforced in England prior to the enactment of the statute in 1601. The courts were compelled to rely upon secondary authorities, and the authorities to which they resorted were the ill-considered dicta of English judges. It is astonishing how frequently courts rely upon the words of other courts, not merely as indications of the law but as proof of facts. The words which fall from judges are seldom a sound foundation for historical research. It was this historical error which led the Supreme Court of the United States to hold invalid a charitable disposition made by a testator who was domiciled in Virginia.

THE HART WILL CASE. The case referred to by Professor Scott, decided in 1819, involved the interpretation of the following provision in the will of Silas Hart:

> What shall remain of my military certificate at the time of my decease, both principal and interest, I give and bequeath to the Baptist Association. . . . Which I allow to be a perpetual fund for the education of youths of the Baptist denomination.[6]

The Philadelphia Baptist Association named in the will was unincorporated, that is, without legal entity. The Legislature of Virginia had repealed all English statutes in 1792, including the Statute of Uses, sometimes referred to as the Statute of Elizabeth.[7] From all available historical material, the members of the Supreme Court assumed that it was not possible, under the common law, to create a charitable trust, that is, that they owed their existence to the enactment of the Statute of Charitable Uses by the English Parliament. Since this had been repealed in Virginia and since the Virginia Legislature had not seen fit to enact similar legislation, there was no law in force in that state un-

---

[5] 4 Scott 2567–68.

[6] The Trustees of the Philadelphia Baptist Association v. Hart's Executors, 17 U.S. (4 Wheat.) 1, 3 (1819).

[7] 43 Eliz. 1, c. 4 (1601).

der which a charitable trust could be created. According to the common law of private trusts, the Philadelphia Baptist Association could have taken title to the property bequeathed by the will of Silas Hart if it had had corporate legal entity. Since it was not incorporated, it could not take title in its own name, and the intended trust thereby failed, with the property reverting to the heirs.

THE GIRARD WILL CASE. The doctrine of the Hart will case, that statutory authority is essential to the creation of a charitable trust, was repudiated by the same high court in 1844 in a famous case involving the estate of Stephen Girard.[8] By this time, better historical material had been made available for judicial consideration. The court came to the conclusion that charitable trusts had been enforced in England long before the enactment of the Statute of Elizabeth in 1601. Consequently, they were obviously not dependent upon statutory authority, that is, the law of charitable trusts is, in fact, an integral part of the common law of this country.[9]

THE LONG-RANGE EFFECTS OF THE HART WILL CASE. Unfortunately, the damage had been done. Courts in a number of jurisdictions continued to echo and re-echo the rule of law enunciated in the Hart will case long after it had been repudiated at its source. In 1866 the Court of Appeals of New York[10] justified its refusal to uphold the validity of a charitable trust in that jurisdiction on the following grounds: (1) the Statute of Charitable Uses had been repealed in New York; (2) when the New York statutes were revised in 1828, no mention was made therein of charitable trusts; (3) the court was persuaded that it would be better public policy not to recognize charitable trusts but to compel those desiring to dedicate funds to charitable purposes to give them to a charitable corporation rather than to individual trustees. In this way, the legislature, by granting or refusing to grant the privilege of incorporation to those planning to devote funds to purposes considered undesirable, could exercise a degree of public control over the use of charitable funds.

THE NEW YORK DOCTRINE. Under this New York doctrine that only a charitable corporation should be permitted to administer funds intended for charitable purposes, it was but a logical corollary that a

---

[8] Vidal v. Girard Executors, 43 U.S. (2 How.) 127 (1844).
[9] See "The Reception of the Common Law in the United States," pp. 3–4.
[10] Bascom v. Albertson, 34 N.Y. 584 (1866).

gift or bequest to a charitable corporation, even with restrictions on its use, did not create a charitable trust, even though the words "in trust" were used in the will or other instrument of gift. As late as 1916, a Maryland court could disregard[11] the following language, usually considered indicative of an intent to create a trust:

> I give and devise unto Trinity Reformed Church . . . my hotel property . . . in trust to the support of the minister, who may, from time to time, be in charge of said church.

Concerning this, the court said:

> . . . there was no intention on the part of the testator to create a trust, . . . the corporation takes the legal and beneficial title to the property, and . . . therefore, its estate is one in fee simple.

If it were really true that the church corporation took title to the property in fee simple, that is, as absolute owner and not as trustee, what law was there to prevent it from disregarding the express instruction of the testator to hold the principal as an endowment and to use the income therefrom for the support of the minister? Shortly after the publication of the first restatement of the law of trusts in 1935, the author called attention to the possible adverse effect a general acceptance of this doctrine might have upon the administration of charitable trusts in this country.[12] In doing so, he was merely reflecting a number of judicial opinions, directly contrary to the New York doctrine. For example, the Supreme Court of Wisconsin, in repudiating the doctrine in 1910, had this to say:

> It seems highly improbable that the testatrix had in mind the giving of this splendid donation in such a way that it might be dissipated or disposed of for any purpose the city saw fit as soon as it came in possession of the property. It is likewise improbable that the donation would have been made had the donor understood that any such result could legally follow.[13]

The general counsel for the University of Illinois, when asked in 1937 his opinion of the possible effect upon future donations to the uni-

---

[11] Conner v. Trinity Reformed Church, 129 Md. 360, 99 Atl. 547 (1916). Note the erroneous assumption implicit in the line of reasoning of the court. A charitable corporation is not the beneficiary of the funds it administers. The real beneficiaries are the members of the general public, especially those in a position to accept the services offered by the charitable corporation. Therefore, a charitable corporation does not take both legal and beneficial titles to funds or property given it to administer.

[12] Blackwell, "The Charitable Corporation and the Charitable Trust," 24 *Wash. U.L.Q.* 1 (1938).

[13] Maxcy v. City of Oshkosh, 144 Wis. 238, 249, 128 N.W. 899, 904 (1910).

versity of an acceptance of the rule of law that an educational corporation holds its endowments as absolute owner and not as trustee,
replied as follows:

If it were known that the University of Illinois, in situations of the type
described, treated the gifts as its absolute property and not encumbered in
any sense with a trust, I am clearly of the opinion that friends, who otherwise might have considered donations for purposes near their hearts, would
hesitate, and probably place their bounty elsewhere.[14]

THE FINAL REPUDIATION OF THE NEW YORK DOCTRINE. Gradually, the
courts of New York began to evidence a desire to escape from the
logical consequences of their doctrine that charitable corporations hold
their restricted funds as absolute owners and not as trustees. Stray
dicta suggested that restrictions imposed by the donor would be enforced by the courts even though no trust had been thereby created.[15]
However, in 1939 the appellate division of the New York Supreme
Court, in the St. Joseph's Hospital case, ruled[16] that a charitable corporation could use its endowment fund for any corporate purpose and
that neither the state nor the donor's representatives could interfere to
require a strict compliance with the donor's expressed intentions. This
decision was reversed in the court of appeals. Judge Finch, speaking
for the majority of his brethren on the bench, said:

The charitable corporation is not bound by all the limitations and rules
which apply to a technical trustee. It may not, however, receive a gift made
for one purpose and use it for another, unless the court, applying the cy pres
doctrine, so commands.

The dissenting opinion of Judge Hubbs reiterated the old New York
doctrine that the bequest to the charitable corporation for the establishment of an endowment was, in fact, an absolute gift to the corporation and that the request or direction that it be held in trust for
a special purpose was merely precatory and did not, in law, compel
the corporation to use and administer the fund in the way directed by
the testator.

---

[14] Letter to the author dated Dec. 7, 1937, from Mr. Sveinbjorn Johnson, general
counsel, University of Illinois.

[15] In the Matter of Griffin, 167 N.Y. 71, 78, 60 N.E. 284, 285 (1901); *cf.* Corporation of the Chamber of Commerce of N.Y. v. Bennett, 143 Misc. 513, 257 N.Y. Supp.
2 (Sup. Ct. 1932).

[16] St. Joseph's Hospital v. Bennett, 256 App. Div. 120, 8 N.Y.S.2d 922 (1933),
rev'd, 281 N.Y. 115, 22 N.E.2d 305, 311 (1939). See 23 *Minn. L. Rev.* 670 (1939)
for an adverse comment on the effects of this decision.

In an annotation to this case, one of the editors of the *American Law Reports* makes this comment:

In-as-much as New York has long since had a statute which permits the creation of charitable trusts, the continued adherence to the view that no trust is created by a gift to a charitable, religious, or educational corporation may be somewhat embarrassing to the New York courts as in *St. Joseph's Hospital v. Bennett,* in which the minority have great difficulty in seeing how the gift can, at the same time, be "absolute," and yet subject to enforceable restrictions on its use.[17]

The following is from an annotation on this same case in the *Columbia Law Review:*

The decision is of practical importance to a host of heavily endowed universities and other charitable organizations and is a substantial clarification of what has heretofore been a moot and disturbing point in this state and in others affected by its decisions.[18]

That the old New York doctrine on this issue has been repudiated by the courts of that state in substance, if not *in toto,* is evidenced by the following from the opinion of Judge Van Voorhis of the Court of Appeals of New York, handed down in July 1957:

It is well established New York law that charitable gifts for designated uses and purposes cannot be diverted or applied to uses other than those specified in the will or instrument of gift.[19]

Thus ends a long and unhappy chapter in the history of the law. In every state, it is now well-established law that colleges and universities, as educational or charitable corporations, hold their restricted gifts and bequests as trustees, in fact if not in name. Those seeking legal justification for diverting restricted gifts from the purposes designated by the donors without the approval of a court of equity can now find no support, either in the cases or in authoritative texts. It is significant that Professor Scott, serving again as editor of the second restatement of the law of trusts, published in 1959, omitted the Introductory Note in the first restatement to the effect that charitable corporations do not hold their restricted funds as trustees. Instead we find the following:

Where property is given to a charitable corporation and it is directed by the terms of the gift to devote the property to a particular one of its purposes, it is under a duty, enforceable at the suit of the Attorney General, to

[17] Annot., 130 *A.L.R.* 1101, 1115 (1941).
[18] 40 *Colum. L. Rev.* 550, 553 (1940).
[19] *In re* Ablett's Will, 3 N.Y.2d 261, 144 N.E.2d 46 (1957).

devote the property to that purpose. Where property is given to a charitable corporation and it is provided by the terms of the gift that it retain the principal and devote the income only to the accomplishment of its purposes or one of its purposes, the corporation is under a duty, enforceable at the suit of the Attorney General, to retain the principal and to use the income for the designated purpose.[20]

It is true, of course, that there are a few important legal distinctions between the duties of the governing board of a charitable corporation holding restricted funds and those of individual trustees of charitable trusts.[21] For instance, a charitable corporation, upon receipt of a bequest for the establishment of a scholarship fund, was not required to seek appointment and to qualify as a trustee by giving bond to the probate court.[22] Since a charitable corporation is not required to qualify with a court as trustee and to submit periodic reports thereto as to its administration of its restricted funds, what assurance does the public have that such funds are being administered in accordance with the terms and conditions in the will or instrument of gift? The public does have an interest in the administration of charitable trusts. This is indicated by the fact that they are sometimes designated as public trusts, in contradistinction to private trusts.

PUBLIC SUPERVISION OF CHARITABLE TRUSTS

At common law, it is the duty of the attorney general of each state to represent the public interest and to enforce the provisions of charitable trusts.[23] In practice, however, this official usually is in no position to do so. In the first place, he has many other duties more demanding of his time. In the second place, he has not the staff that would be required to police the administration of the myriad of charitable trusts in the more populous states. And, more to the point, in the absence of statutory provisions requiring the filing of detailed reports with his office with respect to such funds, he lacks the requisite information to perform the task.

There has been remarkably little recorded litigation in this country involving the maladministration of funds by colleges and universities. In view of the vast sums held by them, this could be construed as a

---

[20] *Restatement (Second), Trusts* § 348 (1959).

[21] 4 Scott 2559 (1956).

[22] American Institute of Architects v. Attorney General, 332 Mass. 619, 127 N.E.2d 161 (1955).

[23] 4 Scott 2755.

tribute to their wise and meticulous administration of such funds. However, the lack of litigation does not always connote good behavior; it may be merely the result of a lack of information.

PERIODIC AUDIT OF THE ADMINISTRATION OF RESTRICTED FUNDS. The published financial report of a typical college contains much fiscal data, but it provides very little information with respect to the degree of care that institution has exercised in fulfilling the requirements of donors as to the administration of the funds they have contributed. Only a careful review of the provisions of the wills and instruments of gift establishing such funds and an analysis of current internal administrative procedures would disclose significant deviations from the terms and conditions thus imposed.

Every reputable institution subjects its administration of cash and other tangible assets to an annual audit by independent accountants. How many have ever had an independent audit and survey of the administration of their endowments and other restricted funds?[24] We are not concerned here with the question of personal dishonesty. A college administrator is under constant pressure to utilize every available resource of his institution to the best advantage. Every college board of control has a duty to provide the best possible educational facilities for the present generation. When these duties and responsibilities seem to come into conflict with restrictions imposed by donors upon the

---

[24] The following is an excerpt from a letter, dated June 20, 1959, to the author from George G. Bogert, one of the leading authorities on the law of trusts:

"With reference to possible ways of checking the use by educational institutions of funds held absolutely but given for a restricted purpose, and also funds held in trust for one or more educational purposes, I would have the following comments:

"(1) My guess is that in some cases funds of these types are administered in a rather loose way and not carefully applied to the special purposes only, but rather under pressure of need from other departments or purposes the special funds are either temporarily or permanently diverted to purposes outside the terms on which they were given.

"(2) I feel that it would be desirable for the authorities of educational institutions to submit such funds to an audit annually by accountants, and also to permit the Attorney General of the state to check on the handling of such funds from a legal point of view. I believe provision for this latter type of inspection is often made in the statutes regarding supervision of charities by the Attorney General, as for example, the statute which has been in force in California and I believe is likely to be continued under a bill introduced at the current session of the legislature.

"Provision for an accountant's audit would have to be made by the governing board of the institution, but the legal audit should be under a statute similar to the Uniform Law for the Supervision of Charitable Trusts, now in force in several states."

use of certain funds, we have, in the words of the General Education Board, the problem of that "duality of interest and motive which is the bane of all good trusteeship."[25] Mr. Justice Jackson of the United States Supreme Court has phrased it very aptly: "Men are more often bribed by their loyalties and ambitions than by money."[26]

PUBLIC SUPERVISION OF CHARITABLE TRUSTS IN GREAT BRITAIN. To what extent have those entrusted with the administration of charitable trusts been faithful to the instructions of donors? Perhaps the record compiled on this subject in England may shed some light. Evidence of maladministration of certain charitable trusts during the reign of Elizabeth I was the real reason for the enactment of the Statute of Charitable Uses discussed at the beginning of this chapter. The remedial portion of the statute gave the chancellor power to appoint commissioners to inquire into and to correct any abuses of charitable bequests or donations. This remedy was in addition to an older one, a petition to the court of chancery. The new procedure gradually fell into disuse. As Professor Scott informs us: "The result was that charitable trusts were left very largely without supervision. Great abuses naturally resulted."[27]

During the reign of Queen Victoria, further legislation on this subject was considered essential. A permanent Charity Commission was created to supervise charitable trusts other than those established for educational purposes; responsibility for these was entrusted to the Board of Education.[28] By the Education Act of 1944,[29] this jurisdiction was conferred upon the Ministry of Education. The Nathan Report advocated further strengthening of the enforcement of charitable trusts.[30]

STATUTORY AUTHORITY FOR THE SUPERVISION OF CHARITABLE TRUSTS IN AMERICA. Professor Scott was one of the first to direct attention to the fact that we have lagged far behind Great Britain in the public supervision of charitable trusts.[31] In 1943 Ernest R. D'Amours, at that time attorney general for the State of New Hampshire, responded to this call

---

25 See p. 203.
26 United States v. Wunderlich, 342 U.S. 98, 103 (1951).
27 4 Scott 2565.
28 62 & 63 Vict. c. 33 (1899).
29 7 & 8 Geo. 6 c. 31 (1944).
30 4 Scott 2755.
31 *Ibid.* § 391.

to action from Professor Scott and drafted proposals to his legislature that resulted in the establishment of a model system of supervision and enforcement.[32]

In addition to New Hampshire,[33] Rhode Island,[34] Ohio,[35] South Carolina,[36] Indiana,[37] Wisconsin,[38] and North Carolina[39] have adopted similar legislation. The Commissioners on Uniform State Laws adopted[40] in 1954 a model act entitled "Uniform Supervision of Trustees for Charitable Purposes Act." This was adopted by California in 1955.[41] According to a survey in 1957,[42] legislation on this subject was under consideration in ten states. The attorney general for New Hampshire found, as the result of his investigation, that approximately 25 percent of the charitable trusts in his state showed evidence of unsatisfactory administration. In Rhode Island, many neglected trusts were discovered.[43]

Although Professor Bogert recommended that legislation of this type include public supervision of charitable corporations holding restricted funds,[44] they have been specifically exempted in every instance. This exclusion in the Ohio Charitable Trusts Act was criticized by Ralph Klapp and Neva Wertz:

> Should not the vast amount of funds so held be specifically subjected to all the provisions of the Act except possibly registration? The language now appearing in the section, if interpreted literally, would seem to free from any powers of the Attorney General all of the vast sums now held by charitable corporations in trust. . . . That such widespread exclusion was not intended is clearly apparent; the Act itself provides that the Attorney General is, "in addition to all his common law and statutory powers," to prepare and maintain a register of charitable trusts. Then, too, the legislature

---

[32] Bogert, "Proposed Legislation Regarding State Supervision of Charities," 52 *Mich. L. Rev.* 635, 639, 641 (1954).

[33] *N.H. Laws* ch. 181 (1943); *N.H. Laws* ch. 92 (1945); *N.H. Laws* ch. 94 (1947); *N.H. Laws* ch. 39 (1949).

[34] *R.I. Laws* ch. 2517 (1950); *R.I. Laws* ch. 2852 (1951).

[35] *Ohio Rev. Code* §§ 109.23–.33, 109.99.

[36] *S.C. Laws* No. 274 (1953).

[37] *Ind. Stat.* §§ 31–712, –713 (1959).

[38] *Wis. Stat.* § 317–06 (1957).

[39] *N.C. Stat.* § 36–19 (1950).

[40] *1958 Report of the National Conference of Commissioners on Uniform State Laws* (Chicago: National Conference of Commissioners on Uniform State Laws, 1959), pp. 339, 364.

[41] *Cal. Gov. Code* §§ 12, 580–96.

[42] Taylor, "Accountability of Charitable Trusts," 18 *Ohio St. L.J.* 157, 165 (1957).

[43] 2A Bogert 643–44.

[44] *Ibid.* 653.

has, aside from the enactment of the Charitable Trusts Act, shown its awareness of the role of the Attorney General in protecting public interests in relation to charitable funds. It is hardly conceivable that there could have been an intention to diminish, in any way, his inherent common law powers and duties.[45]

THE MISAPPROPRIATION OF RESTRICTED FUNDS

There is very little documentary evidence of misappropriation of restricted funds by institutions of higher education in this country except in one specific regard.[46] The published financial reports of many colleges and universities reveal the fact that endowment funds have been utilized for the construction of dormitories and related facilities. This use of endowment funds is termed, euphemistically, "an investment." Tested by all the usual criteria of sound investments, it fails to qualify. An investment, even one made for a long period of time, should possess some degree of liquidity. If future trends should render its retention in the portfolio inadvisable, it should be salable so the funds thereby represented may be reinvested in a more desirable form.

Where could one find a more "frozen" asset than a college dormitory? Who would willingly purchase such property? If a purchaser could be found, could the college relinquish control of so important a facility? The fact is, of course, that it is not an investment at all. Even though the college goes through the formalities of debiting "interest" as a "cost" of dormitory operation and crediting it as "income" from invested endowment, neither entry represents true expense or true income, according to the standards of good accounting. The use of endowment funds for the construction of units of the educational plant of a college can only be justified on the grounds of expediency. The need for such facilities may be very great; the results may be excellent, in terms of service to students and the community. The fact remains, however, that such an expenditure of restricted funds is a misappropriation of funds entrusted to the college.

---

[45] Klapp and Wertz, "Supervision of Charitable Trusts in Ohio: The Ohio Charitable Trusts Act," 18 *Ohio St. L.J.* 181, 192, 193 (1957).

[46] See John Dale Russell, *The Finance of Higher Education* (2d ed.; Chicago: University of Chicago Press, 1954), pp. 268–71; Dr. Russell declares, p. 268: "The responsibility that is most often violated is that of maintenance of the principal intact. A conservative estimate, based upon extensive experience, indicates that perhaps half the endowed colleges of America, on one or more occasions within the past half-century, have violated this obligation in the management of their trust funds."

THE OPINION OF THE GENERAL EDUCATION BOARD. The General Education Board became so concerned with this problem that it published the following opinion in its annual report for the year 1931–32:

It is the judgment of the General Education Board that funds received by a college earmarked "for endowment" (or by other equivalent phrase) cannot be properly invested in plant or buildings of the college used for any of its general or charter purposes, whether such plant or buildings be income-producing (e.g., dormitories, or laboratories for whose use fees are charged) or not. A donor who has earmarked his gift "for endowment" is thinking of safety of principal and certainty and adequacy of income, to the end that the income may always be available to serve the general purposes of the college. He does not wish the principal of his gift to be so used; he wishes that set aside, "invested"; he sharply distinguishes between the *use* of his principal and its *investment*. Expenditure on a dormitory is not the sort of investment he has in mind, because although it may happen to be an income-producing expenditure, the production of income return is not the sole purpose of the expenditure. The choice of this expenditure is not solely determined by safety of principal and certainty and adequacy of income; it is determined largely by the importance of housing students, a social function. If such an investment be allowed, the trustees have that duality of interest or motive which is the bane of all good trusteeship, and the temptation is offered to them to disregard or override the considerations which solely were present in the mind of the donor.

A dormitory, if it is an investment at all, is a "frozen" one; it would presumably sell to a market buyer at far below its cost to the college; the investment could not be changed into another form without serious loss of principal if the college should wish to move to another site, or if the number of students should be cut down, or other housing become available. The income return is not determined by investment conditions, but by the arbitrary decision of the college authorities to charge so much rent to students over whom they have control. The simple and natural understanding of the words "for endowment" seems to preclude their application to uses which form part of a college's general purposes.

The secretary of the General Education Board, in a letter dated July 24, 1950, stated that the resolution quoted above had not been amended and that it therefore represents the board's present policy.

THE USE OF ENDOWMENT CAPITAL GAINS FOR GENERAL CORPORATE PURPOSES. It is apparent, from an examination of the financial reports of the colleges, that many have realized substantial profits on capital by the sale of common stocks held in their endowment funds. Several of the larger institutions have reported capital gains of millions of dollars. In view of the extreme need on many campuses for funds with which to meet increasing annual deficits, it is understandable why such apparently "free funds" should attract attention.

There is indirect evidence to the effect that at least two large universities have seriously considered the use of endowment capital gains for general corporate purposes. The argument seems to run somewhat as follows: If it is true, as the New York courts have said many times, that charitable corporations hold their restricted funds as absolute owners and not as trustees, why should not a university use such profits for any legitimate corporate purpose, as long as the principal of each endowment is maintained at its original dollar value? The argument obviously disregards the present state of the common law of charitable trusts, even in New York. Those advancing the argument are still reading from the casebooks of the past.

THE USE OF RESTRICTED FUNDS FOR INDIRECT ADMINISTRATIVE COSTS. Another variation on the general theme is a proposal by one university to use a portion of its current restricted funds each year for indirect administrative costs or overhead, without the knowledge or consent of donors. It is quite true that every new fund accepted for administration, every new project undertaken, involves increased costs of administration and operation. If the impact of sponsored research did nothing more to the colleges, it drove this important lesson home. Indirect costs are true costs; they are just as real as direct costs. But they differ from direct costs in one very important particular: by definition, they cannot be directly identified; they must be computed or estimated. In this process of computation or estimate, it is inevitable that a college administrator finds himself subject to a strong conflict of interest.

It is to the interest of the general activities of the college, that is, of the college in its corporate capacity as owner and administrator, that the overhead rate on special projects and special funds be as high as possible. On the other hand, it is to the interest of the college in its capacity as trustee, dedicated to the conservation of the special funds entrusted to it, to set the overhead rate thereon as low as possible. How can this conflict of interest be resolved? In any system of jurisprudence evolved by man, it is axiomatic that one cannot sit in judgment on one's own acts.

In the case of contracts for sponsored research, the question of the overhead rate is settled by negotiation, with opposing interests fully represented. The conflict of interest in the case of contracts with agencies of the Federal Government is so great that it has been the subject of much group discussion over the years between representatives of the federal agencies and of the colleges.

Is it not somewhat unrealistic to assume that a conflict of interest of such magnitude, requiring long and sometimes bitter argument in contract negotiations, can be equitably determined by unilateral decision, as in the case of the overhead rate to be charged against restricted funds? If a college should become convinced that it should not continue to administer certain of its restricted funds without being reimbursed for its overhead costs, it may apply to a court for advice. The court and the attorney general of the state, representing the public interest, can settle the question equitably.

COMPENSATION FOR THE ADMINISTRATION OF CHARITABLE TRUSTS. At common law, a trustee was supposed to serve without compensation. Today, however, it is customary for the trustees of private trusts to ask and to receive a reasonable fee for their services. This fee is usually stated in the trust instrument. If not so stated or if the stated rate is considered excessive by the court, it is determined by the judge. The majority of states have established trustee fees by statute.[47]

By long-established custom and tradition, colleges and universities have accepted endowments and other charitable funds entrusted to them without expecting or requesting compensation for the overhead costs involved in their administration. It is quite possible that a prospective donor would be surprised and shocked if he were asked to include a provision for an administrative or service charge in the instrument of gift establishing an endowment for the support of a professorship. The surrogate's court of New York County, in 1944, granted the Marine Midland Trust Company, serving as the corporate trustee of a charitable trust, the same fee for administration thereof as would have been granted if the trust had been a private one.[48] This allowance, it should be noted, was by court order. Apparently, no college or university has ever petitioned a court for such an allowance. Until there are cases of record on this point, it is impossible to predict the attitude of the courts.

HARVARD UNIVERSITY AND THE ARNOLD ARBORETUM CONTROVERSY. The difficulty of obtaining judicial review of an alleged violation of the terms and conditions of a restricted gift is illustrated by a case involving

---

[47] 2A Bogert § 975.
[48] In the Matter of Belknap, 184 Misc. 272, 50 N.Y.S.2d 228 (Surr. Ct. 1944).

Harvard University. Under the provisions of an indenture dated March 29, 1872, trustees appointed by the will of James Arnold conveyed to Harvard the property received by them for the establishment of a permanent endowment, the net income to be used for

the establishment and support of an Arboretum, to be called the Arnold Arboretum, which shall contain, as far as practicable, all the trees, shrubs, and herbaceous plants, either indigenous or exotic, which can be raised in the open air at the said West Roxbury . . . and to the support of a Professor, to be called the Arnold Professor.

By 1879 the Arnold endowment had increased to $150,000, and Charles Sprague Sargent had been appointed the Arnold Professor, a position which he held until his death in 1927. Under his leadership, an outstanding library and an excellent herbarium were assembled at the West Roxbury location now known as Jamaica Plain. Before Professor Sargent's death and subsequently, friends of the Arboretum, by gift and bequest, increased the book value of the Arnold endowment to more than $4 million.

In June 1945 Professor Irving W. Bailey, of the Department of Biology at Harvard University, prepared and submitted a report entitled "Botany and Its Application at Harvard," usually referred to as "the Bailey Plan." This was a proposal that the nine independently endowed institutions at Harvard concerned with botany coordinate their activities. The Bailey Plan was approved by the Harvard Corporation in 1946. By 1949, as preliminary measures were taken to implement the plan, their effect upon the status and the work of the Arboretum became apparent to certain members of the committee appointed by the Harvard board to review the work of the Arboretum.

They retained counsel to advise them as to whether the Bailey Plan was in violation of the trust upon which the Arnold fund was held. In an opinion dated March 1, 1952, they were advised that there were serious questions as to the legality of the proposed changes. The opinion recommended that a judicial determination of the legal issues be sought.

The Harvard Corporation, early in 1949, as a result of the criticisms of the members of the Arnold committee, requested the Board of Overseers of Harvard to review the controversy. At its meeting of January 19, 1953, the provisions of the Bailey Plan, as they applied to the Arboretum, were rescinded, but the corporation declared, by formal resolution, that the removal to a central building in Cambridge, of the main body of the library and herbarium of the Arboretum relating to research, would be in the best interests of the Arboretum and would promote the purposes of its endowment. The books, approximately eight thousand in number, and the specimens to be left at Jamaica Plain were those required for a working library and museum.

Both before and after this action by the corporation, counsel for the Arboretum committee urged the members of the corporation to file a petition with a court of equity to review impartially the issues involved. The following statement by the president and fellows of Harvard was published in the *Harvard Alumni Bulletin* of December 12, 1953:

We understand that, as a matter of law, instructions will be granted in Massachusetts only when the trustee has "real and serious doubts as to his duty." We have no such doubts as to our duty in respect to matters covered by our resolution of January 19, 1953. On the contrary, we are firmly convinced that the administration of the Arboretum and of its endowment in accordance with that resolution is proper and is within the terms of the endowment and the scope of our discretion as trustee.

When this decision of the Harvard Corporation became known, counsel for certain members of the Arnold committee and others, acting as individuals, decided to take action. Under Massachusetts law, when a trustee declines to file a petition for instructions, persons interested in the trust may request the attorney general of the state to file a petition on his own initiative or, more frequently, to permit the use of his name by "relators," that is, individuals willing to assume the cost of the suit.

THE ATTORNEY GENERAL DECLINES TO ACT. The attorney general requested his assistant to review the matter and submit an opinion. The following is from his opinion:

There is no legal breach of trust. To permit the use of the name of the Attorney General in cases like the present, where it is clear that the trustee is acting in good faith and within the bounds of reasonable judgment and sound discretion, simply because others, equally in good faith, differ with the decision of the trustee, would open the door to unreasonable and vexatious litigations. Accordingly, by the direction of the Attorney General, the application is denied.

Ten alumni of Harvard, eight of whom were members of the Arnold committee, brought suit in the Supreme Judicial Court of Massachusetts for an order directing the attorney general to reconsider his decision and thus permit the controversy to be reviewed by a court of law. The following is from the opinion of the court on the question of judicial review:

In our opinion, the decision of the Attorney General not to permit the use of his name in a suit against the College for alleged breach of a public charitable trust was a purely executive decision which is not reviewable in a court of justice. The duty of taking action to protect public charitable trusts and to enforce proper application of their funds rests solely upon the Attorney General as the representative of the public interest.[49]

THE ASSOCIATION FOR THE ARNOLD ARBORETUM, INC. If one may judge the intensity of interest in this controversy by the volume of published material, it is clear that some friends of Harvard feel very strongly on this matter. The Association for the Arnold Arboretum, Inc., was organized as a nonprofit Massachusetts corporation to oppose Harvard's announced plan for the Arboretum. The following is from a statement published by the association under date of March 31, 1955:

The membership is widely representative of those interested in preserving the Arnold Arboretum as a distinguished horticultural-botanical institution and of those concerned with the reputation of Harvard University as a guardian of trust funds. . . . To many it seems intolerable that, when important questions of legal breach of trust have been raised by eminent lawyers, no way has been found to obtain a judicial ruling through the only means whereby these questions can be determined, i.e., through a hearing on the merits by the courts of Massachusetts.

THE DOCTRINE OF VISITATION. To what extent can the administrators of endowment and other trust funds be relied upon to sit in judgment on their own actions and decisions? Mr. Justice Storey, in the famous Dartmouth College case, remarked that since administrators

are liable . . . to deviate from the end of their institution, . . . there shall somewhere exist a power to visit, inquire into, and correct all irregularities and abuses in such corporations and to compel the original purposes of the charities to be faithfully fulfilled.[50]

The right of a donor, his appointees, and his heirs to visit, inspect, and correct abuses in the administration of endowments established by his philanthropy is an ancient legal concept. A few of the early American colleges and preparatory schools have permanent boards of visitors. Professor Bogert has this to say:

The exact status of the doctrine of visitation in modern American law is not perfectly clear. It seems a relic of earlier times which has not been expressly abolished by statute in most states and has been occasionally recog-

---

[49] Ames v. Attorney General, 332 Mass. 246, 250, 124 N.E.2d 511, 513 (1955).
[50] Trustees of Dartmouth College v. Woodward, 17 U.S. (4 Wheat.) 518, 673 (1819).

nized by decision. It is not believed, however, that it is a feature of charitable trust administration which is either practical or desirable under present conditions. It would seem that the visitorial power should be separated from the managerial power. No genuine check or control on the administration of the charity will come from the very administrators themselves.[51]

The Supreme Court of Pennsylvania in 1954 declared that "The state serves as visitor to all charitable institutions."[52] As authority for this statement it cited an earlier case as follows:

The Commonwealth exercises its visitorial and supervisory powers through the Orphans' Court. . . . That court is therefore not merely a court of competent, but of exclusive, jurisdiction for the control and direction of managers and trustees in the use and disposition of property belonging to incorporated charities.[53]

BUILDINGS GIVEN FOR A SPECIFIC PURPOSE. With the rapid expansion of campus facilities demanded by postwar enrollments, many colleges are faced with the fact that existing buildings are no longer adequate to serve present-day needs, especially where they were designed to provide facilities for a given department, such as physics. If the building was constructed with contributed funds, the will or instrument of gift establishing the building fund should be examined before making any change in its use. The donor or his heirs should, of course, be consulted also, but it should be remembered that their consent to a proposed change is not enough. If the donor of the fund stipulated that the building be used for a specific purpose and if, in the opinion of counsel, the language used was mandatory and not merely "precatory," that is, expressing only a recommendation or request, the consent and approval of a court of competent jurisdiction should be obtained as authorization for any proposed change of occupancy and use.

FUNDS SOLICITED FOR A SPECIFIC PURPOSE. Although there are, apparently, no recorded cases directly in point, it would seem logical to assume that a college is as much bound to apply funds solicited for a specific purpose to the purpose as though the donor had himself demanded the same restraint on their use. For instance, if a college initiates a campaign to raise funds for endowment and buildings and this proposed use of the funds to be raised is widely publicized, such funds,

---

[51] 2A Bogert § 416 (1935).

[52] In the Matter of McKee, 378 Pa. 607, 108 A.2d 214 (1954).

[53] John C. Mercer Home for Disabled Clergymen of the Presbyterian Faith v. Fisher, 162 Pa. 239, 29 Atl. 733 (1894).

when received, would seem to be as much impressed with the stated restrictions as though each individual contributor had inserted the restrictions in his letter of gift. In the law of contracts, it makes no difference who formulates the terms of the bargain; once the contract becomes effective, all parties thereto are bound by its terms. If one may use this same line of reasoning in the law of charitable trusts, then it is a breach of trust for a college to solicit funds for one purpose and use them for another, as, for example, funds solicited for endowment used in part to pay the costs of the campaign of solicitation. Furthermore, it is good public relations to obtain funds for campaign expenses from a few understanding friends of the college. Although everyone knows that it costs money to raise money, the average contributor tends to resent the thought that his modest gift will not be utilized in full for the purpose for which he gave it.

THE EFFECT OF SUBSEQUENT WITHDRAWAL OF RESTRICTIONS BY A DONOR. If a donor should make a grant to a college for the establishment of an endowment fund and, some years later, inform the college that, so far as the donor is concerned, the college is free to use the principal of the fund for any corporate purpose approved by its own governing board, such actions by the donor and the governing board of the college would not, in themselves, be sufficient to convert an endowment fund into an unrestricted fund. It would still be necessary for the college to file a petition with a court of competent jurisdiction, requesting a modification of the terms of the original gift or grant. The fact that the donor had expressed his consent and approval of such modification would be a factor in the court's consideration of the petition. If convinced that, due to changed conditions, it would now be in the public interest to permit the college to use some or all of the principal of the funds for current purposes, it could issue an order to that effect.

THE INVESTMENT OF RESTRICTED FUNDS

There is still some question as to whether the same rules of law governing the investments of individual trustees must be observed by the governing board of a charitable corporation.[54] Consequently, the advice

---

[54] 4 Scott § 389. However, Scott, writing as editor of *Restatement (Second), Trusts* § 389 comment *b* (1959), has this to say: "Where money is given to a charitable corporation for its general purposes, it may make such investments as a prudent man would make. Even in a State in which trustees are restricted, by statute or otherwise, to certain kinds of investments, the restriction is not appli-

of counsel is essential in this matter. In some jurisdictions, trustees are limited by statute to certain types of investment. If, in the opinion of counsel, the statute in the state in which the college is incorporated is not applicable to charitable corporations or if there is no such restrictive statute in force, the governing board of the college is free to make any investment a prudent man would make of his own property, having in mind the preservation of principal and adequacy of income to be derived therefrom.[55]

THE PRUDENT MAN RULE. The case in which the "prudent man" rule for the guidance of trustees was enunciated involved a bequest for the establishment of a professorship at Harvard College. In 1830 Judge Putnam, on behalf of the Supreme Judicial Court of Massachusetts, declared:

> All that can be required of a trustee to invest is, that he shall conduct himself faithfully and exercise a sound discretion. He is to observe how men of prudence, discretion and intelligence manage their own affairs, not in regard to speculation, but in regard to the permanent disposition of their funds, considering the probable income, as well as the probable safety of the capital to be invested.[56]

This Harvard College case has been cited many times. It freed the fiduciaries of Massachusetts from the rigid limitations of precedents imposed by English conservatism of the Victorian era and opened the door to a more effective utilization of the accumulated earnings of the New England merchants and shipowners. It was the primary factor in the development of what came to be known in later years as the "Boston trusteeship." A number of the leading families of Boston achieved fame and considerable fortune by building a reputation for sagacious and effective administration of trust funds, under the protection of the prudent man rule. Trusteeship became a profession.[57]

Prior to 1900, only a few jurisdictions had adopted the prudent man rule of the Massachusetts court. The major economic areas of the coun-

---

cable. Even though the corporation is directed to invest the funds and use only the income, either for any of its purposes or for a particular one of its purposes, the restriction applicable to trustees is not applicable to it, unless it is otherwise provided by the terms of the gift."

[55] This is assuming that the donor of the fund to be invested has not imposed restrictions of his own on the type of securities to be retained or purchased.

[56] Harvard College v. Amory, 26 Mass. (9 Pick.) 446, 461 (1830).

[57] Shattuck, "The Development of the Prudent Man Rule for Fiduciary Investment in the United States in the Twentieth Century," 12 *Ohio St. L.J.* 491, 500, 501 (1951).

try—New York, Ohio, Pennsylvania, Texas, Illinois, California, and the states created from the old Northwest Territory—limited the investment of trustees to what are known as "legal lists." These schedules of eligible securities, prepared in accordance with statutory formulae, include federal, state, and municipal bonds and very high-grade industrial bonds and notes.[58]

After World War I, the accumulation of fiduciary funds seeking investment increased with great rapidity. Paralleling this enormous increase in trust fund assets there was a drastic decrease in the volume of "legal list" securities eligible for investment. Under the irresistible pressure of these two concurring factors, state after state was forced to adopt a more liberal policy. In 1942 the American Bankers Association sponsored the preparation of a model state statute designed to facilitate the enactment of the Massachusetts prudent man rule. In the wording of this model statute, much of the phraseology was taken verbatim from the opinion of the court in the Harvard College case of 1830. Many states have made use of the model act.[59]

THE SALE OF COMMON STOCKS UNDER THE PRUDENT MAN RULE. Under the prudent man rule, a trustee is not only permitted to purchase sound common stocks, but, under certain circumstances, the sale of such stocks may be in violation of his duty as a trustee. In 1956, a California court ruled[60] that, under the California prudent man statute,[61] a trustee must exercise his independent judgment as to whether he should or should not sell certain common stocks. If he fails to do so, and instead, relies upon the advice and judgment of one of the beneficiaries of the trust, he is liable for any loss in value of principal of the trust fund if the other beneficiaries of the trust do not consent to the sale.

THE MERGER OF ASSETS OF ENDOWMENT FUNDS. According to the law of trusts, a trustee must not commingle or merge the assets of two or more trust funds administered by him. Bogert declares:

If the same person is trustee of two trusts, . . . he should set up the trusts separately, tag the property of each with the appropriate name and keep

---

[58] Dean Stanley Samad of the College of Law of the University of Akron suggests: " 'Legal list' requirements can often be obviated by express provision in the trust agreement—at least if the university has any control over its drafting. In Ohio, the legal list is applicable to both testamentary and *inter vivos* trusts."

[59] 4 Scott § 227.13.

[60] *In re* Talbot's Estate, 141 Cal. App. 2d 309, 296 P.2d 848 (S.D. Cal. 1956); see Annot. 58 A.L.R. 2d 674 (1958).

[61] *Cal. Civ. Code* § 2261 (1).

the *res* of each trust distinct, both physically and with respect to all records and marks of identification.

There has been some tendency, however, to permit the mingling of two or more trust funds in an investment, provided the trustee keeps accurate books with regard to the shares of each trust, and each *cestui* is given notice of his exact interest. Modern legislation regarding . . . common trust funds sanctions the mixture of the funds of several trusts under appropriate safeguards.[62]

It should be noted that Bogert is discussing the rights and duties of individual trustees and of trust companies. Scott has this to say:

There is a further question whether a charitable corporation is bound to keep separate from its other funds those which are given to it for restricted purposes, or whether it may mingle all the funds in one common pool. Private trustees are ordinarily not permitted to mingle funds of different trusts. It is believed that, in the absence of restrictions in the terms of the gift as to this matter, such mingling by a charitable corporation is not improper.[63]

As editor of the second restatement of the law of trusts, Scott words his opinion more positively:

Where money is given by separate donors to a charitable corporation, whether the money may be used for any of its purposes or is to be applied to various particular purposes, the corporation can properly mingle the funds in making investments, allocating shares of the mingled fund and its income to the various purposes, unless it is otherwise provided by the terms of the donation.[64]

Unfortunately, Scott does not cite a case directly in point to support his belief. In view of the very large sums involved, it seems strange that there is, apparently, no case of record declaring that a college or university may, without breach of trust, merge or consolidate the assets representing the investment of their endowed and other restricted funds. The advantages of this procedure are obvious. Each individual fund invested in the pool receives the benefit of broader diversification, with its attendant protection of principal and stability of income. For the college itself, merger of investment assets means substantial economies in administrative costs. That the practice is almost universal today is easily proven by a review of college financial reports. If only a few of the larger institutions would file petitions with the courts for advice on this important question and support their petitions with

---

[62] 2 Bogert § 596 (3) (1960).
[63] 4 Scott § 389.
[64] *Restatement (Second), Trusts* § 389 comment *c* (1959).

well-reasoned arguments as to the advantages of merger, the resulting decisions would begin to establish reliable case law on the subject.

THE PURCHASE OF PARTICIPATING SHARES IN INVESTMENT TRUSTS. One of the phenomena of the modern investment market is the enormous increase in investment trusts, both in number and in the total value of their assets. Whether a trustee may legally invest in the certificates of an investment trust is still an open question in many jurisdictions.

Probably the most important duty of a trustee, the one for which he was selected, is the exercise of his personal skill and discretion in the purchase of sound investments for the trust. Duties of such importance cannot be delegated. Bogert has this to say: "In the case of such highly important transactions as would be carried out personally by the average property owner, the trustee must personally make the decisions and perform the acts involved."[65]

Despite this basic rule of law, an Ohio court was of the opinion that the purchase of common and preferred stock of Continental Shares, Inc., by a trustee did not represent an improper delegation of his personal responsibility to select each specific security for his trust.[66]

THE RULE AGAINST ACCUMULATION OF INCOME. In 1946 the Supreme Court of Florida held that a trust instrument stipulating that one half of the income of a trust fund should be added to principal indefinitely and the other half be expended for charitable purposes annually was void as violating the common law rule against perpetuities.[67] The court apparently considered it against public policy to permit an accumulation to charity for an indefinite period. However, in the same year, a Wisconsin court held unobjectionable a provision in a charitable trust for the accumulation of the income of a fund of approximately $25,000 until it should reach a size where it would produce an income of $6,000 a year.[68]

---

[65] 1 Bogert § 92 (1952).

[66] *In re* Estate of Rees, 53 Ohio L. Abs. 385, 85 N.E.2d 563 (Ct. App. 1949), *affirming* 53 Ohio L. Abs. 513, 87 N.E.2d 397 (P. Ct. 1947); see 3 Scott § 227.9A (1956), n. 2, for citations to state statutes permitting fiduciaries, subject to certain restrictions, to invest in stocks or other investment securities of management investment companies. For further discussion of this type of investment, see *College and University Business Administration* (2 vols.; Washington: American Council on Education, 1952; 1955), II, 118.

[67] Porter v. Baynard, 158 Fla. 294, 28 So.2d 890 (1946), *cert. denied* 330 U.S. 844 (1947).

[68] *In re* Robinson's Estate, 248 Wis. 203, 21 N.W.2d 391 (1946); *see also* 2 Bogert § 353 (1953).

LEGAL RESTRICTIONS ON GIFTS TO CHARITY

Individuals in England during the Middle Ages, impelled by religious convictions, bequeathed great wealth to the Church. At one time, religious orders were said to possess nearly one-half of the land of Great Britain.[69]

MORTMAIN STATUTES. A desire to protect the family of the testator from want resulted in the enactment of the so-called Statute of Mortmain during the reign of George II.[70] Twelve jurisdictions in this country have similar restrictions on bequests to religious and charitable organizations: New York, Idaho, Ohio, Missouri, Pennsylvania, Florida, the District of Columbia, Montana, Iowa, Georgia, Maryland, and California.[71] The Louisiana Civil Code stipulates that

donations *inter vivos* (during the lifetime of the donor) or donations *mortis causa* (in anticipation of death) can not exceed two-thirds of the property of the disposer, if he leaves at his decease, a legitimate child; one-half if he leaves two children, and one-third, if he leaves three or more children. The term "child" includes grandchildren and great-grandchildren. Donations . . . can not exceed two-thirds of the property, if the disposer, having no children, leaves a father or mother or both.[72]

ACCEPTANCE OF CERTAIN GIFTS IN NEW YORK MAY CONSTITUTE "UNFAIR EDUCATIONAL PRACTICE." The New York Legislature in 1948 made certain actions by educational institutions "unfair educational practices."[73] In 1953 it was declared to be "an unfair educational practice" for an educational institution, after September 15, 1948, "to accept any endowment or gift of money or property conditional upon teaching the doctrine of supremacy of any particular race."[74]

CORPORATIONS MAY NOW SUPPORT HIGHER EDUCATION. For many years, it was a well-supported rule of law that the directors of commercial corporations had no right to "give away" their stockholders' money.[75]

---

[69] Joslin, "Legal Restrictions on Gifts to Charities," 21 *Tenn. L. Rev.* 761, 762 (1951).

[70] 9 Geo. 2, c. 36 (1736). Mortmain means, literally, "dead hand," and it is frequently used to refer to the holding of property by religious and charitable organizations with perpetual existence.

[71] 2 Bogert § 326 (1953); 4 Scott § 362.4 (1956).

[72] *La. Civ. Code* art. 1493-94 (1945).

[73] *N.Y. Laws* ch. 753 (1948); see "Racial Discrimination in Private Schools," pp. 118–19.

[74] *N.Y. Educ. Law* § 313 (2)(c).

[75] Dodge v. Ford Motor Co., 204 Mich. 459, 170 N.W. 668 (1919); *see also* 6A Fletcher, *Cyclopedia of the Law of Private Corporations* §§ 2 939, 2 940 (1950); Annot., 39 *A.L.R.* 1192 (1955).

Three-quarters of a century ago an English chancellor declared: "Charity has no business to sit at the boards of directors."[76] Less than fifty years later, a chancellor, sitting in the same English court, approved a corporate contribution of £100,000 for the support of scientific education and research.[77] However, the general rule in England and in America, until quite recently, was that donations by corporations to educational and other charitable organizations could be justified as a legitimate use of corporate assets only if it could be shown that direct and substantial benefits would accrue to the corporation as a result of the gift.

As early as 1917, the Legislature of Texas, in a statute restricting the use of corporate funds to "the legitimate business" of the corporations, was far-sighted enough to add the following:

provided that nothing in the Article shall be held to inhibit corporations from contributing to any bona fide association, incorporated or unincorporated, organized for purely religious, charitable or eleemosynary activities.[78]

This was apparently the first statutory declaration that the power of a corporate board to make such donations no longer rested upon the common law doctrine of corporate benefit. By 1945 nine other states followed the trail blazed by Texas: New York (1918), Illinois (1919), Ohio (1920), Tennessee (1925), New Jersey (1930), Massachusetts (1933), Michigan (1935), Missouri (1937), and Delaware (1941).

At the 1948 Annual Meeting of the American Bar Association, Ray Garrett, a Chicago attorney, in his address to the section on corporations, banking, and mercantile law, commented on the growing disparity between the common law on the subject of corporate giving and the need for greater support of educational and other charitable organizations. In March 1949 his Committee on Business Corporations issued a memorandum recommending the adoption, by the various state legislatures, of an act declaring that commercial corporations shall have the power to make donations for charitable, scientific, or educational purposes. This provision is now Section 4(m) of the Model Business Corporation Act, approved by the National Conference of Commissioners on Uniform State Laws.[79]

---

[76] Hutton v. West Cork Ry., 23 Ch. D. 654, 673 (1883).

[77] Evans v. Brunner, Mond & Co., 1 Ch. 359 (1921).

[78] See *Model Business Corporation Act, Annotated* (St. Paul, Minn.: West Publishing Co., 1960), § 4(m), par. 2.01.

[79] Bell, "Corporate Support of Education: The Legal Basis," 38 *A.B.A.J.* 119 (1952); de Capriles and Garrett, "Legality of Corporate Support to Education:

Largely as a result of this action by the American Bar Association, the adoption of statutes authorizing donations by corporations has become widespread. All such statutes enacted prior to 1950, except in West Virginia, were subsequently amended to conform, at least in part, to the provisions of the Model Act. As of February 1960, the only states that had no statutory provisions authorizing corporate donations were Arizona, Idaho, Montana, South Carolina, South Dakota, and Wyoming.[80]

The Supreme Court of New Jersey in 1952 was called upon to interpret a state statute enacted in 1950[81] which declared that it was the public policy of the State of New Jersey that encouragement be given to charitable, educational, and scientific activities, and, to this end, corporate gifts, not in excess of 1 percent of capital and surplus, might be made without the specific authorization of stockholders. The Board of Directors of the A. P. Smith Manufacturing Company had adopted a resolution which set forth the proposition that it was in the corporation's best interest to join with others in the 1951 Annual Giving to Princeton University. A contribution of $1,500 was approved. The action was questioned by certain of the stockholders, and the corporate directors requested a declaratory judgment setting forth their duties and powers under the new statute.

Recognizing the importance of this test case to corporate management as well as to higher education, counsel for the A. P. Smith Manufacturing Company was able to persuade several leaders of American industry to testify, including Frank W. Abrams, at that time board chairman of the Standard Oil Company (New Jersey), and Irving S. Olds, former chairman of the board of the United States Steel Corporation. Mr. Abrams gave as his opinion that

more and more Americans have come to expect corporations to assume an attitude of social responsibility. . . . The people who own corporations, and the personnel whom they employ to manage them, wish to meet and fulfill this public expectation. . . . They feel that it is not good business for corporations to take substantial benefits from their membership in the economic

---

A Survey of Current Developments," 38 *A.B.A.J.* 209 (1952); Bleiken, "Corporate Contributions to Charities: The Modern Rule," 38 *A.B.A.J.* 999 (1952); Rohr, "Corporate Philanthropy: The Changing Law," 33 *Mich. S.B.J.* 14 (1954); Richard Eells, *Corporation Giving in a Free Society* (New York: Harper & Bros., 1956).

[80] The American Bar Foundation, 1155 E. 60th St., Chicago 37, Ill., is prepared to furnish information as to the current status of state legislation authorizing corporate philanthropy and the adoption of Section 4(m) of the Model Business Corporation Act.

[81] *N.J. Stat.* § 14:3–13.1 (1958).

community while avoiding the normally accepted obligations of citizenship in the social community.

Mr. Olds declared:

> The corporations of this state will suffer, if, in the future, these educational institutions should be allowed to wither away, decay or, perhaps, to disappear because of lack of funds to carry on their important functions. . . . Every American business has a direct obligation to support the free, independent, privately endowed colleges of this country to the limit of its financial ability and, unless it recognizes and meets this obligation, I do not believe it is properly protecting the long-range interest of its stockholders, its employees and its customers.

Judge Jacob's opinion is an excellent review of the change that has taken place in common and statutory law on the subject of corporate gifts. The following are excerpts therefrom:

> During the 19th Century, when corporations were relatively few and small and did not dominate the country's wealth, the common law rule did not significantly interfere with the public interest. But the 20th Century has presented a different climate. (Berle and Means, *The Modern Corporation and Private Property* (1948)). Control of economic wealth has passed largely from individual entrepreneurs to dominating corporations, and calls upon the corporations for reasonable philanthropic donations have come to be made with increased public support. In many instances such contributions have been sustained by the courts within the common law doctrine upon liberal findings that donations tended reasonably to promote corporate objectives. (Cousens, "How Far Corporations May Contribute to Charity," 35 *Va. L. Rev.* 401 (1949)).
>
> In the light of all the foregoing, we have no hesitation in sustaining the validity of the donation by the plaintiff. . . . We find that it was a lawful exercise of the corporation's implied and incidental powers under common law principles and that it came within the express authority of the pertinent state legislation.[82]

The Supreme Court of the United States, by its dismissal of the appeal in this case,[83] implicitly upheld the constitutionality of the New Jersey statute and of others similar to it in other jurisdictions.

SUPPORT OF HIGHER EDUCATION BY PUBLIC UTILITIES. Utilities, because of their quasi-monopolistic status, are regulated by public commissions. In return for this regulation, they have been held to be en-

---

[82] A. P. Smith Manufacturing Co. v. Barlow, 13 N.J., 145, 149, 160, 161, 98 A.2d 581, 584, 590.

[83] *Ibid., appeal dismissed,* 346 U.S. 861 (1953).

titled to a reasonable return on their capital assets devoted to public service. If the rates charged the public are not sufficient to provide a reasonable return, the commission must permit them to increase their charges. Consequently, if a public utility is permitted to charge its donations to one of its operating expense accounts, the public will, in the long run, carry the burden of such contributions in the form of higher rates.

This issue was presented in a case decided by the Supreme Court of Utah in 1958.[84] The majority of the court ruled that the Union Pacific Railroad had implied authority to make such contributions. It should be noted that the gift in question had been made before the Utah Legislature had taken action on the question of corporate donations.

The state utility commissions have, with very few exceptions, disallowed such items as operating expenses of a public utility.[85] The reasons given by the members of the commissions for this disallowance may be summarized as follows:

1. The patrons of public utilities should not be forced to become involuntary contributors to charities selected by the governing boards of the utilities. If their customers wish to donate to such organizations, the gift should be a voluntary act.

2. Such contributions by utilities have no direct relation to the development or improvement of services rendered. Whatever benefit may accrue to the utility is primarily in the interest of the stockholders, and they should bear the burden rather than those who make use of the services of the utility.

This question came before the Supreme Court of New Jersey in 1953, but the court declined to rule upon it. The New Jersey Bell Telephone Company had charged, as an operating expense for the year, an item of $77,300, representing charitable contributions. The state board of public utility commissioners had ruled that it was unreasonable to require the consumer to pay for these donations in the form of higher telephone charges. Because the gross amount of the contributions, even if allowed as an item of expense in computing the company's net return for rate-making purposes, was too small to affect the reasonableness of the existing rates, the court declined to rule on the issue.[86]

---

[84] Union Pac. R.R. v. Trustees, Inc., 8 Utah 2d 101, 329 P.2d 398 (1958).

[85] For a summary of decisions on this point, see *Public Utilities Reports Digest*, under "Expenses" § 46, "Donations."

[86] New Jersey Bell Telephone Co. v. Department of Public Utility Commissioners, 12 N.J. 568, 97 A.2d 602 (1953).

PUBLIC REGULATION OF THE SOLICITATION OF
CHARITABLE GIFTS

The New York Legislature, in an effort to protect its citizens from the importunities of the agents of unknown and perhaps unworthy charities, passed the Tomkins Act in 1954.

THE TOMKINS ACT OF NEW YORK. This legislation was enacted at the end of the session without due consultation with representatives of educational institutions. It required every charitable organization intending to solicit contributions from persons in the State of New York, except religious organizations and those confining their solicitations to their own members, or, in the case of educational institutions, to their student body, their families, alumni, and friends, to register with the New York Board of Social Welfare. As administered, the original act resulted in strong protests. It was amended in 1957 to read:

The following persons shall not be required to register with the department:

(a) An educational institution the curriculums of which in whole or in part are registered or approved by the state education department either directly or by acceptance of accreditation of an accrediting body recognized by such department, an educational institution confining its solicitation of contributions to its student body, alumni, faculty and trustees, and their families . . . provided that the annual report of such institutions . . . shall be filed with the state educational department where it shall be open to public inspection.

(b) . . . alumni organizations when solicitation is confined to its membership.[87]

REGULATION OF SOLICITATION IN OTHER STATES. In order that other state legislatures may avoid the mistakes inherent in the original Tomkins Act, the Council of State Governments[88] has prepared a model act entitled, "An Act To Prohibit the Unauthorized Use of Names in the Solicitation of Funds for Charitable Purposes." A substantial number of states have already passed legislation restricting, in some degree, the solicitation of contributions for charitable purposes. The American Alumni Council[89] has published, as Section 60:3 of its *Educational Fund Raising Guide,* a summary of restrictive legislation affecting those soliciting funds for educational institutions.[90]

---

[87] *N.Y. Laws* ch. 276 (1957); *N.Y. Social Welfare Law* § 482(a)(2)(a)–(b).

[88] 522 Fifth Ave., New York, N.Y.

[89] 1785 Massachusetts Ave., N.W., Washington 6, D.C.

[90] See Annot. 128 *A.L.R.* 1361 (1940) and 130 *A.L.R.* 1504 (1941) for a dis-

THE CUMULATIVE LIST OF CHARITABLE ORGANIZATIONS. The Federal Government exerts an indirect, but powerful, control over organizations soliciting contributions from the public. In order that a contributor may be able to deduct his contribution from his gross income in computing his income tax for the year, the organization receiving the gift must have qualified as a "charitable organization," as defined in Section 170 (c)(2) of the Internal Revenue Code. The Internal Revenue Service maintains a cumulative list of all organizations whose status has been reviewed and found to be in accord with this definition. The cumulative list is designated as *I.R.S. Publication 78* and the current edition may be obtained from the Superintendent of Documents, Washington 25, D.C. Approximately forty thousand organizations are listed, and a weekly supplement to the list is published in the *Internal Revenue Bulletin.* Although there can be little doubt of the ability of a recognized college or university to qualify for listing, it would be well for each institution, if it has not already done so, to verify the fact that it is included in this published list. A photocopy of the letter from the Internal Revenue Service to this effect should be included in the manual of procedures prepared for the use of those seeking contributions for the college. Every prospective contributor is entitled to assurance on this point.

THE EFFECT OF ALUMNI ASSOCIATION INCORPORATION. The American Alumni Council in 1959 conducted a survey of the legal status of college alumni associations. Of the 669 institutions replying to the questionnaire, 196 reported that their alumni associations were incorporated as a separate legal entity. Of this number, 65 reported that they had qualified as a "charitable organization" under the provisions of Section 501(c)(3) of the Internal Revenue Code, thus obtaining, not only exemption from the federal income tax, but also the privilege of deductibility of gifts to them for donors. However, 29 had qualified under Section 501(c)(7), which gives exemption to the association but denies deductibility to their contributors.

In a case before the federal Tax Court in 1955, involving a bequest to the California Alumni Association, the incorporated alumni association of the University of California, judicial notice was taken of the fact that "any social or recreational aspects of the Association are

---

cussion of the constitutionality of statutes or ordinances regulating the solicitation of charitable contributions.

merely incidental to its primary purpose of affording a medium through which the alumni can contribute to the welfare of the university."[91]

The sole issue presented for decision was whether a bequest of $60,101.98 to the California Alumni Association was deductible from the gross estate of Philip R. Thayer under Section 812(d) of the Internal Revenue Code of 1939. The Tax Court held that the association was operated exclusively for educational and charitable purposes within the meaning of the code and that the bequest was therefore not subject to the federal estate tax. One judge dissented, on the grounds that, in his opinion, the social and recreational activities of the association were not incidental but substantial.

The Commissioner of Internal Revenue has acquiesced in the Tax Court's decision in this case.[92] All separately incorporated alumni associations planning to solicit and receive gifts and bequests in their own corporate name should, of course, seek qualification under Section 501 (c)(3) rather than under Section 501(c)(7). The current tax regulation on the subject reads as follows:

A gift to an educational institution through an alumni association or class organization which acts simply as a fund-raising or collection agency through which gifts may be made currently to the institution, is a gift to the educational organization if the entire gift inures to its benefit, but not if any part of it inures to the general or operating fund of the agency.[93]

THE LEGAL STATUS OF PLEDGES

Colleges are frequently compelled to rely upon the validity of charitable subscriptions. Plans must be based upon the assumption that courts will enforce, if necessary, the payment of pledges to support the work of the institution undertaken in reliance on such pledges. Although American courts have, within recent years, recognized the validity of charitable subscriptions, their reasons for taking this position have been conflicting and confusing.

MORAL OBLIGATIONS NOT RECOGNIZED BY THE COURTS. This conflict with legal logic arises from the fact that the common law of England and America developed the theory of contracts upon the assumption that moral obligations should not be enforceable in a court of law. The Roman law had provided for the recognition of such obligations of con-

---

[91] Philip R. Thayer, 24 T.C. 384, 391 (1955).

[92] 1956–2 Cum. Bull. 309.

[93] Myers and Quiggle, "Alumni Associations as Organizations Described in Section 501(c)(3) of the Code," 45 A.B.A.J. 392 (1959).

science, but the English common law courts rejected this alien intruder from the civil law. The English judges were willing to hold people to their bargains, but they would not enforce their gratuitous promises unless they were executed in solemn form under seal. In other words, mutuality was of the essence of the bargain, so far as the common law courts were concerned. The value of the consideration to bind the contract need be only nominal; even a peppercorn has been held sufficient.

This necessity for consideration gave the courts grave difficulties when they were confronted with the problem as to whether they should permit an individual to revoke his promise to make a gift to a college or other charitable organization. The English courts usually refused to enforce gratuitous subscriptions.[94] Sir Frederick Pollock, the leading English authority on the law of contracts, has said: "A promise to contribute money to charitable purposes is a good example of the class of promises which, though they may be laudable and morally binding, are not contracts."[95]

THE EARLY AMERICAN CASES. The early American courts were almost unanimous in their refusals to enforce charitable subscriptions.[96] However, public opinion in this country was not satisfied with the English doctrine and the courts were under increasing pressure to hold subscribers to charities legally bound upon their promises. In 1845 Chancellor Walworth, in the Hamilton College case,[97] attempted to inject into the common law of New York the theory that the promises of the various subscribers should be sufficient consideration for each other. The court seemed well aware of the essential fact that performance of the promise by one of the promisors would not, in a legal sense, be beneficial to the others.

The fallacy of the doctrine that consideration for each subscription promise can be found in the promises of the other subscribers has been exposed many times, yet the courts continue to indulge in it.[98] Everyone knows that the subscriber is making a gratuitous promise to make a gift and nothing more. The charity to benefit from the promise is equally aware of the fact that it is not driving a bargain in the commercial

---

[94] *In re* Hudson, 54 *L.J.* ch. 811 (1885).

[95] Pollock, *Principles of Contracts* (3d American ed. 1906), at 186.

[96] Trustees of Bridgewater Academy v. Gilbert, 19 Mass. (2 Pick.) 578 (1824).

[97] Stewart v. Trustees of Hamilton College, 2 Denio 403, 421 (N.Y. Ct. Corr. Err. 1845).

[98] Underwood v. Waldron, 12 Mich. 73 (1863); Higet v. Indiana Asbury University, 53 Ind. 326 (1876).

sense of that word. The court, conscious of the fact that sound public policy demands that charities should be permitted to rely on such promises, gropes in legal darkness for something that bears a reasonable resemblance to the common law concept of consideration.

PROMISSORY ESTOPPEL. Another doctrine relied upon by American courts to support the legal validity of charitable subscriptions is that of the so-called promissory estoppel. This doctrine was first invoked in an early Massachusetts case.[99] A friend of Farmington Academy had agreed to make a contribution to finance the erection of a building on the campus. After he had seen the building constructed in reliance on his promise, he refused to pay his pledge. The court held that, since he had permitted the promisee to incur heavy obligations on the faith of his promise, he should not be permitted to repudiate his pledge, that is, he should be estopped to deny it.

A Vermont court followed this same doctrine of estoppel in 1829 when it held that a subscription, taken to rebuild the University of Vermont after its destruction by fire, was legally enforceable because the university corporation had initiated work of reconstruction in good faith, relying upon the promise to support the work.[100] However, this application of the doctrine of estoppel was so at variance with the fundamental concepts of that word that the term "promissory estoppel" was coined by the legal commentators to designate the anomaly. As one writer has said:

the hundreds of American subscription cases attest the fact that our courts intend to enforce these promises, even though they are compelled to warp either the doctrine of consideration or that of estoppel in order to reach the desired result. . . . Courts do not intend to permit promissors to go scot free because prevailing common law doctrines lack the breadth to hold them bound.[101]

THE COLORADO WOMAN'S COLLEGE CASE. The Colorado Woman's College found itself near bankruptcy in the depression years, with the holders of the first and second mortgages on its campus buildings threatening foreclosure and with over $37,000 of unsecured notes and accounts unpaid. In 1935 the administration of the college organized a campaign to raise funds to free the college of debt. They requested their general

---

[99] Trustees of Farmington Academy v. Allen, 14 Mass. 172 (1817).

[100] University of Vermont v. Buell, 2 Vt. 48 (1829).

[101] Billig, "The Problem of Consideration in Charitable Subscriptions," 12 *Cornell L.Q.* 467 (1927).

creditors and the holder of the second mortgage to pledge one half the amount of their claims against the college as an incentive to the other contributors, pointing out the fact that, if the campaign for funds failed, the holder of the first mortgage would take over and that they, the junior creditors, would lose the entire amount of their claims. All the creditors except one responded to this appeal. A printing company, with a claim of $10,605 against the college, pledged only $2,500.

With this respite, the college was able to continue its activities, and in 1937 it initiated a campaign to raise funds for the construction of a new dormitory. By 1941 the college had raised sufficient funds to pay off all its creditors, less the amounts of their pledges. The college tendered the printing company the amount of its claim, less the $2,500 pledged. The company refused the tender and brought suit for the full amount of its claim. It obtained judgment in the trial court, but the decision was reversed in the Colorado Supreme Court. The court, in reaching its desired conclusion, reasoned as follows:

> The circumstances necessarily support the inference that the college accepted the pledge, incurred expense and devoted effort, and that the other subscribers, in good faith, made contributions, all in reliance on the pledge. . . . The company could not, in good conscience, be permitted knowingly to let the efforts and expenses continue and the other contributions be made, all on the strength of its pledge; by silence inducing the belief that it was still recognized and in force, when, in fact, the company had secretly determined to refuse payment.[102]

THE PLEDGE OF MARSHALL FIELD. By letter dated December 9, 1954, to Edward L. Ryerson, a trustee of the University of Chicago, Marshall Field, Jr., confirmed the oral pledge of his father and of himself, stating, in part, as follows:

> This is a brief note to confirm what I told you on the telephone the other day—namely, that my father and I would attempt to put together a half a million dollar package for the forthcoming University of Chicago fund raising campaign. This amount would be given over a five-year period. The breakdown of this would be:
>
> 1. My own personal contribution would be $50,000, or $10,000 a year.
> 2. My father's personal contribution would be $100,000, or $20,000 a year.
> 3. Field Enterprises, Inc., including the newspaper, would be $100,000, or $20,000 a year.
> 4. The Foundation would be $250,000, or $50,000 a year.

---

[102] Colorado Woman's College v. Bradford-Robinson Printing Co., 114 Colo. 237, 246, 157 P.2d 612, 616 (1945); see Annot. 38 A.L.R. 868 (1925), 95 A.L.R. 1305 (1935), 115 A.L.R. 589 (1938), 151 A.L.R. 1238 (1944).

On or about April 12, 1955, Mr. Field transferred to the university securities with a market value of $20,147.50, and on or about July 10, 1956, he made a second payment on his pledge by a transfer of securities valued at $20,170.50. After his death in 1956, his executors filed a petition in the surrogate's court of Suffolk County, New York, for instructions regarding the validity and enforceability of this and another charitable subscription made by the deceased. The following are from the opinion of the surrogate, handed down on April 3, 1958:

The law of Illinois on the enforceability of a charitable subscription is stated by its Appellate Court (*In re* Estate of Drain, 311 Ill. App. 481, 36 N.E.2d 608, 609 (1941)), as follows:

. . . if the promisee, on the faith of the subscription, and before its withdrawal, performs some act, such as the expenditure of money or incurring liabilities which are enforceable, in furtherance of the enterprise the promisor intended to assist or promote, consideration for the subscription is then supplied, and the same is therefore deemed to be valid, binding and enforceable.

There, the Court also enunciated (36 N.E.2d at page 609) the public policy of Illinois toward charitable subscriptions:

Courts lean toward sustaining such contracts when the same may be done without violating established rules of law. Many of our most beneficent institutions are largely maintained by virtue of voluntary contributions from those who are disposed to encourage and promote such work.

I find that the decedent made the pledge in question, made partial payments thereunder and that the donee, in reliance upon the promise of the decedent donor, as well as the promises of other donors, incurred certain obligations. Accordingly, I hold the decedent's oral promise is valid and enforceable and that this pledge does not come within the prohibitions of the Illinois Statute of Frauds and Perjuries. After deducting the partial payments, the balance of $59,682 remains due the University of Chicago from this estate.[103]

TAX ADVICE TO DONORS

In these days of high taxes, those seeking to persuade others to give must be prepared to advise them as to the tax implications of the gifts. Many colleges have found it desirable to prepare, with the aid of counsel, booklets in which the needs of the college are stated and tax legislation, regulations, rulings, and decisions are discussed in relation to gifts and bequests for the support of higher education. Specific examples permit a prospective donor to visualize more vividly the tax implications of his proposed gift.

---

[103] *In re* Field's Estate, 11 Misc. 2d 427, 172 N.Y.S.2d 740 (Surr. Ct. 1958).

THE EFFECT OF CHARITABLE GIFTS UPON THE AMOUNT OF TAX PAYABLE. Although it is a matter of common knowledge that a charitable gift may be deducted from gross income before the calculation of income tax, those soliciting such gifts should be prepared to cite the exact provisions of federal and state legislation on the subject, and, by carefully prepared tables and examples, show the net cost of gifts to individuals in the various tax brackets.

Section 170(a)(1) of the federal Internal Revenue Code states the general rule: "There shall be allowed as a deduction any charitable contribution . . . payment of which is made within the taxable year." A charitable contribution is defined in Section 170(c) as

a contribution or gift to or for the use of:

(2) A corporation, trust, or community chest, fund, or foundation—

(A) created or organized in the United States or in any possession thereof, or under the law of the United States, any State or Territory, the District of Columbia, or any possession of the United States;

(B) organized and operated exclusively for religious, charitable, scientific, literary, or educational purposes or for the prevention of cruelty to children or animals;

(C) no part of the net earnings of which inures to the benefit of any private shareholder or individual; and

(D) no substantial part of the activities of which is carrying on propaganda, or otherwise attempting to influence legislation.

Institutions are sometimes asked to accept what may be termed a scholarship fund, but with the donor reserving the right to designate the particular individuals to receive the so-called scholarships. Since the very essence of a charitable contribution is the intent of the donor to benefit society in general and not designated individuals, such designated funds should be treated as prepaid tuition rather than as contributions. For tax purposes, the distinction between such private philanthropy and public philanthropy must be maintained. If one makes a gift for the direct benefit of an individual, this is private philanthropy and is not deductible from the taxable income of the donor.

CONTRIBUTIONS BY AN INDIVIDUAL. Although Section 170(b)(1)(B) limits the amount an individual may deduct as a charitable contribution to 20 percent of his adjusted gross income for the year, the 1954 revision of the code, that is, Section 170(b)(1)(A), provides for an additional 10 per cent if the contributions are made to "(i) a church or convention or association of churches, (ii) an educational institution, or (iii) a hospital."

UNLIMITED DEDUCTIONS FOR GENEROUS INDIVIDUALS. Section 170(b)(1)(C) states that the limit on charitable deductions "shall not apply in the case of an individual, if in the taxable year and in eight of the ten preceding tax years, the amount of charitable contributions plus the income tax . . . paid during such year or preceding tax years, exceeds 90% of the taxpayer's taxable income for such years." Prior to the 1954 revision of the code, this test had to be met in each of the ten preceding years in order for the taxpayer to claim the right to unlimited deduction of charitable gifts.

CONTRIBUTIONS BY A CORPORATION. Section 170(b)(2) states that "in the case of a corporation, the total deduction under subsection (a) for any taxable year shall not exceed 5% of the taxpayer's taxable income." If the corporation's gifts are in excess of 5 percent in any one tax year, this section of the code permits the company to apply the excess amount against the two succeeding tax years.

AN EDUCATIONAL INSTITUTION DEFINED. An educational institution is defined in Section 503(b)(2) as one "which normally maintains a regular faculty and curriculum and normally has a regularly enrolled body of pupils or students in attendance at the place where its educational activities are regularly carried on."

Section 1.170.2(b)(3) of the Code of Federal Regulations reads, in part, as follows:

An "educational organization" within the meaning of section 170(b)(1)(A) is one whose primary function is the presentation of formal instruction and which normally maintains a regular faculty and curriculum and normally has a regularly enrolled body of pupils or students in attendance at the place where its educational activities are regularly carried on. The term, therefore, includes institutions such as primary, secondary, preparatory, or high schools, and colleges and universities. It includes Federal, State, and other public-supported schools which otherwise come within the definition. It does not include organizations engaged in both educational and noneducational activities unless the latter are merely incidental to and growing out of the educational activities.

CONTRIBUTIONS OTHER THAN MONEY. In soliciting contributions, college representatives should call attention to the very substantial tax avoidance possibilities offered by gifts in the form of securities or other property. The Code of Federal Regulations states:

If a contribution is made in property other than money, the amount of the deduction is determined by the fair market value of the property at the time of the contribution. The fair market value is the price at which the property would change hands between a willing buyer and a willing seller, neither being under any compulsion to buy or sell and both having reasonable knowledge of relevant facts.[104]

In a Law Opinion, issued by the Treasury Department in 1923, it was held that:

On account of the clear purpose of Congress in enacting the charitable contribution section . . . , it is not considered that Congress intended to tax indirectly any unrealized appreciation in the value of property given to charitable organizations.[105]

THE DONATIVE SALE. In the light of this ruling, declaring that one may claim the unrealized appreciation of donated property without becoming subject to a capital gains tax on the amount of the appreciation, it is possible to make use of what is known as a "donative sale" in reducing one's tax liability. If the donor does not care to give the full amount represented by the present market value of the property, he may sell it to the college at his original cost, or at any price less than its present market value, and claim as a deductible gift the difference between the market value and the amount realized by the sale to the college. The effect of the capital gains tax is to "freeze" an investor in securities which he may not care to retain, but in which he has a large appreciation in value. The donative sale permits him to "unfreeze" his original capital and, in addition, reduce his current tax liability. To many prospective donors, the benefits to be derived from this procedure, when fully explained, may prove surprising.

CONTRIBUTION OF AN UNDIVIDED INTEREST IN PROPERTY. If the property to be given cannot be divided without loss of value, it is possible to give an undivided interest therein each year for several years, thus spreading the deduction over more than one tax period. This procedure was upheld in 1931 by a federal district court of appeals.[106] A tract of land was conveyed by deed to a charitable corporation. The consideration for the transfer was a series of notes maturing over a period of five years. The notes were cancelled by the holder each year as they matured, and their amounts were claimed by him as a charit-

---

[104] 26 C.F.R. § 1.170–1(c) (1958); see also 26 C.F.R. § 86.19(a) (1949).

[105] L.O. 1118, II–2 Cum. Bull. 148 (1923); see also final paragraph of Rev. Rul. 275, 1955–1 Cum. Bull. 295, 297.

[106] Andrus v. Burnet, 50 F.2d 332 (D.C. Cir. 1931).

able deduction. The Board of Tax Appeals disallowed the items as claimed and ruled that the entire gift had been made when the title passed. The district court of appeals reversed this ruling and held that the donor was entitled to use this method to spread the value of his gift over more than one tax year.

LIFE INSURANCE AS A GIFT. It has become traditional, in some colleges, for each member of the senior class to take out an endowment policy with his alma mater as the beneficiary. The face of the policy is made payable on the twentieth anniversary of the class graduation. The class members claim as tax deductions the premiums as paid. In this way, a very substantial gift is spread over a long span of years. In the event of nonpayment of premiums by a member, a class fund is used to maintain the policy as long as possible.[107]

There are, of course, other plans under which life insurance may be used to raise funds for the support of higher education. Representatives of life insurance companies are prepared to offer helpful suggestions.

GIFT OF PROPERTY WITH LIFETIME USE THEREOF RETAINED BY THE DONOR. By calling his attention to the tax savings possible, a college may be able to persuade an individual to give property, with legal title vesting at once in the institution but with retention of the use and enjoyment of the property during the lifetime of the donor, that of his wife, should she survive him, and that of any other designated individuals.[108]

There are many variations possible, each of which should be explored in considering the one most likely to appeal to the prospective donor. The property to be given may consist of cash, securities which have appreciated in value, residences, country estates, business property, farms, works of art, valuable books, or stamp or coin collections.[109]

The donor is entitled to claim as a deduction for tax purposes, not the full market value of the property at the time of the gift, but that value, reduced by the value of the income or use retained, based upon the life expectancy of the beneficiaries, discounted at a stipulated rate of interest. If this amount, when computed, is found to be in excess of the donor's allowable deduction for the current year, title to undivided

---

[107] See Meier, "Charitable Bequests and Life Insurance," 11 *Am. Soc. of Chartered Life Underwriters* 331 (1957); Rev. Rul. 372, 1958–2 *Cum. Bull.* 8.

[108] Ithaca Trust Co. v. United States, 279 U.S. 151 (1929).

[109] Rev. Rul. 293, 1957–2 *Cum. Bull.* 153.

fractions of the property can be given each year for two or more years.[110]

The computation of the value of the gift is made in accordance with Section 1.170–2(d)(2) of the Code of Federal Regulations, which reads, in part, as follows:

> Where the value of a reversionary interest is dependent upon the continuation or termination of the life of one or more persons, it must be determined on the basis of Table 38 of the United States Life and Actuarial Tables 1939–1941, published by United States Department of Commerce, Bureau of the Census, and interest at the rate of 3½% a year, compounded annually. See Table I of §81.10 (i) of Regulations for valuations based upon one life, and Internal Revenue Service Publication No. 11 (1955), (Actuarial Values for Estate and Gift Tax) for values based upon more than one life. In an actual case (not merely hypothetical), the grantor or his legal representative may, upon request, obtain the information necessary to determine such a value from the district director with whom the grantor files his return. The request must be accompanied by a statement showing the date of birth of each person the duration of whose life may affect the value of the reversionary interest and by copies of the instruments relevant to the transfer.[111]

LIFE INCOME AGREEMENTS. The life income agreement is one example of the gift of property with lifetime enjoyment thereof retained by the donor. Many colleges and other charitable institutions have found it a very effective method of raising capital funds. The donor has the pleasure of establishing a named fund during his lifetime and of designating the use of the fund by the college after the death of the last named beneficiary. Many individuals, dependent upon their accumulated savings for present support, can be persuaded to relinquish the task of investment and reinvestment to a responsible institution. The college has the assurance that the fund will eventually be available for the support of its activities. Although the college might receive the equivalent in the form of a bequest, a present gift is always to be preferred to a possible bequest in the future.

A TAX-FREE INCOME POSSIBLE. By instructing the college to invest his fund in tax-free state or municipal bonds, the donor may enjoy the tax benefit therefrom. Although such securities yield less than corporate bonds of equal investment rating, the net yield to those in the higher tax brackets is very attractive. Of course, the donor can pur-

---

[110] Rev. Rul. 58–455, 1958–2 *Cum. Bull.* 30.
[111] T.D. 6285, 1958–1 *Cum. Bull.* 127, 139.

chase such tax-free securities for his own account. If, however, some of his capital is "frozen" in securities in which he has a large unrealized profit, by giving these same securities to the college, subject to a life income, he could, prior to December 2, 1960, obtain this tax advantage without paying the "toll" of the capital gains tax. This and the reduction of his current income tax by virtue of his deduction of the value of his gift to the college made the proposal extremely desirable to anyone in a position to take advantage of it.[112]

However, on December 1, 1960, the Internal Revenue Service announced that it had changed its position with respect to such life-income agreements. The following are excerpts from Ruling 112, published in *Internal Revenue Bulletin* 1960–49, dated December 5, 1960:

> Where a taxpayer transfers appreciated securities or other property to a tax-exempt organization, as trustee, which is under an express or implied obligation to sell such property and invest the proceeds in tax-exempt securities, or exchange the transferred property for tax-exempt securities, and to pay the income therefrom to the transferor (and a secondary beneficiary for life, if any), with the trustee acquiring a remainder interest in the trust corpus, the gain from the sale or exchange of the transferred property by the trustee is includible in the gross income of the transferor. Tax-exempt income realized from trust investments and distributed by the trustee to the transferor beneficiary or to the secondary beneficiary retains its exempt status in their hands.
>
> . . . .
>
> Pursuant to the authority contained in section 7805(b) of the Code, the principles announced in this ruling will be applied only to transfers of property after December 2, 1960, involving an investment of the proceeds of sale of the transferred property in tax-exempt securities or an exchange of the transferred property for tax-exempt securities. Any change in existing Internal Revenue Service position with respect to transfers of property not involving such sale or exchange, and reinvestment in tax-exempt securities, will be prospective only.

A LIFE INCOME AND CAPITAL GAINS TO THE DONOR. The attractiveness of the life income agreement as a means of giving was enhanced by a 1955 tax ruling.[113] The taxpayer had created an irrevocable trust, reserving the income to himself for life with remainder over at his death to a charitable organization. The agreement provided that the trust shall be invested in the stock of regulated investment companies and that dividends received by the trustee which represent profits derived from the sale of securities owned by such investment companies may

---

[112] Rev. Rul. 60–370.
[113] Rev. Rul. 620, 1955–2 *Cum. Bull.* 56.

be considered as income and, as such, distributed to the donor. The ruling held that, despite the possibility of capital gains becoming payable to the donor, the full present worth of the remainder interest passing to the charity may be deducted by the donor in the taxable year in which the property was transferred to the trustee. This ruling also illustrates the point that a trust company, rather than the college, may receive the present legal title to the property donated, with present income retained by the donor and those he may designate; the college to receive both the legal and beneficial titles at the decease of the last named beneficiary.

A GIFT OF ONLY PRESENT INCOME. The reverse of the life income agreement may appeal to some friends of the college. They may be in a position to give the present income from property to the college during their lifetime, but not longer, because of a desire to protect dependents. This result may be accomplished by the creation of a trust, with the income from the property payable to the college, with the principal or income or both payable to designated individuals after the decease of the donor and his wife.

A variation of this plan may fit the need of an individual who has already given or committed his full allowable deduction. He can create a short-term trust, with the income payable to the college for the designated term and the principal reverting to him at the expiration of the trust. By removing, temporarily, the income to be derived from the property thus placed in trust from his current taxable income, he is thereby enabled to increase the amount of his gifts to charity without reference to the statutory limitations.

Prior to the 1954 revision of the code, a taxpayer was required to part with legal title and possession of his property in the trust for a period of ten years in order to enjoy this privilege, but, under the provisions of the present code, the trust need be for a term of only two years or more.[114]

THE SALE OF ANNUITY CONTRACTS BY A COLLEGE. Some individuals may prefer the assurance of a fixed income, to be obtained from an annuity contract, in preference to the variable income provided by the life income agreement. The purchase of an annuity is not a gift, and no deduction may be claimed. However, a portion of the annual income derived from an annuity contract is tax free, whereas all of the income

---

[114] 26 U.S.C. § 673 (b) (1955).

from a life income trust or agreement is taxable to the recipient, unless his fund is invested in tax-exempt securities.

The recipient of an annuity is permitted, under Section 72 of the code, to exclude that portion of the payment which represents the return of capital rather than true income or interest. This return of capital is computed in accordance with the formula known as the "exclusion ratio," as explained in subsection (b) of Section 72. This exclusion is based upon the life expectancy of the annuitant, but, once computed, it remains constant even though the recipient outlives his life expectancy.

From the standpoint of the college, however, the sale of an annuity contract may not be as advantageous as the receipt of a gift, subject to the payment of a life income. Under an annuity contract, the college obligates itself to pay a fixed amount each year during the lifetime of the annuitant. The amount of such payments is calculated from standard tables used by commercial life insurance companies, reduced by whatever factor the college may feel is justified. These tables may be relied upon with some assurance by a life insurance company writing many thousands of life and annuity contracts. The law of averages, however, is reliable only where large numbers are involved. Since an individual may live much longer than his predicted life span, a college, by accepting only a few of such risks, may suffer severe financial loss, due to the failure of the law of averages to function when only a few individuals are involved. Even though a college may attempt to protect itself by using tables more favorable to it than those used by commercial insurance companies in computing annuity benefits, there is still some hazard involved.[115] Moreover, some states require organizations writing annuity contracts to register and to comply with certain statutory regulations. Those contemplating the sale of such contracts should obtain expert legal and actuarial advice.

TESTAMENTARY TRUSTS. If a friend of the college has or plans to make provision for the institution in his will, a frank discussion of its provisions may prove mutually advantageous. It is difficult for a college to reject a bequest, even though the restrictions on the use of the property bequeathed may prove onerous. Important tax savings may be accomplished. For instance, a testamentary trust, with full income

---

[115] The following is the comment of Mr. Grant Nickerson, of counsel for Yale University: "Might also affect tax exemption as possible diversion of charitable funds to private use."

for life to named beneficiaries and the remainder passing to the college, will reduce substantially estate and inheritance taxes. The advice of counsel is essential in the drafting of such agreements.

THE EFFECTIVE DATE OF A GIFT. When a gift is made near the close of a tax year, the actual date title passed to the college becomes of importance to the donor. Moreover, this date is of importance in the case of a gift of securities. The donor is entitled to claim, as the amount of his charitable deduction, the fair market value of his gift on the date his gift becomes effective. According to common law, a gift is not effective until it has been delivered to the donee. What constitutes effective delivery? With respect to shares of stock, the Commissioner of Internal Revenue has ruled that the date of delivery of a properly endorsed stock certificate to the donee or to his agent is the effective date of the gift.[116]

If the donor has the stock certificate transferred on the books of the corporation before delivery to the donee, the date of registration of the stock in the name of the donee is the effective date of gift, not the date of the subsequent delivery of the certificate to the donee or to his agent.[117]

If the payment is by check, the federal Tax Court has ruled that the date of delivery of the check is the controlling one, not the date the check is paid by the donor's bank and charged to his account.[118] In the case in question, one of the checks was not received by the charitable organization until December 31, 1948, after banking hours. It was not paid by the bank that it was drawn on until January 4, 1949. The following are excerpts from the opinion of the court:

> It would seem unfortunate for the Tax Court to fail to recognize what has so frequently been suggested, that, as a practical matter, in everyday personal and commercial usage, the transfer of funds by check is an accepted procedure . . .
> With knowledge of the prevalence of this practice, and of the necessity of treating tax questions from a practical rather than a theoretical viewpoint, it would be astonishing indeed if, by the use of the word "payment" in section 23(O), Congress did not intend to include a check given absolutely and, in due course subsequently presented and paid. . . . We conclude that the decedent, upon the issuance and delivery of the checks in question,

---

[116] Rev. Rul. 554, 1954–2 *Cum. Bull.* 317.

[117] Rev. Rul. 135, 1954–1 *Cum. Bull.* 205.

[118] Modie J. Spiegel, 12 T.C. 524, 527 (1949). The Commissioner of Internal Revenue has acquiesced in this decision; see 1949–2 *Cum. Bull.* 3.

made a conditional payment of the charitable contribution, which, upon the presentation and payment of the checks, became absolute and related back to the time when the checks were delivered.

THE ASSESSMENT OF STATE INHERITANCE
TAXES ON CHARITABLE BEQUESTS

An inheritance or succession tax is not a levy upon property but upon the privilege of receiving property by a bequest. The tax burden is upon the recipient and, since it is not a property tax, an educational institution, even though exempt from property taxation, is subject to a tax on the property it receives by bequest unless the inheritance tax statute of the state in which the testator was domiciled at the time of his death contains an exemption provision for such bequests.[119]

No state levies a tax on bequests to charitable institutions located and incorporated within its borders, but some states tax bequests to charitable institutions located in other states. In order to eliminate this toll upon charitable bequests, efforts have been made to establish, by legislation, a policy of reciprocity, whereby the state in which the testator was domiciled agrees to waive the assessment if the state in which the recipient institution is incorporated has agreed to a similar policy.[120]

---

[119] Washington County Hospital Ass'n v. Mealey's Estate, 121 Md. 274, 88 Atl. 136 (1913).

[120] *In re* Baxter's Estate, 100 Cal. App. 2d 397, 223 P.2d 877 (S.D. Cal. 1950); see 1 *CCH Inh., Est. & Gift Tax Rep.* (7th ed.) ¶ 12,020 (Wash. 1957); for an analysis of federal and state income, inheritance, estate, gift, and franchise taxes of interest to college and university administrators, see Edward T. Applegate, *Tax Deductions and Exemptions of Gifts to Educational Institutions* (Washington: American Alumni Council, 1959).

CHAPTER VIII

Additional Problems of Publicly Controlled Colleges[1]

T H E first state universities in this country, established soon after the Revolution, were in many respects private, rather than public, corporations.

HIGHER EDUCATION AS A FUNCTION OF GOVERNMENT

The concept of an institution of higher education as an instrumentality of the state was slow in evolving in the public consciousness. The courts, during this early period, tended to consider them in the same light as hospitals and other private charitable corporations, chartered by the state but controlled by their own governing boards.

This attitude of the courts is understandable in view of the fact that higher education as a public purpose was, in itself, a novel idea. The medieval universities of continental Europe and England were not considered to be integral parts of the framework of civil government.

---

[1] Many of the legal problems of public institutions of higher education are identical with those subject to private control. However, the fact that the tax-supported institutions are divisions or instrumentalities of the state itself creates many additional problems. Hence, the necessity for this chapter. Nonetheless, it has seemed expedient to discuss some of the problems of the tax-supported colleges in the preceding chapters, under appropriate headings. For instance, in the discussion in chap. 2 of "The Power of Eminent Domain," it was stated that there was no question about the power of a public institution of higher education to invoke the right of eminent domain (p. 38).

In chap. 3, it seemed desirable to include a consideration of loyalty oaths required of state employees in certain jurisdictions (p. 64). The effect of state legislation upon faculty tenure rights was also reviewed in that chapter (p. 68). In chap. 5, the relative difficulty of maintaining law and order on the campuses of private and public institutions was contrasted (p. 132). The fact that unrelated business income of public as well as private colleges and universities is now subject to the federal income tax was also brought out in chap. 5 (p. 165).

Education, even at the primary and secondary levels, was thought to be the responsibility of religious or private institutions and individuals, not that of the state. The use of public funds, raised by taxation, for the support of higher education was challenged in the courts[2] of this country even during the present century in jurisdictions where, under constitutional restrictions on legislative action, public funds must be used solely for public purposes.

THE FIRST STATE UNIVERSITY. The University of North Carolina was founded in 1789 and endowed by the state legislature with a grant of "all property that has heretofore or shall hereafter escheat to the state." In 1800 the legislature decided that it had been too generous and re-pealed this grant of public lands. The new act provided that all escheated lands not already sold by the university should revert to the state. The Trustees of the university refused to comply with the pro-visions of the act, contending that the institution had acquired vested rights under the act of 1789 which could not be impaired by sub-sequent action of the legislature. The state supreme court upheld this contention of the governing board and declared the act of 1800 unconstitutional and void as contrary to Section 10 of Article I of the Bill of Rights of the federal Constitution.[3] This section forbids a state to pass any law "impairing its obligation of contracts." The court was of the opinion that the property of the university was as completely be-yond the control of the legislature as that of a private person. It should be noted that this decision, treating a state university as a private, rather than as a public, corporation, antedated the Dartmouth College case by fourteen years.

One of the North Carolina judges dissented. He was of the opinion that the university corporation was a mere agency of the state and that its property was at the unfettered disposition of the legislature. His view was accepted by the same court nearly fifty years later when it was decided that "the university is a public institution and body politic, and hence, subject to legislative control."[4]

STATE UNIVERSITIES AS PRIVATE CORPORATIONS. The courts in several jurisdictions continued for many years to look upon state universities

---

[2] Higgins v. Prater, 91 Ky. 6, 87 S.W. 1125 (1890); Marsee v. Hager, 125 Ky. 445, 101 S.W. 862 (1907); James, Auditor v. State University, 131 Ky. 156, 114 S.W. 767 (1908).

[3] Trustees of University of North Carolina v. Foy, 5 N.C. 58 (1805).

[4] University of North Carolina v. Maultsby, 43 N.C. 257 (1852).

as private corporations, with certain rights beyond the reach of legislative interference. In 1832 the Legislature of Ohio appointed Thomas Bryce a member of the governing board of Ohio University "to fill the vacancy occasioned by Jacob Linley having removed out of the state." Linley applied for a writ of quo warranto to determine the right of the new appointee to his seat on the board. The Supreme Court of Ohio declined to permit the appointee of the legislature to take his place on the board.[5]

An Illinois court in 1864 held that Illinois State Normal University was a private corporation and that its property was not protected by the sovereign immunity of the state but was subject to a mechanic's lien.[6] The Supreme Judicial Court of Maine, in 1909, held that its state university was a private corporation, in a case involving the taxation of a fraternity house erected on land belonging to the university. Again, in a similar case in 1911, the Maine court reiterated its belief that the University of Maine was a private, and not a public, corporation.[7] The courts of Maryland[8] and of Kentucky[9] have expressed similar views.

The Pennsylvania state normal schools were organized as private associations and the courts of that state felt constrained to rule that they were strictly private corporations until the turn of the century.[10] The Indiana Supreme Court, as late as 1887, ruled that the state legislature, in creating the Trustees of Indiana University and their successors "a body politic," had not thereby created a public corporation. In the words of the court:

The corporation thus organized has none of the essential characteristics of a public corporation. It is not a municipal corporation. Its members are not officers of the government, or subject to the control of the Legislature in the management of its affairs and the university fund . . . does not belong

---

[5] State ex rel. Linley v. Bryce, 7 Ohio (Pt.II) 82 (1836).

[6] Board of Education v. Greenbaum & Sons, 36 Ill. 610 (1864). See also, Board of Education v. Bakewell, 122 Ill. 339, 10 N.E. 378 (1887); and Fitzsimmons v. Miller, 308 Ill. 85, 139 N.E. 18 (1923).

[7] Orono v. Sigma Alpha Epsilon Society, 105 Me. 214, 74 Atl. 19 (1909); Orono v. Kappa Sigma Society, 108 Me. 320, 80 Atl. 831 (1911). This outmoded position of the Maine court has been criticized by Professor Clarence W. Peabody in "The Legal Status of the University of Maine," 13 Me. L. Rev. 187 (1920).

[8] Regents of University of Maryland v. Williams, 9 Gill & J. 365 (Md. 1838).

[9] City of Louisville v. President & Trustees of University of Louisville, 54 Ky. (51 B. Mon.) 642 (1854).

[10] McLeod v. Normal School Ass'n, 152 Pa. 575, 25 Atl. 1109 (1893); Commonwealth v. Yetter, 190 Pa. 488, 43 Atl. 226 (1899).

to the State. . . . The university, although established by public law, and endowed and supported by the State, is not a public corporation, in the technical sense.[11]

THE STATE UNIVERSITY AS A PUBLIC CORPORATION. The University of Virginia, chartered in 1819, was the first state university to be made subject to public control from the date of its establishment. Thomas Jefferson was its sponsor and its first rector. He had intended[12] to convert the College of William and Mary into a state university and introduced bills for this purpose in the state assembly, but the friends of William and Mary were too powerful, politically, to permit the passage of the proposed legislation.

The act of 1819 established a corporation known as "Rector and Visitors of the University of Virginia." Since its form of organization, with a board of control appointed by the legislature, became the prototype of state universities in this country, the following excerpt from the act is of interest:

And the said Rector and Visitors shall, at all times, conform to such laws as the legislature may, from time to time, enact for their government. And said university shall, in all things, at all times, be subject to the control of the legislature.

The Supreme Court of Alabama was the first to recognize and to enunciate the doctrine that a state university is a public corporation. In a case involving the corporate status of the University of Alabama, it declared in 1833:

What is the corporation, consisting of the President and Trustees of the University of Alabama, but "an instrument of government, created for its purposes" . . . This institution is, in every respect, a public one, organized and prosecuted by legislative enactment, towards which no citizen has contributed one cent, either in money, other property, labor or services, even as trustees, without remuneration.

While we would unhesitatingly maintain the doctrine that an act establishing a private corporation forms a contract by which the state is bound, we have no doubt but that the President and Trustees of the University of Alabama constitutes a public corporation and that their charter may be altered, amended or repealed by the General Assembly, at pleasure.[13]

---

[11] State v. Carr, 111 Ind. 335, 12 N.E. 318 (1887).

[12] Herbert B. Adams, *The College of William and Mary*, U.S. Bureau of Education, Circular of Information No. 1 (Washington: Government Printing Office, 1887), p. 38.

[13] Trustees of the University of Alabama v. Winston, 5 Stew. & P. 17 (1833); see Annot., 29 *L.R.A.* 378 (1915). John C. Monk, consulting director of the Asso-

Tɪɪ Noncorporate Status of Some Public Institutions of Higher Education. Today, the majority of tax-supported colleges and universities are considered to be public corporations. Some courts prefer the term "quasi-corporations" to describe this type of legal entity. However, in a few instances, publicly controlled colleges and universities have been denied the dignity of corporate status.

The Supreme Court of Iowa in 1876 was of the opinion[14] that the state university was not a corporation and, hence, lacked legal capacity to take and to hold real property in its own name, and, in the same year, the Supreme Court of Ohio ruled[15] that the Ohio Agricultural and Mechanical College, now the Ohio State University, was not a corporation and therefore was unable to sue or be sued in its own name. In 1926, the Ohio Court of Appeals declared[16] that "The Ohio State University is, by statute, made a body corporate," but five years later, the state attorney general, in two separate opinions,[17] asserted that the university is not a corporation.

The Kansas State Normal College at Emporia was held[18] to be without corporate status in 1891, and the University of Kansas was placed in this same category by the state court in 1917.[19] A state normal school in North Dakota[20] and one in Idaho[21] were also declared to lack the status of a corporation.

A more recent case involving this issue came before the Supreme Court of Appeals of West Virginia in 1957. The will of Floyd Craft, dated February 17, 1947, contained the following statement:

"Ninth: All the rest, residue and remainder of my estate I give to the Bluefield Colored Institute . . ."

The bequest, in the amount of $8,860.30, was accepted by the designated institution, now known as the Bluefield State College. The state auditor challenged the right of the college to utilize the funds repre-

ciation of Governing Boards of State Universities and Allied Institutions and chairman of its Committee on Legislation and Intergovernmental Relations, suggested that emphasis be given to the benefits which may accrue to colleges and universities as a result of their status as public corporations.

[14] Weary v. State University of Iowa, 43 Iowa 335 (1876).

[15] Neil v. Trustees, 31 Ohio St. 15 (1876).

[16] Long v. Trustees, 24 Ohio App. 261, 157 N.E. 395 (1926).

[17] Opinion No. 2929, 1 *Ops. Att'y Gen. Ohio* 212 (1931); Opinion No. 3044, 1 *Ops. Att'y Gen. Ohio* 379 (1931).

[18] State v. Stover, 47 Kan. 119, 27 Pac. 850 (1891).

[19] Garrity v. State Board of Administration, 99 Kan. 695, 162 Pac. 1167 (1917).

[20] State v. McMillan, 12 N.D. 280, 96 N.W. 310 (1933).

[21] Thomas v. State, 16 Idaho 81, 100 Pac. 761 (1909).

sented by the bequest on the ground that the Bluefield State College was without corporate entity, that is, that it was merely an arm of the state, and that a bequest to it was in reality a bequest to the state. The court agreed that the college had no existence independent of the state, but apparently in the interest of good public relations and in the public interest, the college was permitted to make use of the bequest for its own educational needs. The following is from the opinion of the court:

> This court should, if possible, give force and effect to the terms of the will of Floyd Craft, which is not ambiguous with respect to this gift, and which is clear in its intent, to the end that the beneficiary should be given the benefit of the gift thereby made. To do otherwise would defeat the purpose and intention of the testator.
>
> ....
>
> Furthermore, it is not amiss, we think, to say that benefactions in favor of public institutions, or to any particular institution, should be looked on favorably, so that prospective donors may be encouraged to make such gifts.[22]

THE CONSTITUTIONALLY INDEPENDENT CORPORATIONS

A few institutions of public higher education in this country enjoy a very privileged legal status by virtue of having been created and established under specific provisions of their state constitutions. These fortunate few possess a sphere of authority within which neither the legislative nor the executive divisions of state government may interfere. They are, in substance, coordinate with the legislative, executive, and judicial branches and thus represent a fourth arm of state government.

The list of institutions recognized by the courts as having this high degree of autonomy include the University of Michigan, the Michigan State University, the University of California, the University of Idaho, the University of Minnesota, and the Oklahoma State University. Although not yet confirmed by court decisions, it is probable that the University of Colorado and the University System of Georgia possess similar constitutional immunity from interference in their internal affairs.

THE UNIVERSITY OF MICHIGAN, THE FIRST TO GAIN INDEPENDENCE. The University of Michigan was established in 1817 as the University of Michigania. In 1837 the legislature reorganized it and placed it under

---

[22] State *ex rel.* West Virginia Board of Education v. Sims, 101 S.E.2d 190 (W.Va. 1957).

the control of a Board of Regents. Since it was the creature of the legislature, it was subject to its control. This duality of responsibility between the Board of Regents and the legislature retarded its development and members of the legislature drew attention to the contrast between the state institution and colleges under private control.

In 1840 a legislative committee, charged with responsibility for discovering a reason for this difference in development, reported that the state university lacked

that oneness of purpose and singleness of aim (essential to their prosperity) that others have whose trustees are a permanent body, men chosen for their supposed fitness for that very office, and who, having become acquainted with their duties, can and are disposed to pursue a steady course, which inspires confidence and insures success, to the extent of their limited means.[23]

The debate on the subject continued during the constitutional convention of 1850. As a result, the people of the State of Michigan, by the adoption of the constitution drafted by that convention, declared that "The Board of Regents shall have the general supervision of the University and the direction and control of all expenditures from the University Interest Fund."[24]

Despite this direct mandate from the people, the legislature continued to interfere with the internal administration of the institution. The Michigan Supreme Court rebuffed these attempted encroachments upon the duties and responsibilities of the Board of Regents.[25] However, it was not until 1896 that the court handed down its definitive ruling on the constitutional status of the board. The following is from the opinion of the court:

The board of regents and the legislature derive their power from the same supreme authority, namely, the constitution. . . . They are separate and distinct constitutional bodies, with the powers of the regents defined. By no rule of construction can it be held that either can encroach upon or exercise the powers conferred upon the other.[26]

---

[23] Mich. *H.R. Docs. of 1840,* at 470.

[24] *Mich. Const.* art. 13, § 8 (1850). The constitution of 1909 deleted the word "interest," thus granting the Board of Regents control over all university funds.

[25] People *ex rel.* Drake v. University of Michigan, 4 Mich. 98 (1856); People v. Regents of the University, 18 Mich. 469 (1869); People *ex rel.* Attorney General v. Regents of the University, 30 Mich. 473 (1874).

[26] Sterling v. Regents of the University of Michigan, 110 Mich. 369, 68 N.W. 253 (1896). See also Weinberg v. Regents of University of Michigan, 97 Mich. 246, 56 N.W. 605 (1893); Board of Regents of the University of Michigan v. Auditor General, 167 Mich. 444, 132 N.W. 1037 (1911).

THE UNIVERSITY OF CALIFORNIA GRANTED AUTONOMY IN 1879. The next public institution to be granted the dignity of constitutional independence was the University of California. The following is an excerpt from the constitution adopted by the people of that state in 1879:

> The University of California shall constitute a public trust, and its organization and government shall be perpetually continued in the form and character prescribed by the organic act creating the same . . . , subject only to such legislative control as may be necessary to insure compliance with the terms of its endowments, and the proper investment and security of its funds.[27]

The state supreme court has consistently upheld[28] the full scope of authority thus delegated by the voters to the Board of Regents.

THE BILL OF RIGHTS OF THE OKLAHOMA STATE UNIVERSITY. The citizens of Oklahoma adopted a constitution in 1907, just before the territory became a state, making provision for a State Board of Agriculture. The following excerpt from the constitution spells out this grant of autonomy: "Said board shall be maintained as a part of the state government, . . . and shall be the board of regents of all state agricultural and mechanical colleges."[29]

As construed by the Oklahoma courts[30] in 1909, this constitutional provision freed the agricultural and mechanical colleges of the state from legislative and administrative controls. Subsequent litigation[31] and opinions of the state attorney general have confirmed this autonomy.

---

[27] *Cal. Const.* art. IX, §9 (1879).

[28] People v. Kewen, 69 Cal. 215, 10 Pac. 393 (1886); Williams v. Wheeler, 23 Cal. App. 619, 138 Pac. 937 (1913); Tolman v. Underhill, 39 Cal. 2d 708, 249 P.2d 280 (1952); Fraser v. Regents, 39 Cal. 2d 717, 249 P.2d 283 (1952).

[29] *Okla. Const.* art. 6, § 31 (1907).

[30] Trapp v. Cook Construction Co., 24 Okla. 850, 105 Pac. 667 (1909).

[31] Connell v. Gray, 33 Okla. 591, 127 Pac. 417 (1912); Baker v. Carter, 165 Okla. 116, 25 P.2d 749 (1933); *Okla. Ops. Att'y Gen.* Feb. 16, 1946, Feb. 8, 1958, and Sept. 12, 1958.

In an opinion dated November 9, 1959, as yet unpublished, the attorney general of Oklahoma declared that the "mandatory" provisions of Oklahoma Central Purchasing Act of 1959 (ch. 4 of title 74 of the Oklahoma Sessions Laws of 1959) are unconstitutional "insofar as they would have the effect of taking away from the Board of Regents for the Oklahoma Agricultural and Mechanical Colleges the power, duty and authority to acquire, and to contract for the acquisition of, any and all supplies, materials, equipment, or contractual services to be used, consumed or spent by any of the agricultural and mechanical schools and colleges maintained, in whole or in part, by the State of Oklahoma . . ."

THE DECLARATION OF INDEPENDENCE OF THE UNIVERSITY OF IDAHO. The constitution of Idaho, adopted in 1889, has this to say with reference to the administration of the University of Idaho:

The regents shall have the general supervision of the University and control and direction of all funds of and appropriations to, the University, under such regulations as may be prescribed by law.

This language was not, in itself, sufficient to free the board from legislative and administrative interference. An attempt on the part of the legislature in 1920 to bring the fiscal affairs of the university under the direct control of state administrative officers prompted the Board of Regents to draft a comprehensive statement of rights. The following is a summary of this document:

1. The Regents declared that they had the right and that they intended to retain all university income, including that derived from the sale of discarded equipment, under their own control and that they would not deposit it with the state treasurer as required by statute.

2. They declared that they intended to purchase all necessary supplies and equipment through their own purchasing office rather than through the State Department of Public Works.

3. They declared that they intended to pay all proper claims against the university without submitting them for preaudit and review to the State Board of Examiners.

4. They declared that they intended to employ their own legal counsel to aid them in maintaining their legal rights.

The state attorney general petitioned the court for a writ of prohibition to prevent the implementation of this declaration of independence. The Board of Regents was completely vindicated in its position by the state supreme court.[32] Mr. Justice Budge, speaking for the majority of his brethren on the bench, discussed the constitutional autonomy of the University of Michigan and stated that the following sentence from an opinion of the Supreme Court of Michigan accurately described the status of the University of Idaho:

It is made the highest form of juristic person known to the law, a constitutional corporation of independent authority, which, within the scope of its functions, is coordinate with and equal to, that of the Legislature.

THE UNIVERSITY OF MINNESOTA ALSO ACHIEVES INDEPENDENCE. Although the Board of Regents of the University of Minnesota was incorporated by the territorial assembly in 1851, with a mandate to

---

[32] State v. State Board of Education, 33 Idaho 415, 196 Pac. 201 (1921).

"govern" the university, and the constitution of 1858 expressly "perpetuated unto said university" "all the rights, immunities, franchises and endowments heretofore granted or conferred," the question of constitutional autonomy was not raised by the board until 1925. The legislature had created a Commission of Administration and Finance. The Board of Regents submitted a voucher for payment of the cost of a preliminary survey of the feasibility of installing a plan of group insurance for its faculty and staff. The voucher was disapproved by the commission solely on the grounds of policy. The Board of Regents instituted a mandamus proceeding against the state auditor to compel the payment of the voucher. Mr. Justice Stone, speaking for the Supreme Court of Minnesota, said in part:

> The right so to control University finances is the power to dictate University policy and direct every legislative activity . . .
> The legislature cannot transfer any of these constitutionally confirmed powers from the regents to any other board, commission or officer whatever. . . . The Constitution of the state has declared, in effect, that the management of the University shall be, until the people themselves say otherwise, in a relatively small, slowly changing board, chosen for their special fitness for an interest in the work. . . . The purpose of the constitution remains clear. It was to put the management of the greatest state educational institution beyond the danger of vacillating policy, ill-informed or careless meddling and partisan ambition that would be possible in the case of management by either Legislature or executive, chosen at frequent intervals and for functions and because of qualities and activities vastly different from those which qualify for the management of an institution of higher learning.[33]

THE MICHIGAN STATE UNIVERSITY GRANTED INDEPENDENCE. The citizens of Michigan, evidently well satisfied with the excellent record made by the University of Michigan after it was granted its freedom from legislative and executive interference, decided to grant a similar privilege to the Michigan State College, now the Michigan State University. By the provisions of the constitution of 1908, the state board of agriculture was given "the general supervision of the college, and the direction and control of all agricultural college funds."[34] The powers of this board were construed by the state supreme court in

---

[33] State v. Chase, 175 Minn. 259, 220 N.W. 951 (1928).

[34] *Mich. Const.* art. 11, § 7 (1908); at an election held in April 1959, the voters of Michigan conferred upon Wayne State University the same constitutional status as that enjoyed by the University of Michigan and Michigan State University by the adoption of an amendment to the state constitution adding § 16 to art. XI.

1911 to be similar to those of the Board of Regents of the University of Michigan.[35]

THE UNIVERSITY OF COLORADO. The constitution of Colorado, adopted in 1876, vested "the general supervision of the state university" and "the exclusive control and direction of all funds of, and appropriations to, the university" in a Board of Regents.[36] This broad grant of power is quite similar to that given to the governing boards of the other constitutionally independent universities. However, the courts of Colorado have not, as yet, conceded that it was the intention of the people to grant full autonomy to their state university. Furthermore, in another section of the state constitution, the management of the university is declared to be "subject to the control of the state, under the provisions of the constitution, and such laws and regulations as the general assembly may provide."[37]

In 1886 the state supreme court decided that, since the location of the university and that of certain other state schools had been fixed by the constitution, their situs could not be changed by legislative action.[38] In 1893 the court ruled that the legislature had the power under the state constitution "to provide that the proceeds of sales of lands donated by the federal government to the state of Colorado for the benefit of the university shall constitute a University Permanent Fund,"[39] that is, that only the income of the fund and not the principal would be available to the university Regents for the benefit of the university.

The Board of Regents in 1892 determined that it was essential to the conduct of the last two years of instruction in medicine that the clinical work be done in Denver rather than in Boulder, the location of the main campus. The basis for this decision was the fact that a small community could not provide a sufficient number of cases for clinical review and analysis. Despite this obvious educational basis for the decision, the state supreme court declined to permit the Regents to exercise discretion and judgment in this matter.[40] The removal of this portion of

---

[35] Bauer v. State Board of Agriculture, 164 Mich. 415, 129 N.W. 713 (1911).

[36] *Colo. Const.* art. IX, § 14.

[37] *Colo. Const.* art. VIII, § 5.

[38] *In re* Senate Resolution Relating to State Institutions, 9 Colo. 626 21 Pac. 472 (1886).

[39] *In re* University Fund, 18 Colo. 398, 33 Pac. 415 (1893).

[40] People v. Regents of the University, 24 Colo. 175, 49 Pac. 286 (1897).

the medical school to Denver was challenged by a taxpayer of Boulder and the following is from the opinion of Mr. Justice Campbell:

> If the regents have the power to remove a part of any of the departments of the university, it follows that they have the power to remove an entire department. If they have the right to remove an entire department, they have the power to remove all, or such of the departments as they may determine. To say that they have any such power would be equivalent to declaring that they may remove the entire university from Boulder, and thus override the constitution itself.

The state supreme court, in 1937, had an opportunity to rule that the Board of Regents of the university was not subordinate to the regulations of a state administrative agency, that is, the public utility commission, but it declined to do so.[41] The Regents had established a bus service for its students and faculty to and from the Rocky Mountain National Park during the university summer session. Operators of other passenger buses brought an action to enjoin the operation of the university buses on the ground that the Regents had not obtained a certificate of "public convenience and necessity" from the state utility commission. The following is from the opinion of Mr. Justice Bakke:

> It appears that the constitutional body which governs the university and creates, directs and supervises its educational policy has determined the propriety of the operation of these buses in connection with the summer school. This position has been concurred in by the National Park Service, and the P.U.C. said it had no jurisdiction.
>
> Assuming that the latter two were not in agreement with the regents on the legal result, there might be some question as to whether the court should substitute its opinion for that of the regents, but with the two other administrative agencies joining with the regents as to the legality of the operation of the buses, as outlined, all doubt is removed as to the duty of this court. We should not and do not disturb the findings.

THE UNIVERSITY SYSTEM OF GEORGIA. The Georgia Legislature in 1931 vested the "management and government of the University of Georgia, and all of its branches"[42] in the Board of Regents of the University System of Georgia. In 1945 the voters of Georgia adopted a new constitution, and the Board of Regents was thereby raised from legislative to constitutional status, with retention of "the government, control and management of the University System of Georgia and all of its institutions in said system."[43]

---

[41] Burnside v. Regents, 100 Colo. 33, 64 P.2d 1271 (1937).

[42] *Ga. Acts 1931* at 72–73.

[43] *Ga. Const.* art. VIII, § IV, ch. 2–6701.

Even before the Board of Regents had acquired constitutional status, the state supreme court had held that

So long as the board does not exercise its powers capriciously or arbitrarily, or so as to thwart the purpose of the Legislature in establishing a system of university education, the board itself must determine what is necessary for the usefulness of the system, and thus will govern the University of Georgia and its several branches. The powers granted are broad and comprehensive, and, subject to the exercise of a wise and proper discretion, the regents are untrammeled except for such restraints of law as are directly expressed or necessarily implied.[44]

After the adoption of the constitution of 1945, the state supreme court expressly confirmed its opinion that the powers and duties of the Regents "are untrammeled except by such restraints of law as are directly, expressly, or necessarily implied."[45] Whether they are as extensive and plenary as those exercised by other constitutionally independent state universities remains to be tested in the courts.

THE UNIVERSITIES OF MISSOURI AND UTAH FAIL TO ACHIEVE INDEPENDENCE. The Board of Curators of the University of Missouri, in 1916, made an unsuccessful attempt to achieve constitutional independence. The constitution of 1865 had commanded the General Assembly to "establish and maintain a state university."[46] The constitution of 1875 declared that "the General Assembly shall . . . aid and maintain the state university, now established, with its present departments. The government of the university shall be vested in a board of curators."[47]

In 1915 the General Assembly had added certain courses to the curriculum of the university. The Board of Curators declined to comply with the command of the legislature on the ground that the people of the state, by the adoption of the constitution of 1875, had divested the General Assembly of all authority over the internal affairs of the university and that they had constituted the Board of Curators a separate and distinct department of the state government over which the General Assembly had no power "except that of appropriating or withholding public funds, as it deems proper."

The Supreme Court of Missouri declined to thus construe the word "government" in the constitution of 1875 and refused to follow the precedents established by the courts of Michigan, Minnesota, Cali-

---

[44] State v. Regents of University System, 179 Ga. 210, 175 S.E. 567 (1934).
[45] Villyard v. Regents of University System, 204 Ga. 517, 50 S.E.2d 313 (1948).
[46] Mo. Const. art. 9, § 4 (1865).
[47] Mo. Const. art. 11, § 4 (1875).

fornia, and Oklahoma with respect to the administration of their state universities.[48]

The Supreme Court of Utah also refused to follow this trend.[49] The Board of Regents of the University of Utah requested a district court of Salt Lake County to issue a declaratory judgment, "defining the rights, immunities, franchises, and endowments granted, conferred, and perpetuated unto the university by the constitution of Utah."[50] The district court entered judgment holding that the university is "a constitutional corporation free from control of the legislative, administrative bodies, commissions and agencies and officers of the state." On appeal to the state supreme court, this judgment was reversed in 1956. The following is from the opinion of the court, as delivered by Mr. Justice Herriod:

It is inconceivable that the framers of the Constitution . . . intended to place the University above any controls available to the people of this state as to the property, management and government of the University. . . . The University is a public corporation, not above the power of the Legislature to control, and is subject to the Laws of the State from time to time enacted relating to its purposes and government.

THE SITUATION IN OTHER JURISDICTIONS. Specific provisions with respect to public institutions of higher education are to be found in many state constitutions.[51] However, as we have seen, mere mention in the constitution is not sufficient to create a constitutionally independent corporation. The grant of freedom must be explicit, and it must be so interpreted by the highest court of the state.

THE COMMITTEE ON GOVERNMENT AND HIGHER EDUCATION

Recognizing the vital need for greater public understanding of the effect of undue interference in the internal administration of our state

---

[48] State v. Board of Curators, 268 Mo. 598, 188 S.W. 128 (1916).

[49] University of Utah v. Board of Examiners, 4 Utah 2d 408, 295 P. 2d 348 (1956).

[50] *Utah Const.* art. X, § 4.

[51] See Alexander Brody, *The American State and Higher Education* (Washington: American Council on Education, 1935), pp. 215–25; Edward C. Elliott and M. M. Chambers, *The Colleges and the Courts* (New York: Carnegie Foundation for the Advancement of Teaching, 1935), pp. 505–12; Council of State Governments, *Higher Education in the Forty-eight States* (Chicago: The Council, 1952), pp. 131–32; Council for the Study of Higher Education in Florida, *Provisions of State Constitutions for Higher Education* (Tallahassee, Fla.: The Council, 1957).

colleges and universities by the legislature and by state administrative agencies, the Fund for the Advancement of Education in 1957 sponsored the organization of the Committee on Government and Higher Education. Under the chairmanship of Milton S. Eisenhower, president of the Johns Hopkins University, the committee undertook a study of more than three hundred state-supported colleges and universities. The study, under the direction of Malcolm Moos, was concerned primarily "with the impact of state administrative controls upon the management of state colleges and universities. Do state controls tend to have a suffocating effect upon administrative policy under certain conditions?"

The conclusions of the committee may be summarized by the following statement from the final page of its report:

However petty each instance of control may be, in cumulative effect a broad range of restrictions upon the operating freedom of institutions of higher education leaves very little room for imagination and vitality by which truly creative institutions of higher learning are nourished.[52]

INTERFERENCE IN THE INTERNAL ADMINISTRATION OF INSTITUTIONS OF HIGHER EDUCATION

Legislators have, over the years, not hesitated to substitute their judgment for that of the governing boards charged with responsibility for the administration of state colleges and universities. Members of their governing boards, in resisting these intrusions, have built up a vast accumulation of court decisions defining and construing their proper scope of authority. Only a small fraction of this litigation can be considered in this volume.

CONTROL BY STATE ADMINISTRATIVE AGENCIES. The trend toward centralization of function has increased the scope of authority of state budget officers, auditors, comptrollers, and purchasing agents. The pressure to conform to standards and procedures established by state civil service and state architects is strong in many states. How to preserve the values inherent in local autonomy and, at the same time, meet

---

[52] Malcolm Moos and Francis E. Rourke, *The Campus and the State* (Baltimore, Md.: Johns Hopkins Press, 1959), p. 323.

The Association of Governing Boards of State Universities and Allied Institutions has become very active in presenting its objections to the encroachment, by state administrative agencies, upon the powers of the governing boards of institutions of public higher education. In a report as yet unpublished, dated April 4, 1960, its Committee on Legislation and Intergovernmental Relations declares: "Public higher education in America was born free. It should, in all logic, remain as free as the public interest and its unique functions demand."

the demand of the public for economy in administration is a question that will be debated in the legislature and on the campus for years to come.

POWER OF THE STATE AUDITOR TO CONTROL DISBURSEMENTS. A decision of the Supreme Court of Appeals of West Virginia is an example of the refusal of the courts to permit state auditors and other state administrative agencies to go too far in their attempts to substitute their judgment for that of educational officers. The vice-president and comptroller of West Virginia University signed several requisitions, drawn on a special fund, for the purpose of paying certain invoices covering the cost of hospitalization and medical treatment of a student injured while participating as a member of its football team in an intercollegiate game. The fund on which the requisitions were drawn was derived from general admission charges to the games, compulsory student athletic fees, and guarantees paid on behalf of competing teams.

The state auditor refused to honor these requisitions on the ground that there was no balance available in the fund, since the reported profit for the year for intercollegiate athletics was not a true profit in view of the fact that the salary of the athletic director and those of the coaches were not charged against this fund but were paid, in part, from the budget of the department of physical education. The Board of Governors of the university petitioned the court to issue a peremptory writ of mandamus to compel the auditor to pay the claims. The court, in granting the writ, commented in its syllabus of the case:

> In the absence of an abuse of discretion on the part of the board of governors of West Virginia University, the auditor for the state of West Virginia has a mandatory duty to honor requisitions of the board to cover payment of the cost of medical and hospital services rendered to a student athlete, injured in an intercollegiate contest.[53]

In 1939 the same state auditor had refused to honor a voucher for the payment of printing for the athletic department of West Virginia University. The court, in directing him to pay the claim, rebuked him for his attempts to substitute his own judgment for that of the university administration, in the following words: "No one can successfully assert that a proper athletic program is not appropriate to a great educational institution."[54]

---

[53] Board of Governors of West Virginia University v. Sims, 134 W. Va. 428, 55 S.E.2d 505 (1950).

[54] Glover v. Sims, 121 W. Va. 407, 3 S.E.2d 612 (1939).

These two West Virginia cases have an interesting parallel in a 1949 decision of the Supreme Court of Arizona. The court granted a writ of mandamus directed to the state auditor, commanding her to issue warrants in payment of obligations incurred by the Board of Regents of the University of Arizona in the inauguration of a new president of the university. The claims were presented to the state auditor twice for payment and were rejected each time. They were then presented to the governor of the state, who also rejected them. Fortunately for the dignity of the State of Arizona, Chief Justice La Prade and the majority of his associates on the bench had a broader concept of the proper educational functions of a university. The court, in granting the writ, had the following to say to the auditor and to the governor of Arizona:

> In determining whether expenses incurred as incident to the inauguration of a new president of the university are of a kind authorized by law, it should be considered what the event is of inducting into office a new president, the purpose to be served by such a ceremony, and the practice observed by similar institutions with regard to a like event.
>
> . . . .
>
> By common knowledge, the custom is generally followed. . . . A failure to avail the university of the opportunity to signalize the importance of this event in its life when the reins of control are transferred to a new president might more readily subject the board of control to a charge of laxity and indifference to the psychological values inherent in the occasion than with extravagance for providing a ceremonious celebration of so important an event. We have no hesitancy in holding that a reasonable expenditure for the purpose falls into the category of expenditures for a public purpose.[55]

THE DEPOSIT OF UNIVERSITY FUNDS WITH THE STATE TREASURER. A member of the state assembly of Arkansas brought suit, as a taxpayer, to require the deposit of all monies handled by any state institution or department into the state treasury. If sustained, this would have meant that the University of Arkansas and other tax-supported institutions of higher education within the state would have been compelled to deposit all federal funds, private grants and donations, tuition and fees, receipts from auxiliary enterprises, endowments, trust funds, and athletic and student activity fees with the state treasurer. Since the constitution of Arkansas requires that all appropriations shall be item by item, the administrative chaos that would have resulted can well be imagined. Fortunately, the court refused to place higher education of the state into such a fiscal strait jacket. The majority opinion held that

---

[55] Board of Regents v. Frohmiller, 69 Ariz. 50, 208 P.2d 833 (1949).

"there is no language in our present Constitution which requires that all public money shall be paid into the state treasury."[56] In arriving at this conclusion, the court pointed out that, although the Arkansas constitution of 1868 contained such a requirement, the present constitution, adopted in 1874, was silent on this point. The court reasoned that "the absence of such a provision from our present constitution appears to have been a studied and deliberate omission."

However, Chief Justice Smith wrote the following vigorous dissent:

This is the first time since 1836, and the only time during the seventy-five years of rule under the constitution of 1874, that there has been a judicial affirmation of the proposition that a public fund, belonging to the people in their governmental capacity, may be dealt with by boards, commissions, institutions and agencies under a plan giving to them unrestricted authority to act with complete indifference to the public treasury, absent the formality of appropriation.

This dissent of Chief Justice Smith was not unanticipated. He had served for a number of years as the state comptroller and, as such, had taken a definite stand that all monies handled by any division of the state should be deposited with the state treasurer and spent only by virtue of an appropriation by the state assembly.

STATE CIVIL SERVICE LIMITS LOCAL AUTONOMY. Almost half the states have extended civil service procedures and controls to public higher education. The following is from the staff report of the Committee on Government and Higher Education:

In broad terms, difficulties arise where a state personnel agency is given the authority to regulate phases of the hiring and promotion of personnel in the educational institutions, rather than leaving discretion in the hands of the institutions themselves. For many of the rigid rules and procedures laid down by state personnel agencies have no legitimate relation to the actual needs of the institutions. Cumbersome policies, lack of concern for unique jobs, and unrealistic salary scales are particularly upsetting to college authorities.

But there are other tensions that involve more fundamental issues of academic life. As state merit systems extend their influence beyond the purely non-academic employees to include professional, administrative, and even teaching personnel, college governing bodies may lose power over a precious area of discretion—the selection and direction of the personnel who carry out the main program of the institution. Nor is this mere conjecture; the University of Massachusetts, to cite the most prominent example, engaged in

---

[56] Gipson v. Ingram, 215 Ark. 812, 223 S.W.2d 595 (1949).

open combat for several years with state agencies over the right to control
the salaries and promotions of its own members.[57]

MEASURES FOR SELF-DEFENSE. Every public institution of higher education should maintain a permanent, cumulative file of all pertinent constitutional and legislative provisions, with the interpretation of these
provisions by the courts, by the attorney general, and by legal counsel.
Their basic manuals of day-by-day procedures should contain digests
of this material for convenient reference so that administrative officers
may be able to recognize any illegal encroachment or limitation of their
legal rights.

THE DEMAND FOR ECONOMY IN GOVERNMENT

When these encroachments upon the powers and duties of the governing boards are obviously motivated by political pressures, public
opinion and the courts are usually on the side of the boards of control.
However, with the constantly increasing burden of taxation has come
an insistent demand from the taxpayers for greater economy and efficiency in government, at all levels and in every division, including
public higher education.

Surveys and studies have brought to light the high cost of unco-
ordinated decisions. While consolidation of power and authority does
not, in itself, result in greater efficiency and economy, some unification
of effort is clearly called for in education as in other functions of gov
ernment. Furthermore, by increasing the size of an administrative
unit, it is possible to pay the chief administrator a salary sufficient to
attract and hold an individual of superior training and experience.

STATE SYSTEMS OF HIGHER EDUCATION. These considerations led the
voters of South Dakota, by the adoption of the constitution of 1889, to
establish a Board of Regents of Education, with control of all educational institutions "sustained either wholly or in part by the state."[58]
The Legislature of Florida in 1905 abolished all existing state institutions of higher education and set up a new system under the exclusive
control of a single board.[59]

These early steps were the beginning of a trend toward consolidation of control. Some of these consolidated boards were content to
leave the day-by-day administration of the units under their control in

---

[57] Moos and Rourke, *op. cit. supra* note 52, at 151.

[58] *S.D. Const.* art. XIX, § 3.

[59] *Fla. Stat. of 1957*, ch. 240, § 240.04.

the hands of the local administration on each campus. Gradually, a demand for centralized staff work and centralized records led to the appointment of full-time administrative officers to provide continual supervision. In some states, the central board has been given responsibility for all public institutions of higher education with the exception of the state university.

Two-thirds of all state institutions of higher education are governed by boards which have more than one institution under their jurisdiction. Thirteen states—Arizona, Florida, Georgia, Iowa, Kansas, Mississippi, Montana, New Jersey, New York, North Dakota, Oregon, Rhode Island, and South Dakota—have single boards that govern all state institutions of higher education. These boards perform both the coordinating and the governing functions with respect to public higher education.

Six states—Illinois, Oklahoma, New Mexico, North Carolina, Utah, and Wisconsin—have established central state coordinating boards without direct responsibility for control. For example, the New Mexico Board of Educational Finance, established in 1951, exercises no powers of direct supervision but has authority to review and to coordinate budget requests of the several institutions and to recommend appropriate action to the governor and to the legislature.[60]

CONSOLIDATION. The most drastic answer to the demand for greater coordination is, of course, outright consolidation of several institutions into one. In 1931 the North Carolina State College at Raleigh, the Woman's College at Greensboro, and the Chapel Hill campus of the University of North Carolina were consolidated under the control of one Board of Trustees and a president. Each institution is headed by a chancellor. The Texas Agricultural and Mechanical College System is a consolidation of the Agricultural and Mechanical College of Texas and three smaller colleges. The University of California, with campuses at Berkeley, Los Angeles, San Francisco, Santa Barbara, Davis, Riverside, La Jolla, and Upper Newport Bay, is virtually a consolidated system, although its units are considered to be branches and not separate institutions.

---

[60] The Book of the States, 1956–57 (Chicago: Council of State Governments, 1956), XI, 259–70; The Book of the States, 1958–59 (Chicago: Council of State Governments, 1958), XII, 114–15. See also Moos and Rourke, op. cit. supra note 52, 203–26; Encyclopedia of Educational Research (3d ed.; New York: Macmillan Co., 1960), pp. 243–49.

INTERSTATE COMPACTS. One of the most interesting developments of the last decade is the use of interstate compacts to reduce costs and to improve facilities in public higher education. Section 10 of Article I of the federal Constitution reads, in part, as follows: "No state shall, without the consent of Congress . . . enter into any agreement or compact with another state . . ."

Over one hundred interstate compacts have been authorized by Congress. Probably the best known is the one negotiated in 1920 between New York and New Jersey for the creation of the New York Port Authority. Approved by Congress in 1921, this compact permits the two states to share the cost and control of the docks and other facilities required by America's leading harbor.

THE SOUTHERN REGIONAL EDUCATION BOARD. The first use of the interstate compact for the advancement of public higher education created the Southern Regional Education Board. The Meharry Medical College of Nashville, Tennessee, proposed that "its lands, buildings, equipment, and the net income from its endowment be turned over to the Southern States, or to an agency acting in their behalf, to be operated as a regional institution for medical, dental and nursing education . . ." In response to this offer, the Southern Regional Education Compact was drafted and signed by the governors of fifteen Southern states on February 8, 1948, subject to the approval of their respective legislatures. Sixteen Southern states are now members of the compact: Alabama, Arkansas, Delaware, Florida, Georgia, Kentucky, Louisiana, Maryland, Mississippi, North Carolina, Oklahoma, South Carolina, Tennessee, Texas, Virginia, and West Virginia. The Southern Regional Education Board, created by this interstate compact, is a nonprofit, tax-exempt public agency. According to its bylaws, as amended and adopted by its board of control September 22, 1958, "the membership of the board shall consist of the Governor of each State which has approved the Compact, *ex officio*, and four additional citizens of each Compact State, to be appointed by the Governor thereof, at least one of whom shall be selected from the field of education, and at least one of whom shall be a member of the legislature of that State." The bylaws declare that the board shall perform the following functions:

1. Serve as a clearinghouse on information regarding significant activities among institutions and agencies concerned with higher education in the Southern region.
2. Provide a facility and staff for continuous assessment of needs in

higher education within the South and for developing plans and programs to meet those needs.

3. Serve as an administrative device for carrying out interstate arrangements for regional educational services and institutions.

4. Serve as fiscal agent for carrying out interstate arrangements for regional educational services and institutions.

By virtue of contracts negotiated through the board, thousands of students have crossed state lines for training not available within the borders of their own states. The Southern Regional Education Compact became the prototype for other compacts for the advancement of public higher education.

THE WESTERN INTERSTATE COMMISSION FOR HIGHER EDUCATION. The Western Regional Education Compact was formulated at the Western Governors' Conference in 1949 and became effective in 1951. It now includes thirteen states: Alaska, Arizona, California, Colorado, Hawaii, Idaho, Montana, Nevada, New Mexico, Oregon, Utah, Washington, and Wyoming.

In 1957 a resident and taxpayer of the State of Washington brought an action to restrain the state auditor from issuing a warrant upon the state treasurer for the purpose of defraying Washington's share of the operating costs of the Western Interstate Commission for Higher Education as authorized by the state legislature in 1955. The taxpayer challenged the validity of the act of the legislature on the grounds that it was in violation of Article VIII, Section 5, of the state constitution which provides that "the credit of the state shall not, in any manner, be given or loaned to, or in aid of, any individual, association, company or corporation."

The Supreme Court of Washington, in upholding the constitutionality of the legislation in question, had this to say:

The legislature of this state has undertaken to carry out a part of its duty to educate our children residing within its borders by a reciprocal arrangement with its sister states. In return for this state's share of the operating costs of the interstate commission, it receives benefits in educational facilities for the residents of this state. The legislature, in the proper exercise of its discretion, has deemed the benefits received to be a sufficient consideration for the funds expended. . . . The expenditure of funds for such purpose does not constitute the giving or loaning of the credit of this state. . . . We do not find in the state constitution any limitation upon the power of the legislature to contract with its sister states.[61]

---

[61] State *ex rel.* Tattersall v. Yelle, 52 Wash. 2d 856, 329 P.2d 841 (1958).

THE NEW ENGLAND BOARD OF HIGHER EDUCATION. The New England Board of Higher Education was established in 1955 under the provisions of the New England Higher Education Compact, approved by Congress in 1954. The board consists of eighteen members, three from each of six states: Connecticut, Maine, Massachusetts, New Hampshire, Rhode Island, and Vermont. According to its annual report for 1959, the board "serves as a clearing house for information . . . and when necessary, as an administrative and fiscal agent for carrying out interstate agreements for educational services."

INFORMAL REGIONAL COOPERATION. Eugene T. Branch, attorney for the Southern Regional Education Board, has stated that "not every compact or agreement between the states requires the consent of Congress," despite the wording of the Constitution. "Compacts which in no respect concern the United States and do not result in any political combination tending to increase the political power of the states would not, in our opinion, require such consent."[62]

The Committee on Institutional Cooperation of the Council of Ten State Universities and the University of Chicago is an example of informal regional cooperation without the benefit of an interstate compact.

CONSTITUTIONAL DEBT LIMITATIONS

The majority of state constitutions contain drastic limitations on the power of the legislature to authorize the incurrence of public debt. Students of American history will recall the many ill-considered projects for internal improvement sponsored and financed by the states during the first three decades of the nineteenth century. Many of the state legislatures in those early days authorized large bond issues to subsidize the construction of canals, railroads, banks, and private industrial projects.[63] These obligations were issued in excess of the ability and willingness of the citizens to repay them. The panic

---

[62] Letter to the author dated May 24, 1960, from Mr. Eugene T. Branch. The author is also indebted to Mr. Branch for the following references on interstate compacts: Richard H. Leach and R. S. Sugg, *Administration of Interstate Compacts* (Baton Rouge, La.: Louisiana State University Press, 1959); Vincent V. Thursby, *Interstate Cooperation* (Washington: Public Affairs Press, 1953); Dunbar, "Interstate Compacts and Congressional Consent," 36 *Va. L. Rev.* (1950); Zimmerman and Wendell, "The Interstate Compact and Dyer v. Sims," 51 *Col. L. Rev.* 931 (1951).

[63] Lawrence S. Knappen, *Revenue Bonds and the Investor* (New York: Prentice-Hall, 1939); John Francis Fowler, *Revenue Bonds* (New York: Harper & Bros., 1938).

of 1837 forced many of the states to default on their bond issues. There were two other waves of default and repudiation of state debts—those of 1848–60 and 1870–84.

As a result of these unfortunate experiences, the voters in many states demanded and obtained constitutional limitations upon the otherwise plenary power of the legislature to pledge "the full faith and credit of the state" for public improvements.

More recently, there has been an increasing pressure again to finance internal improvements with borrowed money. It has usually been considered politically inexpedient to attempt to amend the state constitutions and thus remove or modify the debt limitations. The revenue, authority, or limited obligation bond was found to be, in many states, a legal detour around the constitutional roadblock of debt limitation. The bondholder was persuaded to accept an obligation secured solely by the income to be derived from the utility or facility constructed with the proceeds of the bond issue or from service charges imposed to retire the bonds. Since the bondholder could not look to any other funds of the state for repayment, it was reasoned that the issuance of such limited obligation bonds did not contravene constitutional debt limitations, that is, for this purpose, they were not to be considered debts of the state or of an instrumentality thereof.

On the other hand, it was important that they be construed as obligations of a sovereign state of the federal union in order that the income therefrom be exempt from the federal tax. Under our American political philosophy of the limitation of federal power, neither the states[64] nor the Federal Government[65] may tax the other nor the instrumentalities thereof. Under this doctrine, state and municipal bonds enjoy complete immunity from the federal income tax. Consequently, they offer the wealthy taxpayer a welcome escape from the high tax brackets of the present Internal Revenue Code. As a result, they can be issued and sold on the basis of a very low interest rate, which means, of course, that the agencies of state governments can frequently borrow money more cheaply than the Federal Government itself.

In order that the revenue bonds of these agencies of state government may not contravene the constitutional limitations on state in-

---

[64] Jaybird Mining Co. v. Weir, 271 U.S. 609 (1926).

[65] Warren v. Paul, 22 Ind. 276 (1864). See also Brown, "Federal and State Taxation," 81 *Pa. L. Rev.* 247 (1933).

debtedness and, at the same time, enjoy constitutional freedom from federal taxation, legal and tax experts are called upon to exercise extreme ingenuity in drafting the legislation creating them. When is a debt not a debt?

THE SPECIAL FUND DOCTRINE. The special fund doctrine, upon which the validity of most revenue bonds depends, is said to have had its origin in the State of Washington in 1895. The city of Spokane had reached its constitutional debt limit but found itself in need of a new waterworks. It issued bonds payable solely from the revenue to be derived from the system. The state supreme court held that the issuance of these revenue bonds did not create a debt as defined by the state constitution.

The revenue bond, as a new financial idea, spread slowly from West to East. Its major period of development came during the depression years of the thirties when the Reconstruction Finance Corporation was authorized by Congress to make loans to finance self-liquidating municipal projects. During the next two decades, many states authorized the issuance of revenue bonds to finance the construction of toll roads. After World War II, the flood of veterans seeking higher education created a similar dilemma for the tax-supported colleges and universities.

THE OKLAHOMA STATE COLLEGE CASE. The reluctance of some judges to accept the sophistry of the special fund doctrine is illustrated by a case decided by the Supreme Court of Oklahoma in 1933. In 1931 the state legislature had authorized the Board of Regents of the Oklahoma Agricultural and Mechanical College to issue $450,000 in revenue bonds for dormitory construction. The Regents agreed to collect rentals and to deposit them with the state treasurer as a special fund from which the interest and principal of these securities would be paid. The act provided that the bonds should be tax exempt and a lawful form of investment for the sinking funds of the state or any of its political subdivisions.

The validity of the issue was questioned on the grounds that the bonds were obligations of the State of Oklahoma and that the issue would exceed the constitutional debt limitation. The majority of the court upheld the validity of the issue after a detailed summary of decisions in other jurisdictions, but there was a strongly worded dissenting opinion signed by the chief justice and two of his associates.

They reminded the court that the special fund theory, relied upon to support its decision

that the obligation so elaborately to be expressed in these proposed bonds is that of nobody, but only of the special fund itself . . . has been definitely and most recently rejected by this court. The agreement to pay . . . creates an indebtedness, no matter from what source the funds are to be derived. . . . These bonds are to be tax exempt securities. Does not that provision of the law contemplate that they are obligations of the state or one of its indivisible counterparts?

These are what are commonly known in the vernacular as "wildcat" bonds. Shortly after the World War this state experienced an epidemic in such public finance, including the investment of sinking funds in such wildcat bonds. Apparently, again the cycle is reached.[66]

Despite this polemic, it is the general rule[67] that constitutional debt restrictions are not applicable to obligations which are payable only out of the fund derived from the specific revenue-producing properties constructed or purchased with proceeds from their sale.

THE SOUTH DAKOTA STATE COLLEGE CASE. The South Dakota Legislature in 1955 authorized the State Board of Regents of Education, with the consent and approval of the governor and the secretary of finance, to issue revenue bonds to finance the construction of necessary student housing at any educational institution under its control. The principal and interest of such revenue bonds were to be secured by a pledge, not only of the income to be produced by the buildings so financed, but, for a period not to exceed ten years, of the net income of student housing then existing at such institutions.

The Board of Regents, by appropriate resolutions, authorized the construction of a women's residence hall, a men's residence hall, and an apartment building for married students on the campus of the South Dakota State College at an estimated cost of approximately $1.9 million.

A taxpayer invoked the original jurisdiction of his state supreme court to arrest the proposed action of the Board of Regents on the ground that the issuance of the revenue bonds to finance the project would create a debt of the state in excess of the limitation established in its constitution.

Judge Smith, delivering the unanimous opinion of the court, pointed

---

[66] Baker v. Carter, 165 Okla. 116, 25 P.2d 747 (1933).

[67] Annot. 146 A.L.R. 328 (1941). See also Lawrence E. Cermack, *The Law of Revenue Bonds* (Washington: National Institute of Municipal Law Officers, 1954).

out that his court had, in the past, upheld the special fund doctrine. However, in the case under consideration, revenue of already existing buildings would be used to pay off the bonds, in addition to the revenue to be derived from the new buildings. This, declared Judge Smith, was going too far. He asserted:

Because of that pledge of additional property and resources of the state, we are solemnly persuaded that such a debt has been incurred. . . . The crucial inquiry is, whether those who framed and adopted our constitution used the term "debt" in some special or limited sense, which fails to comprehend such a debt.

Looking to its context, subject matter and purposes, and to its relationship to the "pay-as-you-go" policy so obviously revealed by the constitution as a whole, we discern no rational basis for a conclusion that this debt limiting provision relates only to debts for the payment of which taxes must be levied.

If, as some sincerely believe, these organic limitations are unrealistic and are hampering progress, the appeal must be to the sovereign people. To amend the constitution is not a function of the court.[68]

THE NORTH DAKOTA CASE. In support of his opinion, Judge Smith referred to a case in the adjoining state of North Dakota. In 1928 a taxpayer of that state had challenged the constitutionality of an act of the legislature creating the University Dormitory Association of Grand Forks for the purpose of erecting residence halls on the campus of the state university and leasing them to the State Board of Administration. Chief Justice Nuessle stated the opinion of his court as follows:

To our minds, the fact that the dormitory income goes into so-called "institutional funds" and not into the state treasury can make no difference. Whether paid into the treasury or not, this income is, nevertheless, the property of the state. . . . We are forced to the conclusion that the contract . . . will result in a debt against the state, within the meaning of the term "debt" as used in the constitution.[69]

THE OKLAHOMA EDUCATIONAL TELEVISION AUTHORITY CASE. A more recent case cited by Judge Smith involved the validity of a proposed issue of revenue bonds, in the amount of $1.45 million, by the Oklahoma Educational Television Authority. In the opinion of the Oklahoma Supreme Court:

When a dollar comes into the possession and ownership of the state, it is of no more or no less value to the state and to its citizens because it comes

---

[68] Boe v. Foss, 76 S.D. 295, 77 N.W.2d 1 (1956).
[69] Wilder v. Murphy, 56 N.D. 436, 218 N.W. 156 (1928).

from the cigaret tax or the gasoline tax . . . or from the rental of lands owned by the state. We consider it beyond question that the state and the people of the state have the power, by constitutional provision, to protect all funds belonging to the state from future debt.[70]

CONTRASTING COURT VIEWS ON STATE BUILDING AUTHORITIES. In order to provide much-needed student housing and other educational facilities, the Wisconsin Legislature created the Wisconsin University Building Corporation. The Regents of the university leased land to the building corporation for a term of fifty years. The building corporation arranged to borrow funds to finance the construction of student housing for approximately 1,500 students and an athletic practice building. The Regents agreed to rent these properties for the fifty-year term on a basis that would retire the loan.

In a friendly suit to determine the legality of these transactions, the Supreme Court of Wisconsin declared:

> We are constrained to determine that the assignment and pledging of the state's rental obligation did not create a state debt, and that, by consenting to such an arrangement, the state did not loan its credit, contrary to the constitutional provision in question.
>
> For the reason that there is no enforceable legal obligation on the part of the state to pay the obligations of the building corporation, even though good judgment may dictate that it do so voluntarily . . . , no state debt is involved.[71]

On the other hand, the University of Washington was not successful in its attempt to make use of a building authority to finance the cost of campus improvements. Justice Schwellenback, in his opinion for the Supreme Court of Washington, stated the issues as follows:

> We recognize the housing problem with which the state is confronted. Nevertheless, we cannot permit the exigency of the situation to override the constitutional safeguard against improvidence and the integrity of the state's economy. We cannot resort to the dexterity of judicial thinking in order to assist the state in its problem. We cannot close our eyes to what is actually being attempted. When we strip the plan down to fundamentals, we find that it is not a leasing arrangement between landlord and tenant, but the installment purchase, by the state, of certain buildings and facilities, with state moneys raised by taxation, far in excess of constitutional limitation.[72]

---

[70] Application of Oklahoma Educational Television Authority, 272 P.2d 1027 (Okla. 1954).

[71] State v. Giessel, 271 Wis. 15, 72 N.W.2d 577 (1955).

[72] State v. Yelle, 46 Wash. 2d 166, 289 P.2d 355 (1955).

THE UNIVERSITY BOARD AS A SEPARATE LEGAL ENTITY. The Supreme Court of Louisiana in 1933 took a more direct approach to the problem of constitutional debt limitations.[73] It declared that, since the Board of Supervisors of the Louisiana State University and Agricultural and Mechanical College is a separate legal entity, bonds issued by the board are not bonds of the state. Consequently, a debt or liability of the board is not a debt or liability on behalf of the state.

THE RESIDENT STUDENT AND HIS RIGHTS

The majority of tax-supported institutions of higher education in this country are required by statute to charge nonresident students a special fee or a higher tuition fee than that paid by resident students. Who is a nonresident? How is he to be distinguished from a resident? Is the word "resident" synonymous with "citizen"? A 1954 decision[74] of the Supreme Court of Ohio sheds some light on these questions.

The son of an alien named Halaby brought an action for a judgment against the governing board of the University of Cincinnati to declare his rights under the provision of an Ohio statute[75] granting free tuition in the academic departments of the university to citizens of the city of Cincinnati. His parents, although citizens of Israel, had declared, by formal action, their intention of becoming citizens of the United States. Both parents owned property located within the city limits and paid taxes thereon. The case reached the supreme court of the state. The following is from the opinion of the court:

It is apparent from a study of legislation and court decisions that, except where a citizen of the United States is referred to, a variety of meanings is loosely given to the term "citizen," and that such use creates legal ambiguity. It is to be observed that the term "citizen" is often used where "domicile" is meant.

The University of Cincinnati is a public institution organized for the purpose of rendering a public service to the residents of the city of Cincinnati. It is supported, in part, by public taxation and, in this respect, stands in the same category as the city's water service, garbage collection service, fire department service, and the public school service. For the support of these services, even though they be aliens, the parents of the plaintiff are required, and if the plaintiff were a property owner, he would be required, to pay property taxes in the same manner as other residents of the city. In these

[73] Caldwell Bros. v. Board of Supervisors, 176 La. 825, 147 So. 5 (1933).
[74] Halaby v. Board of Directors of University of Cincinnati, 162 Ohio St. 290, 123 N.E.2d 3 (1954).
[75] Ohio Gen. Rev. Code 3349.22 (1958).

respects, alien residents are entitled to the same privileges as other residents of the city.

THE CONSTITUTIONALITY OF THE NONRESIDENT FEE. Does a state university have the constitutional right to discriminate against the citizens of other states by the establishment of a higher scale of tuition and fees for nonresidents? The leading case on this point was decided in 1922.[76] The state statute in question defined the term "nonresident" as one who had not been a bona fide resident of the state for one year prior to his admission to the university. The court held that the imposition, by the Regents of the University of California, of a $75 admission fee for nonresidents, was neither unreasonable nor unconstitutional.

RESIDENT STUDENT DEFINED. The New Mexico Board of Educational Finance adopted the following definitions, in compliance with Opinion 58–68, dated June 10, 1958, of the attorney general of the State of New Mexico:

A resident student is defined as one who shall be a bona fide resident of and domiciled within the State of New Mexico for a reasonable period, not less than one year, immediately preceding his or her registration for a term or semester in any State-supported college or university in the State of New Mexico. A minor will generally be presumed to be a resident of the place of his parents' or guardian's domicile.

Domicile is a person's permanent home, to which he intends to return at the termination of any temporary residence at another place. A person can have but one domicile at any time. In changing domiciles, he retains his old one until he fully acquires a new one. "Permanent home" means that place which the person considers to be his home either permanently or for the indefinite foreseeable future.

The residence of a minor (male or female under 21 years of age) is that of his father; or of his mother, if his father be not living or if the parents are separated and the minor habitually resides with the mother; or, if both parents are dead, of his legally appointed guardian or any one else with whom he habitually resides in the absence of formal legal adoption.

A minor may become emancipated (freed from parental domicile) through marriage, formal court action, abandonment by parents, death of both parents and lack of legally appointed guardian, or positive action on his own and his parents' part evidential of his release from parental control. To qualify under this last category, the minor must have completely separated himself from the parental domicile and prove that such separation is complete and perma-

---

[76] Bryan v. Regents of University of California, 188 Cal. 559, 205 Pac. 1071 (1922).

nent. Mere absence from the parental domicile is not proof of its complete abandonment.

The residence of a married woman is that of her husband if they are living together, except as noted further in this paragraph. A wife not living with her husband may establish separate domicile. A non-resident woman who marries a resident of New Mexico shall become a resident at the beginning of the next semester or term following such marriage.

A resident woman who marries a non-resident shall keep her resident status as long as she maintains residence in New Mexico, but loses it if her husband establishes a family home elsewhere. If a resident woman marries an alien, she shall not, by that act alone, be deemed to have alienated her New Mexico residence.

Residence or non-residence status once established shall be presumed to continue, but such status may be reviewed upon the application of the school officials or of the student on any occasion of registration or re-registration for any term or semester.

THE CONSTITUTIONAL IMMUNITIES OF PUBLIC INSTITUTIONS OF HIGHER EDUCATION

Tax-supported colleges and universities, as instrumentalities of sovereign states, enjoy certain valuable legal immunities. Under our system of jurisprudence, a sovereign state cannot be brought into a court of justice without its consent,[77] and, as we have seen in our discussion of the tax-free status of state revenue bonds, neither the state nor the Federal Government may tax the other or the instrumentalities thereof.

THE KING CAN DO NO WRONG. The historical basis for the theory of the irresponsibility of the state for wrongs committed by its officers, agents, and employees is the ancient dictum that the king can do no wrong. It is indeed an anomaly that this concept, based upon the discarded claim of the divine rights of royalty, repugnant to American ideals, should have become so firmly embedded in the very structure of our common law. However, a review of the speeches of Alexander Hamilton, James Madison, and John Marshall, urging the ratification of the Constitution, will reveal the importance placed upon this doctrine of the sovereign immunity of the states of the federal union at

---

[77] The author is indebted to Dean Stanley Samad of the College of Law of the University of Akron for the following annotation: "The statement that 'a sovereign state cannot be brought into a court of justice' is subject to the exception that the United States may sue a state without its consent: *United States v. Texas*, 143 U.S. 621 (1892); but without its consent the United States is not subject to a suit by a state: *Kansas v. United States*, 204 U.S. 331 (1907)."

the very beginning of our national existence. Some authorities believe that it was the fear of the newly created and financially insecure state governments of being overwhelmed by a flood of claims that prompted the adoption of this rule of law. Gradually, the states have accepted a certain degree of responsibility for the wrongs of their agents and have provided various methods for compensating those injured thereby.

THE LEGISLATIVE METHOD OF ADJUDICATING CLAIMS AGAINST THE STATE. The right of the people to petition their government for redress of grievances is a very ancient doctrine, a right guaranteed by the First Amendment to the federal Constitution and by many state constitutions.

In states where this method is in use, the claim is usually introduced as a special bill in the legislature by the representative of the one seeking compensation. The bill, along with others of similar character, is reviewed and rejected or approved by an appropriate legislative committee. This process is obviously time-consuming and costly. For this reason, every state has, to some degree, delegated the details of review to designated officials or administrative agencies.

ADMINISTRATIVE ADJUDICATION. Nineteen states[78] have established a claims board or commission, and three[79] have designated state officials to review claims against the state. These boards or officials are usually given jurisdiction over claims for compensation based upon contractual rights, but not over those based upon personal injury or death. In the majority of states, the tort claims of state employees are adjudicated in accordance with the regular workmen's compensation act.

In twelve states[80] the administrative boards are authorized to hear the claims of citizens based upon the alleged negligent acts of state employees. In addition, the California board has also been granted jurisdiction over claims based upon negligence, but the state supreme court has restricted it to situations in which the state has engaged in industrial or business activities.[81] Tennessee limits the tort jurisdiction of its Board of Claims to personal injury or property damage caused by the negligence of employees in the construction or main-

---

[78] *The Determination and Payment of Claims against the State* (Tallahassee, Fla.: Florida Legislative Council and Reference Bureau, 1957), pp. 17–18.

[79] *Op. cit. supra* note 78, at 18.

[80] *Op. cit. supra* note 78, at 21.

[81] People v. Superior Court, 29 Cal. 754, 178 P.2d 1 (1947).

tenance of its state highways, buildings, or property and the negligence of state employees in the operation of state-owned motor vehicles.[82] It should be noted that a state does not waive its sovereign immunity by the creation of a board of claims. The usual procedure is for the board to investigate the claim and to transmit all the facts, together with its approval or disapproval and its recommended award, to the legislature.

JUDICIAL REVIEW. Although many states now utilize their courts in the adjudication of claims against the state and its instrumentalities, the jurisdiction and duties of the courts in this area are usually sharply restricted by the legislature or by the state constitution. Four states— Illinois, New York, Michigan, and West Virginia—have established special tribunals for reviewing claims against the state.[83] West Virginia abolished her claims court in 1953 and transferred its powers and duties to her attorney general.

The Court of Claims in Michigan was authorized to "hear and determine all claims and demands . . . *ex contractu* and *ex delicto*, against the state and any of its agencies."[84] This act was interpreted by the Michigan Supreme Court as waiving only the state's immunity from suit, not its liability for tort.[85]

As a result of this decision, in 1943 the legislature[86] expressly waived its defense of governmental immunity in tort, but, two years later, this waiver of defense was restricted[87] to actions arising out of the negligent operation of state-owned motor vehicles.

The New York Legislature has gone much further than any other in accepting full liability for the acts of state officers and employees. Here, the state "waives its immunity from liability and action and . . . assumes liability and consents to have the same determination in accordance with the same rules of law as applied to actions in the supreme court against individuals and corporations."[88]

LIABILITY INSURANCE. Although New York is the only state that has waived its tort immunity, many states now either permit or require

---

[82] *Tenn. Code* tit. 9, § 821 (1955).
[83] *Op. cit. supra* note 78, at 25.
[84] *Ibid.*
[85] Manion v. State Highway Commissioners, 303 Mich. 1, 5 N.W.2d 527 (1942).
[86] *Op. cit. supra* note 78, at 25.
[87] *Ibid.* at 26.
[88] N.Y. *Court of Claims Act* § 8; *Laws of N.Y. 1939*, ch. 860, § 8.

state agencies and instrumentalities to carry liability insurance to provide for compensation for personal injuries and property damage caused by the negligent operation of state-owned motor vehicles. The statutes require the insurance company to agree that it will not avail itself of the governmental immunity of its insured. Under the principle of subrogation, an insurer is entitled to all the defenses and immunities of his insured.

Some states prefer to dispense with insurance contracts and become, in effect, self-insurers by the establishment of a reserve fund from which claims are paid. The Bureau of Public Administration of Virginia in 1941 conducted a survey[89] of the relative advantages and disadvantages of state self-insurance.

THE NEW MEXICO COLLEGE CASE. A student enrolled at the New Mexico College of Agriculture and Mechanic Arts was injured as a result of the alleged negligence of an employee in the cafeteria of the college. Her father instituted suit against the Regents of the college and against the employee. In his petition for relief, the father called the attention of the court to the fact that the Regents, at the time of the accident, carried liability insurance. He requested judgment in the amount of $50,000 but agreed to accept a lesser sum as compensation for his daughter's injury if the liability insurance policy had limits of less than the amount demanded.

At the time of the trial, it was disclosed that the liability insurance contract would cover the full amount of the claim. Despite this evidence, the court refused to permit recovery, on the grounds that, under the doctrine of the immunity of a sovereign state and of its instrumentalities from suit, the Regents could not be sued.[90]

The court took judicial notice of the fact that the state legislature, in 1941, had authorized the State Board of Finance to require all officials and administrative heads of departments to purchase and secure public liability and property damage insurance to protect the state against property loss and the public against damage to property or injury to persons because of the negligent operation of automobiles and other motor vehicles of state employees.[91]

This decision of the Supreme Court of New Mexico, handed down

---

[89] George Albro Warp, *Municipal Tort Liability in Virginia* (University, Va.: Bureau of Public Administration, 1941), pp. 98–113.

[90] Livingston v. Regents of New Mexico College of A. & M.A., 64 N.M. 306, 328 P.2d 78 (1958).

[91] *N.M. Stat. Ann.* § 64–25–8 (1953).

in 1958, is in accord with the majority rule that the procurement of liability insurance by a state agency, even with the express consent and authorization of the legislature, does not in itself establish legislative permission to be sued—that is, it does not waive immunity. The reluctance of the courts to abandon the old rule of immunity unless the legislature has, in unequivocal language, expressed an intention to do so, is stated by a judge of the Supreme Court of Montana as follows: "Should the people see fit, they have the power, through the legislature, to consent that the state may be sued, and to determine under what circumstances the state and its agencies shall be answerable to the individual."[92]

The majority rule is followed by the courts of Maryland,[93] Pennsylvania,[94] Kentucky,[95] and Texas,[96] in addition to those of New Mexico and Montana.

The minority rule is exemplified by a decision of an appellate court of Illinois in 1952. This case involved an action in tort for a student injured on a school playground. While upholding the historic rule of sovereign immunity from suit, the Illinois court reasoned that liability insurance, to the extent that it protects public funds, removes the reason for the immunity of the state.[97] The minority rule is followed by the courts of Tennessee[98] as well as by those of Illinois.

THE SOVEREIGN STATE NOT SUBJECT TO STRIKES. As instrumentalities of a state, public institutions of higher education enjoy important immunities in the area of labor law. In 1958 a California district court ruled that a strike against the University of California was illegal since there is, in the opinion of the tribunal, no such thing as the right to strike against the state or one of its agencies.[99]

Some federal labor laws, including the wages and hours law[100]

---

[92] Coldwater v. State Highway Commission, 118 Mont. 65, 162 P.2d 772 (1945).

[93] Jones v. Scofield Bros., 73 F. Supp. 395 (D. Md. 1947).

[94] Kesman v. School District of Fallowfield Township, 345 Penn. 457, 29 A.2d 17 (1942).

[95] Wallace v. Laurel County Board of Education, 287 Ky. 454, 153 S.W.2d 915 (1941).

[96] Texas Prison Board v. Calbeen, 159 S.W.2d 523 (Tex. Civ. App. 1942).

[97] Thomas v. Broadlands Community School District, 344 Ill. App. 567, 109 N.E.2d 636 (1952).

[98] Williams v. Town of Morristown, 32 Tenn. App. 274, 222 S.W.2d 607 (1949).

[99] Newmarker v. Regents of University of California, 160 Cal. App. 2d 640, 325 P.2d 558 (1958). See also Annot., 31 A.L.R.2d 142 (1953).

[100] Fair Labor Standards Act of 1938, 29 U.S.C. §§ 203(d), (e) (1953).

and the Taft-Hartley Act,[101] expressly exempt states and their political subdivisions from their operation and scope. Certain federal agencies, including the Armed Forces[102] and the Atomic Energy Commission,[103] have by administrative regulations excluded state agencies from the purview of the eight hours law of 1912.[104]

THE TAX IMMUNITIES OF PUBLICLY CONTROLLED COLLEGES. As we have seen, under our dual system of federal and state governments, neither can burden the other with taxation. Chief Justice Marshall established federal immunity from state taxation in the celebrated case of McCulloch v. Maryland[105] in 1819, and in 1871 the Supreme Court of the United States declared that the salary of a state officer could not be subjected to a federal income tax. The decision established the general principle that Congress may not impose a tax which impairs the sovereign rights of the states.[106]

Under this doctrine, professors and other employees of the publicly controlled institutions of higher education enjoyed immunity from the federal income tax for many years. Gradually, the tax immunity of the state and of its agencies was eroded by a series of court decisions, and in 1939 the high federal court ruled that the salaries of officers and employees of both the national and state governments are now subject to taxation by the state and national government, respectively.[107]

According to an authority[108] on the subject, the intergovernmental

---

[101] *Labor-Management Relations Act of 1947, 29 U.S.C.* §§ 152(2), (3) (1953).

[102] *Armed Services Procurement Regulations* ¶ 12–302(b).

[103] *Atomic Energy Commission Procurement Manual* § 16–203. In a letter dated November 14, 1958, the general counsel of the Board of Regents of the University of California informed the author that his office has always taken the position that federal labor legislation is inapplicable to the university and that the federal administrative agencies have never seriously challenged this view.

[104] 40 *U.S.C.* § 321. The statute applies only to work done under contract with the Federal Government.

[105] McCulloch v. Maryland, 17 U.S. 316 (1819).

[106] Collector v. Day, 78 U.S. 113 (1871).

[107] Graves v. O'Keefe, 306 U.S. 466 (1939).

[108] Robert Eugene Cushman, *Leading Constitutional Decisions* (9th ed.; New York: Appleton-Century-Crofts, 1950), pp. 377–78.

Dean Stanley Samad adds the following words of caution: "The statements from Cushman regarding the principle of immunity are too doctrinaire. The 'governmental-proprietary' dichotomy has no application to the federal government. It has been rejected in determining the validity of federal taxes against state instrumentalities (*State of New York v. United States*, 326 U.S. 572 (1946)). The problem facing the courts is overcoming the overly broad statement in the McCulloch case that 'The power to tax involves the power to destroy.' The in-tax doctrine, as today defined by the Supreme Court of the United States, is approximately as follows:

1. The federal or state government, together with its functions, property, instrumentalities, and processes—anything reasonably regarded as an attribute of sovereignty—is absolutely immune from any tax levied by the other government.

2. However, this immunity is limited in matters where a state engages in a business enterprise, in contrast to a function traditionally governmental in nature.

3. Such immunity does not extend to persons who merely have business or other relations with the government, unless such persons can show that to tax them is to impose a direct and substantial burden on the government itself.

THE IMPOSITION OF A FEDERAL TARIFF ON THE IMPORTS OF A STATE UNIVERSITY. The University of Illinois challenged the right of the Federal Government to levy and collect import duties on scientific equipment it had purchased abroad for use in its laboratories. The case reached the Supreme Court of the United States in 1933. The following is from the opinion of Chief Justice Hughes:

The principle invoked by the petitioner, of the immunity of state instrumentalities from federal legislation, has its inherent limitation. . . . It is a principle implied from the necessity of maintaining our dual system of government. . . . Springing from that necessity, it does not extend beyond it. Protecting the functions of government in its proper province, the implication ceases when the boundary of that province is reached. The fact that the state, in the performance of state functions, may use imported articles, does not mean that the importation is a function of the state independent of federal power. The control of importation does not rest with the state but with Congress. In international relations and with respect to foreign intercourse and trade, the people of the United States act through a single government with unified and adequate national power. There is thus no violation of the principle which petitioner invokes, for there is no encroachment of the power of the state as none exists with respect to the subject over which the federal power has been exerted. To permit the states and their instrumentalities to import commodities for their own use, regardless of the requirements imposed by the Congress, would undermine, if not destroy, the

vidious feature of the Maryland tax was its *discriminatory* nature. The federal government can grant or withdraw immunity of its instrumentalities by legislation ('necessary and proper' clause) whereas the states can't. Thus, 'implied inter-governmental immunity is not reciprocal.' As to point 3 in Cushman, in several cases involving governmental contractors, the 'direct and substantial' burden on the federal government was not the test, but upon whom did the legal (not economic) tax incidence fall."

single control which it was one of the dominant purposes of the Constitution to create. It is for Congress to decide to what extent, if at all, the states and their instrumentalities shall be relieved of the payment of duties on imported articles.[109]

A FEDERAL EXCISE TAX ON ADMISSION FEES TO ATHLETIC EVENTS. The Regents of the University System of Georgia declined to pay a federal excise tax on income derived from admission charges to athletic events, as required by the Revenue Act of 1932. When the case reached the Supreme Court of the United States, the justices were divided on the question. The following is from the majority opinion:

> The important fact is that the state, in order to raise funds for public purposes, has embarked in a business having the incidents of similar enterprises usually prosecuted for private gain. If it be conceded that the education of its prospective citizens is an essential governmental function of Georgia, as necessary to the preservation of the state as is the maintenance of its executive, legislative, and judicial branches, it does not follow that if the state elects to provide the funds for any of these purposes by conducting a business, the application of the avails in aid of necessary governmental functions withdraws the business from the field of federal taxation.[110]

This decision was the subject of much debate and discussion in Congress, and in 1954 educational institutions, both public and private, were granted freedom from federal taxation on their gate receipts from athletic games and exhibitions, provided they are held during the regular athletic season for the particular activity involved and provided that the proceeds were exclusively for the benefit of the participating educational institutions.[111]

FEDERAL AID FOR PUBLIC INSTITUTIONS OF HIGHER EDUCATION

The first state universities, established shortly after the United States of America gained its independence from the Crown of England, tended to follow the pattern of English universities as to their curriculum. They were not essentially different from the private colleges established during our colonial period. College education here, as in England, was essentially for the members of the leisure classes, governmental leaders, and members of the professions.

---

[109] University of Illinois v. United States, 289 U.S. 48 (1933).

[110] Allen v. Regents of University System of Georgia, 304 U.S. 439 (1938).

[111] *Excise Tax Reduction Act of 1954*, 68A *Stat.* 498, 26 *U.S.C.A.* 4233 (a)(1)(c) (1955).

By the middle of the ninteenth century, a strong demand for a different type of education began to make itself heard. Farmers, through their organizations, were insisting that agriculture have a place in the list of subjects taught by the colleges.

THE MORRILL LAND-GRANT ACT OF 1862. The discussion reached the floor of Congress, and a bill introduced by Justin Smith Morrill, representative from the State of Vermont, was passed in both houses of Congress in 1859. However, it was vetoed by President Buchanan, on the ground that it was in violation of the traditional policy of the Federal Government, which had, up to that time, left the financing of education entirely to the several states. In 1862, the Morrill Act was again passed and was signed into law by President Lincoln.

President Buchanan's veto message to the contrary, the Federal Government began the practice of making public lands available to the states for university purposes with a grant to the State of Ohio in 1802. After that date, it was customary for the enabling acts under which territories were admitted as states to the federal union to include grants of public lands in aid of higher education. The Morrill Act, however, was the first general act offering such aid to all states and territories.

The wording of these federal land-grant acts was not explicit as to just what should be considered to be permanent funds and what might be expended as current funds. The courts have generally held that proceeds from the sale of land or land scrip must be held as permanent endowment but that the interest thereon and proceeds from ordinary rentals of unsold lands are current funds.[112] However, oil royalties have been held to constitute additions to principal, not current income.[113]

As we have seen, a few states, notably New York, New Jersey, Delaware, and Pennsylvania, utilized privately controlled institutions already established as their land-grant colleges.[114] In order to qualify for these allocations of public funds, some of these private institutions accepted a degree of public control.

Rutgers University has been cited as an example of the ultimate

---

[112] State v. Barrett, 26 Mont. 62, 66 Pac. 504 (1901).

[113] Regents of University of New Mexico v. Graham, 33 N.M. 214, 264 Pac. 953 (1928).

[114] See the discussion in chap. 2 of "Allocation of Federal Land-Grant Funds to Nonpublic Institutions," p. 29.

effect of the acceptance of public funds by a private institution of higher education.

In response to a petition of Dutch settlers, George III of Great Britain granted a royal charter in 1766 to the "Trustees of Queen's College in New Jersey." One of the provisions of the charter was that the president of the college should be a member of the Dutch Reformed Church. After the American Revolution, the royal charter was confirmed by the State of New Jersey upon petition of the Board of Trustees of the college. In 1825 the board voted to change the name of the corporation to the "Trustees of Rutgers College in New Jersey" in recognition of the generous gifts of Colonel Henry Rutgers.

When federal funds became available for the support of instruction and research in agriculture under the provisions of the Morrill Act of 1862, the Trustees of Rutgers requested the New Jersey Legislature to designate Rutgers Scientific School as the "New Jersey Land-Grant College." As such, it was made subject to the supervision and control of a Board of Visitors created for the purpose and appointed by the governor of the state. In 1917 the legislature changed the name of the land-grant college to "The State University of New Jersey."

In 1920 the Trustees of Rutgers deleted from its charter all religious and sectarian qualifications and in 1927 increased the number of its *ex officio* Trustees to include five state officials for the purpose of promoting "a closer cooperation in educational work between this institution and other educational agencies of the state of New Jersey." The legislature in 1928 appointed a special commission to investigate and report on "the most effective procedures to be followed in coordinating the educational work of the state with that of Rutgers College."

By 1945 Rutgers was recognized by the state and by its own Board of Trustees as the state university, that is, as an instrumentality of the State of New Jersey. All its divisions became subject to a public trust for higher education under the supervision of the State Board of Education.

A much more drastic revision of its charter was proposed in an act of the legislature in 1956. The name of the institution would become "Rutgers, The State University of New Jersey." The act created a Board of Governors to take over the duties of its Board of Trustees in the general supervision and conduct of the university. However, the identity and name of the old corporation, "Trustees of Rutgers College in New Jersey," would be preserved intact, and the Trustees would retain custody and control of its endowments and other assets. The Trustees were given until September 1, 1956, to accept or to reject the provisions of the act.

The Trustees, doubtful of their right as charitable trustees to consent to this reduction of their authority and responsibilities, requested a declaratory judgment of the Chancery Division of the Supreme Court of New Jersey as to the constitutionality of the act of reorganization. They also requested a bill of instructions from the court.

Justice Schettino delivered the opinion of the court.[115] He reviewed the history of Rutgers and the urgent need for increased public financial support in order to meet the growing demand for higher education. He emphasized the point that the court was not called upon to determine the wisdom of the plan but merely to pass upon its legal validity. The following are from his opinion:

> The first inquiry is directed to determining the nature of the charitable trusts held and administered by the trustees of Rutgers College in New Jersey. It is created by charter and must pursue the charitable purposes outlined in its charter and amendments thereto.
>
> The board of trustees retains power to withdraw and withhold the use and income of the trust property, presently of the value of $89,000,000, from the board of governors in the event that its trust duties for the accomplishment of the trust purposes are not adequately discharged.
>
> The board of governors, to whom substantial managerial powers would be delegated, is controlled, through a majority representation, by persons designated by the governor of the state of New Jersey, with the advice and consent of the senate.
>
> Thus, we find here created a hybrid institution—at one and the same time private and public, with the state being granted a major voice in management and the designation "State University"; and the institution being granted private autonomy and control of physical property and assets.
>
> I conclude that the court has jurisdiction to grant a final judgment . . . and that the board of trustees of Rutgers College in New Jersey has power and authority to adopt chapter 61 of the Laws of 1956 as a valid and constitutional act.

LEGISLATION SUBSEQUENT TO
THE MORRILL ACT OF 1862

Federal legislation providing for the financial support of public higher education and research in the fields of agriculture and engineering, subsequent to the Morrill Act, includes the following:

---

[115] Trustees of Rutgers College v. Richmond, 41 N.J. Super. 259, 125 A.2d 10 (1956).

1. The Hatch Act of 1887, setting up, in the land-grant institutions, a system of agricultural experiment stations.[116]

2. The Second Morrill Act, of 1890, supplementing, by direct appropriations, the income from the proceeds from the sale of the original grant of public lands.[117]

3. The Smith-Lever Act of 1914, establishing, in cooperation with the states, a program of adult education courses in agriculture.[118]

4. The Bankhead-Jones Act of 1935, providing for research in basic scientific laws and principles relating to agriculture and for further development of adult extension courses in agriculture.[119]

---

[116] 7 *U.S.C.A.* § 362 (1952).
[117] *Ibid.* § 322.
[118] *Ibid.* §§ 341–48.
[119] *Ibid.* §§ 329, 343c, 427–427g.

Appendix

STATE CONSTITUTIONAL AND STATUTORY PROVISIONS ON
THE TAX STATUS OF THE PROPERTY OF PRIVATELY CON-
TROLLED INSTITUTIONS OF HIGHER EDUCATION,
WITH COMMENTARY ON SPECIFIC CASES

ALABAMA

Ala. Const. art. 4, § 91

"The Legislature shall not tax . . . lots in incorporated cities and towns,
or within one mile of any city or town to the extent of one acre, nor lots
one mile or more distant from such cities or towns to the extent of five
acres, with the buildings thereon, when same are used exclusively . . . for
schools . . ."

Ala. Code Ann. tit. 51, ch. 2, § 2 (1940)

"(a) The following property . . . shall be exempt from ad valorem taxation . . . : all property, real and personal, used exclusively for . . . schools;
provided, however, property, real or personal, owned by any educational . . .
institution . . . , let for rent or hire or for use for business purposes shall not
be exempt from taxation, notwithstanding the income from such property
shall be used exclusively for educational . . . purposes."

"(k) No license or taxation of any character, except franchise taxes . . .
shall be collected or required to be paid to the state . . . by any . . . athletic
stadiums owned and controlled by universities, schools or colleges, and
which are used exclusively for the purpose of promoting intercollegiate or
interstate athletics. Provided that the revenue received from athletic stadiums, when admission is charged, shall be used for the benefit of athletic
associations of such universities, colleges or schools . . ."

[April–June 1944] *Rep. Att'y Gen. Ala.* 65

"The property of the Alabama Research Institute, a nonprofit scientific
institution organized under Title 10, par. 150, when used in regular business
is exempt.

"The property of a college fraternity or sorority is not exempt under Alabama statutes."

ALASKA

Alaska Const. art. IX, § 4

"All, or any portion of property used exclusively for nonprofit . . . educational purposes, as defined by law, shall be exempt from taxation."

279

ARIZONA

Ariz. Const. art. 9, § 2

"Property of educational . . . institutions not used or held for profit may be exempt from taxation by law."

Ariz. Rev. Stat. Ann. art. 3, §§ 42–271 (1956)

"All property in the state shall be subject to taxation except . . . colleges . . . and other buildings used for education, with their furniture, libraries and equipment, and the lands appurtenant thereto and used therewith, as long as they are used for the purpose of education and are not used or held for profit, but when such property is private property from which a rent or valuable consideration is received for its use, it shall be taxed as other property."

CASE

Louis Grunow Memorial Clinic v. Oglesby, 42 Ariz. 98, 22 P.2d 1076 (1933). According to this decision of the Arizona Supreme Court an "educational institution," as this term is used in the state constitution, is one which teaches and improves its pupils—a school, seminary, college, or educational establishment. It held that a clinic used by physicians and surgeons who rent offices to derive profit therefrom in connection with their practice, some of which is charitable and incidentally used for the purpose of scientific research, is not exempt, either as an educational or as a charitable institution.

ARKANSAS

Ark. Const. art. 16, ¶ 5

". . . the following property shall be exempt from taxation: . . . school buildings and apparatus; libraries and grounds used exclusively for school purposes."

Ark. Stat. Ann. § 84–206 (Supp. 1953)

"All property described in this section, to the extent herein limited, shall be exempt from taxation: All public colleges . . . , all buildings connected with the same and all houses connected with public institutions of learning, not used with a view to profit. This provision shall not extend to leasehold estates, or to real property held under the authority of any college or university of learning in this State."

CASE

Phillip Co. v. Estelle, 42 Ark. 536 (1884). The exemption as to school buildings applies to private schools as well as public schools.

CALIFORNIA

Cal. Const. art. 13, § 1a

"Any educational institution of collegiate grade within the State of California, not conducted for profit, shall hold exempt from taxation its buildings and equipment, its grounds within which its buildings are located, not

exceeding 100 acres in area, its securities and income used exclusively . . .
for the purposes of education.

"The exemption granted by this section applies to and includes building
in the course of construction on or after the first Monday of March, 1950,
and the land on which the building is located, if the property is intended,
when completed, to be used exclusively for the purpose of education."

Cal. Rev. & Tax Code § 203

"The college exemption is as specified in Section 1a of Article XIII of the
Constitution.

"An educational institution of collegiate grade is an institution incorporated as a college or seminary of learning under the laws of this State, which
requires for regular admission the completion of a four-year high school
course or its equivalent, and confers upon its graduates at least one academic
or professional degree, based on a course of at least four years in liberal
arts and sciences, or on a course of at least three years in professional
studies, such as law, theology, education, medicine, dentistry, engineering,
veterinary medicine, pharmacy, architecture, fine arts, commerce, or journalism.

"An educational institution of collegiate grade is one not conducted for
profit when it is conducted exclusively for scientific or educational purposes
and no part of which inures to the benefit of any private person."

CASES

Lutheran Hospital Soc'y of So. California v. Los Angeles County, 25 Cal. 2d
254, 153 P.2d 341 (1944). A school of nursing conducted as an incident
to hospital operations was held to be not "an educational institution of
collegiate grade."

Pasadena Playhouse Ass'n v. Los Angeles County, 69 Cal. App. 2d 611,
159 P.2d 679 (N.D. Cal. 1945). An association devoted to developing the
histrionic talents of students was held to be "an educational institution of
collegiate grade" and, hence, exempt from taxation.

Church Divinity School of the Pacific v. Alameda County, 152 Cal. App. 2d
496, 314 P.2d 209 (S.D. Cal. 1957). Property used to provide a parking lot
for students and staff, to provide rent-free residences for its faculty members, and to provide housing for married students and their families, was
held to be exempt from taxation. See 24 *So. Cal. L. Rev.* 252 (1951);
9 *Hastings L.J.* 215 (1958).

COLORADO

Colo. Const. art. 10, § 5

"Property, real and personal, that is used solely and exclusively for . . .
schools . . . shall be exempt from taxation, unless otherwise provided by general law."

Colo. Rev. Stat. Ann. ¶ 137–12–3 (1953)

"The following . . . shall be exempt from taxation . . ."

"(7) Property, real and personal, that is used solely and exclusively for schools, other than schools held or conducted for private or corporate profit. School is hereby defined to mean an educational institution having a curriculum comparable to a grade, grammar, junior high, high school or college or a combination thereof, requiring daily attendance, having an enrollment of at least forty students, and charging a tuition fee."

CASE

Denver v. Gunter, 63 Colo. 69, 163 Pac. 1118 (1917). Rental from property held in trust for Clayton College was held to be exempt.

CONNECTICUT

Gen. Stat. of Conn. ch. 203, § 12–81 (1958)

"(7) Subject to the provisions of sections 12–87 and 12–88, the real property of, or held in trust for, a Connecticut corporation organized exclusively for scientific, educational . . . purposes . . . and used exclusively for carrying out such purposes, and the personal property of, or held in trust for, any such corporation, provided (a): any officer, member or employee thereof does not receive or, at any future time, shall receive, any pecuniary profit from the operation thereof, except reasonable compensation for services . . . and provided (b): in 1961 and quadrennially thereafter, a statement on forms prepared by the tax commissioner shall be filed . . . with the local assessor of any town . . . in which its property claimed to be exempt is situated."

"(9) Personal property, while it is loaned without charge or leased at a nominal charge of one dollar per year to any tax-exempt educational institution above the secondary level and used exclusively by such institution for teaching, research or teaching demonstration purposes."

CASES

Yale University v. Town of New Haven, 71 Conn. 316, 42 Atl. 87 (1898). Buildings of Yale University which were occupied exclusively as dormitories and dining halls for its students were nontaxable, but a dwelling owned by the university but occupied by one of its professors was not exempt.

New Canaan County School, Inc. v. New Canaan, 138 Conn. 347, 84 A.2d 691 (1951). Homes owned by a school but used as living quarters for some of its teachers were not exempt from taxation.

Arnold College v. Milford, 144 Conn. 206, 128 A.2d 537 (1957). The gymnasium and playing fields of a college are exempt.

DELAWARE

Del. Const. art. 10, § 3

". . . all real or personal property used for school purposes, when the tuition is free, shall be exempt from taxation and assessment for public purposes."

Del. Code Ann. tit. 9 (1953)

"§ 8103: Property belonging . . . to any college or school . . . and used for educational or school purposes and not held by way of investment, except as otherwise provided, shall not be liable to taxation and assessment for public purposes . . ."

"§ 8105: No real property owned or used . . . for the purposes stated, except that which is held by way of investment, shall be liable to taxation and assessment for public purposes. . . . Incorporated college fraternities (limit $10,000 per fraternity)."

CASE

Burris v. Tower Hill School Ass'n, 36 Del. 577, 179 Atl. 397 (1935). Residence owned by a day school and used as a residence by the headmaster was held to be subject to taxation.

DISTRICT OF COLUMBIA

D.C. Code Ann. tit. 47, § 47–801a (1951)

"The real property exempt from taxation in the District of Columbia shall be the following and none other:"

"(j) Buildings belonging to and operated by schools, colleges, or universities which are not organized or operated for private gain and which embrace the generally recognized relationship of teacher and student."

"(g) Buildings belonging to organizations which are charged with the administration, coordination, or unification of activities, locally or otherwise, of institutions or organizations entitled to exemption under provisions of sections 47–801a . . . and used as administration headquarters thereof."

"(r) (1) Grounds belonging to and reasonably required and actually used for the carrying on of the activities and purposes of any institution or organization entitled to exemption under provisions of sections 47–801a . . .

(2) Additional grounds belonging to and forming a part of such institutions or organizations as of July 1, 1942 . . ."

CASES

Howard University v. District of Columbia, 81 U.S. App. D.C. 40, 155 F.2d 10 (1946). Property held as an investment by university was ruled subject to taxation.

District of Columbia v. The George Washington University, 100 U.S. App. D.C. 140, 243 F.2d 246 (1957). Parking lots owned by the university and used by its students were held to be exempt from taxation.

FLORIDA

Fla. Const. art. IX, § 1

"The Legislature shall provide for a uniform and equal rate of taxation . . . excepting such property as may be exempted by law for . . . educational purposes."

Fla. Const. art. XVI, § 16

"The property of all corporations . . . shall be subject to taxation unless such property be held and used exclusively for . . . educational purposes."

Fla. Stat. ch. 192, § 192.06 (1957)

"The following property shall be exempt from taxation . . ."

"(3) Such property of educational . . . institutions within this state as shall be actually occupied and used by them for the purpose for which they may have been or may be organized; provided that not more than seventy-five per cent of the floor space of said building or property is rented and the rents, issues and uses of said property are used for the educational purposes of said institutions; provided further that nothing in this subsection shall be construed as applying to special assessment . . . for sidewalks, curbing, street paving or other local improvements."

See also § 192.061 for provisions with respect to exemptions of real property held by educational corporations under long-term leases.

GEORGIA

Ga. Const. art. 7, ch. 2–5, § 2–5405

"The General Assembly may, by law, exempt from taxation, . . . all intangible personal property owned by or irrevocably held in trust for the exclusive benefit of . . . educational . . . institutions, no part of the net profit from the operation of which can inure to the benefit of any private person; all buildings erected for and used as a college . . . , and also all funds or property held or used as endowment by such colleges . . . , provided the same is not invested in real estate; and provided further that such exemptions shall only apply to such colleges . . . as are open to the general public; provided further, that all endowments to institutions established for white people, shall be limited to white people, and all endowments to institutions established for colored people, shall be limited to colored people . . . ; all books and philosophical apparatus and all paintings and statuary . . . ; provided the property so exempted be not used for the purposes of private or corporate profit or income . . . ; this exemption shall not apply to real estate or buildings other than used for the operation of such institutions and which is rented, leased or otherwise used for the primary purpose of securing an income therefrom; and also provided that such donations of property shall not be predicated upon an agreement, contract or otherwise that the donors shall receive or retain any part of the net or gross income of the property."

Ga. Code Ann. ch. 92–2, § 92–201 (1937)

"The following shall be exempt from taxation, to wit:" [wording of the statute identical with provisions of the state constitution quoted above].

Letter to the author from the Office of the Attorney General, dated May 15, 1959. A proposed amendment to the state constitution that would have granted exemption to college fraternity and sorority houses was defeated November 4, 1958, by a vote of 31,516 to 72,044.

CASES

Elder v. Atlanta-Southern Dental College, 183 Ga. 634, 109 S.E. 254 (1936).
A dental college, provided none of its physical properties were used for private or corporate gain, was held to be exempt.

Elder v. Trustees of Atlanta University, 194 Ga. 716, 22 S.E.2d 515 (1942).
Athletic fields and faculty housing owned by the college were held to be exempt.

HAWAII

Hawaii Rev. Laws ch. 128, § 128–18 (1955)

"The following real property shall be exempt from real property taxes; real property actually, and except as otherwise specifically provided, exclusively used by:

"(1) Any incorporated or private school not operated for profit, the property exempt from taxation being limited to such property as may be used for buildings, campus grounds and camp sites, with not more than twenty additional acres for agricultural or dairying purposes in connection with the activities of such schools." A number of designated educational institutions are specifically exempted from property taxation.

IDAHO

Idaho Const. art. 7, § 5

". . . the legislature may allow such exemptions from taxation from time to time as shall seem necessary and just . . ."

Idaho Code, tit. 63, ch. 1, § 63–105 (1955)

"The following property shall be exempt from taxation:"

"13: All property used exclusively by the owner for school or educational purposes, from which no profit is derived, and property from which no profit or rental is derived is held or used exclusively for endowment, building or maintenance purposes of schools or educational institutions."

ILLINOIS

Ill. Const. art. IX, § 3

". . . such other property as may be used exclusively for . . . school purposes . . . may be exempted from taxation, but exemption shall only be by general law . . ."

Ill. Ann. Stat. ch. 120, § 500 (1934)

"All property described in this section, to the extent herein limited, shall be exempt from taxation, that is to say: (1) all property of schools, including the real estate on which the schools are located and any other real estate used by such schools exclusively for school purposes, not leased by such schools or otherwise used with a view to profit. . . . The property described in this paragraph shall be exempt from taxation whether owned by . . . a corporation, whether incorporated in this state or in any other state in the United States, and not leased or otherwise used with a view to profit."

CASES

City of Chicago v. University of Chicago, 228 Ill. 605, 81 N.E. 1138 (1907). The dormitories, dining hall, and the Reynolds Club of the University of Chicago used for study, living, and social purposes by students, alumni, and faculty and operated on a nonprofit basis were held to be exempt from city water taxes.

Monticello Seminary v. Board of Review, 249 Ill. 481, 94 N.E. 938 (1911). Endowment funds for college scholarships were held to be exempt from taxation.

Knox College v. Board of Review, 308 Ill. 160, 139 N.E. 56 (1923). The home of the college president owned by the college is subject to taxation; college fraternity houses also are subject to taxation.

People v. Alpha Pi of Phi Kappa Sigma Educational Ass'n, 326 Ill. 573, 158 N.E. 213 (1927). College fraternity houses are subject to taxation.

People v. North Central College, 336 Ill. 263, 168 N.E. 269 (1929). Dormitories and dining halls used exclusively by students were held to be essential parts of a college and exempt from taxation.

People v. University of Illinois Foundation, 388 Ill. 363, 58 N.E.2d 33 (1944). Buildings owned by the University of Illinois Foundation, a nonprofit educational corporation, including residence halls, dining rooms, clubhouses, and recreational facilities necessary and proper in conducting the University of Illinois, were held to be exempt from taxation.

Coyne Electrical School v. Peachen, 12 Ill.2d 387, 146 N.E.2d 73 (1957). A nonprofit corporation providing a course of study in electronics which did not fit into the scheme of education offered by public schools or colleges was held not to be exempt from property taxation.

INDIANA

Ind. Const. art. 10, § 1

"The General Assembly . . . shall prescribe such regulations as shall secure a just valuation for taxation of all property, both real and personal, excepting such only used for . . . educational, literary, scientific . . . or charitable purposes, as may be specifically exempted by law."

Ind. Stat. ch. 2, § 64–201 (1951)

"The following property shall be exempt from taxation:"

"*Fourth:* The personal property and real estate of . . . any college incorporated within this state when used and actually occupied for the purpose for which such institution was incorporated; such real estate not to exceed eight hundred acres in any one county of this state.

"*Fifth:* . . . including the campus and athletic grounds of any educational institution not exceeding fifty acres; also the lands purchased with the bona fide intention of erecting buildings for such use thereon, not exceeding forty acres; also the personal property endowment funds and interest thereon, belonging to any such institution . . . and connected with, used or set apart for any of the purposes aforesaid."

"*Twelfth:* Any part, parcel or tract of land, not exceeding one acre, and the improvements thereon, and all personal property, owned by any Greek-letter or other fraternity or sorority, which is connected with any college, university, or other institution of learning, and under the supervision thereof, and which is used exclusively by such Greek-letter or other fraternity or sorority to carry out the purposes of such organization."

"*Twenty-second:* All annuities payable by . . . educational institutions located in this state, to any person or persons who have made gifts, bequests or devises to any such . . . institution and which shall have been accepted heretofore for the purpose of such . . . institution under the provisions of any law of this state: Provided, that any such annuity payable by any such . . . institution to any person or persons who hereafter may make any such gifts, bequests or devises to any such . . . institution shall not be exempt from taxation."

[1939] *Ops. Att'y Gen. Ind.* 146

"Farms owned by colleges, . . . operated by students, products of which are used by the institution, are not tax exempt, except as to colleges using the farms as part of their educational procedures."

CASE

State v. Allen, 189 Ind. 369, 127 N.E. 145 (1920). A 1914 statute exempting the property of college fraternities was held to be constitutional. The word "fraternity," in its generic sense, includes organizations composed of either or both sexes.

IOWA

Iowa Const. art. VIII, § 2

"The property of all corporations for pecuniary profit shall be subject to taxation, the same as that of individuals."

Code of Iowa ch. 427, § 427.1 (1958)

"9. All grounds and buildings used by literary, scientific, charitable . . . institutions . . . solely for their appropriate objects, not exceeding three hundred twenty acres in extent and not leased or otherwise used with a view to pecuniary profit.

"10. Money and credits belonging exclusively to institutions named in [subsection] . . . 9 and devoted solely to sustaining them, but not exceeding in amount or income the amount prescribed by their charters or articles of incorporation; and the books, papers, pictures, works of art, apparatus and other personal property belonging to such institutions and used solely for the purposes contemplated in said subsection and the like property of students in such institutions used for their education.

"11. Real estate owned by any educational institution of this state as a part of its endowment fund, to the extent of one hundred sixty acres in any civil township."

CASE

Trustees of Griswold College v. Iowa, 46 Iowa 275, 26 Am. Rep. 138 (1877). Faculty housing at Griswold College was held to be exempt from taxation.

KANSAS

Kan. Const. art. 11, § 1

"All property used exclusively for . . . educational purposes . . . shall be exempt from taxation."

Kan. Gen. Stat. ch. 79, art. 2, § 79–201 (1949)

"That property described in this section, to the extent herein limited, shall be exempt from taxation.

"First: . . . all buildings with furniture and books therein contained and used exclusively for the accommodation of schools . . . together with the grounds owned thereby, not exceeding in any one case ten acres, if not leased or otherwise used with a view to profit . . ."

"Fourth: All moneys and credits belonging exclusively to universities, colleges . . . , appropriated solely to sustain such institutions . . . not exceeding in amount or income arising therefrom the limit prescribed in the charter of such institution."

Kan. Gen. Stat. ch. 79, art. 2, § 79–208

"All property used exclusively for the housing of the regularly matriculated students of any denominational college or university erected upon the regular campus ground of such college or university, shall be exempt from taxation."

CASE

Kansas Wesleyan University v. Saline County Commissioners, 120 Kan. 496, 243 Pac. 1055 (1926). A building owned by a college and occupied as a residence by its president was held to be exempt from taxation.

KENTUCKY

Ky. Const. § 170

"There shall be exempt from taxation . . . institutions of education not used or employed for gain by any person or corporation, and the income of which is devoted exclusively to the cause of education . . . their endowments and the income of such property if used exclusively for their maintenance."

Ky. Rev. Stat. § 132.190 (1956)

"The property subject to taxation, unless exempted by the Constitution, shall be as follows . . ."

CASE

Commonwealth v. Berea College, 149 Ky. 95, 147 S.W. 929 (1912). The laundry, waterworks, printing plant, supply store, and hotel owned and used by the college were held to be exempt from taxation.

LOUISIANA

La. Const. art. 10, § 4

"The following property, and no other, shall be exempt from taxation . . . :"

"2. . . . schools and colleges . . . ; but the exemption shall extend only to property, and grounds thereto appurtenant; used exclusively for the above mentioned purposes, and not leased for profit or income."

La. Rev. Stat. § 1703 (1950)

"There shall be exempt from taxes levied by this chapter all property which is declared to be exempt from taxation by section 4 of article X . . . of the constitution of 1921, and no other."

MAINE

Me. Rev. Stat. ch. 92, § 6 (1954)

"III. . . . real and personal property owned and occupied or used solely for their own purposes . . . by literary and scientific institutions . . . ; provided further, however, as a further condition of the right of exemption that no director, trustee, officer or employee of any organization claiming exemption shall receive directly or indirectly any pecuniary profit from the operation thereof, excepting reasonable compensation for services in effecting its purposes or as a proper beneficiary of its strictly benevolent or charitable purposes, and that all profits derived from the operation thereof and the proceeds from the sale of its property are devoted exclusively to the purposes for which it is organized . . ."

"Any college in this state authorized to confer the degree of bachelor of arts or bachelor of science and having real estate liable to taxation shall, upon the payment of such tax . . . be reimbursed . . . to the amount of the tax so paid, provided however, that the aggregate amount so reimbursed to any college in any one year shall not exceed $1,500 and that this right of reimbursement shall not apply to real estate bought after April 12, 1889."

CASE

Orono v. Kappa Sigma Society, 108 Me. 320, 80 Atl. 831 (1911). The building of a fraternity erected on the campus of the University of Maine under a contract of purchase for its own use is not exempt from taxation.

MARYLAND

Md. Code Ann. art. 81

"The following shall be exempt from assessment and from state, county and city taxation in this state, each and all of which exemption shall be strictly construed:"

"§ 7(8). Buildings, furniture, equipment and libraries of educational . . . institutions, no part of the net income of which inures to the benefit of any private shareholder or individual, and the grounds, not exceeding (outside of any city) one hundred acres in area, appurtenant thereto, and necessary for the respective uses thereof."

"§ 9. Tangible personal property in the form of machinery, tools and scientific apparatus, including nuclear reactors, particle accelerators and radiation sources and associated measuring, controlling, material handling, pumping, cooling and containment equipment and special nuclear material which is part of or necessary for the efficient operation of a nuclear research or testing facility . . . the same is or may be exempt from county and/or city taxation; . . . this exemption shall not be construed to apply to any nuclear reactors for the commercial production of electric power."

MASSACHUSETTS

Mass. Ann. Laws ch. 49, § 5(3) (1953)

"The following property and polls shall be exempt from taxation: Personal property of any charitable organization, which term, as used in this clause, shall mean (1) a literary, benevolent, charitable or scientific institution . . . and (2) a trust for literary, benevolent, charitable, scientific . . . purposes and solely carried out within this Commonwealth, or its literary, benevolent, charitable, scientific . . . purposes are principally and usually carried out within this Commonwealth; and real estate owned or held in trust for a charitable organization and occupied by it or its offices for the purposes for which it is organized . . . ; and real estate purchased by a charitable organization with the purpose of removal thereto, until such removal, but not for more than two years after such purchase; provided however, that:— (a) If any of the income or profits of the business of the charitable organization is divided among the stockholders, the trustees or the members, or is used or appropriated for other than literary, benevolent, charitable, scientific . . . purposes, its property shall not be exempt . . ."

CASES

President & Fellows of Harvard College v. Assessors of Cambridge, 175 Mass. 145, 55 N.E. 844 (1900). Dormitories, the president's house, and faculty housing were declared exempt. The basis for the exemption of the faculty housing was the fact that the professors performed a substantial portion of their university duties in the homes thus provided for them by the college.

Williams College v. Assessors of Williamstown, 167 Mass. 505, 46 N.E. 394 (1897). In this case, faculty housing was declared to be taxable property on the grounds that the occupation was strictly private.

Amherst College v. Assessors, 173 Mass. 232, 53 N.E. 815 (1899). The president's house at Amherst College was held to be exempt from taxation if, in the trial court, there was evidence warranting a finding of fact that the dominant purposes of the president's occupation thereof were not private but were those for which the college was incorporated.

MICHIGAN

Mich. Comp. Laws § 211.7 (1948)

"The following property shall be exempt from taxation:"
"Fourth: Such real estate as shall be owned and occupied by . . . educational or scientific institutions . . . incorporated under the laws of this state, with the buildings and other property thereon while occupied by them solely for the purposes for which they were incorporated."

CASE

Webb Academy v. City of Grand Rapids, 209 Mich. 523, 177 N.W. 290 (1920). The fact that members of the faculty and staff of an educational institution are housed in buildings owned by the institution does not render them taxable.

MINNESOTA

Minn. Const. art. IX, § 1

". . . colleges and universities . . . shall be exempt from taxation."

Minn. Stat. Ann. § 272.02 (1946)

"All property described in this section to the extent herein limited shall be exempt from taxation:"
"(4) All . . . colleges and universites . . ."

[1930] 355 *Op. Att'y Gen. Minn.* **301**

To render an employee's residence tax-exempt, there must be proof of reasonable necessity that the college must furnish residence for a particular employee in order that he may better perform his duties.

[Apr. 13, 1933] *Op. Att'y Gen. Minn.* **414–B–2**

Renting of part of a college building to a newspaper did not destroy tax exemption if such use was subordinate to use as college building.

CASES

Rice County v. Bishop Seabury Mission, 90 Minn. 92, 95 N.W. 882 (1903). College endowment invested in farm mortgages was held to be exempt.
Ramsey County v. Macalester College, 51 Minn. 437, 53 N.W. 704 (1892). Faculty housing was declared to be exempt from taxation. However, a tract of unimproved land, held for possible future use as a student recreational area, was not exempt.
State v. Carleton College, 154 Minn. 280, 191 N.W. 400 (1923). Residences owned by the college and occupied by the president and professors are not subject to taxation.

State v. Carleton College, 154 Minn. 280, 191 N.W. 400 (1923). College
dormitories are exempt, but farms operated or leased to provide revenue
for the college are not exempt.

MISSISSIPPI

Miss. Code Ann. (1942)

"§ 6193. Any person desiring in his lifetime, to promote the public welfare
by founding, endowing . . . an educational institution within the state, to be
operated without profit, may, to that end, grant . . . such real property in
this state as shall be necessary to the operation of such . . . educational
institutions, and any personal property wherever situated . . ."

"§ 6196. Every institution founded hereunder, and its property, money,
stock, bonds, notes, certificates of indebtedness, other evidence of indebtedness and all other personal property so far as is devoted exclusively to
carrying out objects and purposes of such institution, shall be exempt from
all state, county and municipal taxes; provided however, such institution
shall own only such real property as shall be necessary to the fulfillment of
the objects and purposes of such institution."

"§ 9697. The following shall be exempt from taxation:
All property, real and personal, belonging to any college . . . used directly
and exclusively for such purpose, provided that no college . . . shall have
exempt from taxation more than six hundred forty acres of land; provided
further that this exemption shall not apply to commercial schools and colleges or trade institutions or schools where the profits of same inure to
individuals, associations or corporations."

CASE

Jackson v. Belhaven College, 195 Miss. 734, 15 So. 2d 621 (1943). The fact
that college land, not in excess of six hundred and forty acres, was used
for farm purposes did not destroy its tax-exempt status.

MISSOURI

Mo. Const. art. X, § 6

". . . all property, real and personal, not held for private or corporate
profit and used exclusively for . . . colleges . . . may be exempted from
taxation by general law."

Mo. Rev. Stat. § 137.100 (1951)

"The following subjects shall be exempt from taxation for state, county
or local purposes:"

"(6) All property, real and personal, actually and regularly used exclusively
for . . . colleges, and not held for private or corporate profit, shall be exempted from taxation for state, city, county, school, and local purposes;
provided, however, that the exemption herein granted shall not include real
property not actually used or occupied for the purposes of the organization,

but held or used as investment even though the income or rental received therefrom be used wholly for . . . educational . . . purposes."

CASES

State v. Board of Trustees of Westminster College, 175 Mo. 52, 74 S.W. 990 (1903). Where a will granting real and personal property to a college subjected the property to an annuity, but the annuity was actually paid from income derived from the personal property alone and the land thus granted was used by the college for its educational purposes, the land was tax exempt.

Midwest Bible & Missionary Institute v. Sestric, 364 Mo. 167, 260 S.W.2d 25 (1953). A college building used as a dormitory for students and housing for faculty was held to be exempt.

MONTANA

Mont. Const. art. XII, § 2

". . . such other property as may be used exclusively . . . for educational purposes . . . may be exempt from taxation."

Rev. Code of Mont. tit. 84, § 202 (1947)

". . . such other property, as is used exclusively . . . for educational purposes . . . are exempt from taxation, but no more land than is necessary for such purposes is exempt."

NEBRASKA

Neb. Const. art. VII, § 2

"The legislature by general law may exempt property owned by and used exclusively for . . . educational purposes, when such property is not owned or used for financial gain or profit to either owner or user."

Neb. Rev. Stat. tit. 77, § 202 (1943)

"The following property is exempt from taxation:"

"(c) Property owned and used exclusively for educational . . . purposes, when such property is not owned or used for financial gain or profit to either owner or user."

CASE

Iota Benefit Ass'n v. County of Douglas, 165 Neb. 330, 85 N.W.2d 726 (1957). Property of a fraternity for medical students was held to be subject to taxation, despite the argument that its members received valuable training from older members of the fraternity.

NEVADA

Nev. Const. art. 8, § 2

". . . the property of corporations formed for . . . educational purposes may be exempted by law."

Nev. Rev. Stat. (1957)

"§ 361.105. Nonprofit private schools, with lots appurtenant thereto and furniture and equipment, shall be exempt from taxation."

"§ 361.100. All real property owned by any fraternity or chapter thereof, when the same is composed of students of the University of Nevada and used as a home for its members, shall be exempt from taxation, but such exemption shall in no case exceed the sum of $5,000 for any one fraternity or chapter thereof."

NEW HAMPSHIRE

N.H. Rev. Stat. Ann. ch. 72, § 72:23 (1955)

"The following real estate and personal property shall be exempt from taxation:"

"The buildings and structures of . . . colleges . . . and universities organized or incorporated or carrying on their principal activities in this state and owned, used and occupied by them for the purposes for which they are established, including but not limited to the dormitories, dining rooms, kitchens, auditoriums, classrooms, infirmaries, administrative and utility rooms and buildings connected thereto, athletic fields and facilities and gymnasiums, boat houses and equipment belonging to them and used in connection therewith, and the land thereto appertaining but not including land and buildings not used and occupied directly for the purposes for which they are organized or incorporated, and the personal property used by them for the purposes for which they are established, provided none of the income or profits are divided among the members or stockholders or used or appropriated for any other purposes than those for which they are organized or established; provided further that if the value of the dormitories, dining rooms and kitchens shall exceed one hundred and fifty thousand dollars, the value thereof in excess of said sum shall be taxable. A town . . . or city may vote to increase the amount of the exemption upon dormitories, dining rooms and kitchens."

NEW JERSEY

N.J. Stat. Ann. § 54:4–3.6 (1939)

"The following property shall be exempt from taxation under this chapter: All buildings actually used for colleges . . . ; the furniture and personal property in said building if used in and devoted to the purposes above mentioned; provided in case of all the foregoing, the buildings, or the lands on which they stand . . . are not conducted for profit. . . . The foregoing exemptions shall apply only when the . . . corporation . . . claiming the exemption owns the property in question and is incorporated . . . under the laws of this state and is authorized to carry out the purposes on account of which the exemption is claimed."

CASES

Piscataway Township v. State Board of Tax Appeals, 131 N.J.L. 158, 35 A.2d 711 (Sup. Ct. 1944). A house owned by the university and used as a residence for its president was exempt from taxation.

City of Hoboken v. Division of Tax Appeals, 134 N.J.L. 594, 49 A.2d 587 (Sup. Ct. 1944). College dormitories, gymnasium, athletic fields, president's residence, fraternity residences (if rented on a nonprofit basis), garages, storehouses, tool houses, and a research laboratory used for sponsored research were declared exempt from taxation.

State v. Ross, 4 N.J. 497, 24 N.J.L. 497 (1854). Dwelling houses and grounds occupied by the president, vice-president, professors, and steward of the college were held to be exempt from taxation.

Trustees of Rutgers University v. Piscataway Township, 134 N.J.L. 85, 46 A.2d 56 (1946). A million-dollar stadium of Rutgers University was refused tax exemption on the grounds that it was in excess of the actual instructional requirements of the physical education department of the university.

NEW MEXICO

N.M. Const. art. VIII, § 3

". . . all property used for educational . . . purposes . . . shall be exempt from taxation."

N.M. Stat. ch. 72, § 72–1–1 (1953)

"All property, real and personal and intangible shall be subject to taxation, except as in the Constitution and existing law otherwise provided."

NEW YORK

N.Y. Const. art. 16, § 1

"Exemption from taxation may be granted only by general law. Exemptions may be altered or repealed except those exempting real or personal property used exclusively for . . . educational purposes as defined by law and owned by any corporation or association organized or conducted exclusively for one or more of such purposes and not operating for profit."

N.Y. Tax Law art. 1, § 4, ¶ 6

"The following property shall be exempt from taxation:

"(a) The real property of a corporation or association organized exclusively for . . . educational purposes . . . and used exclusively for carrying out thereon one or more of such purposes . . .

"(b) But no such corporation shall be entitled to any such exemption if any officer, member or employee thereof shall receive or may be lawfully entitled to receive any pecuniary profit from the operation thereof, except as reasonable compensation for services . . . or is a proper beneficiary of its strictly charitable purposes.

"(c) The real property of any such corporation or association entitled to such exemption . . . from which no rents . . . or income is derived, shall be exempt, though not in actual use . . . if construction in good faith is contemplated . . ."

"(j) No educational corporation or association that holds itself out to the public to be nonsectarian and exempt from taxation pursuant to the provisions of this section shall deny the use of its facilities to any person otherwise qualified, by reason of his race, color or religion.

"(k) The real property of a membership corporation . . . used exclusively to provide housing and auxiliary facilities for faculty members or students and their immediate families of the college or university at which such housing is provided. Such exemption shall be upon condition that the property of such corporation shall upon dissolution, vest in such college or university and that no part of the net earnings of such college, university or membership organization shall inure to the benefit of any private individual."

CASES

Cornell University v. Thorne, 184 Misc. 630, 57 N.Y.S.2d. 6 (Sup. Ct. 1945).
College dormitories, but not college fraternity houses, are exempt.

People v. Haggett, 300 N.Y. 595, 89 N.E.2d 882 (1949). Faculty housing is exempt.

Pace College v. Boyland, 4 N.Y.2d 528, 176 N.Y.S.2d 356 (1958). The portion of a building occupied by a cafeteria operated by an independent contractor but owned and under general control of a college was exempt.

In re *Syracuse University,* 124 Misc. 788, 209 N.Y. Supp. 329 (Sup. Ct. 1925). Dormitories, dining halls, student infirmary, storehouse, university farm, and the residence of the chancellor were exempt from taxation. Property held for future expansion was declared to be subject to taxation.

NORTH CAROLINA

N.C. Const. art. V, § 5

"The General Assembly may exempt . . . property held for educational . . . purposes."

Gen. Stat. N.C. (1958)

"§ 296. The following real property and no other, shall be exempt from taxation: . . . (4) Buildings, with the land actually occupied, wholly devoted to educational purposes, belonging to, actually and exclusively occupied and used for colleges . . . or other institutions of learning, together with such additional land owned by such . . . educational institutions as may be reasonably necessary for the convenient use of such buildings; and also buildings thereon used as residences by the officers or instructors of such educational institutions."

CASE

Rockingham County v. Board of Trustees of Elon College, 219 N.C. 342, 13 S.E.2d 618 (1941). Property held by a college as an investment is subject to taxation.

NORTH DAKOTA

N.D. Const. art. XI, § 176

". . . the Legislative Assembly shall, by a general law, exempt from taxation property used exclusively for . . . school . . . purposes."

N.D. Rev. Code tit. 57, § 0208 (1943)

"All property described in this section, to the extent herein limited, shall be exempt from taxation:"

"(6) All . . . colleges, institutions of learning, with the books and furniture therein, and the grants attached to such buildings necessary for their proper occupancy, use and enjoyment and not otherwise used with a view to profit, and all dormitories and boarding halls, including the land on which they are situated, owned and managed by any religious corporation for educational or charitable purposes for use of students in attendance upon any educational institution, if such dormitory and boarding halls shall not be managed or used for the purpose of making a profit over and above the cost of maintenance and operation."

"(11) . . . all the real and personal property owned by any fraternity, sorority, or organization of college students, if such property shall be used exclusively for such purposes."

"(16) Real and personal property now owned, or hereafter acquired, by a corporation organized, or hereafter created, under the laws of this state for the purpose of promoting athletics and educational needs and uses at any state educational institution in this state, and not organized for profit."

OHIO

Ohio Const. art. XII, § 2

". . . general laws may be passed to exempt . . . institutions used exclusively for charitable purposes . . ."

Ohio Rev. Code § 5709.07 (1953)

". . . public colleges . . . and all buildings connected therewith, and all lands connected with public institutions of learning, not used with a view to profit, shall be exempt from taxation. This section shall not extend to leasehold estates or real property held under the authority of a college or university of learning in this state."

Ohio Rev. Stat. § 2732 (1908) (now Ohio Rev. Code § 5709.07 (1953))

Residences occupied by its president and professors and janitor are exempt, but the college farm is not exempt.

CASES

Kenyon College v. Schnebly, 12 Ohio C.C.R. (n.s.) 1, 21 Ohio C.C. Dec. 150 (1909); *aff'd without opinion,* 81 Ohio St. 513 (1909). A pumping station owned and operated by the college and which supplied water to outsiders at a profit was refused tax exemption.

Kenyon College v. Schnebly, 81 Ohio St. 514, 91 N.E. 1138 (1910). Kenyon

College, although privately controlled, is a "public college" within the meaning of this statute.

OKLAHOMA

Okla. Const. art. X, § 6

". . . property used exclusively for . . . colleges . . . shall be exempt from taxation."

Okla. Stat. Ann. tit. 68, § 15.2 (1951)

"The following property shall be exempt from taxation:"

"3. All property of any . . . college . . . , providing such property is devoted exclusively and directly to the appropriate objects of such institution, college . . . , provided however that any such . . . college . . . shall be allowed an exempted valuation not to exceed $2,500 on property not used exclusively and directly for scientific or educational purposes within this state.

"4. The books, papers, furniture and scientific or other apparatus pertaining to any . . . college and the like property of students . . . while such property is used for the purposes of their education."

CASES

Board of County Commissioners v. Phillips University, 144 Okla. 57, 289 Pac. 720 (1930). Property held as an investment by the university is exempt from taxation.

In re *Park College*, 170 Okla. 132, 38 P.2d 105 (1934). Property of a college incorporated in another state is not exempt.

State v. Oklahoma Beta of Pi Beta Phi Sorority, 176 Okla. 186, 55 P.2d 133 (1936). Property of college fraternities and sororities is tax exempt.

OREGON

Ore. Rev. Stat. tit. 29, ch. 307 (1953)

"§ 307.170. Upon compliance with O.R.S. 307.170, the following property owned by incorporated . . . charitable and scientific institutions shall be exempt from taxation:

"(a) . . . only such real or personal property, or proportion thereof, as is actually and exclusively occupied or used by the charitable or scientific work carried on by such institutions.

"(b) Parking lots maintained solely for the use, without charge, of persons going to and from the property exempted under (a) of this subsection."

"§ 307.145. If not otherwise exempted by law, the . . . student housing accommodations, owned by incorporated eleemosynary institutions used exclusively by such institutions or organizations for or in immediate connection with educational purposes, are exempt from taxation."

CASE

Willamette University v. Knight, 35 Ore. 33, 56 Pac. 124 (1889). College farms operated or leased to provide revenue for the college are not exempt from taxation.

PENNSYLVANIA

Pa. Const. art. IX, § 1

"The General Assembly may, by general law, exempt from taxation . . . institutions of purely public charity."

Pa. Stat. Ann. tit. 72, § 5020–204 (1930)

"The following property shall be exempt from all . . . tax to wit:"

"(c) All . . . universities, colleges . . . with the grounds thereto annexed and necessary for the occupancy and enjoyment of the same, founded, endowed, and maintained by public or private charity. Provided: That the entire revenue derived by the same shall be applied to the support and to increase the efficiency and facilities thereof, the repair and the necessary increase of grounds and buildings thereof and for no other purpose."

CASES

Northampton County v. Lafayette College, 128 Pa. 132, 18 Atl. 516 (1889). An incorporated college admitting students of every religious belief is a charity and is exempt from taxation.

In re *Hill School,* 370 Pa. 21, 87 A.2d 259 (1952). A school is a "public charity" despite the fact that it charges a tuition for its services.

Northampton County v. Lehigh University, 13 Pa. County Ct. 659 (1893). Two houses owned by the university and occupied by its employees were held to be exempt from taxation.

Haverford College v. Rhoads, 6 Pa. Super. 71 (1897). A machine shop, pumping station, and ice house owned and used by the college were exempt from taxation.

Mercersburg College v. Poffenberger, 36 Pa. Super. 100 (1908). The college was denied exemption for its property used for educational purposes on the grounds that, for a period of five years, its receipts from student fees were in excess of its operating expenses.

RHODE ISLAND

R.I. Gen. Laws tit. 44, ch. 3, § 44–3–3 (1956)

"The following property shall be exempt from taxation:"

"(8) the buildings and personal estate owned by any corporation used for a school, academy or seminary of learning . . . , and the land upon which said buildings stand and immediately surrounding the same to the extent not exceeding one acre, so as the same is used exclusively for educational purposes . . . , but no property shall hereafter be exempt from taxation in any case where any part of the income or profits thereof . . . is divided among its owners or stockholders.

"(9) . . . the estates, persons, and families of the president and professors for the time being of Brown University for not more than $10,000 for each officer, his estate, person and family included."

CASE

In re *Pawtucket*, 24 R.I. 86, 52 Atl. 679 (1902). A building partly used as a residence for teachers was not exempt as an educational building.

SOUTH CAROLINA

S.C. Const. art. X

"§ 1. The General Assembly shall provide by law for . . . the taxation of all property . . . excepting such property as may be exempted by law for . . . educational purposes."

"§ 4. There shall be exempted from taxation . . . the property of all . . . colleges and institutions of learning . . . except where the profits of such institutions are applied to private use."

Code of Laws of S.C. § 65–1522 (1952)

"The following property shall be exempt from taxation to wit:"

"(4) All incorporated public colleges . . . and institutions of learning, with the funds provided for their support and the grounds and buildings actually occupied by them and not used with a view to pecuniary profit; but this provision shall not extend to leasehold estates held by others under the authority of any college . . . or other institution of learning."

SOUTH DAKOTA

S.D. Const. art. XI, § 6

"The legislature shall, by general law, exempt from taxation, property used exclusively for school . . . purposes."

S.D. Code tit. 57, § 57.0311 (1939)

"The following property described in this section, to the extent herein limited, shall be exempt from taxation:"

"(2) All the property, real and personal, belonging to any educational institution in this state, and all property used exclusively by and for the support of such institution; but if any such property shall consist of farm lands or improvements thereon or any property not occupied or directly used in the carrying out of the primary object of the institution owning the same, it shall be taxed . . ."

TENNESSEE

Tenn. Const. art. II, § 28

"All property . . . shall be taxed, but the Legislature may exempt such as may be held and used for purposes purely . . . educational."

Tenn. Code § 67–502 (1959)

"The property herein enumerated shall be exempt from taxation:"

"(2) The real estate owned by any . . . educational institution occupied by such institution or its officers exclusively for carrying out . . . the purposes for which such institution was created or exists, and the personal property of such institution used exclusively for . . . the purposes for which such institution was created or exists.

"But the property of such institution shall not be exempt if the owner, officers, members or employees . . . shall receive any pecuniary profit from the operation of the property . . . except reasonable compensation for service in effecting . . . such purposes. . . . The real property of such institution . . . leased . . . shall not be exempt."

CASES

State v. Fisk University, 87 Tenn. 233, 10 S.W. 284 (1889). A college farm used to supply food for faculty and students was exempt from taxation.
State v. Waggoner, 162 Tenn. 172, 35 S.W.2d 389 (1931). A residence belonging to a college but occupied by its business manager is not exempt.

TEXAS

Tex. Const. art. VIII, § 2

". . . the legislature may, by general laws, exempt from taxation . . . all buildings used exclusively and owned by persons or associations of persons for school purposes and the necessary furniture of all schools. . . . Also the endowment funds of such institutions of learning . . . not used with a view to profit; and when the same are invested in bonds or mortgages, or in land or other property which has been and shall hereafter be bought in by such institutions under foreclosure sales made to satisfy or protect such bonds or mortgages, that such exemption on such lands and property shall continue only for two years after the purchase of the same at such sale by such institutions and no longer."

Tex. Civ. Stat. tit. 122, § 7150 (1955)

"The following property shall be exempt from taxation, to wit: all public colleges . . . , and all endowment funds of institutions of learning [language identical with that in the state constitution on the subject]. The provision shall not extend to leasehold estates of real property held under any authority of any college or university of learning."

CASES

St. Edward's College v. Morris, 82 Tex. 1, 18 S.W. 512 (1891). A college farm used to supply food for faculty and students was denied exemption.
Smith v. Feather, 234 S.W.2d 418 (Tex. Civ. App. 1950). The property of a private school of commercial art and design owned and operated for private profit was held to be exempt from taxation. See also W. V. Geppert, "A Discussion of Tax Exempt Property in the State of Texas," 11 *Baylor L. Rev.* 133 (1959).

UTAH

Utah Const. art. VIII, § 2

". . . lots, with the buildings thereon, used exclusively . . . for charitable purposes . . . shall be exempt from taxation."

Utah Code Ann. tit. 59, § 59–2–1 (1953)

The wording is identical with that of the state constitution on the subject.

VERMONT

Vt. Stat. Ann. tit. 32, § 3802 (1959)

"The following property shall be exempt from taxation . . ."

"(4) . . . lands owned or leased by colleges . . . The exemption of lands owned or leased by colleges . . . shall not apply to lands or buildings rented for general commercial purposes, nor to farming or timber lands owned or leased thereby; but this provision shall not affect the exemption of so called school or college lands sequestered to such use prior to January 28, 1911.

"(5) Real or personal property held by and for the benefit of college fraternities and societies and corporations owning such property, but this exemption shall not apply to property held for investment purposes. The exemption from taxation of real and personal property held by and for the benefit of college fraternities and societies and corporations shall not be construed as exempting lands, buildings or property other than a fraternity or society house, the land occupied thereby, the land adjacent thereto and used as a lawn, playground or garden, and the household furniture and equipment in actual use in such fraternity or society house."

CASE

Troy Academy v. Poultney, 115 Vt. 480, 66 A.2d 2 (1949). A college dormitory and dining hall was held to be exempt from taxation.

VIRGINIA

Va. Const. art. XIII, § 183

"Unless otherwise provided in this Constitution, the following property and no other shall be exempt from taxation . . . :"

"(d) Property owned by . . . incorporated colleges . . . not conducted for profit, together with the endowment funds thereof not invested in real estate."

Code of Va. tit. 58, art. 3, § 58–12 (1950)

"The following property shall be exempt from taxation:"

"(4) Property owned by . . . incorporated colleges . . . including incorporated alumni associations thereof beneficially owned by or organized and operated exclusively for the benefit of such incorporated institutions of learning not conducted for profit, together with the endowment funds thereof, not invested in real estate."

CASES

Commonwealth v. Trustees of Hampton Normal and Agricultural Institute,
106 Va. 614, 56 S.E. 594 (1907). College land held and used as income-
producing property is not exempt from taxation.

Commonwealth v. Smallwood Memorial Institute, 124 Va. 142, 97 S.E. 85
(1919). An electric power plant owned and operated by the institute but
also serving the public was denied exemption.

WASHINGTON

Wash. Rev. Code tit. 84, ch. 84.38, § 84.36.050 (1957)

"The following property shall be exempt from taxation: Property owned
by or used for any . . . college in this state, supported in whole or in part
by gifts, endowment or charity, the entire income of which said . . . college, after paying the expenses thereof, is devoted to the purposes of such
institution, and which is open to all persons on equal terms. To be exempt,
such property must be devoted exclusively for college or campus purposes,
or for dormitories or as a community residence for teachers or employees.
Where the college is under the direction or control of any religious denomination, the exemption shall be allowed to one college only directed by such
religious denomination. Real property owned or controlled by such institution or leased or rented by it for the purpose of deriving a revenue therefrom shall not be exempt from taxation under this statute."

CASE

Wilson's Modern Business College v. King County, 46 Wash. 2d 636, 104
P.2d 580 (1940). The property of a nonprofit business college is exempt.

WEST VIRGINIA

W. Va. Const. art. X, § 1

". . . property used for educational . . . purposes . . . may be exempted
from taxation."

W. Va. Code § 678(9) (1955)

"All property described in this section and to the extent herein limited,
shall be exempt from taxation, that is to say:"

". . . property belonging to or held in trust for colleges . . . , if used for
educational . . . purposes, including books, apparatus, annuities, money and
furniture . . . all real estate not exceeding one-half acre in extent, and the
buildings thereon, and used exclusively by any college or university society
as a literary hall, or as a dormitory or club room, if not leased or otherwise
used with a view to profit.

"Notwithstanding any other provisions in this section, however, no language herein shall be construed to exempt from taxation any property owned
by, or held in trust for, educational corporations or organizations, unless
such property is used primarily and immediately for the purposes of such
corporations or organizations."

CASE

In re *Mountain State College,* 117 W. Va. 819, 188 S.E. 480 (1936). The property of a commercial college conducted for profit or private gain is exempt.

WISCONSIN

Wis. Stat. § 70:11 (1957)

"The property described in this section is exempt from general property taxes:"

"(3)(a) Grounds of any incorporated college or university, not exceeding 80 acres.

"(b) The fact that college or university officers, faculty members, teachers, students or employees live on the grounds does not render them taxable. The leasing of land by a university or college, for educational or charitable purposes, shall not render it liable for taxation provided the income derived therefrom is used for the maintenance of the institution or for charitable purposes."

42 Ops. Att'y Gen. Wis. 149 (1953)

College faculty housing is exempt from taxation.

WYOMING

Wyo. Const. art. XV, § 12

"The property of the United States, the state, counties, cities . . . shall be exempt from taxation, and such other property as the legislature may, by general law, provide."

Wyo. Comp. Stat. tit. 32, § 104 (1945)

"Lands, with the buildings thereon, used for schools . . . shall be exempt from taxation, so long as those portions of said lands and buildings so exempt are not used for private profit."

Table of Cases

Bibliography

ADMINISTRATIVE LAW

DAVIS, KENNETH CULP. *Administrative Law Treatise.* St. Paul, Minn.: West Publishing Co., 1958.

FORKOSCH, MORRIS D. *Administrative Law.* Indianapolis, Ind.: Bobbs-Merrill Co., 1956.

HEWART, GORDON. *The New Despotism.* London: E. Benn, 1945.

PARKER, REGINALD. *Administrative Law: A Text.* Indianapolis, Ind.: Bobbs-Merrill Co., 1952.

ARCHITECTS, CONTRACTORS, AND ENGINEERS

DUNHAM, CLARENCE W., and YOUNG, ROBERT D. *Contracts, Specifications, and Law for Engineers.* New York: McGraw-Hill Book Co., 1958.

NORD, MELVIN. *Legal Problems in Engineering.* New York: John Wiley & Sons, 1956.

SIMPSON, LAURENCE P., and DILLAVON, ESSEL R. *Law for Engineers and Architects.* 4th ed. St. Paul, Minn.: West Publishing Co., 1958.

TOMSON, BERNARD. *Architectural and Engineering Law.* New York: Reinhold Publishing Corp., 1951.

WERBIN, I. VERNON. *Legal Guide for Contractors, Architects, and Engineers.* 1st ed. New York: McGraw-Hill Book Co., 1952.

CHARITIES AND CHARITABLE TRUSTS

Charitable Contributions: Legal Restrictions

JOSLIN, G. STANLEY. "Legal Restrictions on Gifts to Charities," 21 *Tennessee Law Review* 761 (1951).

Charitable Contributions: Public Regulation of Solicitation

"Validity of Statutory or Municipal Regulation of Soliciting of Alms or Contributions for Charitable, Religious or Individual Purposes," 128 *American Law Reports Annotated* 1361 (1940); 130 *Ibid.* 1504 (1941).

Charitable Corporations: Tort Immunity

BROWN, W. "Stare Decisis Is Worth Its Weight in Reason: Abolish the Charitable Immunity Doctrine," 46 *American Bar Association Journal* 629 (1960).

314

"Charitable Institutions—Hospitals' Liability to Paying Patients," Note, 72 *University of Pennsylvania Law Review* 443 (1924).

JOACHIM, A. "Charitable Immunity: Why Abandon the Doctrine of Stare Decisis?" 45 *American Bar Association Journal* 822 (1959).

"Liability of Privately Conducted Charity for Personal Injuries," 14 *American Law Reports Annotated* 572 (1921).

SIMEONE, JOSEPH J. "The Doctrine of Charitable Immunity," 5 *St. Louis University Law Journal* 357 (1959).

"Tort Responsibility of Charitable Corporations," Note, 34 *Yale Law Journal* 316 (1925).

ZOLLMAN, CARL. "Damage Liability of Charitable Institutions," 19 *Michigan Law Review* 395 (1921).

Charitable Trusts: Public Supervision

BALL, RALPH K. "Accountability of Charitable Trustees," 98 *Trusts and Estates* 970 (1959).

BOGERT, GEORGE G. "Proposed Legislation Regarding State Supervision of Charities," 52 *Michigan Law Review* 635 (1954).

CRAIG, ARLO F., JR. "Charitable Trusts in Iowa," 9 *Drake Law Review* 90 (1960).

KARST, KENNETH L. "The Efficiency of the Charitable Dollar: An Unfulfilled State Responsibility," 73 *Harvard Law Review* 433 (1960).

KLAPP, R., and WERTZ, N. H. "Supervision of Charitable Trusts in Ohio: The Ohio Charitable Trusts Act," 18 *Ohio State Law Journal* 181 (1957).

SCHMIDT, J. DWAIN. "Trusts: The Charitable Trust," 13 *Oklahoma Law Review* 354 (1960).

TAYLOR, E. K. "Accountability of Charitable Trusts," 18 *Ohio State Law Journal* 157 (1957).

Restricted Gifts to Charitable Corporations

BLACKWELL, THOMAS E. "The Charitable Corporation and the Charitable Trust," 24 *Washington University Law Quarterly* 1 (1938).

"Charitable Donations: Gift or Trust?" Note, 40 *Columbia Law Review* 550 (1940).

"Legal Effect of Gifts to Charitable Corporations," Note, 23 *Minnesota Law Review* 670 (1939).

"Nature of Estate Created by, and Enforceability of, Provision in Devise or Bequest to Charitable, Religious, or Educational Corporation as to Particular Purpose of the Corporation for Which It Shall Be Used," 130 *American Law Reports Annotated* 1101 (1941).

SCHMIDT, J. DWAIN. "The Charitable Trust," Note, 13 *Oklahoma Law Review* 354 (1960).

CONSTITUTIONAL LAW

General

ALLOWAY, CLIFFORD CHARLES. *United States Constitutional Law.* Coral Gables, Fla.: University of Miami Press, 1958.

COOLEY, THOMAS M. *Constitutional Limitations.* 8th ed. Boston: Little, Brown & Co., 1927.

CORWIN, EDWARD S. *The Constitution and What It Means Today.* 12th ed. Princeton, N.J.: Princeton University Press, 1958.

CORWIN, EDWARD S., and PELTASON, JACK W. *Understanding the Constitution.* Rev. ed. New York: Dryden Press, 1958.

CUSHMAN, ROBERT E. *Leading Constitutional Decisions.* 9th ed. New York: Appleton-Century-Crofts, 1950.

DUMBAULD, EDWARD. *The Bill of Rights and What It Means Today.* Norman, Okla.: University of Oklahoma Press, 1957.

McCLOSKEY, ROBERT GREEN. *Essays in Constitutional Law.* New York: Alfred A. Knopf, 1957.

MASON, A. T., and BEANEY, W. M. *American Constitutional Law.* Englewood Cliffs, N.J.: Prentice-Hall, 1954.

MUSSATTI, JAMES. *The Constitution of the United States: Its Origins, Principles and Problems.* Princeton, N.J.: D. Van Nostrand Co., 1956.

PRITCHETT, CHARLES HERMAN. *The American Constitution.* New York: McGraw-Hill Book Co., 1959.

SCHWARTZ, BERNARD. *American Constitutional Law.* Cambridge, England: Cambridge University Press, 1955.

WILLIS, HUGH E. *Constitutional Law in the United States.* Bloomington, Ind.: Principia Press, 1936.

Civil Rights: Due Process

"Expulsion or Suspension from Private School or College," 50 *American Law Reports Annotated* 1497 (1927).

Civil Rights: Freedom from Discrimination

BERGER, MORROE. "The New York State Law against Discrimination: Operation and Administration," 35 *Cornell Law Quarterly* 747 (1950).

CUSHMAN, ROBERT E. *Civil Liberties in the United States: A Guide to Current Problems and Experience.* Ithaca, N.Y.: Cornell University Press, 1956.

"Discrimination Because of Race, Color or Creed in Respect of Appointment, Duties, Compensation, etc., of Schoolteachers or Other Public Officers or Employees," 130 *American Law Reports Annotated* 1512 (1941).

ELSON, ALEX, and SCHANFIELD, LEONARD. "Local Discriminatory Employment Practices," 56 *Yale Law Journal* 431 (1947).

MILLER, ARTHUR S. "Racial Discrimination and Private Schools," 41 *Minnesota Law Review* 145 (1957).

"The New York State Commission against Discrimination: A New Technique for an Old Problem," 56 *Yale Law Journal* 837 (1947).

SHAD, PATRICIA P. "Constitutionality of Restricted Scholarships," 33 *New York University Law Review* 604 (1958).

THALER, ALWIN. "With All Deliberate Speed," 27 *Tennessee Law Review* 510 (1960).

ZIEGLER, BENJAMIN MUNN. *Desegregation and the Supreme Court.* Boston: D. C. Heath & Co., 1958.

Civil Rights: Freedom from Self-Incrimination

"Adequacy of Immunity Offered as a Condition of Denial of Privilege against Self-Incrimination," 53 *American Law Reports Annotated* 1030 (1957).

BYSE, CLARK. "Teachers and the Fifth Amendment," 102 *University of Pennsylvania Law Review* 871 (1954).

CLAFLIN, BEECHER N. "The Self-Incriminating Clause of the Fifth Amendment: Its Interpretation, Use and Misuse," 42 *American Bar Association Journal* 935 (1956).

GRISWOLD, ERWIN NATHANIEL. *The Fifth Amendment Today.* Cambridge, Mass.: Harvard University Press, 1955.

KRONER, JACK. "Self-Incrimination: The Extreme Reach of the Privilege," 60 *Columbia Law Review* 816 (1960).

PITTMAN, R. CARTER. "The Fifth Amendment: Yesterday, Today and Tomorrow," 42 *American Bar Association Journal* 509 (1956).

Constitutional Debt Limitations

CERMACK, LAWRENCE E. *The Law of Revenue Bonds.* Washington: National Institute of Municipal Law Officers, 1954.

FOWLER, JOHN FRANCIS. *Revenue Bonds.* New York: Harper & Bros., 1938.

KNAPPEN, LAWRENCE S. *Revenue Bonds and the Investor.* New York: Prentice-Hall, 1939.

"Pledge or Appropriation of Revenue from Utility or Other Property in Payment Therefor, as Indebtedness of Municipality or Other Political Subdivision," 146 *American Law Reports Annotated* 328 (1941).

Constitutional Prohibition of Impairment of Contractual Rights

ZUMBALEN, JOSEPH H. "The Federal Constitution and Contract Exemption from Taxation," 17 *St. Louis Law Review* 191 (1932).

Constitutional Restrictions on Use of Public Funds

BARKER, ERNEST. *Church, State and Education.* Ann Arbor: University of Michigan Press, 1957.

BUTTS, R. FREEMAN. *The American Tradition in Religion and Education.* Boston: Beacon Press, 1950.

CAGEL, A. P. "Public Aid for Sectarian Schools," 2 *Baylor Law Review* 159 (1950).

MOEHLMAN, C. H. "Wall of Separation: The Law and the Facts," 38 *American Bar Association Journal* 281 (1952).

SCANLAN, E. F. "Providing Publicly Financed Benefits to Private Schools," 11 *University of Pittsburgh Law Review* 318 (1950).

WALTER, ERICH ALBERT. *Religion and the State University.* Ann Arbor: University of Michigan Press, 1958.

Interstate Compacts

"Cooperative Progress." A study prepared for the Committee on Institutional Cooperation of the Council of Ten and the University of Chicago. Mimeographed. November 1959.

DUNBAR, L. W. "Interstate Compacts and Congressional Consent," 36 *Virginia Law Review* 21 (1950).

LEACH, RICHARD H., and SUGG, R. S. *Administration of Interstate Compacts.* Baton Rouge, La.: Louisiana State University Press, 1959.

"Regional Cooperation in Higher Education in the United States and Its Meaning for the Midwest." A study prepared for the Committee on Institutional Cooperation of the Council of Ten and the University of Chicago. Mimeographed. June 1959.

"Regional Cooperation in Higher Education: Aid or Hindrance." A study prepared for the Committee on Institutional Cooperation of the Council of Ten and the University of Chicago. Mimeographed. September 1959.

THURSBY, VINCENT V. *Interstate Cooperation: A Study of the Interstate Compact.* Washington: Public Affairs Press, 1953.

ZIMMERMAN, F. L., and WENDELL, M. "The Interstate Compact and *Dyer v. Simms,*" 31 *Columbia Law Review* 931 (1931).

CONTRACTS

General

CLARK, GEORGE LUTHER. *Contracts.* Indianapolis, Ind.: Bobbs-Merrill Co., 1954.

CORBIN, ARTHUR LINTON. *Contracts.* St. Paul: West Publishing Co., 1952.

POLLOCK, SIR FREDERICK. *Principles of Contracts.* 3d American ed. New York: Baker, Voorhis & Co., 1906.

Consideration for Charitable Subscriptions

BILLIG, T. C. "The Problem of Consideration in Charitable Subscriptions," 12 *Cornell Law Quarterly* 467 (1927).

"Consideration for Subscription Agreements," 38 *American Law Reports Annotated* 868 (1922).

"Consideration for Subscription Agreements," 95 *Ibid.* 1305 (1935); 115 *Ibid.* 589 (1938); 151 *Ibid.* 1238 (1944).

Contracts of Employment

HILLWAY, TYRUS. "When Hiring Professors, Hasn't the Time Arrived To Supplant the Gentleman's Agreement with a Legal Contract?" *College and University Business,* XXVI (February 1959), 27.

COPYRIGHT

General

AMDUR, LEON. *Copyright Law and Practice.* New York: Clark Boardman & Co., 1936.

BALL, HORACE G. *The Law of Copyright and Literary Property.* New York: Matthew Bender & Co., 1944.

HOWELL, HERBERT A. *The Copyright Law.* 3d ed. Washington: Bureau of National Affairs, 1952.

NICHOLSON, MARGARET. *A Manual of Copyright Practice for Writers, Publishers, and Agents.* 2d ed. New York: Oxford University Press, 1956.

"Symposium: Intellectual Property," 9 *Cleveland-Marshall Law Review* 1 (1960).

WITTENBERG, PHILIP. *The Law of Literary Property.* Cleveland, Ohio: World Publishing Co., 1957.

Employee Copyrights

FIDLER, WILLIAM P. "Educational Television: A Faculty Point of View," *Quarterly Journal of Speech*, XLV (April 1959), 121.

YOUNGDAHL, JAMES E. "Copyright Law and the Employment Relation," 5 *St. Louis University Law Journal* 510 (1959).

Fair Use

"The Gentlemen's Agreement and the Problem of Copyright," 2 *Journal of Documentary Reproduction* 1 (1939).

LATMAN, ALAN. "Fair Use of Copyrighted Works," General Revision of the Copyright Law, Study No. 10. Multilithed. Washington: Copyright Office, 1958.

SMITH, LOUIS CHARLES. "The Copying of Literary Property in Library Collections," 46 *Law Library Journal* 197 (1953); 47 *Ibid.* 204 (1954).

Universal Copyright

KUPFORM, THEODORE R., and FONER, MATHEW (eds.). *Universal Copyright Convention Analyzed.* New York: Federal Legal Publications, 1955.

PINNER, H. L. *World Copyright: An Encyclopedia.* Leyden, Holland: A. W. Sijthoff, 1958.

CORPORATIONS

General

ANDERSON, WALTER HOUSTON. *Limitations of the Corporate Entity: A Treatise of the Law Relating to the Overriding of the Corporate Fiction.* St. Louis, Mo.: Thomas Law Book Co., 1931.

BALLANTINE, HENRY WINTHROP. *Corporations.* Chicago: Callaghan & Co., 1946.

BERLE, ADOLF A., JR., and MEANS, GARDINER C. *The Modern Corporation and Private Property.* New York: Macmillan Co., 1933.

DORIS, LILLIAN, and FRIEDMAN, EDITH J. *Corporate Secretary's Manual and Guide.* Rev. ed. New York: Prentice-Hall, 1949.

FLETCHER, WILLIAM M. *Cyclopedia of the Law of Private Corporations.* 20 vols. Chicago: Callaghan & Co., 1954.

HORNSTEIN, GEORGE DAVID. *Corporation Law and Practice.* St. Paul, Minn.: West Publishing Co., 1959.

OLECK, HOWARD LEONER. *Modern Corporation Law.* 2 vols. Indianapolis, Ind.: Bobbs-Merrill Co., 1958–59.

Power To Make Charitable Donations

BELL, LAIRD. "Corporate Support of Education: The Legal Basis," 38 *American Bar Association Journal* 119 (1952).

BLEICKEN, GERARD D. "Corporate Contributions to Charities: The Modern Rule," 38 *American Bar Association Journal* 999 (1952).

DE CAPRILES, MIGUEL A., and GARRETT, RAY, JR. "Legality of Corporate Support to Education: A Survey of Current Developments," 38 *American Bar Association Journal* 209 (1952).

EELLS, RICHARD. *Corporate Giving in a Free Society.* New York: Harper & Bros., 1956.

"Power of a Business Corporation to Donate to a Charitable or Similar Institution," 39 *American Law Reports Annotated* 2d 1192 (1955).

ROHR, R. D. "Corporate Philanthropy: The Changing Law," 33 *Michigan State Bar Journal* 14 (1954).

RUML, BEARDSLEY (ed.). *The Manual of Corporate Giving.* Washington: National Planning Association, 1952.

ENCYCLOPEDIAS

American Jurisprudence. 38 vols. San Francisco: Bancroft-Whitney Co.; Rochester, N.Y.: Lawyers Co-operative Publishing Co., 1936–48.

Corpus Juris Secundum. 101 vols. Brooklyn, N.Y.: American Law Book Co., 1836–.

Encyclopedia of Educational Research. 3d ed. New York: Macmillan Co., 1960.

HIGHER EDUCATION

Accreditation

BLAUCH, LLOYD E. (ed.). *Accreditation in Higher Education*, U.S. Office of Education. Washington: Government Printing Office, 1958.

Manual of Information about Recognized Accrediting Agencies. Washington: National Commission on Accrediting, 1957.

Report on Workshop Conference on Accrediting, June 25–26, 1957. Washington: National Commission on Accrediting, 1957.

Business Administration

College and University Business Administration. 2 vols. Washington: American Council on Education, 1952 and 1955.

MARTIN, KENNETH F. "Keeping Records—How Many and How Long?" *College and University Business*, XXVII (1959), 59.

RUSSELL, JOHN DALE. *The Finance of Higher Education.* 2d ed. Chicago: University of Chicago Press, 1954.

WHELAN, ROBERT B. *Corporate Record Retention.* New York: Controllership Foundation, 1958.

Educational Administration

CAPEN, SAMUEL P. *The Management of Universities.* Buffalo, N.Y.: Foster & Stewart Publishing Corp., 1953.

DEUTSCH, MONROE E. *The College from Within.* Berkeley: University of California Press, 1952.

EELLS, WALTER CROSBY, and HOLLIS, ERNEST V. *Administration of Higher Education: An Annotated Bibliography.* U.S. Office of Education. Washington: Government Printing Office, 1960.

LINDSAY, ERNEST E., and HOLLAND, E. O. *College and University Administration.* New York: Macmillan Co., 1930.

WOODBURNE, LLOYD S. *Faculty Personnel Policies in Higher Education.* New York: Harper & Bros., 1950.

History of Higher Education

ADAMS, HERBERT B. *The College of William and Mary.* U.S. Bureau of Education Circular of Information No. 1. Washington: Government Printing Office, 1887.

CLAPP, MARGARET A. (ed.). *The Modern University.* Ithaca, N.Y.: Cornell University Press, 1950.

FLEXNER, ABRAHAM. *Universities: American, English, German.* New York: Oxford University Press, 1930.

Higher Education in the Forty-eight States. Chicago: Council of State Governments, 1952.

HOFSTADTER, RICHARD, and HARDY, C. DEWITT. *The Development and Scope of Higher Education in the United States.* New York: Columbia University Press, 1952.

ROGERS, FRANCIS MILLET. *Higher Education in the United States.* Cambridge, Mass.: Harvard University Press, 1952.

WORKS, GEORGE A., and MORGAN, BARTON. *The Land-Grant Colleges.* Prepared for the Advisory Committee on Education, Staff Study No. 10. Washington: Government Printing Office, 1939.

YOUNG, BURNS B. "What Is a College?" *Educational Record,* XXX (October 1949), 385.

Legal Problems of Higher Education

BRIND, C. A. "Legal and Administrative Problems of the Board of Regents and the New York State Education Department," 24 *Albany Law Review* 80 (1960).

BRODY, ALEXANDER. *The American State and Higher Education.* Washington: American Council on Education, 1935.

ELLIOTT, EDWARD C., and CHAMBERS, M. M. *The Colleges and the Courts.* New York: Carnegie Foundation for the Advancement of Teaching, 1935.

HOLLIS, ERNEST V.; LAND, WILLIAM G.; and MARTORANA, S. W. *Survey of State Legislation Relating to Higher Education, July 1, 1956 to June 30, 1957.* U.S. Office of Education Circular No. 511. Washington: Government Printing Office, 1957.

RAUH, MORTON A. *College and University Trusteeship.* Yellow Springs, Ohio: Antioch Press, 1959.

SPURLOCK, CLARK. *Education and the Supreme Court.* Urbana: University of Illinois Press, 1955.

Supervision and Control of Public Higher Education

The Efficiency of Freedom: Report of the Committee on Government and Higher Education. Baltimore: Johns Hopkins Press, 1959.

Moos, Malcolm, and Rourke, Francis E. *The Campus and the State.*
Baltimore: Johns Hopkins Press, 1959.
Provisions of State Constitutions for Higher Education. Tallahassee, Fla.:
Council for the Study of Higher Education in Florida, 1957.

Public Supervision of Privately Controlled Institutions

Beach, Fred F., and Will, Robert F. *The State and Nonpublic Schools.*
U.S. Office of Education Misc. No. 28. Washington: Government Printing Office, 1958.
Reid, Robert H. *American Degree Mills.* Washington: American Council
on Education, 1959.

IMMUNITIES OF THE STATE AND ITS AGENCIES

Labor Stoppages

"Union Organization and Activities of Public Employees," 31 *American Law
Reports Annotated* 1142 (1953).

Tort Immunity

The Determination and Payment of Claims against the State. Tallahassee,
Fla.: Florida Legislative Council and Reference Bureau, 1957.
Warp, George Albro. *Municipal Tort Liability in Virginia.* University,
Charlottesville, Va.: Bureau of Public Administration, 1941.

INCOME TAX

General

Federal Taxes. 16 vols. Englewood Cliffs, N.J.: Prentice-Hall, 1956– .
Lasser, Jacob K. (ed.). *Encyclopedia of Tax Procedures.* Englewood Cliffs,
N.J.: Prentice-Hall, 1956.
Paul, Randolph E. *Taxation in the United States.* Boston: Little, Brown &
Co., 1954.

Exempt Status of Alumni Associations

Myers, John Holt, and Quiggle, James W. "Alumni Associations as Organizations Described in Section 501(c)(3) of the Code," 45 *American
Bar Association Journal* 392 (1959).

Retirement and Death Benefits

"Gift v. Income: Discord in the Supreme Court Compounds Confusion,"
13 *Journal of Taxation* 165 (1960).
Nimms, Arthur L., III. "Deferred Compensation Agreements," 45 *American
Bar Association Journal* 1204 (1959).
"Payment Made to Employees upon Retirement in Appreciation of Services
Is Not a Gift," 13 *Vanderbilt Law Review* 819 (1960).

PELISEK, FRANK J. "Tax Treatment of Payments to the Widows of Corporate Officers and Employees," 44 *Marquette Law Review* 16 (1960).

"Use of a Salary-or-Annuity Option under the Technical Amendments Act of 1958," *November 1960 Memorandum*. New York: Teachers Insurance and Annuity Association, 1960.

WALLACE, J. PAUL A. "Taxation of Private Annuities," 40 *Boston University Law Review* 349 (1960).

Scholarship and Fellowship Stipends

GORDON, DONALD H. "IRS's Use of Gift v. Compensation Test Delays Practical Fellowship Income Rule," 13 *Journal of Taxation* 272 (1960).

———. "Scholarship and Fellowship Grants as Income: A Search for Treasury Policy," 1960 *Washington University Law Quarterly* 144 (1960).

Tax Advantages of Charitable Gifts

APPLEGATE, EDWARD T. *Tax Deductions and Exemptions of Gifts to Educational Institutions*. Washington: American Alumni Council, 1959.

GOLDBERG, PHILIP J. "Funding a Charitable Program with Life Insurance," 99 *Trusts and Estates* 788 (1960).

LOWNDES, CHARLES L. B. "Tax Advantages of Charitable Gifts," 46 *Virginia Law Review* 394 (1960).

MEIER, WALTER H. "Charitable Bequests and Life Insurance," 11 *American Society of Chartered Life Underwriters* 331 (1957).

QUIGGLE, JAMES W., and MYERS, JOHN HOLT, "Tax Advantages Spur Charitable Gifts of Unusual Properties," 13 *Journal of Taxation* 96 (1960).

WOOD, DAVID P., JR. "Lifetime Gifts Offer Larger Tax Savings than Charitable Bequests of Art Works," 13 *Journal of Taxation* 202 (1960).

Unrelated Business Income

"Charitable Exemption and Business Profits," Note, 35 *Cornell Law Quarterly* 922 (1950).

"Colleges, Charities and the Revenue Act of 1950," Note, 60 *Yale Law Journal* 851 (1951).

FIKELSTEIN, MAURICE. "Tax Exempt Charitable Corporations: Revenue Act of 1950," 50 *Michigan Law Review* 427 (1952).

"Net Lease Income Is Taxable as Unrelated Business Income," 13 *Journal of Taxation* 229 (1960).

SUGGARMAN, NORMAN A., and POMEROY, HARLAND. "Business Income of Exempt Organizations," 46 *Virginia Law Review* 424 (1960).

LABOR LAW

Complete Social Security Law, 1956. Chicago: Commerce Clearing House, 1956.

FORKOSCH, MORRIS D. *A Treatise on Labor Law*. Indianapolis, Ind.: Bobbs-Merrill Co., 1953.

GREENE, BRUCE ALDEN. *State Workmen's Compensation Laws as of September 1950.* U.S. Bureau of Labor Standards Bulletin No. 125. Washington: Government Printing Office, 1952.

LEGAL HISTORY AND GENERAL JURISPRUDENCE

BLACKSTONE, SIR WILLIAM. *Commentaries on the Laws of England.* 1st ed. 4 vols. Oxford: Clarendon Press, 1765–69.

CARDOZO, BENJAMIN N. *The Nature of the Judicial Process.* New Haven, Conn.: Yale University Press, 1921.

CARPENTER, WILLIAM SEAL. *Foundations of Modern Jurisprudence.* New York: Appleton-Century-Crofts, 1958.

DOUGLAS, WILLIAM O. *Stare Decisis.* New York: Association of the Bar of the City of New York, 1949.

GOODHART, A. L. "Precedent in English and Continental Law," 50 *Law Quarterly Review* 40 (1934).

GOODRICH, HERBERT F. "The Story of the American Law Institute," 1951 *Washington University Law Quarterly* 283.

GRAY, JOHN CHIPMAN. *The Nature and Sources of the Law.* 2d ed. New York: Macmillan Co., 1921.

GRINNELL, FRANK W. "Stare Decisis and the Supreme Court of the United States," 27 *Journal of American Judicature Society* 183 (1944).

HAINES, CHARLES GRAVES. *The American Doctrine of Judicial Supremacy.* New York: Russell & Russell, 1959.

HALL, FORD W. "The Common Law: An Account of Its Reception in the United States," 4 *Vanderbilt Law Review* 791 (1951).

HOLDSWORTH, WILLIAM S. *History of English Law.* 13 vols. London: Methuen, 1922-52.

HOLMES, OLIVER WENDELL, JR. *The Common Law.* Boston: Little, Brown & Co., 1881; rev. ed., 1923.

LEWIS, WILLIAM DRAPER. *History of the American Law Institute and the First Restatement of the Law.* Philadelphia: American Law Institute, 1954.

PLUCKNETT, THEODORE FRANK THOMAS. *Concise History of the Common Law.* 5th ed. Boston: Little, Brown & Co., 1956.

POUND, ROSCOE. *The Spirit of the Common Law.* Boston: Marshall Jones Co., 1921.

———. "The Theory of Judicial Decision," 36 *Harvard Law Review* 641 (1923).

Restatement in the Courts. St. Paul, Minn.: American Law Institute, 1945.

VETTER, GEORGE M., JR. "Who Is Supreme: People, Court or Legislature?" 45 *American Bar Association Journal* 1051 (1959).

LIBEL AND SLANDER

ASHLEY, PAUL P. *Say It Safely: Legal Limits in Journalism and Broadcasting.* Seattle: University of Washington Press, 1956.

SPRING, SAMUEL. *Risks and Rights in Publishing, Television, Radio, Motion Pictures, Advertising and the Theatre.* 2d rev. ed. New York: W. W. Norton & Co., 1956.

PATENTS

General

SEIDEL, ARTHUR H. *What the General Practitioner Should Know about Patent Law and Practice.* Philadelphia: Committee on Continuing Legal Education of the American Law Institute, 1956.

Nonprofit Research

PALMER, ARCHIE M. *Administration of Medical and Pharmaceutical Patents.* Washington: National Academy of Science—National Research Council, 1955.

———. *Medical Patents.* Washington: National Academy of Science—National Research Council, 1949.

———. *Nonprofit Research and Patent Management Organization.* Washington: National Academy of Science—National Research Council, 1955.

———. *Nonprofit Research and Patent Management in the United States.* Washington: National Academy of Science—National Research Council, 1956.

———. *Nonprofit Research Institutes.* Washington: National Academy of Science—National Research Council, 1961.

———. *Patents and Nonprofit Research.* Washington: Government Printing Office, 1957.

———. *Supplement to University Patent Policies and Practices.* Washington: National Academy of Science—National Research Council, 1955.

———. *University Patent Policies and Practices.* Washington: National Academy of Science—National Research Council, 1952.

Shop Rights

MORRIS, C. ROBERT, JR. "Patent Rights in an Employee's Invention: The Shop Right Rule and the English View," 39 *Texas Law Review* 41 (1960).

PROPERTY INSURANCE

General

MAGEE, JOHN H. *Property Insurance.* 3d ed. Homewood, Ill.: Richard D. Irwin, 1955.

MOWBRAY, ALBERT H., and BLANCHARD, RALPH H. *Insurance, Its Theory and Practice in the United States.* 4th ed. New York: McGraw-Hill Book Co., 1955.

PATTERSON, ERWIN W. *Essentials of Insurance Law.* 2d ed. New York: McGraw-Hill Book Co., 1957.

RODDA, WILLIAM H. *Fire and Property Insurance.* Englewood Cliffs, N.J.: Prentice-Hall, 1956.

Coinsurance Clause

"Valuation and Measure of Recovery under Fire Insurance Policies," Note, 49 *Columbia Law Review* 818 (1949).

PROPERTY TAX EXEMPTIONS

COFFMAN, RALPH L. "Exemption of Property Owned by Educational Institutions in California," 9 *Hastings Law Journal* 215 (1958).

"Exemption from Taxation of Religious and Charitable Organizations in Pennsylvania," Note, 21 *University of Pittsburgh Law Journal* 656 (1960).

GEPPERT, W. V. "A Discussion of Tax Exempt Property in the State of Texas," 11 *Baylor Law Review* 133 (1959).

HOLBROOK, W. SUMNER, JR., and O'NEILL, FRANCIS H. "California Property Tax Trends: 1850–1950," 24 *Southern California Law Review* 252 (1951).

"Leasehold Estate in Exempt Property as Subject of Tax or Special Assessment," 23 *American Law Reports Annotated* 248 (1923).

PETRIE, RICHARD E., and LANGENHEIM, ROGER A. "Tax Exempt Property in Nebraska: An Analysis of Methods To Control Exemptions," 39 *Nebraska Law Review* 676 (1960).

PUBLIC CORPORATIONS

FRIEDMANN, WOLFGANG (ed.). *The Public Corporation: A Comparative Symposium.* Toronto, Canada: Carswell, 1954.

"Nature of Incorporated Institutions Belonging to the State," 29 *Law Reports Annotated* 378 (1915).

PEABODY, CLARENCE W. "The Legal Status of the University of Maine," 13 *Maine Law Review* 187 (1920).

REAL PROPERTY

KRATOVIL, ROBERT. *Real Estate Law.* 3d ed. Englewood Cliffs, N.J.: Prentice-Hall, 1958.

TENURE

"Academic Freedom and Tenure in the Quest for National Security," *AAUP Bulletin,* XLII (Spring 1956), 49–107.

BYSE, CLARK. "Academic Freedom, Tenure, and the Law: A Comment on Worzella v. Board of Regents," 73 *Harvard Law Review* 304 (1959).

BYSE, CLARK, and JOUGHIN, LOUIS. *Tenure in American Higher Education.* Ithaca, N.Y.: Cornell University Press, 1959.

"1940 Statement of Principles on Academic Freedom and Tenure," *AAUP Bulletin,* XLIV (Spring 1958), 290.

REUTTER, E. EDMUND, JR. *The School Administrator and Subversive Activi-*

ties. New York: Bureau of Publications, Teachers College, Columbia University, 1951.

STEWART, GEORGE. *The Year of the Oath.* Garden City, N.Y.: Doubleday & Co., 1950.

"Teacher Tenure Statutes," 110 *American Law Reports Annotated* 791 (1937); 113 *Ibid.* 1495 (1938); 127 *Ibid.* (1940).

TORTS

HARPER, FOWLER VINCENT, and JAMES, FLEMING, JR. *The Law of Torts.* 3 vols. Boston: Little, Brown & Co., 1956.

POLLOCK, SIR FREDERICK. *Law of Torts.* 15th ed. London: Stevens, 1951.

PROSSER, WILLIAM L. *Handbook of the Law of Torts.* 2d ed. St. Paul, Minn.: West Publishing Co., 1955.

TRUSTS AND TRUSTEES

General

BOGERT, GEORGE G. *The Law of Trusts and Trustees.* 4 vols. Kansas City: Vernon Law Book Co., 1946–55.

Restatement of the Law of Trusts. St. Paul, Minn.: American Law Institute, 1955.

Restatement of the Law, Second: Trusts. 2d ed. Philadelphia: American Law Institute, 1959.

SCOTT, AUSTIN W. *The Law of Trusts.* 2d ed. 5 vols. Boston: Little, Brown & Co., 1956.

Investment of Trust Funds

SHATTUCK, MAYO ADAMS. "The Development of the Prudent Man Rule for Fiduciary Investment in the United States in the Twentieth Century," 12 *Ohio State Law Journal* 491 (1951).

UNIFORM STATE LAWS

Model Business Corporation Act, Annotated. St. Paul, Minn.: West Publishing Co., 1960.

1958 Report of the National Conference of Commissioners on Uniform State Laws. Chicago: National Conference of Commissioners on Uniform State Laws, 1959.

YEARBOOKS

The Book of the States, 1956–57. Chicago: Council of State Governments, 1956.

The Book of the States, 1958–59. Chicago: Council of State Governments, 1958.

Britannica Book of the Year, 1954. Chicago: Encyclopaedia Britannica, 1954.

Index

Abrams, Frank W., 217
Abstract of title, 135
  See also Title, evidence of
Academic credits, right of student to receive, 120, 121
Academic degree, right of student to receive, 121, 122
Academic freedom, 66
  See also Tenure
Accident and health insurance premiums paid by employer, 95
Accreditation in higher education, 26, 56
Accrediting organizations, influence upon higher education, 26, 55, 56
Accumulation of trust fund income, rule against, 214
Acquiescence of the Commissioner of Internal Revenue, 15, 16, 90, 94, 98, 222
Actuarial tables of the Internal Revenue Service, 88, 231
Adelphi College, 162
Adjudication of claims against the state, 30, 149, 268
Administration of restricted funds, 191
Administrative law, 4, 5, 20
Admission fees, federal excise tax, 274
Admission restrictions, effect upon power of eminent domain, 39, 40
  tax exemption, 164
Affiliated corporations, 52, 167, 178, 189, 221
Agencies, administrative, 4, 5, 6, 13, 26
Agency, law of, 59, 141
Agency of government, 24
Agent, implied power to bind principal, 59, 141
Agricultural and Mechanical College of Texas, 110
Akron, University of, 120, 212, 267
Alabama, University of, 113, 240
Alfred University, 29
Allocation of federal land-grant funds to nonpublic institutions, 29
Alumni associations, effect of incorporation, 221

American Academic Freedom Project, 73
American Alumni Council, 220, 221
American Association of Colleges, 58
American Association of University Professors, 58, 63, 189
American Bankers Association, 212
American Bar Association, 97, 216
American Bar Center, 5
American Bar Foundation, 5, 217
American Civil Liberties Union, 72
American Council of Learned Societies, 185
American Council on Education, 25, 28, 57, 138, 139
American Federation of Labor, 72
American Institute of Architects, 142
American judicial system, 19
American Law Institute, 7, 8
American Law Reports, 197
Amherst College, 119, 160
Amicus curiae, defined, 80
Anglo-American system of jurisprudence, 17
Annuity contracts
  donative, 233
  employee, 84
  See also Life income agreements; Retirement benefits
Appraisal, property, 146
Appropriation of public funds for nonpublic institutions of education, 27, 28, 29, 30, 34, 238
  purposes, 27, 28, 29, 30, 34, 153, 238, 258
Approximation, doctrine of, 192
Arbitration agreements, 141
Architect
  as agent, 141
  as arbiter, 141
  certificate, 141
  professional competency, 141
Architecture, regulation of the practice, 26, 141
Arizona, University of, 253
Arkansas, University of, 253
Armed services, 6

329

AMERICAN COUNCIL ON EDUCATION

ARTHUR S. ADAMS, *President*

The American Council on Education is a *council* of national associations; organizations having related interests; approved universities, colleges, teachers colleges, junior colleges, technological schools, and selected private secondary schools; state departments of education; city school systems and private school systems; selected educational departments of business and industrial companies; voluntary associations of higher education in the states; and large public libraries. It is a center of cooperation and coordination whose influence has been apparent in the shaping of American educational policies and the formation of educational practices during the past forty-three years.